FRENCH
PÂTISSERIE

Design and Typesetting: Alice Leroy
Editorial Collaboration: Estérelle Payany

Project Coordinator, FERRANDI Paris: Audrey Janet
Pastry Chefs, FERRANDI Paris: Stévy Antoine,
Carlos Cerqueira, Claude Chiron, Bruno Ciret,
Régis Ferey, Alain Guillaumin, and Edouard Hauvuy

Editor: Clélia Ozier-Lafontaine, assisted by Déborah Schwarz

ENGLISH EDITION
Editorial Director: Kate Mascaro
Editor: Helen Adedotun
Translated from the French by Carmella Moreau,
Ansley Evans, Caitilin Walsh, and Rachel Doux
Copyediting: Wendy Sweetser, with Anne McDowall
Proofreading: Nicole Foster
Production: Christelle Lemonnier
Color Separation: IGS-CP, L'Isle d'Espagnac
Printed in China by Toppan Leefung

Simultaneously published in French as *Pâtisserie:*
Toutes les techniques et recettes d'une école d'excellence
© Flammarion, S.A., Paris, 2017

English-language edition
© Flammarion, S.A., Paris, 2017

24 25 26   12 11 10
ISBN: 978-2-08-020318-2
Legal Deposit: 10/2017

FERRANDI

PARIS

PHOTOGRAPHY BY RINA NURRA

FRENCH
PÂTISSERIE

MASTER RECIPES AND TECHNIQUES FROM
THE FERRANDI SCHOOL OF CULINARY ARTS

Flammarion

FERRANDI

L'ÉCOLE FRANÇAISE DE GASTRONOMIE

PARIS

PREFACE

Famous throughout the world, French pâtisserie is renowned, and deservedly so, for its excellence and ingenuity and has been taught at the **FERRANDI Paris** school of culinary arts for almost one hundred years.

At the heart of our school's teaching philosophy is the desire to both transmit traditional skills and encourage creative innovation, a dual approach that is made possible by our unrivaled industry connections, which have made the school the benchmark institution.

Following the publication of our first book in French, *Le Grand Cours de Cuisine* by **FERRANDI Paris**—a best seller that has been translated into several languages and awarded numerous prizes—it was a natural choice to devote our next book to pâtisserie.

As pastry making is a profession that is both artistic and artisanal, this book needed to be more than simply a recipe book. In line with the school's philosophy, it will teach you the basic techniques, but it will also whet your appetite for creativity and reflection—essential ingredients in the meticulous and expressive art of pâtisserie.

The passion and high standards with which we teach pâtisserie to our students—whether young or mature, or keen amateur cooks taking specialized classes—have enabled us to share this art with the world. The prestige enjoyed by French pâtisserie is today greater than ever, and we hope that this book will add to its credit.

I would like to thank the contributors at **FERRANDI Paris** who helped create this book, in particular Audrey Janet, who coordinated it, as well as many of the school's pastry chefs who have devoted time and effort to share their knowledge: Stévy Antoine, Carlos Cerqueira, Claude Chiron, Bruno Ciret, Régis Ferey, Alain Guillaumin, and Edouard Hauvuy.

I would like to thank all the chefs, friends, former students, associate professors, and members of the Advisory Board, who did us the honor of contributing recipes: Ophélie Barès, Christelle Brua, Christine Ferber, Nina Métayer, Christophe Adam, Julien Alvarez, Nicolas Bacheyre, Nicolas Bernardé, Nicolas Boussin, Yann Brys, Frédéric Cassel, Gontran Cherrier, Philippe Conticini, Yann Couvreur, Christophe Felder, Cédric Grolet, Pierre Hermé, Jean-Paul Hévin, Arnaud Larher, Gilles Marchal, Pierre Marcolini, Carl Marletti, Yann Menguy, Christophe Michalak, Angelo Musa, and Philippe Urraca. Their influence on our school's teaching remains invaluable and precious.

Bruno de Monte
Director of FERRANDI Paris

CONTENTS

FERRANDI
PARIS

FOR NEARLY 100 YEARS

FERRANDI Paris has trained countless chefs, pâtissiers, and foodservice and hospitality professionals, with a focus on excellence. Generations of renowned chefs have been influenced by the innovative FERRANDI approach to teaching, which is based on close ties to the industry. What makes FERRANDI Paris unique? The school prides itself on providing top-notch training for students of all levels, whether undergraduate or graduate, apprentice or career changer, and its international programs offer the same high level of training to students from around the world. FERRANDI Paris students have diverse backgrounds and goals: young learners on work/study training programs, the full spectrum of culinary and hospitality management professionals, career changers, and food enthusiasts looking to hone their skills. The strength of FERRANDI Paris lies in this diversity and in its creative approach to teaching, combining technical rigor with experience in the field. The school is known for keeping abreast with the industry professionals, and continually evolving to remain a pioneer and leader at the peak of excellence: it was the first school to offer a bachelor's degree program more than thirty years ago.

Much more than a school, **FERRANDI Paris** is a hub of French gastronomy and a center of innovation and exchange for the entire culinary industry.

A COMMITMENT TO EXCELLENCE

FERRANDI Paris is one of twenty-one schools affiliated with the Paris Île-de-France Regional Chamber of Commerce and Industry, and it is the only school in France to offer the full range of degree and certification programs in the culinary and hospitality arts, from vocational training to master's degree level. FERRANDI Paris continually revises and updates its teaching methods to ensure that students receive the best education possible, from internships (tuition-free and remunerated) to expert pâtisserie programs. All students—whether they study catering, the art of table setting (*arts de la table*), bread-making, pâtisserie, or hospitality management—share the same dedication to hard work and high standards, which are the keys to excellence.

DEDICATION TO DIVERSITY
—

FERRANDI **Paris** has three campuses: one in the heart of Paris and two in the Paris suburbs of Jouy-en-Josas and Saint-Gratien. The school also has a training center in Bordeaux, with plans to open more in the future. Each year, FERRANDI **Paris** trains 2,300 apprentices and vocational and degree students, 300 international students in designated programs, and around 2,000 adults in career transition or in continuing education courses. The school is dedicated to its mission as a French public institution, and seventy percent of FERRANDI **Paris**'s students in apprenticeship-based programs receive a free education, combining theory with practical work in the field, thanks to the school's many industry partners. The hands-on approach to teaching fosters student success, which is reflected in the ninety-eight percent exam pass rate, which is the highest in France for degrees and certifications in the sector.

A TEACHING CENTER WITH STRONG TIES TO THE PROFESSIONAL WORLD
—

FERRANDI **Paris**'s 100 permanent instructors are all highly qualified, and all have at least ten years of professional experience in prestigious establishments in France and abroad. Several have received prominent culinary awards and distinctions, including the prestigious Meilleur Ouvrier de France (Best Craftsman in France) title. In addition to this brigade of highly talented instructors on staff, many renowned chefs and pastry chefs also contribute to the FERRANDI **Paris** team by teaching master classes or specialized training sessions throughout the year. The school also regularly hosts chefs from around the world to give students a cosmopolitan understanding of food culture and to better prepare them for the professional world. The school's international program instructors often receive invitations to travel abroad to teach French culinary techniques all across the globe. A solid relationship between the academic and professional worlds is one of the school's core features and one of the keys to student success.

A CULINARY HUB IN PARIS
—

FERRANDI **Paris** is located in the beautiful Saint-Germain-des-Prés district in the heart of the city. Students attend classes in historic buildings with some 270,000 square feet (25,000 m²) of teaching space, equipped with state-of-the-art facilities, including thirty-five technical laboratories and two student-staffed restaurants open to the public. A true gastronomic hub in Paris, the school hosts conferences and events for the public on occasions such as the Fête de la Gastronomie and also has a culinary studio where individuals can take private classes with **FERRANDI Paris** professionals. Throughout the year, the school hosts between thirty and fifty professional competitions organized by prestigious French chefs' associations, along with many other professional events. Over the years, **FERRANDI Paris** has trained countless culinary professionals, and many return frequently to hone their skills through continuing education programs, helping the school maintain its unrivaled connections with the professional world.

HANDS-ON LEARNING Practice, precision, and the fundamental techniques and savoir-faire of the French gastronomic tradition are the pillars of a **FERRANDI Paris** education. Rather than passively observing amphitheater demonstrations, students instead learn to master the techniques of top professionals through intensive, hands-on practice. From 6 a.m. onward, the labs and kitchens at **FERRANDI Paris** are abuzz with the activity of students of different ages and backgrounds

learning and perfecting a wide range of culinary skills. The on-site training restaurants allow students to learn by working in the front and back of house in a real-life setting with genuine customers. In addition, students have numerous opportunities to put their training to work at prestigious professional events held throughout the year.

AN INTERNATIONAL SCHOOL France's historical expertise in the culinary arts was recognized internationally in 2010 when the French gastronomic meal was awarded with the UNESCO Intangible Cultural Heritage of Humanity distinction. French culinary and pâtisserie savoir-faire is sought after around the globe, and **FERRANDI Paris** plays a key role in meeting this demand by training international students and preparing all students to put their skills to work worldwide. Every year, around 300 students from more than thirty countries attend **FERRANDI Paris**, drawn by the school's reputation for excellence. They come for intensive professional programs in French cuisine, pâtisserie-making, or bread-baking, or for topical training weeks designed for culinary professionals, and they share what they have learned around the world. At **FERRANDI Paris**, students discover the rich traditions of French gastronomy not only through practice at the school but also through excursions, tastings, and visits to food businesses throughout France, discovering wines, terroirs, growers, producers, and major markets. In this spirit of international exchange, **FERRANDI Paris** is currently collaborating with the Cité Internationale de la Gastronomie et du Vin in Dijon to create a school of French cuisine and pâtisserie for international students, which is due to open in 2019. International program instructors at **FERRANDI Paris** also regularly receive invitations to deliver short training courses for other instructors or culinary professionals around the world.

AND A SCHOOL FOR PROFESSIONALS

Through continuing education classes at **FERRANDI Paris**, culinary arts professionals can acquire new skills and knowledge throughout their careers to keep abreast with evolving techniques and trends. The school offers more than sixty short courses for professionals every year on topics including pâtisserie, bread-making, the art of table setting (*arts de la table*), business and financial management, food safety, and industry requirements. These classes are continually updated to follow innovations and trends in the field (such as vegan and sous-vide cuisines) and to support entrepreneurship in France and abroad. **FERRANDI Paris** also offers customized courses and counsel for a wide range of clients, including restaurants and businesses in the food and agriculture industries.

DRIVEN BY INNOVATION

In creating the bachelor's degree program thirty-five years ago and in continually updating its training courses, **FERRANDI Paris** has become known for its ability to anticipate changes in the food and hotel management industries. In many sectors, it is a pioneer, blazing the trail and earning a reputation as a benchmark school. The spirit of **FERRANDI Paris** is always open, welcoming the world, new technologies, and knowledge from other fields that enhance the culinary arts. To give students maximum opportunities and the chance to connect with the wider community, **FERRANDI Paris** has formed collaborative partnerships with several other French institutions, including the François Rabelais University in Tours and the Institut Français de la Mode (the French fashion institute). With GOBELINS, the school of visual communication in Paris, **FERRANDI Paris** organized a food-photography workshop, in which students from both schools worked together, exchanging knowledge and expertise.

The general public can also benefit from **FERRANDI Paris**'s enterprise via Massive Open Online Courses (MOOC)—intense, tuition-free classes open to all and fully accessible online. The school's first MOOC was offered in 2015, devoted to food design—an emerging field in the world of gastronomy. The second, in 2017, examined culinary trends, enabling participants to acquire monitoring strategies to help them anticipate future changes and innovate accordingly. The next one will cover food styling.

PRESTIGIOUS PARTNERS

In addition to its strong ties to industry, **FERRANDI Paris** also enjoys partnerships with the principal culinary organizations in France, including the Académie Culinaire de France, Cuisiniers de France, Cuisiniers de la République, Les Toques Françaises, the Les Toques Blanches International Club, Maîtres Cuisiniers de France, Maîtres Restaurateurs, the Académie Nationale des Cuisiniers, Club Prosper Montagné, and Euro-Toques France. These partnerships give **FERRANDI Paris** students the

opportunity to participate in a number of recognized events and demonstrate their skills and knowledge. **FERRANDI Paris** is also a partner to many private businesses, which the school assists via auditing and customized consulting services.

PÂTISSERIE ACCORDING TO FERRANDI

At all levels, from enthusiast to professional, pâtisserie remains one of the pillars of **FERRANDI Paris**. For the school, a love of pastries and cakes is only the first step in becoming an excellent pastry chef. Rigor and precision, important in all cooking, are even more crucial in pâtisserie-making, and are indispensable in mastering the wide range of techniques in the field, including bread-baking, ice cream–making, and chocolate work. Creativity is also essential, not only in decorative work, but also in experimenting with the flavors, textures, and colors of new desserts. Pastry chefs must therefore be multifaceted artists, for their work demands a wide range of skills and meticulous work habits. These include speed and dexterity, stellar organization, and careful attention to food safety and hygiene: qualities that **FERRANDI Paris** instructors instill in all their students. Many celebrated pastry chefs have trained at **FERRANDI Paris**, including several who have participated in this book: Gontran Cherrier, Nicolas Bernardé, Nina Métayer, Ophélie Barès, Yann Menguy, and Yann Couvreur.

FRENCH PÂTISSERIE WORLDWIDE

The French savoir-faire in pâtisserie is highly appreciated throughout the world. This reputation not only gives students of French pâtisserie countless career opportunities abroad, but also attracts many international students to **FERRANDI Paris** to receive top-level training in pâtisserie. The school offers French pâtisserie classes in English specifically designed for international students, sixty percent of whom come from Asia. Thanks to small class sizes (twelve to fifteen students per instructor) and a hands-on approach to teaching (including internships with renowned pastry chefs), **FERRANDI Paris**'s international students acquire the essential skills and techniques of classic French pâtisserie-making and finish their programs ready to share what they learned at the school with the world at large.

A BOOK FOR ALL LEVELS

French Pâtisserie celebrates **FERRANDI Paris**'s savoir-faire in a fundamental discipline of French cuisine. Following the school's successful book, *Le Grand Cours de Cuisine* **FERRANDI**, this innovative book—and the first **FERRANDI** title to be published in English—is grounded in the teaching philosophy developed by the school, which is based on practice and close collaboration with professionals. The **thematic introductions** that precede each chapter lay a foundation, providing explanations of the ingredients used, historical information, tips to avoid common pitfalls, and keys to success. The recipes are presented by level of difficulty, a progressive approach inspired by the **FERRANDI Paris**'s bachelor's degree program. The **Level 1 recipes** explain how to make the traditional, classic versions of French pastries. The **Level 2 recipes** are for more sophisticated versions—or reinventions—of the classics. The **Level 3 recipes** were provided by celebrated pastry chefs (some of whom are also associated chefs at the school, class sponsors, board members, or former **FERRANDI Paris** students) and reflect each chef's unique approach and vision. The home chef can choose the appropriate level according to their own ability.

THE FUTURE

Continually innovating to meet the demands of an ever-evolving industry, **FERRANDI Paris** has many exciting projects planned in anticipation of the school's 100th anniversary, including a student-staffed five-star hotel for the hospitality management program and a culinary and pâtisserie training center for students from around the world at the Cité Internationale de la Gastronomie et du Vin in Dijon. At the heart of French cuisine and driven by innovation, **FERRANDI Paris** will continue to share its expertise and passion, sparking inspiration and delight around the world.

EQUIPMENT

UTENSILS

UTENSILS

1——— Copper jam pan
2——— Glass jam jars
3——— Skimmers
4——— Ladles
5——— Stainless steel mixing bowls
6——— Digital kitchen scale

7——— Whipping siphon with nozzles
     and N2O gas cartridges
8——— Small fine-mesh sieves or strainers
9——— Fine-mesh strainer
10——— China cap strainer
11——— Drum sieve or sifter
12——— Candy thermometer
     (176°F–428°F/80°C–220°C)
13——— Glass milk thermometer for custards
     (14°F–248°F/-10°C–120°C)
14——— Digital instant-read thermometer
     (-40°F–392°F/-40°C–200°C)

N.B. When using a new piece of kitchen equipment, especially one that needs to be assembled, it is important to read the manufacturer's instructions carefully to ensure the equipment works efficiently and to avoid potential injuries.

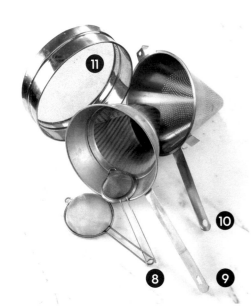

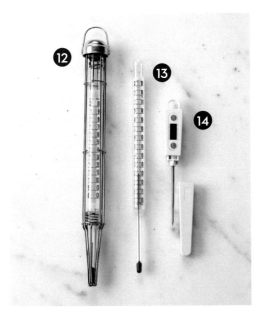

ELECTRICAL APPLIANCES

1 ——— Stand mixer with dough hook (A), whisk (B), and paddle beater (C) attachments
2 ——— Food processor with a chopper blade, also called an S-blade or blade knife
(for grinding and chopping)
3 ——— Stick or immersion blender (for mixing and emulsifying)

MOLDS & BAKING ACCESSORIES

MOLDS & BAKING ACCESSORIES

1 —— Stainless steel charlotte mold
2 —— Nonstick loaf pan
3 —— Stainless steel madeleine mold
4 —— Nonstick fluted tart pan
5 —— Nonstick round cake pans
6 —— Brioche molds
7 —— Copper canelé molds
8 —— Flexible silicone molds
9 —— Traditional earthenware kougelhopf mold or regular Bundt pan
10 —— Ramekins or individual soufflé dishes

11 —— Dessert or cake rings
12 —— Tart ring
13 —— Square pastry, cake, or baking frame
14 —— Rectangular pastry, cake, or baking frame
15 —— Silicone baking mat
16 —— Silicone macaron baking mat
17 —— Fluted stainless steel apple turnover cutter
18 —— Plain round stainless steel cookie cutter
19 —— Plain round cutters made of Exoglass (heatproof)

20 —— Plastic wrap
21 —— Food-grade acetate roll (for assembling entremets)
22 —— Food-grade acetate sheets (for chocolate work)
23 —— Parchment paper
24 —— Stainless steel rectangular cooling rack
25 —— Stainless steel round cooling rack
26 —— Stainless steel baking sheet
27 —— Stainless steel perforated baking sheet
28 —— Stainless steel candy cooling grid, with a tightly-spaced grid

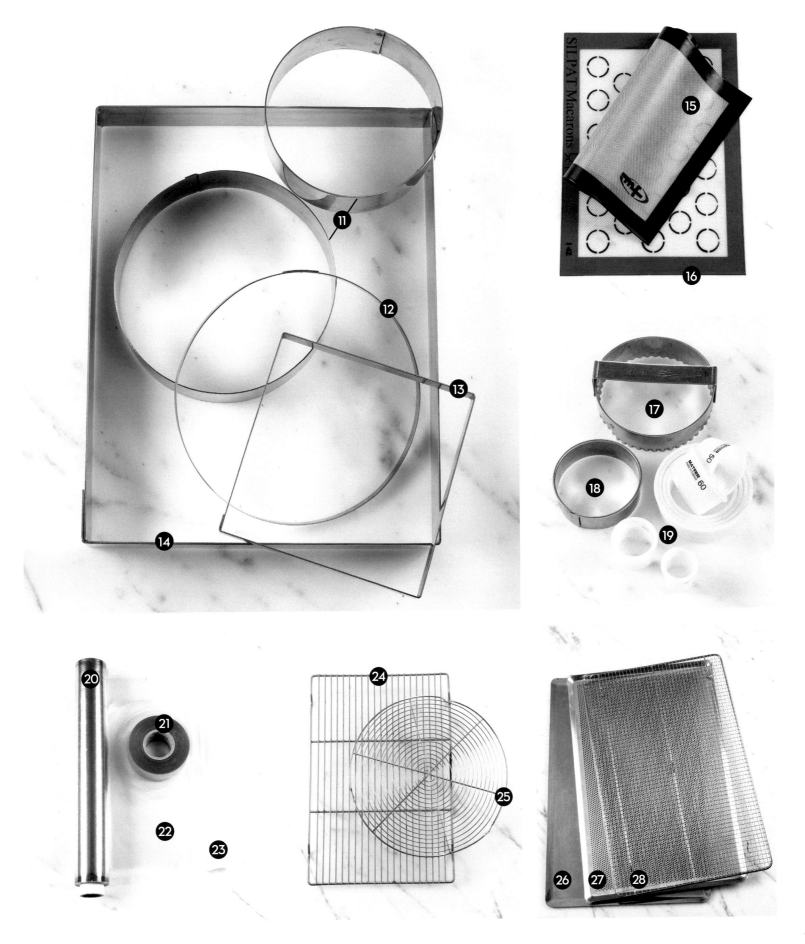

SILPAT Macarons

19

SMALL KITCHEN TOOLS

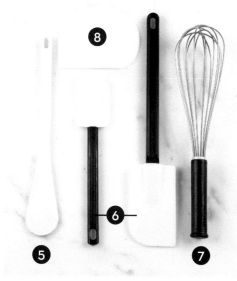
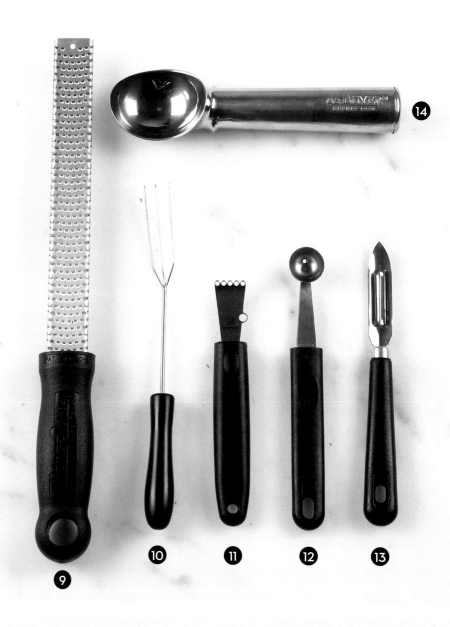

SMALL KITCHEN TOOLS

1 —— Chef's knife
2 —— Serrated knife (for slicing puff pastry and sponge cakes and chopping chocolate)
3 —— Long, thin-bladed knife (filleting or boning knife) (for decorations and chocolate)
4 —— Paring knife
5 —— Exoglass or heatproof spatula
6 —— Flexible spatulas
7 —— French or elongated whisk
8 —— Bowl scraper
9 —— Microplane grater

10 —— Chocolate dipping fork
11 —— Zester with a channel knife
12 —— Melon baller
13 —— Peeler
14 —— Ice cream scoop
15 —— Rolling pin
16 —— Pastry scraper
17 —— Pastry pincher (for decorating the edges of tarts and pies)
18 —— Dough docker (for pricking dough)
19 —— Large drum sieve or sifter

20 —— Flour brush
21 —— Pastry brushes
22 —— Palette knives or straight icing spatulas
23 —— Angled palette knives or offset spatulas
24 —— Disposable polyethylene or acetate pastry bags (more hygienic than reusable bags)
25 —— Pastry tips (preferably polycarbonate)

BASIC TECHNIQUES

Using a Rolling Pin

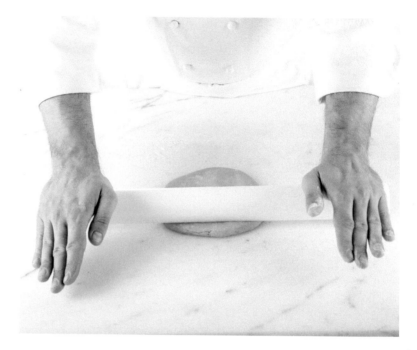

1 • Flour the dough and work surface, as lightly as possible, to prevent sticking. Place your fingertips on either end of the rolling pin.

2 • Keeping your fingers flexed, apply pressure on the pin to roll it across the dough and into the palm of your hands.

3 • Roll the pin back to the initial position. If making a circle, rotate the dough one-eighth of a turn; if making a rectangle or square, make a quarter turn.

4 • Repeat these movements until the desired thickness of the dough is reached.

Lining Tartlet Pans by Patting Down

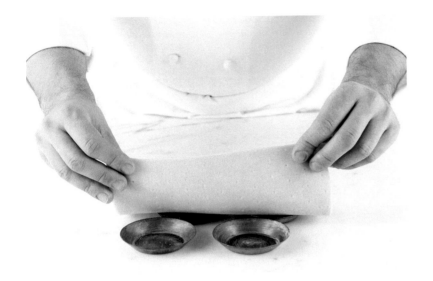

1 • Butter the pans and set them close together. Prick the dough with a fork or dough docker and lay it across the surface of the pans.

2 • Make a ball with any excess dough, dip it in flour, and use it to gently press the sheet of dough against the sides and bottoms of the tart pans.

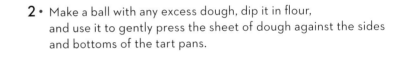

3 • Run a rolling pin across the tops of the pans to remove excess dough. Using 2 rolling pins makes this easier.

4 • This will give you perfectly lined tartlet pans.

Lining a Tart Ring — TECHNIQUE 1

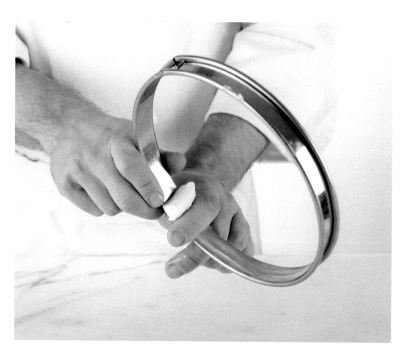

1 • Butter the inside of the tart ring well (this helps the dough to cling to the sides when lining and makes it easier to slip the ring off after baking).

2 • Roll out the dough into a circle larger than the tart ring. When you set the ring on the dough, there should be a border of about two fingers in width.

5 • Carefully lay the dough over the top of the tart ring. Make sure the dough is centered.

6 • Ease the dough into the ring, pressing it into the corners and against the sides.

3 • Remove the ring and lightly flour the dough, removing any excess using a flour brush.

4 • Use a dough docker or fork to prick the dough.

7 • Working around the ring, lift the base up slightly and use your thumb to gently press down on the dough so it reaches the base, taking care not to stretch or mark the dough.

8 • Form a small rim inside the tart ring along the entire upper edge. ⊕

Lining a Tart Ring — TECHNIQUE 1 (continued)

9 • Run a rolling pin across the top of the tart ring to remove excess dough.

10 • Use your thumb and index finger to gently pinch the rim of dough so it extends above the edge of the tart ring.

11 • Using a pastry pincher, crimp the border at regular intervals, turning the ring as you go to maintain the same angle.

12 • Continue crimping until you have an attractive border all the way around the ring.

Lining a Tart Ring — TECHNIQUE 2

1 • Follow steps 1–3 of technique 1. Carefully lay the dough over the top of the ring. Press into the corners and against the sides and prick with the tip of a paring knife.

2 • Run a rolling pin across the top of the tart ring to remove excess dough.

3 • Use your thumb and index finger to gently pinch the dough up and against the sides of the ring.

4 • Run the blade of a paring knife along the top of the ring to trim off excess dough.

Filling and Using a Pastry Bag

1 • Insert the tip to be used into the pastry bag and ensure it is snugly in place.

2 • Using a knife, cut off the end of the pastry bag about halfway up the sides of the tip.

3 • Twist the bag all the way around just above the tip to prevent the filling from escaping.

4 • Tuck the twisted portion into the tip while filling the bag.

5 • Grasp the middle of the pastry bag with one of your hands and fold the top over your hand to make a large cuff.

6 • Use a bowl scraper or large spoon to fill the bag with the piping mixture (cream, mousse, meringue, etc.). The bag should never be more than half filled.

7 • Unfold the cuff.

8 • Hold the top of the bag with one hand and use the other to squeeze the mixture down toward the tip.

9 • Gently pull on the bag to release the twist.

10 • Push the piping mixture into the tip.

11 • Take hold of the bag at the top of the filled part and fold the empty part over the back of your thumb.

12 • Apply equal pressure with the palm of your hand and fingers to control the flow of the mixture.

INGREDIENTS

To make perfect cakes and pastries,
it is essential to start with the best ingredients
you can find. This introduction provides an overview
of the main ingredients used in this book
to help you bake like a professional.

DAIRY PRODUCTS

Milk, cream, and butter are basic building blocks of flavor and texture in pastry making and therefore play a key role in pastry quality.

MILK

References to milk in these recipes are always to cow's milk, which is the most commonly used variety. If the type is not specified, you can choose from whole or low-fat milk.

—— **PURCHASING TIPS:** It is best to use either pasteurized milk from the refrigerated section of the supermarket or ultra-pasteurized (UHT) milk rather than raw milk. Pasteurized milk can have a more pronounced flavor, which may vary seasonally, depending on what the cows have eaten. UHT milk produces identical results throughout the year. Many recipes work just as well with whole or low-fat milk, but in certain types of desserts, such as custard, clafoutis, or flan, whole milk will produce creamier and richer results.

—— **STORAGE TIPS:** Pasteurized milk should be stored in the refrigerator at or below 38°F (3°C) and used before the sell-by date printed on the label. Unopened, shelf-stable UHT milk can be stored at room temperature until the sell-by date. After opening, UHT milk must also be stored in the refrigerator at or below 38°F (3°C), and it should be consumed within about 3–5 days. In all cases, be sure to check the label for the suppliers' recommendations.

CREAM

It is important to choose the right type of cream according to what you are making. Higher fat creams are thicker and easier to whip, and they are less likely to curdle when mixed in with hot ingredients. When a minimum fat content is required for a recipe to work, the recommended percentage is specified in the ingredients list. The table on p. 36 will help you determine which cream is best.

—— **PURCHASING TIPS:** If possible, avoid using ultra-pasteurized cream, which tends to be less flavorful and have more additives than pasteurized cream.

—— **STORAGE TIPS:** Cream should be stored in the refrigerator at a maximum temperature of 40°F (4°C) and used by the sell-by date. Be sure to check the label for the suppliers' recommendations.

CRÈME FRAÎCHE

Crème fraîche is a common product in French supermarkets, but is not always readily available elsewhere. A substitute can be made at home by adding 1 tablespoon of buttermilk to 1 cup (250 ml) of heavy cream. Mix well, cover, and then allow the mixture to sit at room temperature for up to 24 hours, until thickened. Refrigerate until ready to use.

—— **PURCHASING TIPS:** In the US and elsewhere, more and more dairies are producing crème fraîche, which can be found in the refrigerated sections of many well-stocked supermarkets or online.

—— **STORAGE TIPS:** Both store-bought and homemade crème fraîche should be kept in the refrigerator at a maximum temperature of 40°F (4°C). Homemade crème fraîche will keep in the refrigerator for about 1 week. Check the label of store-bought crème fraîche for the sell-by date and the suppliers' storage recommendations.

MASCARPONE

This Italian triple-cream cheese with a minimum fat content of 50% has a soft and spreadable consistency and a mildly sweet flavor. It gives desserts a rich, velvety texture. Mascarpone is a key ingredient in tiramisu, and it can also be used to make whipped cream more stable. To do so, replace 30% of the total cream called for in the recipe with mascarpone and whip as usual.

—— **STORAGE TIPS:** Mascarpone should be kept in the refrigerator at a maximum temperature of 40°F (4°C).

POWDERED MILK

Powdered milk is simply milk that has been dried to a powder; it does not contain any additives, and it retains the same proteins, fats, vitamins, and minerals as liquid milk. In pastry making, powdered milk contributes dry matter and in some cases fat content to recipes without adding water, which makes it possible to experiment with texture and flavor. Powdered milk is used in this book most notably in certain ice creams and viennoiseries (breakfast pastries).

—— **STORAGE TIPS:** Powdered milk should be stored in a cool, dry place away from direct sunlight.

SWEETENED CONDENSED MILK

Sweetened condensed milk is made by cooking milk at high heat until more than half of the water content evaporates. Sugar is then added, resulting in a thick, sweet syrup that works well in shiny glazes.

—— **STORAGE TIPS:** Before opening, sweetened condensed milk should be stored in a cool, dry place. After opening, it should be kept in the refrigerator at a maximum temperature of 43°F (6°C) and consumed within about 3 days. Check the label for the manufacturers' storage recommendations.

EVAPORATED MILK

Evaporated milk is made in the same way as sweetened condensed milk, but no sugar is added. It is called unsweetened condensed milk in many countries. Evaporated milk contributes creaminess to preparations like caramels and glazes.

—— **STORAGE TIPS:** Evaporated milk should be stored in the same conditions as sweetened condensed milk.

BUTTER

As butter contains such a high level of fat, the quality you use is all-important, for the texture and flavor it imparts. In pâtisserie, both pasteurized unsalted and salted butters are used. Try to get butter with as high a butterfat content as you can (preferably a minimum of 82%): the higher the fat content, the less water the butter contains, which equates to creamier, more flavorful butter and flakier crusts. Successful pastries also depend on the temperature and texture of the butter used, so always take care to prepare the butter as indicated in a given recipe before mixing it together with the other ingredients (see the Butter Techniques table on p. 36).

—— **PURCHASING TIPS:** In the US, look for high-fat European-style or cultured butters with at least 82% butterfat, which are increasingly available from small creameries and major brands alike. Both can be found in most well-stocked supermarkets and online. Although most regular butter in the US has a butterfat content of around 80%, this will still produce good results.

—— **STORAGE TIPS:** Butter should be stored in the refrigerator at a temperature of between 32°F and 40°F (0°C and 4°C). Be sure to wrap your butter well, because it easily absorbs odors.

WHY DO SOME RECIPES CALL FOR BUTTER WITH 84% BUTTERFAT?

A high butterfat content is particularly important when making laminated doughs like those for croissants and puff pastries. For such doughs, French pastry chefs use a special butter called *beurre de tourage*, or laminating butter, which has a minimum butterfat content of 84%. This high-fat butter is also sometimes called dry butter (*beurre sec*), because it contains less water than lower-fat butters. One of the advantages of "dry" butter is that it melts more slowly than other butters and is thus easier to work with when making doughs requiring lots of folds and turns. It also results in flakier pastries and superior flavor. If you cannot find *beurre de tourage*, cultured European-style butters with at least 84% butterfat are the best substitute.

WHAT IS BROWNED BUTTER (BEURRE NOISETTE)?

Browned butter is made by heating butter beyond the melting point until the milk proteins begin to caramelize, resulting in a golden brown color and a slightly nutty aroma. To make browned butter, gently heat your butter, stirring frequently, until it is light brown, then carefully submerge the bottom of the saucepan in cold water to quickly stop the cooking process and prevent burning. Strain the melted butter through cheesecloth or a fine-mesh strainer and use it to give an irresistible nutty flavor to cookies and cakes like financiers or madeleines.

WHAT IS CLARIFIED BUTTER?

Clarified butter is pure butterfat obtained by melting regular butter and removing the milk solids, water, and other impurities. Because clarified butter is 100% fat, it has a higher smoke point than regular butter and does not burn as easily. Clarified butter can be purchased, but you can also make it at home. To make your own, melt unsalted butter in a saucepan over very low heat and let it simmer gently, without stirring, until a foamy white layer forms on top. Skim as much of the foam off the surface as you can. Once the butter stops foaming, remove the pan from the heat. Carefully pour the top layer of clear golden butterfat through a strainer into a separate container, leaving the milk solids at the bottom of the pan.

BUTTER TIPS

• When a recipe calls for room-temperature or softened butter, remember to remove the butter from the refrigerator at least 30 minutes before starting.

• Dice butter into small ¼-in. (6-mm) pieces to make it easier to mix into doughs and batters.

• Cut butter into pieces for melting.

• Pay close attention to melting butter, as it easily burns once the temperature reaches 248°F (120°C).

• In pastry making, there is no substitute for butter. Do not be tempted to use spreadable or light butter, margarine, or other similar products.

MILK

TYPE	FAT CONTENT
Whole milk	3.25% (US); 3.5% (UK); 3.6% (France)
Low-fat (reduced-fat) or 2% milk (US)	about 2%
Semi-skimmed milk (UK)	1.5%–1.8%
Low-fat (US) or 1% milk	about 1%
Skim milk	0%–0.5%

CREAM

NAME	FAT CONTENT	CHARACTERISTICS
Clotted cream (UK)	Min 55%	Thick, rich cream made by heating unpasteurized milk, traditionally served with scones; also known as Devonshire or Devon cream
Double cream (UK)	48%	Thick cream that withstands boiling, whips well, and holds its shape; easy to over-whip, resulting in a grainy texture
Heavy cream (US)	36%–40%	Whips easily, producing thick, stable whipped cream; sometimes referred to as heavy whipping cream
Whipping cream	30%–38%	Produces lighter whipped cream than double or heavy cream but does not hold its shape quite as well
Crème fraîche	Min. 30%	Rich and thick cultured cream with a mild tangy flavor; but not curdle when heated
Sour or soured cream	18%–20%	Regular cream fermented with lactic acid cultures to make it thick and tangy
Light cream (US)	18%–30%, generally 20%	Pouring cream; does not whip if the fat content is less than 30%
Single cream (UK)	Min. 18%	Pouring cream; will not whip and curdles if boiled
Half-and-half (US)	10.5%–18%	Pouring cream made with equal parts whole milk and cream; cannot be whipped or boiled

BUTTER TECHNIQUES

DESCRIPTION	PREPARATION	PROPERTIES	USES
Pounded butter (*beurre malaxé*)	Pound cold butter with a rolling pin to make it more malleable	Contributes to the signature texture of certain pastries	Short pastry, puff pastry, brioches, croissants
Softened butter (*beurre pommade*)	Work room-temperature butter with a spatula or using a stand mixer fitted with the paddle beater attachment until smooth and creamy, but not melted	Combines easily with other ingredients, prevents lumps, and gives creams and sauces a velvety consistency that melts on the tongue	Loaf cakes and cookies (cigarettes and cats' tongue cookies); creams such as buttercream, almond cream, and mousseline cream
Room-temperature butter	Remove butter from the refrigerator and let it sit at room temperature until it is malleable but still holds its shape (about 30 minutes depending on the climate)	Combines easily with other ingredients	Cakes, cookies, and creams that call for creaming butter together with sugar (almond cream, mousseline buttercream, pastry cream)
Melted butter	Cut butter into small pieces and heat in a saucepan over low heat or in the microwave until just melted but not browned	Produces a moist texture and prevents cakes from drying out	Cakes and cookies (babas, genoises, madeleines, Genoa bread); buttering baking pans
Beurre manié	Mix equal parts butter and flour together to make a smooth paste	Makes the laminating process (*tourage*) easier and helps ensure a crisp finish	Inverse puff pastry

EGGS

All of the recipes in this book have been made with hen's eggs equivalent in size to "large" eggs in the US and Canada and "medium" eggs in the UK, with an average weight of about 2 oz. (55–60 g) per egg. Because precision is crucial in pastry making, most egg quantities in this book are given by weight and volume, with a guide in brackets as to how many eggs you will need (with the exception of level 3 recipes, in which weight only is indicated). The following table will help you determine the approximate number of 2-oz. (55-g) whole eggs, egg whites, and egg yolks needed, but you can use any size egg you want as long as you weigh or measure them.

AVERAGE COMPOSITION OF A 2-OZ. (55-G) EGG

DESCRIPTION	AVERAGE WEIGHT	APPROXIMATE VOLUME MEASURE
Whole egg without the shell	1.75 oz. (50 g)	3 ½ tablespoons
Egg white	1 oz. (30 g)	2 tablespoons
Egg yolk	0.7–0.75 oz. (18–20 g)	1 tablespoon

—— **PURCHASING TIPS:** The way hens have been raised will influence the quality of their eggs and is therefore an important factor to consider when purchasing. It is best to use free-range or organic eggs whenever possible.

—— **STORAGE TIPS: Eggs in their shells:** To maintain freshness for longer and prevent cross-contamination, these should be stored in the refrigerator at a maximum temperature of 45°F (7°C). Refrigerated eggs are at their best when used within several weeks, although egg quality deteriorates over time. Fresher eggs have firmer yolks and thicker, more viscous whites. As eggs age, the yolks flatten out and the whites get runnier. **Separated eggs:** Stored in an airtight container in the refrigerator, egg whites will keep for up to 3 days and egg yolks for up to 1 day. Yolks tend to dry out and are more susceptible to spoilage. Egg whites freeze well and will keep for up to 3 months in the freezer in an airtight container. Yolks can be frozen for up to 2 weeks in an airtight container, but they must be mixed with 10% of their weight in sugar before freezing to maintain proper consistency.

RULES TO FOLLOW WHEN HANDLING EGGS

– When a recipe calls for eggs, remove the necessary quantity from the refrigerator about 30 minutes ahead of time so the eggs will be the same temperature as the other ingredients.
– You should not wash eggs, because this removes the natural barrier that protects the inside of the egg from bacteria.
– If you discover a crack in an egg you have purchased, it may not be safe to eat and should be discarded. If you later accidentally crack an egg you can still use it for making batters and doughs. Pour it into a clean, airtight container and store in the refrigerator for up to 2 days before using.
– It is best to break eggs into a separate bowl rather than directly into a bowl containing the ingredients they are to be mixed with, so any shell fragments can be easily removed.

WHAT ARE EGG PRODUCTS?
The term "egg products" refers to eggs that have been removed from their shells and processed for commercial, professional, and home use. This includes products such as refrigerated liquid eggs, frozen eggs, concentrated eggs, and dried eggs. Egg white powder, for example, can be used when making macaron shells to make the meringue more stable. Egg products can be found in well-stocked supermarkets, specialty shops, or online.

EGG TIPS

• Once you beat egg whites into peaks, do not wait too long before mixing them together with the other ingredients, as they will gradually lose air and turn liquid again.

• Be sure to whisk egg yolks and sugar together as soon as they are put into the same bowl, and do not allow them to sit. When these two ingredients come into contact, the sugar begins to absorb the water from the yolks, causing the proteins in the yolk to clump together, which results in an unpleasant texture.

SUGAR AND SWEETENERS

Of the many different types of sugar, including glucose, fructose, and lactose, sucrose is the most widely used in cooking and pastry making. Sucrose is the chemical name for table sugar that has been extracted from sugar cane or beets; it is often referred to simply as sugar. The sweetness of sucrose (usually assigned a value of 100) serves as a reference point for determining the relative sweetening power of other types of sugar, which also have a role in pastry and candy making. When the word "sugar" appears in an ingredient list, use regular superfine or caster sugar.

—— **PURCHASING TIPS:** The more difficult-to-find and alternative sugars used in this book can be purchased in specialty shops and online.
—— **STORAGE TIPS:** Moisture is the main enemy of sugar, so be sure to store your sugar in an airtight container in a cool, dry place.

GLUCOSE

In liquid or powder form, glucose is an important ingredient for pastry chefs, particularly when making ice cream or candies. Much of the commercial glucose produced today is made from cornstarch, although liquid glucose, also known as glucose syrup, contains less moisture than regular corn syrup. Glucose powder is sometimes referred to as atomized glucose.

—— **PROPERTIES:** Glucose helps retain moisture and prevents sugar from re-crystallizing, so it can increase the storage time and improve the texture of the items it is used in.
—— **SWEETENING POWER:** About 50% less sweet than sugar

INVERT SUGAR

Invert sugar, sometimes sold as Trimoline, is a pasteurized viscous syrup composed of glucose and fructose. It is made by heating sucrose with enzymes or an acid like cream of tartar or lemon juice, causing the sucrose to split into its component sugars, glucose and fructose. If you are unable to find invert sugar, you can use honey instead, which is a natural invert sugar. Keep in mind, however, that honey has a stronger and more distinctive flavor.

—— **PROPERTIES:** Retains moisture in baked goods like loaf cakes, preventing them from drying out, and helps ensure golden crusts. Often used in combination with glucose, invert sugar helps increase the storage time of frozen desserts, and it improves the texture of ice creams and sorbets by lowering the freezing point and preventing crystallization.
—— **SWEETENING POWER:** 1.2 times sweeter than sugar

HONEY

Honey is a natural invert sugar that offers a remarkable variety of flavors and textures. The flavor depends largely on the bees' nectar source, and the texture can be liquid, crystallized, or creamy.

—— **PROPERTIES:** The properties of honey are nearly identical to those of invert sugar, except that honey has a stronger flavor.
—— **SWEETENING POWER:** 1.3 times sweeter than sugar

WHAT IS POURING FONDANT?
Made of sugar, glucose syrup, and water, pouring or pastry fondant (not to be confused with rolled fondant, which contains additional ingredients) is used to decorate or glaze a variety of cakes and pastries or coat candied fruits. It can be purchased ready to use in specialty shops and online.

TYPES OF SUGAR

TYPE	DESCRIPTION	ADVANTAGES AND USES
Superfine sugar (caster or castor sugar in the UK)	Very finely granulated white sugar	The most common sugar in pâtisserie; dissolves quickly and is easy to incorporate into other ingredients
Granulated sugar	Standard, all-purpose white sugar	Helps keep baked goods moist and tender; used to coat *pâtes de fruits* and add texture to pastries like shortbread cookies
Jam sugar	Sugar to which pectin has already been added	Can be used with low-pectin fruit but not with fruit that has a natural high pectin level
Pearl sugar	Crunchy, pearly-white sugar with large grains of different sizes	Used for decorating and adding crunch to pastries like sugar-crusted choux puffs, brioches, and Tropézienne tarts
Confectioners' sugar (also known as powdered or icing sugar)	Powdered white sugar made by grinding granulated sugar; may contain cornstarch to prevent lumping	Often used for decorating; easy to incorporate into sweet tart doughs
Brown sugar (light and dark)	Processed granulated sugar with added molasses; either light or dark, depending on the amount of molasses added	Adds more moisture and flavor to baked goods than white sugar
Vergeoise sugar	Brown beet sugar made by adding syrup from the beet refining process to sugar crystals	Soft and moist with a light or dark brown color and licorice notes
Muscovado sugar	Unrefined brown cane sugar rich in molasses	Moist, with a tendency to clump together; tastes of molasses with notes of licorice and spice
Molasses	A thick, dark syrup separated from sugar crystals in the cane sugar refining process	Strong flavor with distinctive licorice notes

COOKED SUGAR

See the Sugar Cooking Stages table on p. 516.

COCOA AND CHOCOLATE

Chocolate begins with cocoa beans produced by cacao trees, which are transformed to produce one of our most beloved treats. A favorite ingredient of those with a sweet tooth, chocolate in all of its varieties is one of the key products to master in pastry making.

CHOCOLATE

Different types of chocolate are categorized according to the amount of cocoa solids they contain. For example, bittersweet chocolate must contain at least 35% cocoa solids. Depending on the type, chocolate may also contain sugar, cocoa butter, emulsifiers, powdered milk, flavorings, and more.

TYPE	COMPOSITION
Bittersweet chocolate	Cocoa solids, sugar, cocoa butter, flavoring(s), emulsifier(s)
Milk chocolate	Cocoa solids, sugar, cocoa butter, powdered milk, flavoring(s), emulsifier(s)
White chocolate	Cocoa butter, sugar, powdered milk, flavorings, emulsifier(s)

—— **PURCHASING TIPS:** The best chocolate to buy depends on what you are making. A creamy mousse, for example, requires a different kind of chocolate than shiny molded chocolates. The following two criteria are important to consider:

- Cocoa butter content
Chocolates with a greater percentage of cocoa butter are more fluid when melted and are better for making molded chocolates. If the cocoa butter percentage is not directly indicated on the label, look for the nutritional information and find the total fat per serving in grams. Divide this amount by the total serving size in grams for a good estimation of the cocoa butter percentage. In Europe, look for the amount of fat per 100 g of finished chocolate, which is the percentage of cocoa butter the chocolate contains.

- Cocoa percentages
We tend to associate higher cocoa percentages with a stronger flavor. While it is true that chocolates with higher cocoa percentages contain less sugar, the flavor of the chocolate depends on a number of additional factors. The variety of the cocoa bean, where it was grown, and the roasting and manufacturing processes all have an impact on flavor, and chocolate with 60% cocoa can have a more pronounced flavor than those with even higher percentages. Try different chocolates to determine their strengths and characteristics in order to choose the right ones according to your needs and preferences.

WHAT IS "COUVERTURE" CHOCOLATE?

Couverture chocolate is particularly rich in cocoa butter (containing at least 31%), which means it melts more readily and is more fluid than other chocolates, resulting in a superior texture when it cools. Tempered couverture chocolate can be used for making molded chocolates and chocolate bars, for coating bonbons, and more.

WHAT IS *PÂTE À GLACER* (GLAZING PASTE)?

This is a compound chocolate used for coating, glazing, and dipping. It does not contain cocoa butter and therefore does not need to be tempered. When *pâte à glacer* sets, it is semi-firm and glossy.

—— **STORAGE TIPS:** All chocolates should be stored in an airtight container, in a dry place away from direct sunlight, at a temperature of 60°F–70°F (15°C–20°C).

COCOA POWDER

Cocoa powder is made from roasted and ground cocoa beans that have been pressed to remove most of the cocoa butter and then ground again into a fine, brown powder. Cocoa powder tends to clump together, so always sift it before using.

—— **PURCHASING TIPS:** Look for unsweetened 100% cacao cocoa powder.
—— **STORAGE TIPS:** Store cocoa powder in an airtight container in a cool, dry place away from sunlight.

COCOA BUTTER

Cocoa butter, the fat pressed from roasted cocoa beans, has a neutral flavor and can help in the chocolate tempering process. You can add cocoa butter to chocolate that has been melted over a hot water bath to make the chocolate more fluid.

—— **PURCHASING TIPS:** Be sure to purchase 100% pure cocoa butter, which is available in solid or powdered (freeze-dried) form in specialty shops and online.
—— **STORAGE TIPS:** Store cocoa butter as you do chocolate.

CACAO PASTE

Also known as chocolate liquor or cocoa (or chocolate) mass, cacao paste is chocolate in its purest form, with no added sugar. It is ideal for flavoring creams or mixing into praline paste.

—— **PURCHASING TIPS:** This pure chocolate is available in block form, which is best for professional kitchens that require large quantities, or in chunks or disks, which are better when only small quantities are needed. It can be purchased in specialty shops or online.
—— **STORAGE TIPS:** Store cacao paste in an airtight container in a dry place away from direct sunlight, at a temperature of between 60°F–70°F (15°C–20°C).

FLOURS, GRAINS, AND STARCHES

WHEAT FLOUR

Along with butter, sugar, and eggs, flour is one of the most important ingredients in pastry making. For successful results, be sure to use the type of flour indicated. Unless stated otherwise, "flour" means all-purpose flour.

TYPE	APPROXIMATE PROTEIN CONTENT	DESCRIPTION	USES
Cake flour	7%–9%	Finely-milled soft wheat flour	Well suited for soft-textured cakes
Pastry flour	8%–10%	Finely-milled soft wheat flour with slightly more protein than cake flour	Produces a fine crumb and delicate texture in various viennoiseries and cakes
Self-rising flour (self-raising flour in the UK)	8%–11%	Soft wheat flour blended with baking powder and salt	Pastries and cakes
All-purpose flour (plain flour in the UK)	10%–12%	Versatile flour made from a blend of hard and soft wheats	Pastries, puff pastries, pie and tart crusts, cookies, and certain traditional French breads
Bread flour (strong flour in the UK)	11%–13%	Hard wheat flour, containing more gluten than all-purpose flour	Yeasted breads and brioches; helps breads rise and improves the texture
High-gluten flour	13%–14%	Hard wheat flour milled from high-protein wheat	Yeasted breads and brioches; gives dough more structural integrity, resulting in a particularly airy crumb and pleasantly chewy texture

WHAT IS GLUTEN?

Gluten is formed by two proteins, glutenin and gliadin, which occur naturally in certain grains, including wheat, rye, barley, spelt, and oats. When liquid is added to flour, these two proteins bind together to make gluten, which plays a crucial role in the leavening and texture of baked goods. Kneading or mixing develops the web-like gluten network, which is particularly important for yeasted bread and brioche-type doughs. Gluten gives such doughs elasticity and traps gas as the dough bakes, helping it rise. In the case of delicate cakes, pastries, and tart crusts, you need to avoid overmixing, because if too much gluten develops, it can make the texture dense and tough. The type of flour used in a given recipe, particularly the protein content (a good indicator of the gluten content), is also critical to successful results. Flours with more gluten, sometimes referred to as "strong" or "hard," produce lighter, airier breads with a pleasant chewy texture. Lower-protein flours, on the other hand, are better for more delicate pastries and cakes.

—— **STORAGE TIPS:** Flour should be stored in the following conditions:
- In a cool, dry, and well-ventilated place, to prevent it from turning rancid
- In an airtight container, to protect it from humidity

ALTERNATIVE FLOURS

There are many flavorful alternative flours made from grains or nuts, like buckwheat, rye, spelt, or chestnuts, which are sometimes used in breads or regional specialties. Such flours should be stored in the same conditions as wheat flour.

STARCHES

Many different grains, roots, and tubers naturally contain starch, although cornstarch (or cornflour) is the most widely used in cooking and baking. Potato starch, as the name implies, is extracted from potatoes, and it can be used in place of cornstarch in many recipes. Both cornstarch and potato starch are fine white powders that thicken when heated, and both are gluten-free.

CUSTARD POWDER

Custard powder is a blend of cornstarch, sugar, vanilla flavoring, and a touch of yellow coloring. It gives custard-based desserts and sauces like flan and pastry cream a particularly rich and creamy texture.

NUTS

Walnuts, hazelnuts, almonds, pistachios, and chestnuts are among the most flavorful nuts and they are basic ingredients in pastry making. Used whole, powdered, or in paste or oil form, they provide pastry chefs with a wide range of delectable tastes and textures.

—— **STORAGE TIPS:** Nuts are high in fat, which makes them particularly susceptible to going rancid. It is therefore best to purchase nuts as you need them rather than store them. If you have nuts left over, keep them in an airtight container, preferably in the refrigerator or freezer. Otherwise, store them in a cool, dry place away from sunlight. Pine nuts, Brazil nuts, macadamia nuts, and pecans should be stored in the same manner.

ALMONDS

Whether ground, sliced, slivered, chopped, or whole (blanched or unblanched), almonds play a key role in a number of French pastries, including *galettes des rois* (kings' cake), financiers, macarons, and more.

—— **PURCHASING TIPS:** Get the freshest almonds you can find, preferably of premium quality, and buy them as you need them. Most almond varieties are sweet, which are best for pastry making, but there are some bitter varieties, typically used to make almond extract.

Almond Flour
This is made by grinding blanched (skinned) whole almonds very finely. If you have trouble buying almond flour—available from whole food stores and online—ground almonds (almond meal) can be substituted. The results will not be quite as fine, as ground almonds are produced by milling the nuts with their skins left on to produce a slightly coarser meal.

Marzipan and Almond Paste
In the US, almond paste and marzipan (both called *pâte d'amande* in French) are two different items, whereas both terms refer to the same product in the UK. Marzipan has more sugar and less almonds than almond paste, and it has a smooth, malleable texture. It is used principally for decorating, as it can be modeled into decorative shapes or rolled into a thin, fondant-like layer to cover cakes. Products labeled "almond paste" in the US contain more almonds and less sugar than marzipan, so they are less sweet and have a coarser texture. Almond paste works better for filling tarts or pastries or for blending into other ingredients. Both marzipan and almond paste can be purchased ready-to-use from specialty shops or online. Almond pastes with a higher ratio of almonds to sugar will have a superior taste to pastes with more sugar than almonds, but they will also be more expensive and will not keep as well.

HAZELNUTS

Whole or ground, hazelnuts marry particularly well with chocolate. To make hazelnuts even more flavorful and easier to skin, roast them briefly in the oven.

—— **PURCHASING TIPS:** Look for premium hazelnuts, and buy the freshest you can find. If you wish to use whole hazelnuts, try to find nuts that are more or less the same size.

Praline
Made with hazelnuts and/or almonds that are caramelized and ground into a powder or paste, praline can be prepared at home (see techniques pp. 548 and 550) or purchased in specialty shops or online. If you purchase a French brand, the word *"praliné"* alone on the label indicates that the mixture contains equal amounts of nuts and sugar; otherwise, the percentage of nuts must be clearly indicated. When praline paste is stored for a while, the oil tends to rise to the surface, so it may be necessary to mix it to make it uniform and smooth again. Praline paste should be kept in a cool, dry place away from sunlight.

WALNUTS

Whole, chopped, or ground, walnuts add texture, crunch, and a sweet, nutty flavor to many cakes and pastries.

—— **PURCHASING TIPS:** Buy walnut halves for decoration, or walnut pieces, which are less expensive, for chopping and grinding, and always get the freshest you can find. Avoid purchasing ground walnuts, as they go rancid quickly. It is best to grind them yourself and use them right away.
—— **STORAGE TIPS:** Walnuts are particularly susceptible to going rancid, so buy small quantities and store them in the refrigerator or freezer.

PISTACHIOS

Because pistachios are costly, pastry chefs typically use them in small quantities for decoration only. Pistachio paste is used most notably for making ice cream, but it also adds a luxurious flavor and texture to a number of cakes and pastries.

—— **PURCHASING TIPS:** Be sure to buy unsalted pistachios for pastry making. When purchasing pistachio paste, the higher the percentage of pistachios, the better the flavor. Check the label to confirm the composition.
—— **STORAGE TIPS:** It is best to store pistachios in an airtight container in the refrigerator. Keep pistachio paste in a cool, dry place away from sunlight. Like other nut pastes and butters, pistachio paste tends to separate, so mix it before using.

CHESTNUTS

The natural sweetness of chestnuts makes them perfect for pastries, cakes, and candies. Unlike other nuts, chestnuts are high in carbohydrates and moisture and low in fat, and they must be cooked before being eaten.

Chestnut paste, spread, and purée
Pastry chefs typically use chestnuts in the form of a paste, spread, or purée, all of which are commercially produced in France. The product known as *pâte de marrons* (chestnut paste) typically contains chestnuts, sugar, glucose syrup, and vanilla extract. *Crème de marrons* (chestnut spread) has the same basic ingredients as chestnut paste, as well as crushed candied chestnuts and a tiny amount of water. *Purée de marrons* (chestnut purée), on the other hand, is unsweetened and contains only chestnuts and water.

—— **PURCHASING TIPS:** Chestnut pastes, spreads, and purées produced in France can be purchased in specialty shops and online.

YEAST AND BAKING POWDER

BAKER'S YEAST

Baker's yeast, a living, microscopic fungus, is a vital ingredient in leavened breads. Through the process of fermentation, yeast transforms the sugars in flour into carbon dioxide, which in turn makes dough and bread rise. Yeast also gives bread a distinctive aroma and flavor. Baker's yeast comes in many forms: fresh (also known as cake or compressed yeast); active dry; instant; and rapid- or quick-rise. Most professional bakers and pastry chefs use fresh yeast, although active dry and instant yeasts (both dried) also produce excellent results if used properly. If a recipe calls for fresh yeast, use 50% of the weight in active dry yeast or 40% of the weight in instant yeast. Fresh and instant yeasts can be directly added to doughs, but active dry yeast must first be proofed in warm water to activate the dormant yeast cells. Rapid- or quick-rise yeast works faster than other yeasts, but it is not recommended for the recipes in this book because it also produces an inferior flavor.

—— **PURCHASING TIPS:** Fresh yeast is more widely available in the UK and Europe than in the US. Look in the refrigerated sections of well-stocked supermarkets or online, or check with your local bakery or pizzeria. Active dry and instant yeasts are less perishable and easier to find, although be careful not to confuse instant yeast with rapid- or quick-rise yeast.

—— **STORAGE TIPS:** Fresh yeast is highly perishable and must be stored in an airtight container in the refrigerator, for no longer than 2–3 weeks. It can also be frozen. Store unopened dry yeast in an airtight container in a cool, dry place away from direct sunlight. Once opened, dry yeast should be kept in a sealed container in the refrigerator or freezer, where it will last for several months.

BAKER'S YEAST TIPS

• Although fresh and instant yeasts do not need to be proofed, it is a good idea to always dilute your yeast in a little bit of lukewarm or warm water (no hotter than 122°F/50°C) before mixing it in to distribute the yeast cells more evenly throughout the dough.

• Too much yeast will give your baked goods an unpleasant flavor, so it is important to respect the quantities given in the recipes.

• Both sugar and salt draw water out of yeast cells, which can decrease or totally inhibit yeast activity. It is therefore important to avoid direct contact between yeast and salt or sugar and to knead or mix your dough as soon as you add these ingredients to the bowl.

• Take account of the temperature of the dough and of the room in which the dough will be left to rise: the warmer the room, the more quickly the yeast will act.

BAKING SODA

Baking soda, or bicarbonate of soda, is one of the ingredients in baking powder, but it can also be used as a leavener on its own, although it is not often used in French pâtisserie. Baking soda is alkaline, so it needs to be mixed with an acidic ingredient like yogurt or milk to react and form the carbon dioxide bubbles that make cakes rise. As with yeast and baking powder, be sure to respect the quantity called for in a given recipe. Too much baking soda can result in a soapy taste.

—— **STORAGE TIPS:** Baking soda should be kept in a cool, dry place and replaced after 6 months or so, once opened.

BAKING POWDER

Baking powder is a chemical leavener composed of a mild acid (such as cream of tartar or tartaric acid); a mild alkali (usually baking soda, also known as bicarbonate of soda); and a drying element (like cornstarch or potato starch). When the acid and alkali come into contact with moisture, they react to produce carbon dioxide. This gas produces bubbles in the batter, which make your baked goods rise. Double-acting baking powders in the US also react a second time when exposed to the heat of the oven.

—— **STORAGE TIPS:** Baking powder should be kept in an airtight container in a cool, dry place. It gradually loses its strength, so should be used within several months and before the use-by date.

BAKING POWDER TIPS

• Respect the quantities given in the recipes. Too much baking powder can give your baked goods an unpleasant taste or make them rise too much.

• Baking powder begins to act as soon as it is mixed into the batter, so you must get it into the oven quickly, before the reaction slows.

• It is not necessary to dilute baking powder in liquid before use.

ADDITIVES

These additives serve to improve certain characteristics of foods, such as taste or texture, or to increase the storage time. Some, like salt, have been used for millennia. Others have been more recently put to use in cooking after years of research and experimentation.

SALT

Salt is essential for balanced flavor. Unless otherwise specified, use fine sea salt, which easily dissolves into other ingredients. Fleur de sel is excellent for finishing and adding a pleasant crunch to French shortbread cookies (sablés). If you cannot find fleur de sel, use fine sea salt flakes instead.

CREAM OF TARTAR

Cream of tartar is tartaric acid that has been ground and partially neutralized. The resulting fine white powder is often used as the acidic component in baking powder. Alone, cream of tartar can help stabilize beaten egg whites—just add a pinch while the whites are being whipped.

—— **STORAGE TIPS:** Store tightly sealed in a cool, dry place.

TARTARIC ACID

The tartaric acid used in cooking is a white crystalline powder extracted from the tartar that forms on wine casks in the winemaking process. It is more acidic than cream of tartar. Tartaric acid is also used to help the gelling process in certain candies like fruit jellies (*pâtes de fruit*).

—— **STORAGE TIPS:** Store tightly sealed in a cool, dry place.

CITRIC ACID

Citric acid, which naturally occurs in many fruits, particularly those in the citrus family, is used in the form of a crystalline white powder for cooking. This powder, also known as "sour salt," gives jams, jellies, and certain candies a pleasantly tart flavor.

—— **STORAGE TIPS:** Store tightly sealed in a cool, dry place.

THICKENING AND GELLING AGENTS

AGAR-AGAR

Agar-agar is a plant-based thickener extracted from red algae. It is typically sold in powder or flake form and has remarkable gelling power: 1 tsp (4 g) of powder is enough for 4 cups (1 liter) of liquid. Agar-agar must first be mixed with a cold liquid, and the mixture must then be brought to a boil for 1 minute, or until the agar-agar is fully dissolved. This plant-based gelatin substitute can be used to thicken jams and to set different creams, coulis, and candies. It can also be used with fruits that are not compatible with gelatin.

—— **STORAGE TIPS:** Store tightly sealed in a cool, dry place.

GELATIN

Gelatin, available in sheet and powder form, is derived from the collagen found in the skins, hides, and bones of certain animals, particularly pigs and cows. Gelatin sheets and powder can be used interchangeably, although most professional pastry chefs prefer sheets, because the results are cleaner tasting and perfectly transparent. Gelatin is typically identified according to its setting power—called its Bloom strength—which can range from 50 to 300. The Bloom strength of gelatin sheets is indicated by their grade, which can be bronze, silver, gold, or platinum. Gold strength sheets, which generally weigh 0.1 oz. (2 g) each and have a Bloom strength of between 200 and 220, are recommended for the recipes in this book.

—— **GOOD TO KNOW:** Before use, both powdered and sheet gelatin must first be hydrated in about six times their weight of cold water and then fully dissolved in a warm, but not boiling, liquid (no hotter than 158°F/70°C). Mixtures containing gelatin should never be boiled, because they will not set properly. High amounts of acidity and sugar in a given recipe can also inhibit the setting power of gelatin.
—— **STORAGE TIPS:** Store tightly sealed in a cool, dry place.

PECTIN

Naturally occurring in fruits—such as apples, quince, citrus fruits, and currants—pectin is used in pastry making as both a thickener and gelling agent. The pectin used for cooking comes in powder form and can be divided into two broad categories: high methoxyl (HM) and low methoxyl (LM). Yellow pectin, or apple pectin, is a type of HM pectin used in fruit jellies. Once set, it has a firm texture, and it cannot be re-melted.

Pectin NH, on the other hand, is a special kind of LM pectin that has been processed to make it thermally reversible, meaning that it can be melted and reset as needed. This is particularly useful for certain glazes. Pectin has many applications in pâtisserie, including as a thickener in jams, glazes, creams, and fillings.

—— **GOOD TO KNOW:** Always mix pectin with sugar before adding it to the other ingredients to ensure even distribution.

—— **PURCHASING TIPS:** Most pectin found in regular supermarkets is either high methoxyl (for full-sugar jams or jellies) or low methoxyl (for low-sugar preparations). Yellow pectin and pectin NH can be purchased in specialty shops or online.

—— **STORAGE TIPS:** Store tightly sealed.

FOOD COLORING

Natural food coloring can come from animal sources (such as carmine); plant sources (including beet red and annatto); or mineral sources. Many food colorings used today are synthetically produced, and certain colors can only be made by artificial means. Use natural food dyes whenever possible, and choose between liquid, gel, or powder depending on the recipe, strength of color required, and whether or not any extra liquid can be added.

—— **GOOD TO KNOW:** Always add food coloring little by little to your recipe to avoid adding too much. It is always easy to add more, but impossible to take any away! Suggested quantities are provided in the recipes in this book, but keep in mind that the intensity of different brands can vary, so you may need more or less than the amount called for.

TYPE	USES	STORAGE
Liquid food coloring	Decorations, certain creams, cake batter (loses intensity when baked), almond paste, candies	Away from direct sunlight, for up to 3 months after opening
Gel food coloring (liquid or paste)	Concentrated color with minimal liquid for decorations, creams, icings, and cake batters	Tightly sealed in a cool, dry place
Powdered food coloring (water-soluble)	Dry color for sugar work (pulled and blown sugar), meringues, macarons	Tightly sealed in a cool, dry place, for up to 1 year after opening
Powdered food coloring (fat-soluble)	Dry color for chocolate	Tightly sealed in a cool, dry place, for up to 1 year after opening

FLAVORINGS

In addition to spices and herbs (like vanilla beans, cinnamon, saffron, and aromatic herbs), pastry chefs use a wide range of other natural flavorings to make their creations deliciously distinct. Natural flavorings include extracts (such as vanilla and coffee), flower waters (like orange blossom and rose), and natural essences sold in liquid form. Other examples include bitter almond, anise, bergamot, peppermint, coconut, and many more, all available as liquid extracts or essences. Such flavorings can be directly mixed in with the other ingredients in a given recipe. When flavorings are labeled "natural," it means they are derived from natural sources: they may be extracted directly from animals or plants or biologically produced in a laboratory using enzymes and microbes. Spirits such as rum, kirsch, and eaux-de-vie can also be used to flavor pastries, desserts, and soaking syrups for cakes.

—— **GOOD TO KNOW:** Add flavorings little by little and taste as you go until you obtain the desired strength.

—— **PURCHASING TIPS:** Look for pure extracts, which provide a much better flavor than essences.

STABILIZERS AND EMULSIFIERS FOR ICE CREAMS AND SORBETS

Professional ice cream and sorbet recipes often call for added stabilizers and emulsifiers. These additives help make ice cream extra smooth and creamy, but they also improve the texture by inhibiting the formation of ice crystals. Ice cream with stabilizers and emulsifiers is more resistant to melting and stays in peak condition for longer than additive-free ice cream.

Sorbet stabilizers
Sorbet stabilizers are typically made from natural products like carob, agar-agar, carraghenates, or guar gum. They come in powder form and do not contain emulsifiers, as sorbet contains little to no fat. One of their main roles is to stabilize the water contained in the fruit used, which reduces the formation of ice crystals and helps keep the texture smooth.

Ice cream stabilizers
These additives contain both a stabilizing agent (to stabilize the water in the milk) and emulsifiers, often derived from egg yolks—the original ice cream emulsifier. Emulsifiers help the fat particles bind to the water in the ice cream while it is being churned, resulting in a smooth emulsion.

STABILIZER AND EMULSIFIER TIPS

• Sorbet and ice cream stabilizers and emulsifiers can be purchased in specialty shops or online.

• When you are making ice cream or sorbet at home for immediate consumption, stabilizers and emulsifiers are not essential. The recipes in the ice cream chapter can be made successfully without these additives.

FRUIT

FRESH FRUIT BY SEASON

In recipes calling for fresh fruit, choose the best seasonal fruit you can find. Bear in mind that there may be early or late varieties available.

TYPE	NORTHERN HEMISPHERE SEASON	SOUTHERN HEMISPHERE SEASON
Apple	July–March	December–September
Apricot	May–September	December–February
Banana	January–December	October–August
Black currant	June–August	December–February
Blueberry	May–September	December–February
Cape gooseberry	June–July	September–November
Cherry	June–August	November–January
Chestnut	November–January	March–June
Clementine	November–January	April–February
Fig	June–September	December–April
Grape	September–October	December–May
Grapefruit	September–November	June–February
Kiwi	January–August	February–August
Lemon	January–March	All year round
Lime	September–December	January–August
Lychee	April–June	November–February
Mandarin orange	November–May	April–October
Mango	March–September	October–March
Melon	July–October	October–February
Orange	January–March	All year round
Papaya	All year round	All year round
Passion fruit	July–March	October–June
Peach/nectarine	June–September	December–April
Pear	September–January	January–June
Pineapple	March–July	October–February
Plum	May–October	December–April
Quince	October–December	February–June
Raspberry	June–September	December–March
Red currants	July–August	January–February
Rhubarb	January–May	February–August
Strawberry	June–August	October–February
Wild strawberry	August	January–February

FRUIT PURÉES

Many recipes in this book call for fruit purées, which are made with freshly picked, uncooked fruit and typically contain about 10% sugar. Prepared fruit purées help ensure consistent results. They are often sold frozen for maximum freshness and can be purchased in certain specialty shops and online. You can also make your own in a blender or food processor.

MEASURING AND CONVERSIONS

THE IMPORTANCE OF PRECISION

For successful pastries, it is always advisable to weigh your ingredients; for optimal results, use a digital scale and the metric weights. Volume and imperial measures are included throughout—with the exception of level 3 recipes, where precision is crucial and volume measures are only given for liquid ingredients—but have been rounded up or down to avoid awkward or unmeasurable amounts. When using cups and spoons, remember that they must be level unless stated otherwise.

LIQUID MEASURES

1 tsp	5 ml
1 tbsp	15 ml
¼ cup	60 ml
⅓ cup	75 ml
½ cup	125 ml
1 cup	250 ml

BUTTER EQUIVALENTS

1 tbsp	0.5 oz.	15 g
½ US stick (4 tbsp or ¼ cup)	2 oz.	60 g
1 US stick (8 tbsp or ½ cup)	4 oz.	115 g
2 US sticks (1 cup)	8 oz.	230 g

COMMON DRY INGREDIENT EQUIVALENTS

INGREDIENT	1 US TSP	1 US TBSP	1 US CUP
All-purpose flour	3 g	0.3 oz. /8 g	4.5 oz. /125 g
Superfine/caster sugar	4 g	0.5 oz. /12 g	6.75 oz. /195 g
Confectioners' sugar	3 g	0.3 oz. /8 g	4.5 oz. /130 g
Baking powder	4 g	0.4 oz. /11 g	
Fine sea salt	5 g	0.5 oz. /15 g	

OVEN TEMPERATURE CONVERSIONS

Fahrenheit	225°F	250°F	275°F	300°F	325°F	350°F	375°F	400°F	425°F	450°F	475°F
Celsius	105°C	120°C	140°C	150°C	160°C	180°C	190°C	200°C	220°C	230°C	245°C
Gas mark	¼	½	1	2	3	4	5	6	7	8	9

PASTRIES

DOUGH AND PASTRY

A WIDE VARIETY

Doughs and pastries can be grouped into five main types:
- **Flaky pastries:** shortcrust pastry and sweet short pastry
  (made using either the creaming or rubbing-in method)
- **Puff pastries:** including classic puff pastry and inverse puff pastry
- **Yeast doughs:** including bread dough, brioche dough, and baba dough
- **Leavened puff pastries:** for making croissants and kouign amann (Breton pastries)
- **Choux pastry**

FLAKY PASTRY AND TART CRUSTS

These doughs are light-textured and not elastic. When making them, it is important to avoid activating the gluten in the flour as this would make the dough stretchy, difficult to roll out, and it would shrink when baked. Two techniques are used to prevent the dough becoming elastic: **rubbing in,** which incorporates the butter into the flour, and **creaming,** where butter, sugar, and eggs are beaten together. The two methods produce different textures, with rubbed in pastries being more crumbly, and creamed ones being crisper.

CREAMING AND RUBBING IN: GETTING THEM RIGHT

When making pastry by the creaming method, the temperature of the ingredients is very important. Butter must be softened and eggs at room temperature but although the butter and sugar are emulsified, you are not making mayonnaise. Combine them at low speed so as not to beat in too much air, as this would make the dough fragile, and it would lose its shape during baking. For rubbing in, it is better to use the paddle beater of your mixer rather than your hands to avoid melting the butter, which should be cold and diced beforehand.

HANDLE WITH CARE

As these doughs are light they must not be overworked once the flour has been incorporated. To combine ingredients means just that—so no kneading! The best way to ensure a smooth dough is to work the ingredients together with your hand, without using undue pressure. The French verb for this technique is *fraser*.

CHILLING TIME

When making flaky pastries, the chilling stage is essential as it gives the butter in the dough time to firm up again. A dough that is too cold will crack and be difficult to roll out, while a dough that is too soft will be hard to handle, so follow the chilling times given in the recipe. To ensure your dough chills rapidly and evenly, flatten it into a disk rather than shape it into a ball, as this will make it much easier to roll out. Cover the dough in plastic wrap before placing it in the refrigerator.

ROLLING OUT THE DOUGH

A light dusting of flour, barely visible to the eye, is all that's needed. Chilling the rolling pin will also help keep the dough cold and prevent it becoming sticky. Should this happen, simply re-wrap the dough and return it to the refrigerator to firm up again. It's better than adding flour as that would dry out the dough. The thickness of the rolled-out dough depends on how it will be used and for how long you plan to keep it. A blind baked pastry crust does not need rolling out as thinly as one filled with almond cream. The longer you store the tart crust, the thicker it should be.

BLIND BAKING: IS IT ALWAYS NECESSARY?

A tart crust can be pre-baked, or baked without a filling, which is called "blind baking." To prevent the crust shrinking in the oven, it is important not to stretch the pastry when you line it into the tart pan. The crust needs to be lined with baking paper and filled with weights (pie weights, baking beans, or dried beans that can be re-used). Weighing the pastry down is important when baking basic tart dough, but is not necessary for sweet and short pastries if you butter the tart pan (or ring) before lining it with the dough.

STORAGE

If chilling, cover the dough in several layers of plastic wrap or, if freezing, place it in a freezer bag, label, and date. Store in the coldest part of the refrigerator, well away from strong-smelling foods such as fish and cheeses. Adding a few drops of white vinegar or lemon juice to the dough will extend the storage time of basic and short pastries.

TYPE OF DOUGH	REFRIGERATING	FREEZING
Shortcrust pastry	Up to 3 days	Up to 3 months
Creamed sweet short pastry	Up to 3 days	Up to 3 months
Crumbled sweet short pastry	Up to 3 days	Up to 3 months

THE RIGHT FIT

TO SERVE	4	4–6	6–8	8–10
Ring or pan size	7 in. (18 cm)	8 in. (20 cm)	9 in. (23 cm)	10 in. (25 cm)
Diameter of rolled-out dough	9 in. (23 cm)	10 in. (25 cm)	11 in. (28 cm)	12 in. (30 cm)
Weight of dough	7 oz. (200 g)	9 oz. (250 g)	10 oz. (280 g)	10.5 oz. (300 g)

DIFFERENT PASTRIES TO SUIT DIFFERENT RECIPES

TYPE OF TART	PASTRY
Baked fruit (apples, pears, etc.)	Shortcrust and sweet short pastry (creamed and crumbled)
Tarts with juicy fruit (plums, peaches, etc.)	Shortcrust pastry (must be blind baked)
Tarts with cream fillings (pastry cream, lemon cream, etc.)	Sweet short pastry (creamed and crumbled)
Cheesecakes	Shortcrust pastry
Custard tarts	Shortcrust or puff pastry
Tartes fines	Puff pastry

PUFF PASTRIES

There are records dating back to the 14th century of cakes being made with puff pastry, but it wasn't until the 17th century that François Pierre La Varenne showed how to make the pastry, using the folding technique, in his book Le Cuisinier Français (The French Cook). Later, Antonin Carême improved on this by developing five-turn puff pastry.

QUALITY BUTTER

To make puff pastry successfully, it is essential to use the finest butter, preferably unsalted and with a high butterfat content, ideally 84% as it contains less water. In French this is called *beurre de tourage* and is malleable and softens more quickly. However, away from professional kitchens it can be difficult to buy so use butter with the highest fat content you can find.

TEMPERATURE CONTROL

Work in a cool environment and make sure your equipment and your hands are cold, as the butter will be easier to handle. Using a marble slab also helps, particularly for making inverse puff pastry.

THE SECRETS OF PUFF PASTRY: FOLDING AND TURNING

Creating the leaves in puff pastry is done by folding the dough over itself (making what are known as "turns") and rotating the dough 45 degrees each time. Puff pastry is defined by the number of times it is rolled and folded and this can be four, five, or six. A single turn involves folding the dough in three, while a double turn requires four folds. The greater the number of turns, the lighter and crisper the pastry will be due to the greater number of leaves—a total that can reach 1,024!

A SWISH OF THE BRUSH AND A FLOURISH OF THE ROLLING PIN

Between each turn, it is important to remove the dusting of flour on the work surface used to roll out the dough. Brush it away with a dry pastry brush so the pastry leaves adhere to each other.
Before resting the dough in the refrigerator, roll the pin over it one final time to seal the pastry layers and ensure they are even.

CLASSIC	
Advantages	Easier to make than inverse puff pastry. All uses.
Disadvantages	Requires numerous resting periods. Must be made a day ahead.
Storage	3 days
INVERSE (sometimes known as inside-out puff pastry)	
Advantages	Has a more buttery taste. Shrinks less when baked. Shorter resting periods. Very crisp. Softens less quickly when filled.
Disadvantages	Trickier to make. Essential to work in a cool room with cool hands and preferably on a marble slab that has been chilled first.
Storage	4 days
QUICK (also known as rough puff pastry)	
Advantages	Quick and easy to make. Perfect for tart crusts and petits fours.
Disadvantages	Does not have as many leaves. Irregular appearance.
Storage	1 day (but preferably use immediately)

ROLLING AND CUTTING PUFF PASTRY
—

Puff pastry tends to shrink back when it is rolled out, so it should never be rolled out just once, but two or three times, and left briefly on the work surface each time to shrink back. Roll alternately down the length and across the width to prevent the pastry becoming misshapen. When it is fully rolled out, the pastry should be lifted up briefly from the work surface so it can relax. If the kitchen has become warm, return the pastry to the refrigerator for a few minutes before cutting it to the required shape.

A LONGER STORAGE TIME
—

Dissolve the salt in the water being used to make the dough or add a drop of white vinegar to the water to prevent the pastry from oxidizing. You will be able to refrigerate the dough for up to 3–4 days without it spoiling.

FREEZING
—

Puff pastry can be frozen for up to 2 months, if covered tightly with plastic wrap or put in a sealed freezer bag. If you freeze puff pastry, it is advisable to stop after 4 turns. Once defrosted in the refrigerator, give the pastry a final turn before rolling it out and baking.

LEAVENED DOUGHS AND VIENNOISERIES

Unlike flaky doughs, these use yeast to activate the gluten contained in the flour, giving them their elasticity. They are best made with bread flour, which has a high gluten content.

BRIOCHE DOUGH	
Storage	Up to 2 days in the refrigerator, covered in plastic wrap.
Freezing	After the first rising. Defrost in the refrigerator and let rise again. Brush with egg wash and bake.
LEAVENED PUFF PASTRY	
Storage	24 hours in the refrigerator, covered in plastic wrap.
Freezing	After shaping, freeze uncooked. Defrost in the refrigerator and let rise for 1 hour. Brush with egg wash and bake.

KNEADING: GETTING IT RIGHT
—

Kneading is done in two stages. Start at low speed until all the ingredients are evenly combined and then increase the speed to medium to develop the gluten and incorporate air so the dough rises. Only knead until the dough is smooth and holds its shape, as excessive kneading will make it too elastic.

RISING THE DOUGH
—

Fresh yeast is available from artisan bakers and some pizzerias but, if you are unable to buy it, active dried or quick-rise yeast can be substituted. Both are widely available but dried yeast is twice as strong as fresh so the quantity in recipes should be halved. Follow the package instructions as to usage. The recipes in this book suggest a very cool oven (75°F/25°C) for rising doughs but it can also be done in a warm room. It's imperative not to let the dough get too hot when rising as yeast cells die at 130°F (55°C).

To make egg wash, strain the egg to remove the rope-like white strands and add a pinch of salt to make the egg wash more liquid. When brushing puff pastry, don't use too much, and avoid brushing along the pastry edges as the leaves will "glue" together and prevent the pastry rising evenly in the oven.

UNMOLD IMMEDIATELY

Brioches baked in molds are very moist so turn them out straight away to avoid them reabsorbing any steam, as the moisture will soften them.

CHOUX PASTRY

AVOID EVAPORATION

The butter should be cut into small dice so it melts quickly while the milk and water are coming to a boil. This ensures the liquids evaporate less so the proportions of the ingredients do not change.

WHY MARK THE CHOUX WITH A FORK?

Pressing the prongs of a fork lightly on the top of choux buns and éclairs makes them rise evenly, without any unsightly bumps. Some pastry chefs use a ¾-in. (20-mm) fluted or open star decorating tip to do this.

DON'T DELAY

Uncooked choux pastry has to be shaped as soon as it's made so it rises evenly. Once choux pastries are baked, transfer them to a cooling rack straight away, as they will go soggy if left to reabsorb any steam.

AVOID COLLAPSING

Don't open the oven door while choux pastry is baking—if the temperature inside drops, the pastries will deflate, so don't let them collapse!

CAN CHOUX PASTRY BE FROZEN?

Once choux pastry has been shaped or piped onto a baking sheet, it can be frozen. Baked, unfilled choux buns, such as éclairs, can also be frozen. To defrost, spread them out on a cooling rack and let them thaw in the refrigerator. You might need to heat them briefly in a 200°F (100°C/Gas mark ¼) oven to evaporate any moisture and make them crisp again.

TOPPINGS AND FILLINGS

All sorts of toppings can be used for choux pastry: fondant, ganache, praline paste, or caramel. *Craquelin* has become popular over the last few years; this paste of flour, butter, and light brown sugar is rolled out as thinly as possible, chilled in the freezer, and cut into shapes, which are placed on choux buns and éclairs before being baked. The crisp *craquelin* contrasts with the soft choux pastry, and the brown sugar adds a hint of caramel. As for fillings, vanilla, chocolate, or coffee-flavored pastry creams are traditional for iced éclairs and choux buns, but you can experiment with any flavor of your choice. Round choux puffs are versatile as you can simply fill them with Chantilly cream, and for profiteroles, sandwich small buns with vanilla ice cream, and cover in molten chocolate sauce.

This pastry originated in Italy but was introduced into France in the 16th century by Catherine de Medici's pastry chef. Known as pâte à chaud (hot dough), as it was cooked directly over the heat, it was used to make fritters. In the 18th century, Avice, Talleyrand's pastry chef, devised a way of baking it in the oven, when it became known as pâte à choux, as the baked buns resembled small cabbages—choux in French. It is an integral part of classic French pâtisserie, being made into religieuses, éclairs, salambos, profiteroles, and grand cakes such as Paris-Brest and gâteau Saint-Honoré.

Sweet Short Pastry, Creaming Method

Pâte Sucrée

Makes 1 × 9-in. (23-cm) tart base to serve 6

Active time
15 minutes

Chilling time
2 hours

Storage
Up to 3 days in the refrigerator, well covered

Ingredients
3 tbsp (1.75 oz./50 g) butter, diced, at room temperature
⅓ cup (1.75 oz./50 g) confectioners' sugar, sifted
2 tbsp (1 oz./30 g) lightly beaten egg (about 1 egg)
⅛ tsp (0.5 g) salt
1 cup (4.5 oz./125 g) flour, sifted

1• Whisk the butter in a mixing bowl until soft and creamy.

4• Whisk in the flour.

5• Turn out the dough onto the work surface and finish combining the ingredients, using your hand and a pastry scraper, until you have a smooth dough.

2 • Add the confectioners' sugar.

3 • Whisk until the mixture is smooth. Combine the egg and salt and whisk into the mixture.

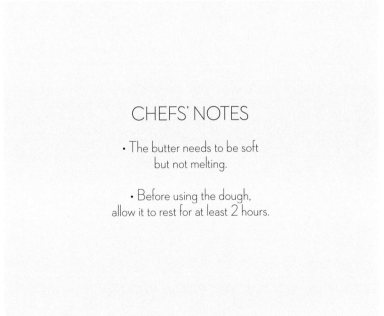

CHEFS' NOTES

• The butter needs to be soft but not melting.

• Before using the dough, allow it to rest for at least 2 hours.

6 • Shape into a flat disk, cover with plastic wrap, and chill in the refrigerator for 2 hours.

Sweet Short Pastry, Crumbling (Rubbing-In) Method

Pâte Sablée

Makes 1 × 9-in. (23-cm) tart base to serve 6

Active time
15 minutes

Chilling time
2 hours

Storage
Up to 3 days in the refrigerator, well wrapped

Ingredients
1 tbsp plus 2 tsp (1 oz./25 g) lightly beaten egg (about ½ egg)

⅛ tsp (0.5 g) salt

1 cup (4.5 oz./125 g) flour

½ cup (2.25 oz./65 g) confectioners' sugar

5 tbsp (2.25 oz./65 g) butter, diced and well chilled

1• Lightly whisk the egg and salt together in a mixing bowl.

4 • Rub the mixture between your hands until it has the texture of coarse sand.

5 • Make a well in the center and pour in the beaten egg. Using a pastry scraper, draw the dough toward the center and gently mix the egg in.

CHEFS' NOTES

Before adding the egg, it's important to rub in the butter until the dough has a rough, crumbly texture, as this is the secret of success with this pastry.

2 • Sift the flour and the confectioners' sugar onto the work surface.

3 • Add the cold butter and rub it into the dry ingredients with your fingertips.

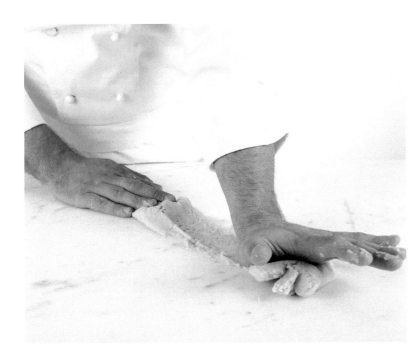

6 • Knead with the palm of your hand until completely smooth.

7 • Shape the dough into a ball, flatten it slightly, and cover with plastic wrap. Chill in the refrigerator for 2 hours.

Shortcrust Pastry, Using a Stand Mixer

Pâte Brisée

**Makes 1 × 9-in. (23-cm)
tart base to serve 6**

Active time
10 minutes

Storage
Up to 3 days in the refrigerator,
well covered

Equipment
Stand mixer

Ingredients
5 ¼ tbsp (2.75 oz./75 g)
butter, diced
1 ¼ tsp (6 g) sugar
½ tsp (2.5 g) salt
1 cup (4.5 oz./125 g) flour, sifted
2 tbsp plus 2 tsp (1.5 oz./40 g)
lightly beaten egg (about 1 egg)

CHEFS' NOTES

Take care not to overwork the dough,
as it will become too elastic.

1 • Fit the stand mixer with a paddle beater and add the butter,
sugar, salt, and flour to the bowl.

2 • Beat until the mixture has the texture of coarse sand,
and then add the egg.

3 • Mix until you have a smooth dough. Shape into a disk,
cover with plastic wrap and chill until needed.

Breton Short Pastry

Pâte à Sablé Breton

Makes 1 × 9-in. (23-cm) tart base to serve 6

Active time
30 minutes

Chilling time
2 hours

Storage
Up to 7 days in the refrigerator, well covered

Ingredients

2 ¾ tbsp (1.4 oz./40 g) egg yolk (about 2 yolks)

½ cup minus 1 ½ tbsp (2.75 oz./80 g) sugar

¾ stick (2.75 oz./80 g) butter, diced and softened

Scant ½ tsp (2 g) salt

Scant 1 cup (4 oz./115 g) flour

¾ tsp (3.5 g) baking powder

1• Whisk the egg yolks and sugar together in a mixing bowl until pale and thick.

2• Add the softened butter and salt and mix in with a flexible spatula. Sift the flour with the baking powder and stir in with the spatula, taking care not to overwork the mixture.

3• When the dough is smooth, shape into a ball and cover with plastic wrap or roll out and line your tart pan. Chill in the refrigerator for 2 hours.

Classic Puff Pastry

Pâte Feuilletée Classique

Makes 1 ¼ lb. (600 g)

Active time
2 hours

Chilling time
About 1 ¾ hours

Storage
Up to 3 days in the refrigerator,
well wrapped

Ingredients
1 tsp (5 g) salt
½ cup (125 ml) water
2 cups (9 oz./250 g) strong
white bread flour, sifted
2 tbsp (1 oz./25 g) butter,
melted and cooled
1 ¾ sticks (7 oz./200 g) butter,
preferably 84% butterfat

1 • In a mixing bowl, mix together the salt and water.
Add the flour and melted butter.

CHEFS' NOTES

• If you add a dash of white vinegar to the water
when making the initial dough, it will prevent oxidation
and extend the storage time by several days.

• Mark the dough lightly with your finger for each turn
so you can keep track of how many you have made.

4 • With a knife, cut a criss-cross pattern in the dough to relax it.

2 • Using a pastry scraper, work the ingredients together until they form a dough, taking care not to overwork it.

3 • Gather the dough together and shape it into a ball.

5 • Cover in plastic wrap and chill in the refrigerator for at least 20 minutes.

6 • Using a rolling pin, soften the butter containing 84% fat, which is to be incorporated into the dough during the folding process. Shape the butter into a square—it should still be cold but needs to be as malleable as the dough you have just made. ⊕

Classic Puff Pastry (continued)

7 • Roll out the dough so it is twice as long as the square of butter.

8 • Place the butter on the dough and wrap the dough around it to enclose it completely.

11 • Roll out the dough again and fold into 3, giving it another single turn. Cover the folded dough with plastic wrap and chill in the refrigerator for 30–40 minutes. At this stage, the dough has been given 2 turns.

12 • Place the chilled dough on the floured work surface, making sure the flap is on one side.

9 • Dust the work surface very lightly with flour and roll the dough into a rectangle measuring 10 × 24 in. (25 × 60 cm).

10 • Fold the dough into 3: this is known as a single turn. Rotate the folded dough 90° to the right.

CHEFS' NOTES

• As a general rule, puff pastry needs to be given 5 or 6 turns. For the optimum rise, give the dough 5 turns.

• Puff pastry made with 4 turns can be used for puff-pastry straws, while 6 turns are needed for vol-au-vents.

13 • Repeat steps 9–12, so the dough has been given 4 turns. Repeat steps 9–10 for the 5th and final turn. Cover in plastic wrap and chill for 30–40 minutes before using.

Quick Puff Pastry

Pâte Feuilletée Rapide

Makes 1 ½ lb. (675 g)

Active time
30 minutes

Chilling time
1 ¾ hours

Storage
Up to 2 days, well wrapped
(but best used on the day
it is made)

Ingredients
2 cups (9 oz./250 g) strong
white bread flour, sifted
1 tsp (5 g) salt
½ cup (125 ml) water
1 ¾ sticks (7 oz. /200 g) butter,
well chilled, cut into 1-in.
(2-cm) dice

1 • Shape the flour into a mound on a cool work surface
and make a well in the center. Dissolve the salt in the water
and pour it into the well. Add the diced butter.

4 • Roll the chilled dough to a rectangle measuring 10 × 28 in.
(25 × 70 cm).

5 • Fold the shorter ends of the dough toward the center, one-third
of the way down from the top and two-thirds up from the bottom,
then fold the dough in half.

· Mark the dough lightly with your finger after each turn
so you can keep track of how many you have made.

· This is a rough-and-ready puff pastry that is ideal to make
when time is short. Although nothing can beat classic puff pastry,
the result is perfectly acceptable as long as the pastry
is used soon after it is made.

2 · Working with your fingertips, draw the flour gradually into the well. Continue working with a pastry scraper to combine the ingredients into a rough dough. The pieces of butter should marble the dough and they should still be cold. Shape the dough into a ball.

3 · Lightly dust the work surface with flour and roll the dough into a rectangle. Fold the dough in 3 to bind the ingredients together. Cover the folded dough in plastic wrap and chill for 20 minutes.

6 · The dough now has 4 folds. Cover the dough in plastic wrap and chill for 30–40 minutes. Repeat steps 4–6 twice more. Cover in plastic wrap and chill for 30–40 minutes.

7 · Give the dough one final single turn (folding it in 3) before using.

Inverse Puff Pastry

Pâte Feuilletée Inversée

Makes 2 lb. (900 g)

Active time
2 hours

Chilling time
About 2 ¾ hours

Storage
Up to 4 days in the refrigerator, well wrapped

Ingredients
Beurre manié
1 cup (4.5 oz./130 g) strong white bread flour
3 ½ sticks (14 oz./400 g) butter, preferably 84% butterfat, well chilled

Water dough
2 cups plus 2 tablespoons (9.5 oz./270 g) flour
½ cup plus 1 tablespoon (140 ml) water
1 ¼ tsp (6 g) salt

1 • Work the flour and butter together with your hands to make the beurre manié (this is the French term for a flour and butter paste).

4 • Working with your fingertips, gradually draw the flour into the well so it absorbs the water.

2 • Roll the beurre manié into a rectangle, cover with plastic wrap, and chill in the refrigerator for about 20 minutes.

3 • Make the water dough by shaping the flour into a mound on a cool surface and making a well in the center. Pour the water into the well and add the salt.

5 • Using a pastry scraper, work the ingredients together to make a smooth dough.

6 • Gather together and shape into a ball. Make criss-cross cuts in the top of the dough with a knife to relax it. Cover with plastic wrap and chill in the refrigerator for about 20 minutes. ⊕

Inverse Puff Pastry (continued)

7 • Roll the dough into a rectangle 8 × 12 in. (20 × 30 cm). Soften the beurre manié with a rolling pin and roll into a rectangle the same width but twice the length of the dough (see Chefs' Notes). Place the dough on the beurre manié.

8 • Enclose the dough by folding the beurre manié over it, pressing down firmly on all sides to seal the edges.

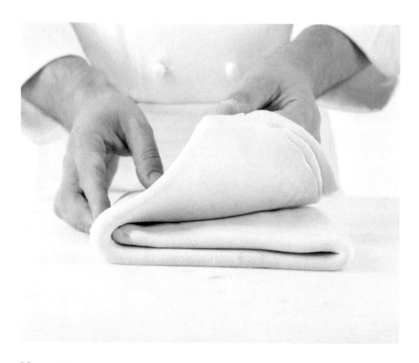

11 • Place the dough on the floured work surface, making sure the flap is on one side. Roll it out and fold in 4 again. At this stage, the dough has undergone 4 turns. Cover in plastic wrap and chill for 30–40 minutes.

12 • Making sure the flap is on one side, roll out the dough again and fold in 3, to make a single turn (see technique, p. 69, step 10). This is the 5th and final turn. Cover in plastic wrap and chill for 30–40 minutes before using.

9 • Lightly dust the work surface with flour.
Roll the dough into a rectangle 10 × 24 in. (25 × 60 cm).

10 • Fold the dough in 4 to make a double turn (see technique, p. 70, steps 4–6). Cover in plastic wrap and chill for 30–40 minutes.

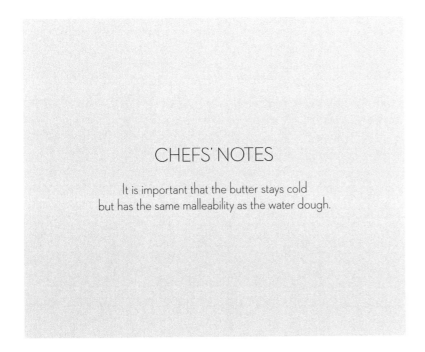

CHEFS' NOTES

It is important that the butter stays cold
but has the same malleability as the water dough.

Apple Turnovers

Chaussons aux Pommes

Makes 5–6

Active time
2 ½ hours
(including making pastry)

Resting time
2 ¾ hours
(including making pastry)

Cooking time
30 minutes

Storage
Up to 24 hours

Equipment
5-in. (13-cm) fluted round
pastry cutter

Ingredients
Inverse puff pastry
Beurre manié
1 ¾ sticks (7 oz./200 g) butter,
preferably 84% butterfat
¾ cup plus 2 tbsp (3.5 oz./100 g) flour
Water dough
1 cup plus 2 tbsp (5.25 oz./150 g) flour
1 tsp (5 g) salt
⅓ cup (85 ml) water

Apple filling
2 cups (1 lb./500 g) applesauce,
preferably homemade

Egg wash
3 ½ tbsp (1.75 oz./50 g) lightly beaten
egg (about 1 egg)
2 ½ tbsp (1.4 oz./40 g) egg yolk
(about 2 yolks)
Scant ¼ cup (50 ml) whole milk

Simple syrup made with 2 tbsp (30 ml)
water and 2 tbsp (1 oz./30 g) sugar

1 • Make the inverse puff pastry using the quantities listed (see technique p. 72). Roll out the dough so it is large enough to cut out 5–6 disks using the cutter.

3 • Spoon 3–4 tbsp (2.5 oz./70 g) applesauce into the center of each oval of dough.

4 • Fold the pastry over the filling and press the edges together to seal firmly.

CHEFS' NOTES

You can spread a thin layer of pastry cream in the center of the ovals of dough before adding the applesauce, or fill the turnovers with poached fruits, such as cherries, apricots, pineapple, plums, or pears.

2 • Flatten the centers of the disks (not the edges) with the rolling pin to make them oval. Brush the pastry edges with egg wash so they can be sealed later in step 4.

5 • Turn the parcels over, place on a baking sheet and brush with egg wash. Chill for 30 minutes and then brush again. Preheat the oven to 400°F (200°C/Gas mark 6).
With a small knife, mark lines in a feather pattern on top of each turnover and pierce 5–6 small holes so steam can escape.

6 • Put the turnovers in the oven and reduce the temperature to 375°F (190°C/Gas mark 5). Bake for about 30 minutes until golden brown. As soon as they come out of the oven, brush with the syrup.

Lemon Pastry Cream Turnovers

Bichons

Makes 12

Active time
3 hours (including making pastry and pastry cream)

Resting time
2 ¾ hours
(including making pastry)

Cooking time
20 minutes

Storage
Up to 2 days

Equipment
Disposable pastry bag without a tip

Ingredients
Inverse puff pastry
Beurre manié
1 ¾ sticks (7 oz./200 g) butter, preferably 84% butterfat
¾ cup plus 2 tbsp (3.5 oz./100 g) flour
Water dough
1 cup plus 2 tbsp (5.25 oz./150 g) flour
1 tsp (5 g) salt
⅓ cup (85 ml) water
Sugar for sprinkling

Lemon pastry cream (*crème bichon*)
2 cups (500 ml) whole milk
Finely grated zest of 1 unwaxed lemon
Generous ⅓ cup (2.5 oz./75 g) sugar
1 tbsp (0.75 oz./20 g) egg yolk (about 1 yolk)
4 tbsp plus ¾ tsp (1.5 oz./40 g) cornstarch

1 · Make the inverse puff pastry using the quantities listed (see technique p. 72). Sprinkle with sugar and roll into a 10 × 20-in. (25 × 50-cm) rectangle, ¼ in. (5 mm) thick.

4 · Sprinkle a work surface with sugar and roll the dough spirals into ovals ¹⁄₁₆ in. (2 mm) thick.

5 · Make the lemon pastry cream using the ingredients listed (see technique p. 196), adding the lemon zest to the milk. Spoon the cream into the pastry bag and pipe over half of each oval.

2 • Roll up the dough from one short side and chill for 30 minutes.

3 • Cut the dough into 12 × ¾-in. (2-cm) slices.

6 • Preheat the oven to 400°F (200°C/Gas mark 6). Line a baking sheet with parchment paper. Dampen the pastry edges with water and fold over to enclose the filling, pressing the edges together to seal. Bake for 20 minutes, until golden brown.

Palmiers

Makes 8–10

Active time
2 ½ hours (including making pastry)

Resting time
2 ¼ hours (including making pastry)

Freezing time
30 minutes

Cooking time
20 minutes

Storage
Up to 3 days
in an airtight container

Ingredients
Inverse puff pastry
Beurre manié
1¾ sticks (7 oz./200 g) butter, preferably 84% butterfat
¾ cup plus 2 tbsp (3.5 oz./100 g) flour
Water dough
1 cup plus 2 tbsp (5.25 oz./150 g) flour
1 tsp (5 g) salt
⅓ cup (85 ml) water

¾ cup (5 oz./140 g) sugar for dusting
Butter for greasing

Egg wash
3 ½ tbsp (1.75 oz./50 g) lightly beaten egg (about 1 egg)
2 ½ tbsp (1.4 oz./40 g) egg yolk (about 2 yolks)
Scant ¼ cup (50 ml) whole milk

1• Make the inverse puff pastry using the quantities listed (see technique p. 72). Before you give the pastry its 5th turn, sprinkle the dough liberally with sugar, and then give it the final turn.

3• Fold them over again toward the center, making sure the two halves meet but do not overlap.

4• Press lightly on the top of the dough with a rolling pin and then fold in two so the dough is about 4 in. (10 cm) wide and 1 ¼ in. (3 cm) thick. Freeze for 30 minutes.

CHEFS' NOTES

The more sugar you add, the more the palmiers will crisp up and caramelize.

2 • Roll the dough into a 10 × 32-in. (25 × 80-cm) rectangle, ¼ in. (5 mm) thick. Fold the 2 short sides inward so they almost meet in the center (leave a ½-in./1-cm gap), to obtain 2 layers.

5 • Preheat the oven to 400°F (200°C/Gas mark 6). Lightly butter a baking sheet. Cut the dough into slices about ½ in. (1 cm) thick. Lay them flat on the baking sheet, with space between them, and brush with the egg wash.

6 • Bake in the oven for 20 minutes, turning the palmiers over after 10 minutes so they brown and caramelize on both sides. When baked, transfer immediately to a rack to cool.

LEVEL

1

LEMON TART

Tarte au Citron

Serves 6

Active time
1 hour

Freezing time
20 minutes

Chilling time
2 hours

Cooking time
15–20 minutes

Storage
Up to 2 days in the refrigerator

Equipment
9-in. (23-cm) tart ring
or pan with a removable base
Citrus zester
Stick blender

Ingredients
9 oz. (250 g) sweet short pastry
(creaming method)
(see technique p. 60)

LEMON CREAM
⅔ cup (150 ml) fresh lemon juice
⅔ cup (5.25 oz./150 g) lightly
beaten egg (about 3 eggs)
Scant ⅔ cup (4.25 oz./120 g) sugar
1½ sheets (0.1 oz./3 g) gelatin
5 tbsp (2.5 oz./75 g) butter,
softened

GLAZE
Clear neutral glaze

MAKING THE CRUST
Line the tart ring with the dough and freeze it for about 20 minutes to prevent the sides collapsing when the crust is baked. Preheat the oven to 325°F (160°C/Gas mark 3). Blind bake the crust for 15–20 minutes until golden. Allow to cool and then, using the zester, file down the edges of the pastry so the rim is perfectly smooth.

MAKING THE LEMON CREAM
Put the lemon juice, eggs, and sugar in a heatproof mixing bowl and stand the bowl over a pan of hot water. Whisk continuously until the mixture has thickened. Meanwhile, soak the gelatin sheets in a bowl of cold water. When the lemon mixture reaches 140°F (60°C), remove the bowl from the heat. Squeeze the water from the gelatin sheets and stir them in until dissolved. Stir in the softened butter and process with the stick blender until smooth.

ASSEMBLING THE TART
Pour the lemon cream into the tart crust, filling it to the rim. Smooth the top with a spatula (or palette knife) and leave to set. Brush the warmed clear neutral glaze over the top.

CHEFS' NOTES

To ensure the base of the tart crust stays crisp, you can "waterproof" it with a little melted white chocolate or, better still, cacao butter. Simply brush the inside of the cooled crust with the chocolate or cacao butter and leave to set before pouring in the lemon cream.

LEVEL

2

LEMON MERINGUE TART

Tarte au Citron Meringuée

Serves 6

Active time
1 ½ hours

Chilling time
1 ½ hours

Freezing time
1 ½ hours

Cooking time
15–20 minutes

Storage
Up to 2 days in the refrigerator

Equipment
Stick blender
Half-sphere molds,
diameter 1 ¼ in. (3 cm)
Stand mixer
(for making the Italian meringue)
9-in. (23-cm) tart ring
or pan with a removable base
Instant-read thermometer
2 pastry bags fitted
with plain ⅓-in. (10-mm)
and ½-in. (15-mm) tips

Ingredients

LEMON JELLY
⅓ cup (95 ml) fresh lemon juice
2 tbsp (30 ml) water
1 ½ tsp (6 g) sugar
0.1 oz. (3 g) agar-agar

LEMON-FLAVORED SWEET SHORT PASTRY
5 tbsp (2.5 oz./75 g) butter,
diced, at room temperature,
plus extra for the ring
⅓ cup (1.5 oz./40 g)
confectioners' sugar
2 ½ tbsp (0.5 oz./15 g) almond
flour
⅛ tsp (1 g) salt
1 tsp (5 g) grated lemon zest
2 tbsp (1 oz./30 g) lightly beaten
egg (about 1 egg)
1 cup (4.5 oz./125 g) flour

LEMON CREAM
⅔ cup (150 ml) fresh lemon juice
⅔ cup (5.25 oz./150 g) lightly
beaten egg (about 3 eggs)
Scant ⅔ cup (4.25 oz./120 g) sugar
1 ½ sheets (0.1 oz./3 g) gelatin
5 tbsp (2.75 oz./75 g) butter,
diced, at room temperature

10 oz. (300 g) Italian meringue
(see technique p. 232)

MAKING THE LEMON JELLY
Heat the lemon juice, water, and sugar in a saucepan until the sugar dissolves. Bring to a boil, stir in the agar-agar and let boil for about 2 minutes. Process with the stick blender and then pour the mixture into the molds. Freeze for 1 hour.

MAKING THE LEMON-FLAVORED SWEET SHORT PASTRY
Fit the stand mixer with the paddle beater and add the butter, confectioners' sugar, almond flour, salt, and grated lemon zest to the bowl. Mix to combine. Beat in the egg and then the flour. When the ingredients come together in a ball, flatten the dough into a disk, cover with plastic wrap, and chill in the refrigerator for 30 minutes. Butter the tart ring lightly and line it with the pastry. Place in the freezer to chill for about 20 minutes. Preheat the oven to 325°F (170°C/Gas mark 3) and blind bake for about 20 minutes. Allow to cool before assembling the tart.

MAKING THE LEMON CREAM
Put the lemon juice, eggs, and sugar in a heatproof mixing bowl. Stand the bowl over a pan of hot water and whisk constantly until the mixture has thickened. Meanwhile, soak the gelatin sheets in a bowl of cold water. When the lemon mixture reaches 140°F (60°C), remove the bowl from the heat. Squeeze the water from the gelatin sheets and stir in until dissolved. Add the butter and process with the stick blender until completely smooth. Press plastic wrap over the surface of the cream and chill in the refrigerator for 1 hour.

ASSEMBLING THE TART
Pour the lemon cream into the cooled tart crust, filling it to the rim but reserving a little to decorate the top of the tart, and smooth the top with a spatula or palette knife. Freeze for 20 minutes. Place the remaining lemon cream in a pastry bag fitted with the ⅓-in. (10-mm) tip and pipe small mounds in the center of the tart. Using the ½-in. (15-mm) tip, pipe the Italian meringue in large mounds around the edge (see Chefs' Notes). Unmold the lemon jelly domes and place on the meringue mounds.

CHEFS' NOTES

When you have piped the mounds of meringue, place the tart in a 475°F (250°C/Gas mark 9) oven for 3–5 minutes, until the meringue is lightly colored and set.

TOURBILLON

by Yann Brys

MEILLEUR OUVRIER DE FRANCE, PÂTISSIER, 2011

Serves 6

Active time
2 hours

Cooking time
25 minutes

Chilling time
2 hours

Storage
Up to 2 days
in the refrigerator

Equipment
Instant-read thermometer
Stick blender
8-in. (20-cm) tart ring or
pan with a removable base
Food processor fitted
with the chopper blade
Pastry bag fitted
with a small plain tip
Pastry turntable
Kitchen torch

Ingredients
LEMON AND YUZU CREAM
5 tsp (24 ml) whole milk
Grated zest of
2 organic limes
4.5 oz. (135 g) lightly
beaten egg
3.25 oz. (95 g)
superfine sugar
5 tsp (25 ml) yuzu juice
2 tbsp (30 ml) lemon juice
5 oz. (140 g) butter, diced

SWEET LEMON PASTRY CRUST
3 oz. (90 g) butter
5 oz. (140 g) flour
1 oz. (27 g) superfine sugar

Grated zest
of ½ organic lemon
Generous pinch (0.5 g) salt
1 oz. (27 g) ground almonds
1 oz. (27 g) confectioners'
sugar
1 oz. (25 g) lightly beaten egg

LIME FRANGIPANE
3.5 oz. (110 g) raw
almond paste
2 oz. (57 g) lightly
beaten egg
Grated zest of 1 lime
1 tbsp (9 g) cornstarch
3 tbsp (17 g) ground almonds
0.5 oz. (16 g) egg white
1 ¼ tsp (5 g) superfine sugar
1.5 oz. (38 g) butter

LEMON MARMALADE
4.5 oz. (125 g) fresh organic
lemons (about 2 lemons)
⅛ tsp (1 g) fine-grain salt
2 tsp (10 ml) lemon juice
2 tsp (10 ml) lime juice
1.75 oz. (50 g) superfine
sugar
Grated zest of
½ organic lime

YUZU ITALIAN MERINGUE
5 tsp (25 ml) water
4.25 oz. (120 g) superfine
sugar
2 oz. (60 g) egg white
1 ½ tsp (7 ml) yuzu juice

DECORATION
Finely grated lime zest
Clear neutral glaze

——— MAKING THE LEMON AND YUZU CREAM
Bring the milk and lime zest to a boil in a saucepan. Remove from the heat, cover, and infuse for 5 minutes. Whisk the eggs with the sugar and strain the infused milk through a fine-mesh sieve into the mixture. Heat the yuzu and lemon juices in a saucepan and stir in the egg mixture. Cook to 185°F (85°C) and then allow to cool to 110°F (45°C). Add the butter and process with the stick blender until smooth and glossy. Chill for about 2 hours.

——— MAKING THE SWEET LEMON PASTRY CRUST
Dice the butter and rub it into the flour as lightly as possible until the mixture resembles fine bread crumbs. Add the remaining dry ingredients, mix in the egg, and gently work together to make a dough, taking care not to overwork the dough. Cover in plastic wrap and chill for 1 hour. When ready to use, roll out the dough thinly and line the tart ring.

——— MAKING THE LIME FRANGIPANE
Preheat the oven to 325°F (165°C/Gas mark 3). Cream the almond paste and egg together until soft and stir in the lime zest, cornstarch, and ground almonds. In another bowl, whisk the egg white and sugar until soft peaks form. Fold the whites into the almond mixture using a spatula. Melt the butter and stir into the mixture while warm. Pour the mixture into the tart crust, smooth the surface, and bake for about 25 minutes. To test for doneness, check the underside of the crust. Allow to cool.

——— MAKING THE LEMON MARMALADE
Cut the lemons into small pieces without peeling them. Place in a saucepan, cover with cold water, bring to a boil, and drain. Rinse under cold water, return to the saucepan, cover with cold water, and add the salt. Bring to a boil, drain, rinse under cold water, and return to the saucepan. Cover with cold water, add the lemon and lime juices, bring to a simmer, and cook for about 10 minutes. Drain and rinse under cold water to stop the cooking process. Place in the food processor, add the sugar, and blend to a smooth, fine paste. Add the lime zest and chill in the refrigerator.

——— MAKING THE YUZU ITALIAN MERINGUE
In a saucepan, heat the water and sugar to 250°F (121°C). Whisk the egg whites to soft peak stage and gradually whisk in the syrup until the whites are stiff. Fold in the yuzu juice and spoon into the pastry bag.

——— ASSEMBLING THE TART
Spoon a layer of lemon marmalade into the baked tart shell over the frangipane and then spread a layer of the lemon and yuzu cream over it. Place the tart on the turntable and pipe the still-warm meringue on top, moving the turntable round slowly to make it easier to pipe a tight spiral. Using the kitchen torch, scorch the edge of the meringue and decorate the top with lime zest and a few dots of neutral glaze.

LEVEL

1

STRAWBERRY TART

Tarte aux Fraises

Serves 6

Active time
1 hour

Chilling time
30 minutes

Freezing time
10 minutes

Cooking time
30 minutes

Storage
Up to 24 hours in the refrigerator

Equipment
Stand mixer
9-in. (23-cm) tart ring
or pan with a removable base
2 pastry bags fitted
with plain ½-in. (15-mm) tips
Electric hand beater
Instant-read thermometer

Ingredients
SWEET SHORT PASTRY
¾ cup plus 2 tbsp
(3.5 oz./100 g) flour
2 ½ tbsp (0.5 oz./15 g)
almond flour
⅓ cup (1.5 oz./40 g)
confectioners' sugar
Scant ⅛ tsp (1 g) salt
4 tbsp (2 oz./60 g) butter, diced
½ tsp (3 g) vanilla extract
1 tbsp plus 1 tsp (0.75 oz./20 g)
lightly beaten egg (about ½ egg)

ALMOND-PISTACHIO CREAM
4 tbsp (2 oz./60 g) butter, diced,
at room temperature
Scant ⅓ cup (2 oz./60 g) sugar
Scant ⅔ cup (2 oz./60 g)
almond flour
1 oz. (25 g) pistachio paste
3 ½ tbsp (1.75 oz./50 g) lightly
beaten egg (about 1 egg)

PASTRY CREAM
½ cup (125 ml) milk
2 tbsp (0.9 oz./25 g) sugar
1 ½ tbsp (1 oz./25 g) egg yolk
(about 1 ½ yolks)
1 tbsp plus scant 1 tsp (0.5 oz./12 g)
cornstarch
1 tbsp plus 1 tsp (0.75 oz./20 g)
butter

STRAWBERRY JELLY
2 sheets (0.15 oz./4 g) gelatin
2 oz. (60 g) strawberry purée
2 tbsp (30 ml) water
2 tbsp (30 ml) strawberry syrup
3 ½ tbsp (1 oz./30 g) glucose syrup

DECORATION
1 lb. 2 oz. (500 g) strawberries
0.75 oz. (20 g) unsalted, skinned
pistachios, roughly chopped

MAKING THE SWEET SHORT PASTRY
Fit the stand mixer with a paddle beater and combine the flour, almond flour, confectioners' sugar, and salt in the bowl. Add the butter and beat until the mixture has a crumbly texture, like coarse bread crumbs. Beat in the vanilla and egg until just combined. Shape the dough into a disk, cover with plastic wrap, and chill for 30 minutes. Line the tart ring with the pastry and freeze for 10 minutes.

MAKING THE ALMOND-PISTACHIO CREAM
Preheat the oven to 325°F (170°C/Gas mark 3). Beat the butter with a spatula until creamy. Add the sugar, almond flour, pistachio paste, and egg and beat until very smooth. Spoon the mixture into a pastry bag and pipe it over the base of the tart. Bake for 30–35 minutes and allow to cool.

MAKING THE PASTRY CREAM
Using the ingredients listed, make the pastry cream (see technique p. 196).

MAKING THE STRAWBERRY JELLY
Soak the gelatin in a bowl of cold water until softened. Heat the purée, water, strawberry syrup, and glucose in a saucepan to 122°F (50°C). Squeeze the excess water from the gelatin sheets and stir into the hot strawberry mixture until completely dissolved. Remove from the heat.

ASSEMBLING THE TART
Spoon the pastry cream into a pastry bag and pipe it into the tart crust so the baked almond-pistachio cream is completely covered. Slice the strawberries in half and arrange them in circles on top of the tart, with a whole strawberry in the center. Brush the warm strawberry jelly carefully over the strawberries and scatter with the chopped pistachios.

LEVEL

2

FRUITS OF THE FOREST TART

Tarte aux Fruits Rouges

Serves 6

Active time
1 hour

Cooking time
18–20 minutes

Storage
Up to 24 hours in the refrigerator

Equipment
Stand mixer
2 pastry bags fitted
with plain ⅓-in. (8-mm) tips
2 × 9-in. (23-cm) tart rings,
1 ¼ in. (3.5 cm) high

Ingredients

DACQUOISE BASE*
⅔ cup (5 oz./140 g) egg white (about 5 whites)
1 tbsp (0.5 oz./13 g) sugar
1 heaping cup (5.25 oz./150 g) confectioners' sugar, plus extra for dusting
1 ½ cups (5.25 oz./150 g) almond flour
Scant ½ cup (1.5 oz./40 g) ground hazelnuts

VANILLA CHIBOUST CREAM
1 ¾ tsp (0.25 oz./8 g) powdered gelatin
2 tbsp plus 1 tsp (35 ml) hot water
⅓ cup (75 ml) milk
⅔ cup (150 ml) whipping cream, 35% butterfat
Scant ⅓ cup (2 oz./60 g) sugar, divided
1 vanilla bean, split lengthwise, seeds scraped out
Scant ½ cup (4.25 oz./120 g) egg yolk (about 6 ½ yolks)
1 ½ tbsp (0.5 oz./15 g) cornstarch or custard powder

ITALIAN MERINGUE
Scant ½ cup (3 oz./90 g) superfine sugar
3 tbsp (40 ml) water
¾ cup (6.25 oz. /180 g) egg white (about 6 whites)

FRUIT FOR DECORATION
2 oz. (50 g) blackberries
3.5 oz. (100 g) raspberries
3.5 oz. (100 g) red currants
5 oz. (150 g) strawberries

MAKING THE DACQUOISE BASE
Preheat the oven to 350°F (180°C/Gas mark 4) and line a baking sheet with parchment paper. Fit the stand mixer with the whisk and whisk the egg whites at medium speed until soft peaks form. Add the sugar in 2 equal amounts and whisk at high speed until firm peaks form. Sift the confectioners' sugar with the almond flour and stir in the ground hazelnuts. Fold the meringue mixture into the dry ingredients using a spatula and taking care not to deflate the mixture. Spoon it into a pastry bag fitted with a tip. Place the tart rings on the lined baking sheet and pipe a layer of dacquoise mixture inside each. Dust with confectioners' sugar and bake for 18–20 minutes. Set aside one dacquoise base for another use.

MAKING THE VANILLA CHIBOUST CREAM
Dissolve the gelatin in the hot water. In a saucepan, heat the milk, cream, half the sugar, and the vanilla seeds. Whisk the egg yolks with the remaining sugar and cornstarch until the mixture is pale. Continue in the same way as making a pastry cream, simmering for 3 minutes, and then stir in the dissolved gelatin.

MAKING THE ITALIAN MERINGUE
Make the Italian meringue (see technique p. 232) using the quantities indicated and fold it into the still warm pastry cream, using a spatula.

ASSEMBLING THE TART
Using a pastry bag fitted with a tip, pipe the Chiboust cream over the dacquoise layer. Shape the cream into a dome with a spatula and arrange the fruit attractively on top.

* This recipe makes 2 dacquoise bases as it is difficult to reduce the quantities of ingredients. Use 1 layer for this tart and store the other, covered in plastic wrap in an airtight container, for 2–3 days in the refrigerator or up to 2 weeks in the freezer.

LEVEL

3

RED BERRY TARTLETS

Tartes aux Fruits Rouges

by Nina Métayer

PASTRY CHEF OF THE YEAR, 2016 AND 2017, AND FORMER FERRANDI PARIS STUDENT

Serves 8

Active time
1 ½ hours

Chilling time
1 ¾ hours

Cooking time
4 ¼ hours

Equipment
8 individual oblong tartlet molds with rounded corners
Electric hand beater

Ingredients

RED BERRY JUICE
1 lb. 2 oz. (500 g) strawberries
1 lb. 2 oz (500 g) raspberries
1.75 oz. (50 g) sugar

RED BERRY PARCHMENT
2 ½ sheets (5 g) gold strength gelatin
1 cup (250 ml) water
9 oz. (250 g) strawberries, blended and strained
4.5 oz. (125 g) raspberries, blended and strained
1.75 oz. (50 g) sugar
½ tsp (2.5 g) pectin NH

SWEET PASTRY CRUST
1 lb. 2 oz. (500 g) flour
6.5 oz. (190 g) confectioners' sugar
2 oz. (60 g) almond flour
½ tsp (2 g) vanilla powder
⅛ tsp (1 g) salt
10.5 oz. (300 g) butter
4 oz. (113 g) lightly beaten egg

HAZELNUT SPONGE
8 oz. (225 g) egg white
2.75 oz. (74 g) sugar
8 oz. (225 g) confectioners' sugar
7 oz. (200 g) finely ground toasted hazelnuts
⅔ cup (150 ml) red berry juice (see ingredients above)

PASTRY CREAM
¾ cup (164 ml) whole milk
1 vanilla bean, split lengthwise and seeds scraped out
1 oz. (30 g) egg yolk
3 tbsp (37 g) sugar
4 tsp (13 g) custard powder
1 ¼ tsp (6 g) butter

HEAVY CREAM MOUSSE
⅔ cup (150 ml) whipping cream, 35% butterfat
Scant 1 cup (200 ml) pastry cream (see ingredients above)
Scant 1 cup (200 ml) heavy cream, 38% butterfat

RED BERRY JELLY
2 sheets (4 g) gold strength gelatin
⅔ cup (150 ml) red berry juice (see ingredients above)

DECORATION
9 oz. (250 g) strawberries
9 oz. (250 g) raspberries
3.5 oz. (100 g) red currants

———— MAKING THE RED BERRY JUICE

Place the strawberries, raspberries, and sugar in a heatproof mixing bowl. Cover with plastic wrap and cook over a pan of hot water for 2 hours. Strain the juice through a fine-mesh sieve into a bowl and set aside.

———— MAKING THE RED BERRY PARCHMENT

Preheat the oven to 480°F (250°C/Gas mark 9) and put a baking sheet in the oven. Soak the gelatin in ice-cold water for 10 minutes. In a saucepan, heat the water and blended berries. Mix the sugar and pectin together and add to the mixture. Bring to a boil, stirring constantly, then simmer for 3 minutes. Remove from the heat, add the squeezed gelatin, and stir in until dissolved. Remove the hot baking sheet from the oven and coat it evenly with a thin layer of the fruit mixture. Reduce the heat to 190°F (90°C), or use an *étuve* (drying oven) and, dry out the fruit mixture for 2 hours. Remove from the oven and immediately cut out and peel off the desired shapes.

———— MAKING THE SWEET PASTRY CRUST

Combine the sifted dry ingredients in a bowl and lightly rub in the butter to a sandy texture. Incorporate the beaten eggs. When the dough is smooth, cover in plastic wrap and chill for 20 minutes. Roll out the dough and line the oblong molds. Preheat the oven to 300°F (155°C/Gas mark 2). Chill for 20 minutes, then blind bake for 7 minutes. Cut out an opening in the base of the crust to leave a ¼-in. (5-mm) interior rim.

———— MAKING THE HAZELNUT SPONGE

Increase the oven temperature to 350°F (180°C/Gas mark 4). Using an electric hand beater, whisk the whites to the soft peak stage and beat in the sugar to stiffen them. Sift in the confectioners' sugar and the ground toasted hazelnuts and carefully fold into the meringue using a spatula. Spread onto a parchment-lined baking sheet and bake for 5 minutes. Turn out onto a wire rack. Cut out oval shapes the same size as the pastry shells. Moisten the sponges with the red berry juice.

———— MAKING THE PASTRY CREAM

Place the milk and vanilla bean and seeds in a saucepan and bring to a boil. In a bowl, beat the egg yolks with the sugar and custard powder until pale and thick. Stir a little of the hot milk into the egg mixture until you have a smooth liquid, then pour it back into the saucepan. Bring to a boil, whisking vigorously. Take the pan off the heat and gradually incorporate the butter. Cool quickly, then strain through a fine-mesh sieve.

———— MAKING THE HEAVY CREAM MOUSSE

Using the hand beater, beat the whipping cream until it forms soft peaks. Combine the pastry cream with the heavy cream and carefully fold in the whipped cream.

———— MAKING THE RED BERRY JELLY

Soak the gelatin in ice-cold water for 10 minutes. In a saucepan, heat the red berry juice, add the squeezed gelatin, and stir until dissolved. Pour into a lightly greased mold. Allow the jelly to set for 1 hour in the refrigerator, then cut it into small cubes.

———— ASSEMBLING THE TARTLETS

Finely dice some of the berries and sprinkle over the hazelnut sponges. Pipe a layer of heavy cream mousse over the fruit and place an upside-down tart shell on top. Decorate the center with cream, fruit, jelly cubes, and berry parchment shapes.

LEVEL

1

APRICOT TART

Tarte aux Abricots

Serves 6

Active time
1 hour

Chilling time
2 ½ hours (including pastry)

Cooking time
20 minutes

Storage
Up to 2 days
in the refrigerator

Equipment
9-in. (23-cm) tart ring
or pan

Ingredients

SWEET SHORT PASTRY
4 tbsp (2 oz./60 g) butter, diced
⅓ cup (1.5 oz./45 g) confectioners' sugar
2 ½ tbsp (0.5 oz./15 g) almond flour
1 tbsp plus 2 tsp (1 oz./25 g) lightly beaten egg (about ½ egg)
Scant ⅛ tsp (1 g) salt
1 cup (4.5 oz./125 g) flour

ALMOND CREAM
3 tbsp (1.5 oz./45 g) butter, at room temperature
⅓ cup (1.5 oz./45 g) sugar
2 tbsp plus 2 tsp (1.5 oz./40 g) lightly beaten egg (about 1 egg)
Scant ½ cup (1.5 oz./45 g) almond flour
1 ½ tsp (8 ml) whipping cream, 35% butterfat

TOPPING
1 lb. 2 oz. (500 g) apricots
Apricot glaze

MAKING THE SWEET SHORT PASTRY
Using the ingredients listed, prepare the sweet short pastry using the creaming method (see technique p. 60).

MAKING THE ALMOND CREAM
Microwave the butter for a few seconds to soften it and then whisk until creamy. Whisk in the sugar until just combined, taking care not to beat in too much air. Beat in the egg and almond flour, followed by the cream. Chill for 30 minutes.

MAKING THE APRICOT FILLING
Wash and dry the apricots. Cut them in half and remove the pits.

ASSEMBLING AND BAKING THE TART
Preheat the oven to 325°F (170°C/Gas mark 3). If using a tart ring, line a baking sheet with parchment paper and place the ring on it. Roll out the dough and line it into the ring or pan. Spread the almond cream over the tart base. Arrange the apricot halves attractively over the almond cream in concentric circles. Bake for 20–30 minutes and cool the tart before unmolding. Warm the apricot glaze and brush the glaze over the top.

CHEFS' NOTES

You can also flavor the almond cream with 0.7 oz. (20 g) of pistachio paste, to be added with the cream.

2

APRICOT TART

Tarte aux Abricots

Serves 6

Active time
2 hours

Chilling time
1 hour

Cooking time
20–25 minutes

Freezing time
30 minutes

Storage
Up to 24 hours in the refrigerator

Equipment
Stand mixer fitted
with the paddle beater
8-in. (20-cm) tart ring
7-in. (18-cm) tart ring
Instant-read thermometer
Stick blender
Pastry bag fitted
with a plain ½-in. (15-mm) tip

Ingredients
7 oz. (200 g) puff pastry
(see technique p. 66)

ALMOND-PISTACHIO CREAM
2 oz. (60 g) raw almond paste,
diced
2 tbsp (1 oz./30 g) lightly
beaten egg (about 1 egg)
3 tbsp plus 1 tsp (0.75 oz./20 g)
almond flour
2 tbsp (1 oz./30 g) butter, softened
0.35 g (10 g) pistachio paste
2 tbsp (30 ml) heavy cream,
35% butterfat

ROASTED APRICOTS
1 lb. 2 oz. (500 g) apricots
1 tbsp plus 2 tsp (0.75 oz./20 g)
light brown sugar
1 tbsp (0.75 oz./20 g) honey
1 sprig of rosemary

ALMOND CRÉMEUX
2 sheets (0.15 oz./4 g) gelatin
3 oz. (85 g) raw almond paste
Scant ½ cup (100 ml) whole milk
1 cup (250 ml) whipping cream,
35% butterfat, divided

WHITE GLAZE
3 ½ sheets (0.25 oz./7 g) gelatin
Scant ½ cup (100 ml) whole milk
1 ¼ cups (9 oz./250 g) sugar,
divided
Scant 1 cup (200 ml) whipping
cream, 35% butterfat
3 tbsp plus 1 tsp (2.5 oz./70 g)
glucose syrup
Seeds from ½ vanilla bean
(optional)
1 ½ tbsp (1.5 oz./15 g) potato starch
0.05 oz. (1 g) titanium dioxide
(optional)

Pistachios for decoration

MAKING THE PUFF PASTRY CRUST
Preheat the oven to 350°F (180°C/Gas mark 4). Line the 8-in. (20-cm) tart ring with the pastry and blind bake for 20 minutes.

MAKING THE ALMOND-PISTACHIO CREAM
Increase the oven temperature to 375°F (190°C/Gas mark 5). Beat the almond paste in the stand mixer, gradually beating in the egg so it softens. When smooth, add the almond flour, butter, and pistachio paste. Beat in the cream and whisk until the mixture is velvety. Spoon the mixture into the pastry bag and pipe it over the tart base. Bake for about 40 minutes and then cool before assembling the tart.

ROASTING THE APRICOTS
Increase the oven temperature to 400°F (200°C/Gas mark 6). Line a baking sheet with parchment paper. Wash the apricots and cut each one into 8 wedges. Coat them with the light brown sugar and honey, and roast on the baking sheet with the rosemary sprig for 15 minutes.

MAKING THE ALMOND CRÉMEUX
Soak the gelatin in cold water. In the bowl of the stand mixer, combine the almond paste with the milk and a scant ½ cup (100 ml) of the whipping cream. When smooth, pour one-third of the mixture into a saucepan and heat to 122°F (50°C). Squeeze the water from the gelatin and stir into the warm mixture until melted. Whisk the remaining cream and lightly fold it in. Spread the crémeux into the 7-in. (18-cm) tart ring, set on a baking sheet, and freeze for 30 minutes.

MAKING THE WHITE GLAZE
Soak the gelatin in a bowl of water. In a saucepan, bring the milk to a boil with half the sugar, the cream, glucose syrup, and vanilla seeds if using. Remove from the heat and cool. Combine the remaining sugar with the potato starch and stir in. Return to the heat and bring to a boil. Remove from the heat again, squeeze excess water from the gelatin and stir in, then stir in the titanium dioxide if using, and process with a stick blender. When the glaze has cooled to 68°F (20°C), spread it over the frozen almond crémeux.

ASSEMBLING THE TART
Place the disk of iced, frozen crémeux in the center of the tart base. Remove the tart ring and arrange the roasted apricots attractively around the edge. Scatter with a few pistachios.

APRICOT AND LAVENDER TART

Tarte Abricot et Lavande

by Nicolas Bacheyre

MOST PROMISING PASTRY CHEF OF THE YEAR, 2016

Serves 8–10

Active time
2 hours

Chilling time
6 hours

Infusion time
30 minutes

Cooking time
25 minutes

Storage
Up to 24 hours
in the refrigerator

Equipment
Stick blender
Stand mixer fitted
with the paddle
beater

11-in. (28-cm) tart ring
or large rectangular
tart mold

Bowl scraper
Pastry bags fitted
with plain tips

Ingredients

WHIPPED VANILLA-LAVENDER GANACHE
1 ½ cups (375 ml) whipping cream,
35% butterfat, divided
0.4 oz. (10 g) vanilla beans
(about 2 beans), split lengthwise
and seeds scraped out
2 tbsp (5 g) fresh lavender flowers
3.25 oz. (95 g) white chocolate,
chopped
½ oz. (15 g) bloomed gelatin

SHORTBREAD PASTRY
9.25 oz. (260 g) butter
9.25 oz. (260 g) unrefined cane sugar
2.25 oz. (65 g) almond flour
6.75 oz. (195 g) ground hazelnuts
½ tsp (3 g) fine-grain salt
7.5 oz. (215 g) flour

ALMOND CREAM
2.75 oz. (80 g) butter
2.75 oz. (80 g) confectioners' sugar
3.75 oz. (105 g) almond flour
1 ½ tsp (8 ml) vanilla extract
2.75 oz. (75 g) lightly beaten egg

TOPPING
1 ¾ lb. (800 g) apricots
Fresh lavender flowers
Micro-greens

--------- MAKING THE WHIPPED VANILLA-LAVENDER GANACHE
In a saucepan, bring ½ cup (125 ml) of the whipping cream to a boil with the vanilla beans and seeds and the lavender flowers. Cover and allow to infuse for 30 minutes. After infusion, reheat slightly and strain through a fine-mesh sieve onto the white chocolate. Stir in the bloomed gelatin and blend with the stick blender to make a ganache. Add the remaining cream and then blend. Chill for about 6 hours before use.

--------- MAKING THE SHORTBREAD PASTRY
Cream the butter with the cane sugar in the bowl of the stand mixer. Sift the almond flour and ground hazelnuts together, then add to the creamed butter and sugar and carefully mix. Add the salt and flour, and mix again gently until a dough is formed. Roll out the dough between 2 parchment sheets to a thickness of ⅛ in. (3 mm). Cover in plastic wrap and let rest in the refrigerator for about 2 hours. Line the tart mold with the dough, checking that the corners and the bottom are perfectly perpendicular to each other and regular. Trim off the excess dough with a paring knife.

--------- MAKING THE ALMOND CREAM
Cream the butter with the confectioners' sugar in the bowl of the stand mixer. Add the almond flour and mix well at medium speed. Scrape down the sides and bottom of the bowl for even mixing. Add the vanilla extract and eggs a little at a time, continuing to beat the mixture. Scrape down the bowl again once the eggs are incorporated, and mix until smooth. Fill a pastry bag with the mixture and keep it at room temperature so that it is soft enough to pipe.

--------- BAKING AND ASSEMBLING THE TART
Neatly pipe enough almond cream into the tart shell to come halfway up the sides. Chill for about 1 hour. Preheat the oven to 350°F (180°C/Gas mark 4) and bake the tart for about 25 minutes. Wash the apricots, remove the pits, and cut them into cubes and quarters. Distribute the cubes evenly over the almond cream and arrange the quarters attractively on top. Whip the vanilla-lavender ganache until soft peaks form. Place in a pastry bag fitted with a plain tip and pipe dots of cream. Decorate with lavender flowers and micro-greens.

LEVEL

1

APPLE TART

Tarte aux Pommes

Serves 6

Active time
30 minutes

Cooking time
35 minutes

Storage
Up to 2 days in the refrigerator

Equipment
9-in. (23-cm) tart ring

Ingredients

SHORTCRUST PASTRY
5 ¼ tbsp (2.75 oz./75 g) butter, diced
1 ½ tsp (0.25 oz./6 g) sugar
Heaping ½ tsp (0.1 oz./3 g) salt
1 cup (4.5 oz./125 g) flour, sifted
1 tbsp plus 2 tsp (1 oz./25 g) lightly beaten egg (about ½ egg)
1 tbsp (15 ml) water

APPLE TOPPING
1 ¾ lb. (800 g) Golden Delicious apples
Scant 1 cup (7 oz./200 g) applesauce
Melted butter for brushing
Clear glaze

MAKING THE SHORTCRUST PASTRY TART SHELL
Using the quantities listed, prepare the shortcrust pastry (see technique p. 64), adding the water with the egg. Chill. Roll out the dough and line the tart ring. Crimp the top edge with a decorative pattern, if wished (see technique p. 28).

MAKING THE APPLE TOPPING
Peel and core the apples. Cut them into very thin slices, no more than ⅛ in. (2–3 mm) thick. Reserve any leftover pieces to put in the middle of the tart.

ASSEMBLING AND BAKING THE TART
Preheat the oven to 350°F (180°C/Gas mark 4). Spread the applesauce over the base of the tart and top with the leftover apple pieces. Arrange the apple slices neatly in concentric circles, overlapping the slices and alternating the direction of the circles. Brush melted butter over the apple slices. Bake the tart for about 35 minutes and allow to cool. Once cool, brush the apple slices with the warmed clear glaze.

LEVEL

2

APPLE TART

Tarte aux Pommes

Serves 6

Active time
1 ½ hours

Chilling time
1 ½ hours

Cooking time
30 minutes

Resting time
24 hours

Storage
Up to 2 days in the refrigerator

Equipment
2 × 7-in. (18-cm) tart rings
Silicone baking mat
Instant-read thermometer
Stand mixer fitted with the whisk
Pastry bags fitted with plain ⅓-in.
and ½-in. (8-mm and 15-mm) tips

Ingredients

SWEET HAZELNUT PASTRY
2 tbsp plus 1 tsp (1.25 oz./35 g)
butter
2 ½ tbsp (0.75 oz./20 g)
confectioners' sugar
2 tbsp (0.35 oz./10 g) ground
hazelnuts
2 ¾ tsp (0.5 oz./13 g) lightly
beaten egg (about ½ egg)
A very small pinch of ground
vanilla bean
½ cup (2.25 oz./65 g) flour

HAZELNUT CREAM
2 tbsp (1 oz./30 g) butter
2 ½ tbsp (1 oz./30 g) sugar
⅓ cup (1 oz./30 g) ground
hazelnuts
1 tbsp plus 2 tsp (1 oz./25 g)
lightly beaten egg (about ½ egg)
2 ½ tsp (0.2 oz./5 g) flour

ROASTED APPLES
3.5 oz. (100 g) Belchard
Chanteclerc apples
2 tbsp plus 2 tsp (1.5 oz./40 g)
butter
½ vanilla bean, split in 2
2 ½ tbsp (1 oz./30 g) sugar
2 tbsp plus 2 tsp (40 ml) water

GRANNY SMITH APPLE JELLY
5.25 oz. (150 g) Granny
Smith apples
2.5 oz. (75 g) puréed
Granny Smith apples
2 tbsp (1 oz./25 g) sugar
2 sheets (0.15 oz./4 g) gelatin
1 tbsp (15 ml) ginger juice
1 tsp (5 ml) lemon juice

APPLE MARSHMALLOW
17 ½ sheets (1.25 oz./35 g) gelatin
2 ⅓ cups (1 lb./450 g) sugar
12 oz. (340 g) invert sugar, divided
½ cup plus 1 tbsp (140 ml) water
7 oz. (200 g) puréed Granny
Smith apple
1 vanilla bean, slit lengthwise,
seeds scraped out
Cornstarch for dusting

Granny Smith apple slices and
edible gold leaf for decoration

MAKING THE SWEET HAZELNUT PASTRY CRUST
Prepare the pastry (see technique p. 60), adding the ground hazelnuts to the dough. Chill for 30 minutes. Preheat the oven to 325°F (170°C/Gas mark 3). Roll the pastry into a 7-in. (18-cm) disk, ¼ in. (5 mm) thick, lift into a tart ring the same size on a silicone baking mat and blind bake for about 15 minutes, until lightly browned. Remove and increase the heat to 350°F (180°C/Gas mark 4) to roast the apples.

MAKING THE HAZELNUT CREAM
Make the hazelnut cream using the ingredients listed (see technique p. 208), replacing the almond flour with ground hazelnuts.

ROASTING THE APPLES
Peel, core, and cut the apples into large dice. Heat the butter, vanilla bean, and sugar in a pan until the butter and sugar melt and the mixture caramelizes. Carefully deglaze with the water. Stir in the apple cubes and transfer to an ovenproof dish. Bake for 15–20 minutes and set aside.

MAKING THE GRANNY SMITH APPLE JELLY
Peel, core, and cut the apples into even-sized dice. Bring the puréed apples and sugar to a boil in a pan, stir in the diced apples, and cook until the mixture softens to the texture of applesauce. Soften the gelatin in a bowl of cold water. Stir the ginger and lemon juices into the apples and cook for 3 minutes. Squeeze out the gelatin sheets and stir in until dissolved. Line one of the tart rings with plastic wrap, pour in the mixture, and chill for about 40 minutes, until set.

MAKING THE APPLE MARSHMALLOW
Soften the gelatin in cold water. Add the sugar and 5 oz. (140 g) of the invert sugar to the water in a pan and heat to 230°F (110°C). Put the remaining invert sugar in the stand mixer and add the puréed apple and vanilla seeds. Drizzle in the sugar syrup as you whisk. Squeeze out the gelatin and whisk in until dissolved. Spoon into the pastry bag fitted with the ⅓-in. (8-mm) tip and pipe 5–6-in. (12–15-cm) lines on parchment paper. Dust with the cornstarch and leave at room temperature for 24 hours. Tie into knots.

ASSEMBLING THE TART
Preheat the oven to 350°F (180°C/Gas mark 4). Place the baked hazelnut crust into the other tart ring. Using the pastry bag fitted with the ½-in. (15-mm) tip, pipe the cream over the crust, filling the ring by three-quarters. Arrange the pieces of roasted apple over the hazelnut cream. Bake in the oven for about 15–20 minutes until golden, and then allow to cool. Very carefully lift the apple jelly on top and decorate with the marshmallow knots, apple slices, and edible gold leaf.

CHEFS' NOTES

If Belchard apples are not available, use another variety that keeps its shape
when cooked, such as Golden Delicious.

LEVEL

3

APPLE TARTLETS

Tartes aux Pommes

by Cédric Grolet

BEST PASTRY CHEF OF THE YEAR, 2016

Serves 6

Active time
3 hours

Chilling time
24 hours

Cooking time
40 minutes

Storage
Up to 24 hours
in the refrigerator

Equipment
Stand mixer
6 × 2-in. (5-cm)
tartlet rings,
¾ in. (2 cm) high

Pastry bag fitted
with a plain tip
Mandoline

Ingredients

SWEET PASTRY DOUGH
5.25 oz. (150 g) butter
3.25 oz. (95 g) confectioners' sugar
1 oz. (30 g) almond flour
⅛ tsp (1 g) Guérande salt
¼ tsp (1 g) vanilla powder
2 oz. (58 g) lightly beaten egg
9 oz. (250 g) flour

ALMOND CREAM
5.25 oz. (150 g) butter
5.25 oz. (150 g) superfine sugar
5.25 oz. (150 g) almond flour
5.25 oz. (150 g) lightly beaten egg

APPLE COMPOTE
2 ¼ lb. (1 kg) Granny Smith apples
½ cup (125 ml) lemon juice

TOPPING
3 Gala apples
(or any crisp red apples)
3.25 oz. (100 g) *beurre noisette*

——— MAKING THE SWEET PASTRY DOUGH

In the stand mixer fitted with the paddle beater, beat together the butter, confectioners' sugar, almond flour, salt, and vanilla powder. Beat in the egg, then add the flour and mix to form a dough. Cover in plastic wrap and chill. Roll out the pastry to a thickness of ½ in. (1 cm). Lightly grease the tartlet rings and line with the dough. Allow to dry out for 24 hours in the refrigerator, then blind bake at 325°F (160°C/Gas mark 3) for about 15 minutes.

——— MAKING THE ALMOND CREAM

In the mixer fitted with the paddle beater, beat the butter with the sugar and almond flour. Incorporate the beaten egg a little at a time.

——— MAKING THE APPLE COMPOTE

Dice the Granny Smith apples into ⅛-in. (3-mm) cubes. Add the lemon juice and vacuum pack. Cook in an *étuve* (steamer oven) at 210°F (100°C) for 13 minutes.

——— ASSEMBLING THE TARTLETS

Preheat the oven to 350°F (180°C/Gas mark 4). Using a pastry bag fitted with a plain tip, pipe the almond cream into the tart shells. Bake for 10–15 minutes. Top with a layer of apple compote. For the rosette, slice the unpeeled Gala apples into very thin (1/16-in./2-mm) slices using the mandoline. Dip the slices into the *beurre noisette* and arrange them over the tart in a circular pattern, starting from the outside and working inward to obtain an attractive rosette shape.

LEVEL

1

PEAR AND ALMOND TART

Tarte aux Poires Bourdaloue

Serves 6

Active time
40 minutes

Cooking time
35 minutes

Chilling time
2 hours (including pastry)

Storage
Up to 2 days in the refrigerator

Equipment
Stand mixer
9-in. (23-cm) tart ring
(set on a baking sheet)
or pan with a loose base

Ingredients

SWEET SHORT PASTRY
Generous ½ cup (2.5 oz./75 g) confectioners' sugar
3 ½ tbsp (1.75 oz./50 g) butter
1 tbsp plus 2 tsp (1 oz./25 g) lightly beaten egg (about ½ egg)
1 tsp (5 ml) water
1 cup (4.5 oz./125 g) flour

ALMOND CREAM
3 tbsp (1.75 oz./50 g) butter, softened
¼ cup (1.75 oz./50 g) sugar
2 tbsp plus 2 tsp (1.5 oz./40 g) lightly beaten egg (about 1 egg)
½ cup (1.75 oz./50 g) almond flour
2 ½ tsp (0.2 oz./5 g) flour
1 tsp (5 ml) rum
1 vanilla bean, slit lengthwise, seeds scraped out

PEAR TOPPING
6 poached pear halves
Apricot glaze
Sliced almonds for sprinkling

MAKING THE SWEET SHORT PASTRY TART CRUST
Using the ingredients listed, prepare the sweet short pastry using the creaming method (see technique p. 60). Roll out the dough about ⅛ in. (3 mm) thick and line the tart ring. Prick the base all over with a fork.

MAKING THE ALMOND CREAM
Cream the butter and sugar together until soft and light. Beat in the egg, fold in the almond flour and, when the mixture is smooth, stir in the flour, rum, and vanilla seeds. Transfer to a bowl and chill in the refrigerator.

ASSEMBLING AND BAKING THE TART
Preheat the oven to 350°F (180°C/Gas mark 4). Spread the almond cream over the base of the tart. Slice the pear halves across very thinly, keeping the shape of the halves. Carefully lift them into the tart, arranging them in a star pattern. Press the halves down lightly into the almond cream so the slices fan out. Bake for 35 minutes. Carefully lift the ring away from the tart (or unmold from the pan) and transfer to a rack to cool. Brush the cooled tart with warmed apricot glaze and scatter over the sliced almonds.

PEAR AND GRAPEFRUIT TART

Tarte aux Poires-Pamplemousse

Serves 6

Active time
1 hour

Chilling time
1 hour

Cooking time
40 minutes

Storage
Up to 3 days in the refrigerator

Equipment
Stand mixer
9-in. (23-cm) tart ring
or pan with a loose base

Ingredients

HAZELNUT SWEET SHORT PASTRY
4 tbsp (2 oz./60 g) butter, softened
⅓ cup (1.5 oz./40 g) confectioners' sugar
2 tbsp (1 oz./30 g) lightly beaten egg (about 1 egg)
⅛ tsp (1 g) salt
¾ cup plus 2 tbsp (3.5 oz./100 g) flour
2 tbsp (0.75 oz./20 g) cornstarch
¼ cup (0.75 oz./20 g) ground hazelnuts

ALMOND-PISTACHIO CREAM
3 tbsp (1.75 oz./50 g) butter, softened
¼ cup (1.75 oz./50 g) sugar
3 ½ tbsp (1.75 oz./50 g) lightly beaten egg (about 1 egg)
½ cup (1.75 oz./50 g) almond flour
2 ½ tsp (0.2 oz./5 g) flour
0.75 oz. (20 g) pistachio paste

FRUIT TOPPING
1 pink grapefruit
4 pears, poached in syrup
Apricot glaze
Chopped pistachios

MAKING THE PASTRY
Fit the stand mixer with the paddle beater and beat the butter and sugar until smooth and creamy. Beat in the egg and salt and then sift in the flour, cornstarch, and ground hazelnuts. Continue beating until the mixture forms a dough. Shape into a disk, cover with plastic wrap and chill for 30 minutes. Roll out the dough ⅛ in. (3 mm) thick and line the tart ring.

MAKING THE ALMOND-PISTACHIO CREAM
Cream the butter and sugar together. Beat in the egg and almond flour until smooth. Stir in the flour until it is incorporated and finally stir in the pistachio paste. Spread the cream over the tart base.

PREPARING THE FRUIT
Peel the grapefruit, cut away the white pith, and divide into segments by cutting between the membranes. Lay the segments on sheets of paper towel to absorb excess juice from the grapefruit. Cut the pears into thin slices lengthwise.

ASSEMBLING AND BAKING THE TART
Preheat the oven to 350°F (180°C/Gas mark 4). Arrange alternate grapefruit segments and pear slices in concentric circles over the almond-pistachio cream and bake the tart for about 35 minutes. Remove the tart ring (or unmold from the tart pan) and transfer to a rack. When the tart has cooled, brush the top with warmed apricot glaze and scatter with chopped pistachios around the edge.

CHEFS' NOTES

Draining excess juice from the grapefruit segments before you add them to the tart prevents the juice running out during baking and making the filling too wet.

LEVEL

3

FRENCH PEAR TART

Bourdaloue

by Christelle Brua

BEST PASTRY CHEF OF THE YEAR, 2009 AND 2014

Serves 6

Active time
2 ½ hours

Chilling time
1 hour

Cooking time
1 hour

Equipment
9-in. (23-cm) tart ring or pan with a removable base

Electric hand beater

Ingredients
10.5 oz. (300 g) sweet short pastry dough (see technique p. 60)
1.5 oz. (40 g) flour, for rolling out

ALMOND CREAM
3.25 oz. (95 g) butter, softened
3.25 oz. (95 g) confectioners' sugar
3.5 oz. (100 g) lightly beaten egg
3.25 oz. (95 g) almond flour
3.25 oz. (95 g) flour

FILLING
5 Bartlett pears
4 ¼ cups (1 liter) water
1 lb. 11 oz. (750 g) superfine sugar
1 vanilla bean, split lengthwise and seeds scraped out
Glaze

——————— PREPARING THE SWEET SHORT PASTRY DOUGH
Preheat the oven to 325°F (160°C/Gas mark 3). Roll out the dough on a floured surface to a thickness of 1/16 in. (2 mm). Line the tart ring or pan with the rolled dough. Gently push up and pinch the edges. Prick the tart shell lightly with a fork and place in the refrigerator for 1 hour. Blind bake for 8 minutes, then increase the oven temperature to 340°F (170°C/Gas mark 3) and bake for an additional 10 minutes until the crust is golden brown. Let cool.

——————— MAKING THE ALMOND CREAM
In a mixing bowl, soften the butter. Cream the butter with the sugar, then beat in the eggs. Mix in the almond flour and then the flour until combined. Set aside.

——————— MAKING THE FILLING
Wash, peel, core, and halve the pears. In a saucepan, make a syrup with the water and sugar, then add the vanilla bean and seeds. Poach the pears in the syrup until tender, which should take about 15 minutes. Test for doneness by inserting the tip of a small sharp knife. Set aside.

——————— ASSEMBLING THE TART
Fill the cooled tart shell with the almond cream. Thinly slice the pear halves crosswise and place them attractively on top of the almond cream. Bake in the oven at 325°F (160°C/Gas mark 3) for about 30 minutes until the tart is golden brown. Finish with glaze and serve immediately.

APPLE UPSIDE-DOWN TART

Tarte Tatin

Serves 4–6

Active time
3 hours

Chilling time
2 ½ hours (including pastry)

Cooking time
2 hours 20 minutes

Storage
Up to 2 days in the refrigerator

Equipment
9-in. (23-cm) tart ring
Instant-read thermometer
Nonstick baking sheet
with a rim
7-in. (18-cm) tarte tatin pan

Ingredients

PUFF PASTRY
1 ¾ cups (6 oz./170 g) flour
Heaping ½ tsp (3 g) salt
Generous ⅓ cup (90 ml) water
1 tbsp plus 1 tsp (0.75 oz./20 g)
butter
1 stick (3.75 oz./110 g) butter,
preferably 84% butterfat

HOMEMADE CARAMEL CREAM
2 tbsp (30 ml) water
½ cup (3.5 oz./100 g) sugar
2 tsp (0.5 oz./15 g) glucose syrup
¼ cup (65 ml) whipping cream,
35% butterfat

LIGHT CARAMEL
1 cup (7 oz./200 g) sugar
2 tbsp plus 2 tsp (1.5 oz./40 g)
butter

APPLE TOPPING
10 apples, such as Golden
Delicious or similar
7 oz. (200 g) homemade
caramel cream (see ingredients above)
⅓ cup (75 ml) whipping cream,
35% butterfat
1 tbsp plus 2 tsp (0.75 oz./20 g)
sugar
½ tsp (3 ml) vanilla extract
3 tbsp (1.75 oz./50 g) butter,
melted
Sugar for sprinkling

MAKING THE PUFF PASTRY
Using the quantities listed, make a classic 5-turn puff pastry (see technique p. 66). Preheat the oven to 350°F (180°C/Gas mark 4). Line the tart ring with the pastry and bake for 30 minutes.

MAKING THE HOMEMADE CARAMEL CREAM
Heat the water, sugar, and glucose syrup in a pan and, when the sugar has dissolved, boil to 345°F (175°C). When the syrup is almost ready, bring the cream to a boil in another pan. Remove both pans from the heat and, protecting your hand against splashes with an oven mitt, carefully stir the hot cream into the caramel to prevent it cooking further. Set aside for the apple topping.

MAKING THE LIGHT CARAMEL
Dissolve the sugar in a heavy pan and cook to 330°F (165°C). Carefully stir in the butter to prevent the caramel from cooking any further, again protecting your hand with an oven mitt.

MAKING THE APPLE TOPPING
Reheat the oven to 350°F (180°C/Gas mark 4). Peel, core, and cut each apple into 8 segments. Heat the homemade caramel cream, whipping cream, sugar, vanilla, and melted butter in a saucepan, remove from the heat and, using tongs or a fork, dip the apple segments into the caramel mixture until coated. Lay them on the baking sheet. Sprinkle with sugar and bake for 35 minutes. Cool and then chill in the refrigerator for 30 minutes.

ASSEMBLING THE TART
Reheat the oven to 350°F (180°C/Gas mark 4). Pour the light caramel over the base of the tarte tatin pan. Cut the apple segments in half to make thinner slices and arrange them over the caramel right to the edge, packing them in tightly. Bake for 1 ¼ hours. Cool completely before turning the apples out carefully onto the baked puff pastry base.

CHEFS' NOTES

To make it easier to turn the apples out,
you can heat the outside of the pan with a chef's blowtorch
to melt the caramel.

APPLE UPSIDE-DOWN TART

Tarte Tatin

Serves 4

Active time
4 hours

Chilling time
2 hours

Cooking time
2 hours

Storage
Up to 2 days in the refrigerator

Equipment
Mandolin
3 × 6-in. (8 × 15-cm) shallow
baking pan, lightly greased
Angled spatula
Stand mixer
Silicone baking mat

Ingredients
5 apples

INVERSE PUFF PASTRY
Beurre manié
¾ cup plus 2 tbsp
(3.5 oz./100 g) flour
1 ¾ sticks (7 oz./200 g) butter,
preferably 84% butterfat,
well chilled

Water dough
1 cup plus 2 tbsp
(5 oz./150 g) flour
Generous ⅓ cup (85 ml) water
1 tsp (5 g) salt
Confectioners' sugar for dusting

TATIN CARAMEL
3 tbsp (50 ml) water
1 ½ cups (10.5 oz./300 g) sugar
Generous ¼ cup (3.5 oz./100 g)
glucose syrup

TATIN SAUCE
1 cup (250 ml) water
3 ½ tbsp (1.5 oz. /40 g) sugar
1 ½ tbsp (25 ml) lemon juice
1 tbsp (0.5 oz./15 g) butter
1 vanilla bean, slit lengthwise,
seeds scraped out
½ tsp (2.5 g) fleur de sel
or other sea salt flakes

ALMOND-HAZELNUT STREUSEL
2 oz. (60 g) roasted, ground,
raw hazelnuts
2 oz. (60 g) roasted, ground,
raw almonds
⅔ cup (3 oz./90 g) light
brown sugar
Scant ½ tsp (2 g) fleur de sel
or other sea salt flakes
⅔ cup plus 1 tbsp (3 oz./90 g) flour
6 tbsp (3 oz./90 g) butter, diced
and softened

Clear neutral glaze

MAKING THE INVERSE PUFF PASTRY
Make a 5-turn inverse puff pastry using the quantities listed (see technique p. 72). Preheat the oven to 425°F (220°C/Gas mark 7). Roll the dough into a rectangle measuring 6 × 8 in. (15 × 20 cm) and ⅛ in. (3 mm) thick. Dust with confectioners' sugar. Lift the pastry onto a baking sheet, cover with parchment paper, and lay a rack on top so the pastry rises evenly. Bake for about 15 minutes.

MAKING THE TATIN CARAMEL
Heat the water, sugar, and glucose syrup in a pan until the sugar dissolves and then boil to a light brown caramel. Line the greased baking pan with parchment paper and pour the caramel over the base in a layer about ⅛ in. (3 mm) thick.

PREPARING THE APPLES
Peel and core the apples. Cut them into ⅛-in. (3-mm) slices, using the mandolin. Arrange the slices in neat layers over the caramel until the pan is full.

MAKING THE TATIN SAUCE
Preheat the oven to 325°F (165°C/Gas mark 3). Heat the water, sugar, lemon juice, butter, vanilla bean and seeds, and fleur de sel in a pan, stirring until the sugar and butter have dissolved. Spoon 4 tablespoons over the apple slices. Bake the apples for 35 minutes, press them down firmly with the spatula and bake for another 15 minutes. Allow to cool.

MAKING THE ALMOND-HAZELNUT STREUSEL
Fit the stand mixer with the paddle beater. Mix the dry ingredients in the bowl, add the butter and beat until the texture resembles coarse bread crumbs. Transfer to a work surface and knead with your hand to make a dough. Push the dough through a sieve to make fine-textured crumbs, or crumble using your fingers. Spread out the crumbs on a silicone baking mat and dry them out in a 300°F (150°C/Gas mark 2) convection oven for 25–30 minutes. Keep the oven at the same temperature for the last step.

ASSEMBLING THE TART
When the apples have cooled, return the pan to the oven for a few minutes so the apples turn out easily. Carefully slide out the parchment paper and, using the spatula, lift the apples into the center of the pastry rectangle. Dot the streusel crumbs along the pastry edges and brush the apples with a little neutral glaze.

LEVEL

3

TARTE TATIN REVISITED

Tarte Tatin Revisitée

by Philippe Urraca

MEILLEUR OUVRIER DE FRANCE, PÂTISSIER, 1993

Serves 6

Active time
3 hours

Chilling time
4 ½ hours

Infusion time
30 minutes

Cooking time
2 hours 25 minutes

Storage
Up to 2 days
in the refrigerator

Equipment
9-in. (23-cm) tart pan
with a removable
base

Ingredients
INVERSE PUFF PASTRY
Beurre manié
9 oz. (255 g) butter
3.5 oz. (100 g) flour
Water dough
8 oz. (230 g) flour
1 ¼ tsp (6.5 g) salt
2.75 oz. (75 g) butter, melted
6 tbsp (90 ml) water
2 tsp (9 ml) white vinegar
Confectioners' sugar for sprinkling

APPLE TOPPING
2.75 oz./80 g) lightly salted butter
2 vanilla beans, split lengthwise
and seeds scraped out
2 ¾ lb. (1.2 kg) Golden
Delicious apples
5 oz (140 g) unrefined cane sugar

Chantilly cream (optional)

——— MAKING THE INVERSE PUFF PASTRY
In a mixing bowl, make the beurre manié by working the butter and flour together until well combined. Cover with plastic wrap and place in the refrigerator. Meanwhile, knead the water dough ingredients together to form a smooth dough. Cover and chill for 30 minutes. Roll out the beurre manié into a large rectangle. Roll out the water dough into a rectangle half the length of the beurre manié. Place the water dough rectangle in the center of the beurre manié and fold the 2 flaps over the dough to enclose it completely. Give one single turn, followed by a double one (see techniques pp. 69 and 70–71). Cover in plastic wrap and place in the refrigerator for about 1 hour. Repeat the single and double turn steps. Roll out the pastry dough to a thickness of ⅛ in. (3 mm) and cut out a disk the size of the tart pan. Let rest in the refrigerator for 2–3 hours. Preheat the oven to 350°F (180°C/Gas mark 4). Place the pastry disk on a baking sheet lined with parchment paper. Prick with a fork and place another sheet of parchment paper and baking sheet on top: this will ensure the puff pastry layers rise evenly as they bake. Bake for about 20 minutes. Remove the top baking sheet and paper, sprinkle the crust with confectioners' sugar, and return to the oven at 425°F (220°C/Gas mark 7) for about 5 minutes until caramelized.

——— MAKING THE APPLE TOPPING
In a saucepan, melt the butter with the vanilla beans and seeds. Let infuse for about 30 minutes. Peel the apples, cut them in half, and remove the cores. Using a sharp knife, slice the halves into thin slices and fan out flat. Pour a little of the melted butter into the bottom of the tart pan and sprinkle generously with cane sugar. Arrange the apple slices attractively in a tight, flat layer. Drizzle over some melted butter and sprinkle again with cane sugar. Bake at 340°F (170°C/Gas mark 3) for about 20 minutes. Repeat this procedure, arranging another even layer of apple slices on top, drizzled with melted butter and sprinkled with cane sugar. Return to the oven and bake for 20 minutes. Repeat the procedure 4 times, then allow to cool slightly in the tart pan.

——— ASSEMBLING THE TART
Unmold the topping and carefully place it on the baked tart crust. Serve while it is still warm, with Chantilly cream on the side, if you wish.

LEVEL

1

BAKED CHOCOLATE TART

Tarte au Chocolat

Serves 6

Active time
1 hour

Chilling time
30 minutes

Cooking time
45 minutes–1 hour

Cooling time
about 1 hour

Storage
Up to 2 days in the refrigerator

Equipment
Stand mixer
Instant-read thermometer
9-in. (23-cm) tart ring
or pan
Stick blender

Ingredients

SWEET SHORT PASTRY
1 cup (4.5 oz./125 g) flour
⅓ cup (1.75 oz./50 g)
confectioners' sugar
3 tbsp (1.75 oz./50 g) butter, diced
2 tbsp (1 oz./30 g) lightly
beaten egg (about 1 egg)
Scant ½ tsp (2 g) salt
½ tsp vanilla extract

CHOCOLATE FILLING
⅓ cup (70 ml) whipping cream,
35% butterfat
⅓ cup (70 ml) milk
2 tbsp (1 oz./25 g) sugar
4.75 oz. (135 g) bittersweet
couverture chocolate, 70% cacao
3 ½ tbsp (1.75 oz./50 g) lightly
beaten egg (about 1 egg)
1 tbsp (0.75 oz./20 g) egg yolk
(about 1 yolk)
½ teaspoon vanilla extract

MIRROR GLAZE
1 ½ tbsp (25 ml) milk
2 tsp (10 ml) water
2 ½ tsp (0.35 oz./10 g) sugar
1 oz. (25 g) bittersweet couverture
chocolate, 58% cacao, chopped
1 oz. (25 g) *pâte à glacer brune*
(brown glazing paste), diced

MAKING THE SWEET SHORT PASTRY
Fit the stand mixer with the paddle beater and sift the flour and confectioners' sugar into the bowl. Add the butter and beat until the mix has a coarse, crumbly texture. Mix the egg and salt together in another bowl, add to the ingredients in the stand mixer and beat briefly to make a dough. Cover in plastic wrap and chill for 30 minutes. Preheat the oven to 325°F (170°C/Gas mark 3). Roll out the dough and line the tart ring. Blind bake for 20 minutes. Remove, but leave the oven switched on.

MAKING THE CHOCOLATE FILLING
Heat the cream, milk, and sugar in a pan and, when the sugar has dissolved, boil to 140°F (60°C). Meanwhile, melt the chocolate in brief bursts in the microwave or in a bowl over a pan of barely simmering water. Stir the melted chocolate into the hot cream mixture, followed by the egg, egg yolk (taking care they do not start to scramble), and vanilla. Process with the stick blender until smooth.

MAKING THE MIRROR GLAZE
Bring the milk, water, and sugar to a boil in a small pan. Put the chocolate and glazing paste in a bowl and pour over the hot liquid. Process with the blender until smooth.

ASSEMBLING AND BAKING THE TART
Pour the chocolate filling into the tart crust and bake in the oven until the edges of the chocolate filling begin to rise slightly (about 25 minutes). Allow to cool. Let the glaze cool to 95°F (35°C) before pouring it over the cooled tart.

2

CHOCOLATE TART

Tarte au Chocolat

Serves 6

Active time
1 hour

Chilling time
1 hour 10 minutes

Freezing time
20 minutes

Cooking time
25–35 minutes

Storage
Up to 2 days in the refrigerator

Equipment
Stand mixer
9-in. (23-cm) tart ring or pan
6-in. (16-cm) pastry cutter
Stick blender
Instant-read thermometer

Ingredients

SHORT CHOCOLATE PASTRY
¾ cup plus 2 tbsp
(3.5 oz./100 g) flour
½ tbsp (0.5 oz./15 g) almond flour
1 ¼ tbsp (0.35 oz./10 g)
unsweetened cocoa powder
⅓ cup (1.5 oz./40 g)
confectioners' sugar
⅛ tsp (1 g) salt
4 tbsp (2 oz./60 g) butter, diced,
at room temperature
1 tbsp plus 1 tsp (0.75 oz./20 g)
egg (about ½ egg)
½ tsp vanilla extract

EGG WASH
1 ½ tbsp (1 oz./25 g) lightly
beaten egg (about ½ egg)
1 tbsp (0.75 oz./20 g) egg yolk
(about 1 yolk)
1 ½ tbsp (25 ml) whole milk

PRALINE FEUILLETINE LAYER
0.35 oz. (10 g) milk couverture
chocolate, chopped
1 tsp (0.2 oz./5 g) butter
1.5 oz. (45 g) praline paste
1 oz. (25 g) *feuilletine* flakes
(or use crushed wafers)

GANACHE
Scant 1 cup (200 ml) whipping
cream, 35% butterfat
0.5 oz. (15 g) invert sugar
6 oz. (170 g) bittersweet
couverture chocolate,
58% cacao, chopped
4 tbsp (1.75 oz./55 g) butter,
softened

SUGAR SYRUP
1 heaping tbsp (0.5 oz./15 g) sugar
1 tbsp (15 ml) water

CHOCOLATE GLAZE
1 ½ tbsp (25 ml) whole milk
1 oz. (30 g) bittersweet couverture
chocolate, 58% cacao, chopped
1 oz. (30 g) *pâte à glacer brune*
(brown glazing paste), diced

DECORATION
5 ¼ oz. (150 g) bittersweet
couverture chocolate, 58% cacao
1 can red chocolate velvet spray

MAKING THE SHORT CHOCOLATE PASTRY
Fit the stand mixer with the paddle beater and sift the flour, almond flour, and cocoa powder into the bowl. Add the confectioners' sugar, salt, and butter and beat until combined. Whisk the egg and vanilla together, add to the bowl and beat until you have a smooth dough. Chill for 30 minutes. Roll out the dough and line the tart ring. Chill in the refrigerator for 20 minutes. Preheat the oven to 325°F (170°C/Gas mark 3) and blind bake the tart crust for 20–30 minutes until the pastry is firm. When you estimate the crust needs about 5 more minutes in the oven, whisk together the egg wash ingredients and brush this over the pastry. Bake the crust for 3–5 minutes until dry and crisp. Allow to cool.

MAKING THE PRALINE FEUILLETINE LAYER
Melt the couverture chocolate in the microwave. Stir in the butter, praline paste, and *feuilletine* to make a paste. Roll it out between 2 sheets of parchment paper and freeze (flat and still between the parchment) for 20 minutes. Using the pastry cutter, cut out a disk from the *feuilletine* layer and immediately lift it carefully into the tart crust. Chill until the ganache is ready to be poured in.

MAKING THE GANACHE
Bring the cream and invert sugar to a boil. Put the chocolate in a bowl, pour the hot cream over it, and process with a stick blender until smooth. Cool to between 95°F and 104°F (35°C and 40°C) and then whisk in the butter. Pour the ganache into the tart crust and place in the refrigerator for 20 minutes to set.

MAKING THE SUGAR SYRUP
Add the sugar to the water in a pan and heat until the sugar dissolves, then bring to a boil. Set aside for the chocolate glaze.

MAKING THE CHOCOLATE GLAZE
Bring the milk and sugar syrup to a boil in a small pan. Pour the mixture over the chocolate and glazing paste and process with the stick blender until smooth.

FINISHING THE TART
Allow the glaze to cool to 95°F (35°C) and then pour it over the cooled tart. For the decoration, temper the chocolate (see techniques pp. 570 and 572) and, using a paper piping cone (see technique p. 598), pipe a spiral decoration the same size as the tart on a sheet of parchment paper. Leave to cool, freeze, then spray with the chocolate velvet spray before placing it on top of the tart.

LEVEL

3

"RENDEZVOUS" CHOCOLATE TART

Tarte au Chocolat "Rendez-Vous"

by Jean-Paul Hévin

MEILLEUR OUVRIER DE FRANCE, PÂTISSIER, 1986

**Makes 2 tarts
(serves 10)**

Active time
35 minutes

Chilling time
2 hours

Cooking time
20 minutes

Equipment
2 × 9-in. (23-cm) tart
rings or pans with
removable bases

Ingredients

SWEET CHOCOLATE PASTRY DOUGH
1.5 oz. (40 g) bittersweet chocolate,
68% cacao, chopped
7.5 oz. (210 g) butter, at room
temperature
4.5 oz. (130 g) confectioners' sugar
1.5 oz. (44 g) almond flour
¼ tsp (0.5 g) vanilla powder
1 pinch of salt
2.5 oz. (70 g) lightly beaten egg
12.4 oz. (350 g) flour

CHOCOLATE GANACHE
12 oz. (340 g) bittersweet chocolate,
63% cacao (Origin Peru),
finely chopped
2 cups plus 2 tbsp (500 ml)
whipping cream, 35% butterfat
¾ oz. (20 g) invert sugar

DECORATION
Tempered bittersweet
couverture chocolate
2 meringue kisses
Edible gold dust powder

——— MAKING THE SWEET CHOCOLATE PASTRY DOUGH
Melt the chocolate in a bowl over a pan of hot water. In a separate bowl, carefully combine the butter, confectioners' sugar, almond flour, vanilla, and salt. Incorporate the egg, then the flour and the melted chocolate, reserving a little chocolate to coat the tart shells after baking. Stir until the mixture forms a smooth dough. Cover with plastic wrap and chill for 2 hours. Preheat the oven to 350°F (180°C/Gas mark 4). Roll out the dough as thinly as possible and cut out 2 disks to line the tart molds. Blind bake the tart shells for about 20 minutes. When the tart shells are cool, coat them with a layer of tempered chocolate which, when set, will prevent the crust from absorbing moisture from the filling.

——— MAKING THE CHOCOLATE GANACHE
Place the chopped chocolate in a bowl. Bring the cream to a boil with the invert sugar. Remove from the heat, slowly pour one-third of the hot cream into the chocolate, and stir well. Repeat this step twice more. Stir until the mixture is smooth. Pour the ganache into the prebaked tart shells.

——— ASSEMBLING THE TART
Make clock hands (2 short and 2 long) for the tarts with tempered chocolate (see techniques pp. 570 and 572). Coat the meringue kisses in tempered chocolate and allow to set before dusting them with gold dust powder. To finish the clocks, carefully arrange the chocolate hands and gold-dusted meringues on each tart.

LEVEL

1

WALNUT TART

Tarte aux Noix

Serves 6

Active time
35 minutes

Chilling time
2 hours

Freezing time
20 minutes

Cooking time
30–40 minutes

Storage
Up to 2 days in the refrigerator

Equipment
Stand mixer
9-in. (23-cm) tart ring
or tart pan

Ingredients

SWEET SHORT PASTRY
3 tbsp (1.75 oz./50 g) butter, diced
⅓ cup (1.75 oz./50 g) confectioners' sugar, sifted
2 tbsp (1 oz./30 g) lightly beaten egg (about 1 egg), at room temperature
⅛ tsp (1 g) salt
¼ tsp (1 g) vanilla extract
1 cup (4.5 oz./125 g) flour, sifted

WALNUT CARAMEL FILLING
9 oz. (250 g) walnut halves
2 tbsp plus 1 tsp (1.75 oz./50 g) glucose syrup
1 ¼ cups (9 oz./250 g) sugar
Scant ¾ cup (175 ml) whipping cream, 35% butterfat

MAKING THE SWEET SHORT PASTRY
Fit the stand mixer with the paddle beater and beat the butter and sugar together until soft, light, and creamy. Whisk the egg, salt, and vanilla together and gradually beat into the creamed mixture until smooth. Beat in the flour at low speed until just combined. Remove the dough from the bowl to a work surface and knead lightly with your hand, taking care not to overwork it. Shape into a disk, cover with plastic wrap, and chill for 1 hour. Preheat the oven to 350°F (180°C/Gas mark 4). Roll out the dough, line the tart ring, and freeze for 20 minutes. Bake for 15–20 minutes until a light golden brown.

MAKING THE WALNUT CARAMEL FILLING
Spread out the walnuts on a nonstick baking sheet and roast in the oven at 275°F–300°F (140°C–150°C/Gas mark 1–2) for 10 minutes. Gently heat the glucose syrup and sugar in a pan until the sugar dissolves and then boil to a rich brown caramel. While the syrup is boiling, bring the cream to a boil in another pan. Protecting your hand from splashes with an oven mitt, carefully pour the warm cream into the caramel, stirring constantly to prevent it from cooking further. Stir in the walnuts.

ASSEMBLING THE TART
Pour the filling into the cooled tart shell and chill for at least 1 hour before serving.

WALNUT TART

Tarte aux Noix

Serves 6

Active time
1 hour

Chilling time
1 hour

Cooking time
40 minutes

Storage
Up to 2 days in the refrigerator

Equipment
Stand mixer
9-in. (23-cm) tart ring or pan
Pastry bag fitted with a fluted
½-in. (15-mm) tip

Ingredients

SWEET SHORT PASTRY
3 tbsp (1.75 oz./50 g) butter, diced
⅓ cup (1.75 oz./50 g)
confectioners' sugar, sifted
2 tbsp (1 oz./30 g) lightly
beaten egg (about 1 egg),
at room temperature
⅛ tsp (1 g) salt
¼ tsp (1 g) vanilla extract
¾ cup plus 1 ½ tbsp (3.75 oz./110 g)
flour, sifted
2 ½ tbsp (0.5 oz./15 g) finely
ground walnuts

WALNUT GENOISE SPONGE
Generous ⅓ cup (3 oz./90 g)
lightly beaten egg (about 2 eggs)
¼ cup (1.75 oz./50 g) sugar
1 oz. (25 g) walnuts, chopped
⅓ cup (1.5 oz./ 40 g) flour, sifted
2 tbsp (1 oz./25 g) butter, melted

SYRUP
½ cup (3.5 oz./100 g) sugar
Scant 1 cup (200 ml) water
2 tbsp (30 ml) rum

ALMOND PASTE CROWN
6 oz. (175 g) almond paste,
50% almonds, chopped
1 tbsp plus 2 tsp (1 oz./25 g) egg
white (about 1 white)

SOFT CARAMEL TOPPING
2 tsp (0.5 oz./15 g) glucose syrup
⅔ cup (4.5 oz./125 g) sugar
⅓ cup (85 ml) whipping cream,
35% butterfat
1 vanilla bean, split lengthwise
and seeds scraped out

7 oz. (200 g) walnut halves,
roasted

MAKING THE SWEET SHORT PASTRY
Fit the stand mixer with the paddle beater and beat the butter and sugar together until soft, light, and creamy. Whisk the egg, salt, and vanilla together and gradually beat into the creamed mixture until smooth. Sift the flour with the ground walnuts and beat into the creamed mixture at low speed until combined. Remove the dough from the bowl to a work surface and knead lightly with your hand, taking care not to overwork it. Shape into a disk, cover with plastic wrap, and chill for 1 hour.

MAKING THE WALNUT GENOISE SPONGE
Preheat the oven to 400°F (200°C/Gas mark 6). Fit the stand mixer with the whisk and beat the eggs and sugar at medium speed to the ribbon stage. Mix the chopped walnuts with the flour and fold into the whisked egg mixture. Drizzle in the melted butter and fold in until combined. Set aside.

MAKING THE SYRUP
Add the sugar to the water in a pan and heat until the sugar dissolves, then bring to a boil. Remove from the heat and stir in the rum. Keep hot.

MAKING THE ALMOND PASTE CROWN
Mix the almond paste with the egg white until soft and smooth. Spoon it into the pastry bag.

MAKING THE SOFT CARAMEL TOPPING
Warm the glucose syrup in a pan, add the sugar and, when the sugar dissolves, boil to a rich brown caramel. While the syrup is boiling, bring the cream to a boil in a small pan. Protecting your hand with an oven mitt, slowly pour the hot cream into the caramel to prevent it from cooking further. Stir in the vanilla seeds.

ASSEMBLING THE TART
Line the tart ring with the rolled-out pastry dough and pour in the sponge batter to half-fill the ring. Bake for about 20 minutes, until light brown and firm enough to support the almond paste crown. Remove from the oven and let cool, leaving the oven switched on. Pipe a decorative border of almond paste around the edge of the tart. Return the tart to the oven for about 10 minutes. Remove the tart from the oven and moisten the sponge filling with some of the hot syrup. Allow to cool. Spread out the roasted walnuts over the cooled sponge layer and pour the caramel topping over the nuts.

WALNUT TART

Tarte aux Noix

by Carl Marletti

BEST PASTRY CHEF OF THE YEAR, 2009

Serves 8

Active time
1 hour

Chilling time
1 hour 10 minutes

Cooking time
45 minutes

Equipment
9 ½-in. (24-cm) tart
ring or pan with
a removable base

Stand mixer fitted
with the whisk
attachment

Ingredients

WALNUT CREAM
2.75 oz. (80 g) butter, softened
2.75 oz. (80 g) sugar
2.75 oz. (80 g) ground walnuts
2.25 oz. (65 g) lightly beaten egg
2 tsp (10 ml) rum

SWEET WALNUT-VANILLA
PASTRY DOUGH
4.5 oz. (130 g) flour
1.75 oz. (52 g) confectioners' sugar
0.5 oz. (15 g) ground walnuts
⅛ tsp (1 g) salt
2.75 oz. (75 g) butter, chilled
and diced
1 oz. (25 g) lightly beaten egg
2 tsp (10 ml) vanilla extract

VANILLA FUDGE
10.5 oz. (300 g) superfine sugar
1 oz. (30 g) glucose
3 vanilla beans, split lengthwise
and seeds scraped out
¾ cup plus 2 tbsp (204 ml)
whipping cream
2 tbsp (30 g) chestnut honey
0.5 oz. (15 g) butter

CARAMELIZED WALNUTS
10.5 oz. (300 g) fresh shelled
walnut halves
Scant ½ cup (100 ml) 30° syrup
4.5 oz. (125 g) golden raisins

CHANTILLY CREAM
2 vanilla beans, split lengthwise
and seeds scraped out
2.75 oz. (80 g) mascarpone
¾ cup (160 ml) whipping cream
2 ½ tsp (10 g) superfine sugar

——————— MAKING THE WALNUT CREAM
Cream the softened butter with the sugar until pale. Stir in the ground walnuts.
Gradually add the egg and combine until smooth and uniform. Incorporate the rum and
beat until lightly whipped. Press plastic wrap over the surface of the cream and chill.

——————— MAKING THE SWEET WALNUT-VANILLA PASTRY DOUGH
Sift the dry ingredients together. Add the butter and rub to a sandy texture. Gradually
incorporate the egg and vanilla extract, and combine until a smooth dough is formed.
Cover with plastic wrap and chill. Roll out the dough to a thickness of about ⅛ in.
(3 mm), line the greased tart pan with the dough, and chill for 1 hour. Preheat the
oven to 325°F (160°C/Gas mark 3). Fill the chilled tart shell with the walnut cream
and bake for about 25 minutes. Let cool completely.

——————— MAKING THE VANILLA FUDGE
Make a dry caramel with the sugar and glucose. In a separate saucepan, infuse the
vanilla beans and seeds in the cream. Gently stop the caramel cooking by pouring
in the hot infused cream through a fine-mesh sieve, then add the honey. Bring to
a simmer, then remove from the heat and incorporate the butter. Blend and strain
through a fine-mesh sieve. Allow to cool until lukewarm.

——————— MAKING THE CARAMELIZED WALNUTS
Preheat the oven to 325°F (160°C/Gas mark 3). Mix the fresh walnuts with the syrup.
Drain off any excess syrup and spread the walnuts on a nonstick baking sheet. Bake
for about 15–20 minutes until caramelized. Set aside a few caramelized walnuts and
raisins for decoration, then add the remaining raisins to the walnuts. Set aside.

——————— MAKING THE CHANTILLY CREAM
Using the stand mixer fitted with the whisk attachment, beat the vanilla seeds, mascarpone, whipping cream, and sugar together until stiff.

——————— ASSEMBLING THE TART
Fill the tart shell with the caramelized walnuts and raisins. Cover with the fudge and
decorate with the reserved caramelized walnuts and raisins. Chill in the refrigerator
for 10 minutes. Using a spoon, place quenelles of Chantilly cream on top.

Brioche Dough

Makes 1 lb. 5 oz. (600 g)

Active time
30 minutes

First rising time
30 minutes

Chilling time
2 hours minimum

Second rising time
1 ½ hours

Cooking time
8 minutes for individual
brioches and about 20 minutes
for a large one

Storage
Up to 2 days in the refrigerator

Equipment
Stand mixer
Molds in the sizes of your
choice

Ingredients
2 cups (9 oz./250 g) white
bread flour

½ cup (4.5 oz./125 g) lightly
beaten egg, well chilled
(about 2 ½ eggs)

1 ½ tbsp (25 ml) whole milk,
well chilled

2 tbsp (25 g) sugar

1 tsp (5 g) salt

0.25 oz. (8 g) fresh yeast

3 tbsp (50 ml) crème fraîche
or heavy cream

1 stick plus 1 tsp
(4.25 oz./120 g) butter, diced,
at room temperature

1• Using your hands, roughly combine all the ingredients,
except the butter, in the bowl of the stand mixer,
without letting the yeast come into direct contact with the salt and sugar.

2 • With the dough hook, knead at low speed for 5 minutes. Increase the speed to medium and knead for 15 minutes until the dough pulls away from the sides of the bowl, scraping down the sides regularly. The dough should be elastic.

3 • Gradually knead in the butter and, when incorporated, knead for 5 minutes, until the dough pulls away from the sides of the bowl. Cover the dough in plastic wrap and let rise at room temperature for 30 minutes.

CHEFS' NOTES

• It is important not to let the yeast come into contact with the salt or sugar when you begin the kneading process.

• You may have to vary the quantity of dough according to the capacity of your stand mixer.

4 • Flatten and push away the dough several times, folding it over to burst any air bubbles trapped inside to make the dough stronger. Cover and refrigerate for at least 2 hours. Divide the dough between the molds—each mold should be half-filled. Let rise for about 1 ½ hours before baking.

Small Individual Parisian Brioches

Petites Brioches à Tête

**Makes 6 individual brioches,
or 1 large brioche to serve 4**
(see technique p. 134)

Active time
5–10 minutes

Rising time
1 ½ hours

Cooking time
8 minutes for individual
brioches, and 20 minutes
for 1 large brioche

Storage
Up to 2 days

Equipment
6 × 2 ½-in. (6-cm) brioche molds,
or 1 × 6 ⅓-in. (16-cm) brioche
mold

Ingredients
Brioche dough (see technique
p. 130), well chilled: 8.5 oz.
(240 g) for 6 individual brioches
weighing about 1.5 oz. (40 g)
each, or 10.5 oz. (300 g)
for 1 large brioche

Butter for the molds

Egg wash
1 ½ tbsp (1 oz./25 g) lightly
beaten egg (about ½ egg)
1 tbsp (0.75 oz./20 g) egg yolk
(about 1 yolk)
1 ½ tbsp (25 ml) whole milk

1• To make small brioches, divide the dough into 6 equal pieces
and roll each into a ball. Chill in the refrigerator for 15 minutes.

3• Pinch around the "head" to shape it and place in a lightly greased
mold. Push the head down into the "body" to the base of the mold.

4• Dip a finger in flour and, using the tip like a hook,
release the "head" from the "body."

2 • Shape the balls into small logs. With the side of your hand, press down into each log two-thirds of the way along, working gently back-and-forth to form the brioche "head," and taking care not to twist or break the dough.

5 • Lightly brush the tops of the brioches with egg wash. Place a bowl of boiling water in a cool oven (75°F/25°C), put the brioches above, and let rise for about 1 ½ hours. Carefully brush the tops of the brioches again with egg wash.

6 • Preheat the oven to 425°F (220°C/Gas mark 7) and heat a baking sheet. Place the 6 molds on the hot sheet to help the "heads" rise, and bake for 8 minutes. Immediately turn the brioches out of the molds to stop them reabsorbing any steam.

Large Parisian Brioche

Grosse Brioche à Tête

1 • To make a large brioche, weigh about 3 oz. (80 g) of the dough and shape it into a small ball. Make another ball with the remaining dough. Chill both in the refrigerator for 15 minutes.

2 • With your thumb, make a hole in the larger ball and pull the dough back to enlarge the hole. Place the dough in a lightly greased mold.

4 • Dip a finger in flour and, using the tip like a hook, release the "head" from the "body."

5 • Lightly brush the top of the brioche with egg wash. Place a bowl of boiling water in a cool oven (75°F/25°C), put the brioche above, and let rise for about 1 ½ hours.

3 • Shape the smaller ball of dough into a pear, pinching one end into a point. Insert the point in the hole of the larger ball so it reaches the bottom of the mold.

6 • Preheat the oven to 350°F (180°C/Gas mark 4) and heat a baking sheet. Carefully brush the top of the brioche again with the egg wash. Dip the tips of the blades of a pair of scissors in water and make 4 equally spaced cuts around the edge of the brioche.

7 • Place on the hot baking sheet to help the "head" rise and bake for 5 minutes. Reduce the oven temperature to 330°F (165°C/Gas mark 3) and bake for 15 minutes. Immediately turn the brioche out of the mold to stop it reabsorbing any steam.

Classic Baker's Brioche

Brioche Nanterre

Makes 1 × 8-in. (20-cm) brioche to serve 6

Active time
15 minutes

Rising time
2 hours

Cooking time
25 minutes

Storage
Up to 2 days

Equipment
8 × 4 × 2.5-in. (20 × 10 × 6-cm) traditional brioche pan
or loaf pan

Ingredients
10.5 oz. (300 g) brioche dough (see technique p. 130), well chilled
Pearl sugar (optional)
Butter for the pan

Egg wash
1 ½ tbsp (1 oz./25 g) lightly beaten egg (about ½ egg)
1 tbsp (0.75 oz./20 g) egg yolk (about 1 yolk)
1 ½ tbsp (25 ml) whole milk

1• Divide the dough into 6 equal pieces with a dough cutter and roll each one into a ball.

CHEFS' NOTES

• If you are concerned the brioche will stick to the pan, even after greasing, line the pan with parchment paper.

• The rising time prior to baking can vary; the dough should double in volume.

3• Brush with the egg wash. Place a bowl of boiling water in a cool oven (75°F/25°C), put the pan above, and let the dough rise for 2 hours.

2 • Butter the pan well and place the balls of dough in the pan, staggering them slightly.

4 • Preheat the oven to 350°F (180°C/Gas mark 4). Brush with egg wash again and, if you wish, sprinkle the top with pearl sugar. Bake for 25 minutes.

5 • Immediately remove from the pan to prevent any steam being reabsorbed into the brioche.

Braided Brioche

Brioche Tressée

Serves 4–6

Active time
10–15 minutes

Rising time
2 hours

Cooking time
20 minutes

Storage
Up to 2 days

Ingredients
10.5 oz. (300 g) brioche dough
(see technique p. 130), well chilled
Pearl sugar (optional)

Egg wash
1 ½ tbsp (1 oz./25 g) lightly
beaten egg (about ½ egg)
1 tbsp (0.75 oz./20 g) egg yolk
(about 1 yolk)
1 ½ tbsp (25 ml) whole milk

1 • Using a dough cutter, divide the brioche dough into 3 equal pieces.

4 • Starting in the middle, braid the ropes together. Repeat, braiding the other half.

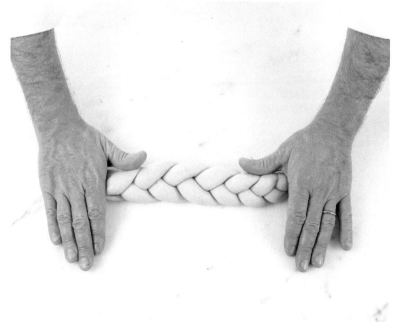

5 • Seal the ends by pressing them down lightly and tucking under the braid.

2 • Shape each one into a ball and roll into a rope 12 in. (30 cm) long, making sure any seam is underneath.

3 • Lightly flour the ropes and place them side by side.

6 • Brush the top with the egg wash. Place a bowl of boiling water in a cool oven (75°F/25°C), put the braid on a baking sheet above, and let the dough rise for about 2 hours, until at least doubled in size.

7 • Preheat the oven to 350°F (180°C/Gas mark 4). Sprinkle with pearl sugar, if using, and bake on a hot baking sheet for 20 minutes. Immediately remove the brioche from the sheet and place it on a rack to cool so it does not reabsorb any steam.

Milk Bread Rolls

Pains au Lait

**Makes 10 small rolls
or 30 *navettes*
(bridge or finger rolls)**

Active time
1 hour

First rising time
45 minutes–1 hour

Second rising time
1 ½ hours

Cooking time
6 minutes

Storage
Up to 24 hours

Equipment
Stand mixer
Pair of long, thin-bladed scissors

Ingredients
2 cups (9 oz./250 g) flour,
preferably white bread flour
0.35 oz. (10 g) fresh yeast
1 tsp (5 g) salt
2 ½ tbsp (1 oz./30 g) sugar
¼ cup plus 1 tsp (2.25 oz./65 g)
lightly beaten egg
(about 1 ½ eggs)
⅓ cup (75 ml) whole milk
4 tbsp (2.25 oz./65 g) butter,
diced, at room temperature
Pearl sugar (optional)

Egg wash
1 ½ tbsp (1 oz./25 g) lightly
beaten egg (about ½ egg)
1 tbsp (0.75 oz./20 g) egg yolk
(about 1 yolk)
1 ½ tbsp (25 ml) whole milk

1 • In the bowl of the stand mixer, quickly combine all the ingredients, except the butter, with your hand. Fit the dough hook and knead at low speed for about 10 minutes, until the dough pulls away from the sides of the bowl. Knead in the butter.

2 • Cover the dough with plastic wrap or a clean, damp cloth and place on a baking sheet. Let rise for 45 minutes–1 hour at room temperature (68°F/20°C).

3 • Firmly flatten the dough with your hand to burst any air bubbles inside. ⊕

CHEFS' NOTES

- To prevent the rolls drying out while rising, keep them in a warm, humid place at a temperature of between 75°F and 85°F (25°C and 30°C).

- You can make the dough a day ahead and store it in the refrigerator, well covered.

4 • Weigh out small pieces of dough: about ½ oz. (15 g) for small rolls or navettes, and about 1 ¾ oz. (50 g) for slightly larger rolls.

5 • Shape the pieces into ovals with pointed ends (known as *navettes* in France as they resemble small boats), or larger oval buns.

6 • Place on a nonstick baking sheet and brush with the egg wash. Place a bowl of boiling water in a cool oven (75°F/25°C), put the baking sheet above, and let the dough rise for about 1 ½ hours, until doubled in size.

7 • Preheat the oven to 425°F (220°C/Gas mark 7). Brush the rolls again with the egg wash and, using scissors, cut a neat herringbone pattern down their length. Sprinkle with pearl sugar, if using, and bake for 6 minutes until golden.

Provençal Epiphany Brioche

Couronne des Rois

Serves 6

Active time
40 minutes

First rising time
1 ½ hours

Second rising time
1 hour

Chilling time
2–12 hours

Third rising time
2 hours

Cooking time
20–25 minutes

Storage
Up to 2 days

Equipment
Stand mixer

Ingredients

Filling
1.75 oz. (50 g) sultanas
(golden raisins)
1.75 oz. (50 g) candied orange
peel, finely diced
1.75 oz. (50 g) candied
strawberries or cherries
1 oz. (25 g) chocolate chips
(about 1 heaping tbsp)
1 ½ tbsp (25 ml) orange liqueur,
e.g. Grand Marnier

Poolish starter
Scant ¼ cup (50 ml) whole milk
⅔ cup plus 1 tbsp (3 oz./90 g)
flour
0.5 oz. (15 g) fresh yeast

Brioche dough
2 cups (9 oz./250 g) flour
1 ¼ tsp (6 g) salt
Scant 1 tsp (4 ml) orange
flower water
Scant ½ cup (3.75 oz./110 g)
lightly beaten egg
(about 2 ½ eggs)
3 tbsp (45 ml) whole milk
0.35 oz. (10 g) fresh yeast
1 stick plus 2 tsp (4.5 oz./125 g)
butter, diced, at room
temperature

Egg wash
1 ½ tbsp (1 oz./25 g) lightly
beaten egg (about ½ egg)
1 tbsp (0.75 oz./20 g) egg yolk
(about 1 yolk)
1 ½ tbsp (25 ml) whole milk

Decoration
Pearl sugar
Nuts and candied fruit
of your choice

1 · Make the filling by soaking the sultanas, candied orange peel, and candied strawberries in a bowl with the orange liqueur.

2 · To make the poolish starter, fit the stand mixer with the dough hook and knead the milk, flour, and yeast in the bowl for no more than 5 minutes, until the dough is smooth. Remove from the bowl, cover with plastic wrap, and let rise for 1 ½ hours at room temperature. ↪

Provençal Epiphany Brioche (continued)

3 • Return the starter to the bowl and add all the ingredients for the dough, except the butter. Knead at low speed for 7 minutes, increase to medium speed and knead for 10 minutes.
Add the butter, drained fruit, and chocolate chips. Mix lightly.

4 • Cover the dough with plastic wrap, transfer it to a baking sheet, and let rise for 1 hour at room temperature. Fold the dough over on itself several times, pushing it down to burst any air bubbles. Re-cover and chill for at least 2 hours or up to 12 hours.

5 • With your thumb, press a hole in the middle of the dough.

6 • Enlarge the hole with your fingers to shape it into a ring. Place a bowl of boiling water in a cool oven (75°F/25°C), put the ring above, and let the dough rise for 2 hours.

CHEFS' NOTES

Don't overmix when you add the soaked fruit to the dough
as you risk reducing the fruit to a purée.

7 • Preheat the oven to 325°F (160°C/Gas mark 3). Brush the top of the dough with egg wash and, with a pair of scissors, cut incisions at regular intervals around the top.

8 • Sprinkle with pearl sugar. Bake for 20–25 minutes. Place on a rack to cool and decorate with the nuts and candied fruit.

Kougelhopf

Makes 1 × 8-in. (20-cm) kougelhopf to serve 4-6

Active time
1 hour

First rising time
1 hour

Chilling time
30 minutes

Second rising time
2 hours

Cooking time
45 minutes–1 hour

Storage
Up to 3 days

Equipment
8-in. (20-cm) traditional earthenware kougelhopf mold
Stand mixer

Ingredients
⅔ cup (3.5 oz./100 g) sultanas (golden raisins)
1 tbsp (15 ml) kirsch
2 cups (9 oz./250 g) flour
0.5 oz. (15 g) fresh yeast
1 ¼ tsp (6 g) salt
¼ cup (1.5 oz/40 g) sugar
3 ½ tbsp (1.75 oz./50 g) lightly beaten egg (about 1 egg)
⅓ cup (75 ml) whole milk
2.75 oz. (75 g) sourdough starter (optional)
1 stick plus 2 tsp (4.5 oz./125 g) butter, diced, at room temperature
2 ½ tbsp (1 oz./25 g) whole, unblanched almonds
A little melted butter for the mold, plus more to brush the kougelhopf
Confectioners' sugar for dusting

Kirsch syrup (see Chefs' Notes)
Scant ½ cup (3 oz./80 g) sugar
Scant ½ cup (100 ml) water
2 tsp (10 ml) kirsch

CHEFS' NOTES

To make the kirsch syrup, dissolve the sugar in the water in a pan and bring to a boil, brushing any crystals from the sides of the pan with a damp brush. Allow to cool and stir in the kirsch.

1· Soak the sultanas in boiling water for 30 minutes and then drain well. Place in a small bowl with the kirsch to macerate.

4· Shape the dough into a ball and cover with plastic wrap to prevent the top crusting. Let rise on a baking sheet for 1 hour at room temperature. Flatten the dough to burst any air bubbles trapped inside and shape into a ball. Cover with plastic wrap and chill in the refrigerator for 30 minutes.

CHEFS' NOTES

- Briefly soak the almonds in boiling water to prevent them burning during baking. This also ensures they stick to the kougelhopf.

- If the yeast comes into direct contact with the salt and sugar before kneading, it will not work efficiently, preventing the dough from rising properly.

2 • Fit the stand mixer with a dough hook and add the flour, yeast, salt, sugar (ensuring the yeast does not come into contact with the salt or sugar), egg, milk, and sourdough starter, if using, to the bowl. Knead at low speed until the mixture pulls away from the sides.

3 • Knead in the butter. As soon as it is fully incorporated, briefly knead in the sultanas.

5 • Brush the mold thoroughly with melted butter, twice.

6 • Arrange the whole almonds around the bottom of the mold and chill so they are firmly set in the butter. ⊕

Kougelhopf (continued)

7 • Weigh 1 lb. 5 oz. (600 g) of the dough, shape it into a ball and use your thumb to press a hole in the center.

8 • Carefully enlarge the hole so the dough becomes ring-shaped.

9 • Lift the dough into the mold. Place a bowl of boiling water in a cool oven (75°F/25°C) and let the dough rise for 2 hours. Bake at 400°F (200°C/Gas mark 6) for 15 minutes, then reduce the heat to 325°F (165°C/Gas mark 3) and bake for 20 minutes, covering the top with foil toward the end of the cooking time to prevent over-browning.

10 • Remove the kougelhopf from the oven and turn it carefully out of the mold. Moisten it generously with the kirsch syrup, brush with melted butter, and dust with confectioners' sugar.

Flaky Brioches

Brioche Feuilletée

Serves 8

Active time
40 minutes

Rising time
2 hours

Chilling time
3 hours plus 30 minutes
freezing time

Cooking time
20–30 minutes

Storage
Up to 3 days,
covered in plastic wrap

Equipment
Stand mixer
Thin sheet of plastic or food-
safe acetate (optional)
2 × 7-in. (18-cm) diameter
brioche molds

Ingredients
2 cups (9 oz./250 g) white
bread flour

1 tsp (5 g) salt

2 ½ tbsp (1 oz./30 g) sugar

1 tbsp plus 1 tsp (0.75 oz./20 g)
butter, plus extra for greasing

¼ cup (2 oz./60 g) lightly beaten
egg (about 1 ½ eggs), well chilled

¼ cup (60 ml) whole milk,
well chilled

0.35 oz. (10 g) fresh yeast

1 stick plus 2 tbsp
(5.25 oz./150 g) butter,
preferably 84% butterfat

Egg wash
1 ½ tbsp (1 oz./25 g) lightly
beaten egg (about ½ egg)

1 tbsp (0.75 oz./20 g) egg yolk
(about 1 yolk)

1 ½ tbsp (25 ml) whole milk

1• Make the dough using all the ingredients listed, except
the 84% butter (see technique p. 130). Roll into a rectangle 8 × 16 in.
(20 × 40 cm) and freeze for 30 minutes.

2• Meanwhile, flatten the 84% butter lightly with a rolling pin
to soften it. Shape it into an 8-in. (20-cm) square.
You can place a sheet of plastic over the butter to do this.

3• Place the butter in the center of the dough and fold the top and
bottom edges over the butter so they meet. Roll the dough into
a rectangle 8 × 32 in. (20 × 80 cm) and fold in 4 (see technique p. 68).
Give the dough a quarter turn to the right and fold in 3 to make
a single turn. Chill in the refrigerator for 1 hour. ⊕

Flaky Brioches (continued)

4 • Roll the dough into a rectangle 4 × 20 in. (10 × 50 cm), ⅛ in. (4 mm) thick and cut in half lengthwise.

5 • Using a pastry brush dipped in water, lightly moisten one of the rectangles.

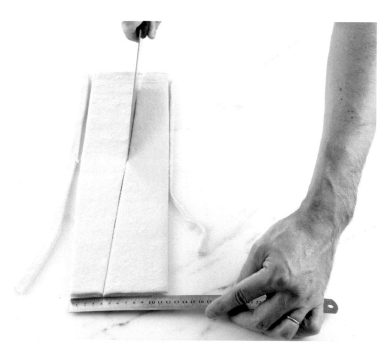

7 • Trim the edges to straighten and neaten them. Make a mark on one short edge one-third from the right and another on the opposite edge one-third from the left. Cut diagonally from top to bottom from one mark to the other.

8 • Butter the brioche molds. Roll up the strips of dough in a spiral and stand one in each mold. Leave to rise in a warm place or in a 75°F (25°C) oven with a bowl of steaming water for about 1 ½ hours, until doubled in size.

6 • Lift the other rectangle on top and press the two lightly together.

9 • Preheat the oven to 325°F (160°C/Gas mark 3). Brush the tops of the brioches with egg wash and bake for 20–30 minutes until golden brown.

Croissants

Makes 12

Active time
2 hours

First rising time
30 minutes

Chilling time
30 minutes plus 30–40 minutes freezing time

Second rising time
2 hours

Cooking time
14 minutes

Storage
Up to 24 hours

Equipment
Stand mixer
Ruler or tape measure

Ingredients
0.35 oz. (10 g) fresh yeast
½ cup (120 ml) whole milk
1 cup (4.5 oz./125 g) flour
1 cup (4.5 oz./125 g) white bread flour
1 tsp (5 g) salt
2 ½ tbsp (1 oz./30 g) sugar
1 tsp (8 g) honey
3 tbsp (1.75 oz./50 g) butter
1 stick plus 2 tsp (4.5 oz./125 g) butter, diced, preferably with 84 % butterfat content, to incorporate into the basic dough (see Chefs' Notes)

Egg wash
1 ½ tbsp (1 oz./25 g) lightly beaten egg (about ½ egg)
1 tbsp (0.75 oz./20 g) egg yolk (about 1 yolk)
1 ½ tbsp (25 ml) whole milk

1 • Whisk the yeast and milk together in the bowl of the stand mixer.

4 • Flatten the dough to burst any air bubbles trapped inside. Place on a baking sheet and freeze for 30–40 minutes until very well chilled. With a rolling pin, flatten the 84% fat butter into a square and place on the chilled dough.

2 • Add the remaining ingredients, except the 84% fat butter which is incorporated later, and fit the mixer with the dough hook. Knead at low speed for 4 minutes and then at medium speed for 6 minutes.

3 • Shape the dough, which should now be elastic, into a ball and cover with plastic wrap. Let rise for 30 minutes, depending on the room temperature.

5 • Fold the dough over to enclose the butter and fold in the edges, sealing them well.

6 • Roll the dough into a 10 × 24-in. (25 × 60-cm) rectangle. Make a double turn and then a single turn (see techniques p. 69, step 10, and pp. 70–71, step 4–6). Chill for 30 minutes in the refrigerator. ⊕

Croissants (continued)

7 • Roll the dough to a 9 ½ × 20-in. (24 × 50-cm) rectangle, ⅛ in. (4 mm) thick. With the tip of a large knife, mark one long side of the pastry at 3-in. (8-cm) intervals and then do the same on the other side, moving the marks by 1 ¼ in. (4 cm).

8 • Cut the dough into triangles and lightly mark the center of the base of each triangle with the knife.

CHEFS' NOTES

• To check the dough is kneaded sufficiently, press down lightly on it with your finger and it should spring back.

• If butter with a fat content of 84% is unavailable, use the best-quality butter you can find with a fat content as close to 84% as possible.

10 • Roll the triangles up from the base to the tip, taking care not to press too hard and squash the dough. Each croissant should weigh about 2 oz. (50–55 g).

9 • Gently stretch each triangle with your hands.

11 • Brush the egg wash evenly over the tops. Place a bowl of boiling water in a cool oven (75°F/25°C), put the croissants above, and let them rise for about 2 hours.

12 • Remove the croissants from the oven and allow to rest for 15 minutes. Brush them again with the egg wash. Preheat the oven to 350°F (180°C/Gas mark 4) and bake for about 14 minutes.

Chocolate Croissants

Pains au Chocolat

Makes 6

Active time
15 minutes

Rising time
2 hours

Cooking time
14 minutes

Storage
Up to 24 hours

Ingredients
14 oz. (400 g) croissant dough
(see technique p. 152)
12 chocolate sticks
(use semisweet or dark *pain au chocolat* sticks)

Egg wash
1 ½ tbsp (1 oz./25 g) lightly beaten egg (about ½ egg)
1 tbsp (0.75 oz./20 g) egg yolk (about 1 yolk)
1 ½ tbsp (25 ml) whole milk

1• Roll out the croissant dough ⅛ in. (4 mm) thick.
Cut into 6 rectangles measuring 3 ½ × 6 in. (9 × 15 cm).
Lay a chocolate stick on each rectangle close to the edge of one short side.

CHEFS' NOTES

When leaving the chocolate croissants to rise, do not exceed 85°F (29°C–30°C), as this is the temperature at which butter melts.

3• Roll up the rectangles and, with the palm of your hand, press down lightly on each to seal the join underneath in the center.

2 • Roll the dough around the chocolate sticks to enclose it, and then place a second chocolate stick on the dough.

4 • Place the chocolate croissants on a nonstick baking sheet and brush egg wash evenly over them. Place a bowl of boiling water in a cool oven (75°F/25°C), put the croissants above, and let them rise for 2 hours until doubled in size.

5 • Preheat the oven to 325°F (165°C/Gas mark 3), using the convection setting for electric ovens. Carefully brush the croissants again with egg wash. Chill briefly to firm up the dough and then bake for 14 minutes, until they are nicely risen and golden.

Raisin Swirls

Pains aux Raisins

Makes 8–10

Active time
15 minutes

Rising time
About 1 hour

Cooking time
12–14 minutes

Storage
Up to 24 hours

Ingredients
Heaping ⅔ cup (3.5 oz./100 g) raisins
1 lb. (500 g) croissant dough, well chilled (see technique p. 152)
5 ¼ oz. (150 g) pastry cream (see technique p. 196)

Egg wash
1 ½ tbsp (1 oz./25 g) lightly beaten egg (about ½ egg)
1 tbsp (0.75 oz./20 g) egg yolk (about 1 yolk)
1 ½ tbsp (25 ml) whole milk

Optional
Rum for soaking
Diced candied orange peel
A little ground cinnamon

1• Soak the raisins briefly in boiling water and drain. If you wish, macerate them in a little rum with candied orange peel and cinnamon. Roll the dough into an 8 × 16-in. (20 × 40-cm) rectangle. Spread the pastry cream evenly over it.

3• Carefully roll up the dough widthwise with the filling inside.

4• Brush the roll with egg wash.

2 • Brush this border with egg wash as this will seal the swirls. Drain the raisins and scatter them evenly over the pastry cream with the candied orange peel, if using.

5 • Cut the roll into ¾–1-in. (2–2.5-cm) slices to make 8–10 equal-sized swirls. Place them flat on a nonstick baking sheet with the pastry join underneath so the swirls don't unwind as they bake.

6 • Place a bowl of boiling water in a cool oven (75°F/25°C), put the swirls above, and let rise for about 1 hour. Preheat the oven to 350°F (180°C/Gas mark 4) and bake for 12–14 minutes.

Sweet Breton Puff Pastries

Kouign Amann

Makes 24

Preparation time
3 hours

Rising time
2 ½ hours

Freezing time
30 minutes

Cooking time
15 minutes

Storage
Up to 2 days in an airtight container

Equipment
Stand mixer fitted with the dough hook
24 × 4-in. (10-cm) nonstick molds or 2 × 12-cup muffin pans

Ingredients
2 cups (9 oz./250 g) flour
0.35 oz. (10 g) fresh yeast
Scant 1 cup (6.5 oz./190 g) sugar, divided
1 tsp (5 g) salt
1 tbsp plus 1 tsp (0.75 oz./20 g) butter
½ cup (4.5 oz./125 g) lightly beaten egg (about 2 ½ eggs)
1 stick plus 2 tbsp (5.25 oz./150 g) lightly salted butter

Pearl sugar for sprinkling

Egg wash
1 ½ tbsp (1 oz./25 g) lightly beaten egg (about ½ egg)
1 tbsp (0.75 oz./20 g) egg yolk (about 1 yolk)
1 ½ tbsp (25 ml) whole milk

1 • In the mixer, knead the flour, yeast, 3 ½ tbsp of the sugar, salt, butter, and eggs (keeping the yeast apart from the salt and sugar) for 10 minutes at low speed, then medium speed for 2 minutes. Cover with plastic wrap and let rise for 1 hour at room temperature.

3 • Roll out the dough about ⅛ in. (4 mm) thick and cut into 24 strips measuring 1 ½ × 5 in. (4 × 13 cm).

4 • Roll up the dough strips tightly and place in the molds. Let rise for 1 ½ hours in a cool oven, at a temperature no higher than 68°F (20°C) or the butter and sugar will melt.

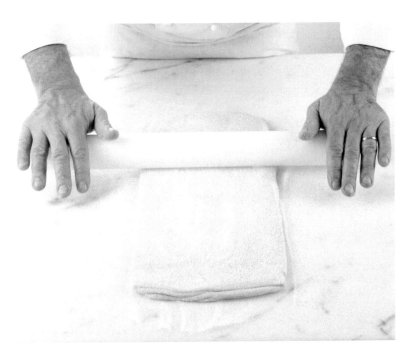

2 • Flatten the dough to a rectangle and freeze for 30 minutes. Enclose the salted butter in the dough and give it 2 single turns (see technique p. 69, step 10). Chill for 30 minutes. Sprinkle over the remaining sugar and give 1 single turn.

5 • Take the risen pastries out of the oven, brush evenly with egg wash, and sprinkle with the pearl sugar. Preheat the oven to 350°F (180°C/Gas mark 4).

6 • Bake the pastries for 12 minutes, then turn them over in the molds and bake for another 2–3 minutes. Turn them out immediately and place on a rack to cool.

Choux Pastry

Pâte à Choux

Makes 15–22 individual pastries

Active time
30 minutes

Storage
Up to 2 days, or freeze unfilled for up to 1 month

Ingredients
½ cup (125 ml) water
½ cup (125 ml) whole milk
Heaping ½ tsp (3 g) salt
1 tsp (5 g) sugar (optional)
1 stick plus 2 tsp (4.5 oz./125 g) butter, diced
1 cup plus 2 tbsp (5.25 oz./150 g) flour, sifted
1 cup (9 oz./250 g) lightly beaten egg (about 5 eggs), at room temperature

Uses
Religieuses, éclairs, Paris-Brest, Saint-Honoré, sugar-crusted choux puffs (*chouquettes*), croquembouches (wedding cakes)

1 • Heat the water, milk, salt, sugar (if using), and butter in a pan and, when the butter has completely melted, bring to a fast boil.

CHEFS' NOTES

• Ensure the butter is completely melted when bringing the mixture to a boil.

• The eggs should be at room temperature.

• Depending on the size of eggs you use, you may need to add a little extra (or less) egg to the mixture. It is important that the choux pastry is the correct consistency or it will not rise properly in the oven.

4 • Beat for 10 seconds or until the mixture is no longer sticking to the sides of the pan. Transfer it to a mixing bowl to prevent further cooking.

2 • Remove from the heat and tip in all the flour, beating vigorously with a spatula until smooth.

3 • Return the saucepan to a low heat and stir constantly to dry out the mixture.

5 • Using the spatula, gradually mix in the beaten eggs, incorporating each addition before you add the next. Beat until the pastry is smooth and glossy.

6 • To check the consistency, draw a line through the pastry with the spatula and it should close up slowly. If necessary, beat in a little extra egg.

Sugar-Crusted Choux Puffs

Chouquettes

Makes 40–60

Active time
25 minutes

Cooking time
20–25 minutes,
depending on size

Storage
Serve as soon as possible
after baking

Equipment
Pastry bag fitted
with a plain ⅓-in. or ½-in.
(10-mm or 12-mm) tip

Ingredients
1 quantity choux pastry
(see technique p. 162)
Pearl sugar for sprinkling

Egg wash
1 ½ tbsp (1 oz./25 g) lightly
beaten egg (about ½ egg)
1 tbsp (0.75 oz./20 g) egg yolk
(about 1 yolk)
1 ½ tbsp (25 ml) whole milk

1 • Butter 2 baking sheets or use nonstick sheets. Preheat
the oven to 425°F (220°C/Gas mark 7). Spoon the choux pastry
into the pastry bag and pipe 1 ¼–1 ½-in. (3–4-cm) mounds
on the baking sheets.

CHEFS' NOTES

Very slightly under-bake the puffs so they remain spongy.

4 • Sprinkle with pearl sugar.

2 • Brush the egg wash over the mounds using a pastry brush.

3 • Dip a fork in cold water and mark the top of each puff.

5 • Tilt the baking sheets to remove the excess pearl sugar
and bake for 20–25 minutes until golden brown.

Piping and Baking Éclairs

Active time
15 minutes

Cooking time
30–40 minutes, depending on size

Storage
Up to 2 days in an airtight container

Equipment
Pastry bag fitted with a plain ½-in. (15-mm) tip
Pastry scraper

Ingredients
1 quantity choux pastry
(see technique p. 162)

Egg wash
1 ½ tbsp (1 oz./25 g) lightly beaten egg (about ½ egg)
1 tbsp (0.75 oz./25 g) egg yolk (about 1 yolk)
1 ½ tbsp (25 ml) whole milk

1 • To make the pastry bag easier to fill without the choux pastry leaking out, fold the end of the bag over and push it into the tip. Stand the bag upright, in a measuring cup, for example.

4 • Preheat the oven to 350°F (180°C/Gas mark 4). Butter a baking sheet. Dip the pastry scraper in flour and mark lines diagonally on the baking sheet to guide you when you pipe the éclairs.

5 • Pipe 5–5 ½-in. (12–14-cm) lengths of pastry over the lines and brush with the egg wash.

CHEFS' NOTES

After the éclairs have been baking for 15–20 minutes, prop the oven door open slightly
with a wooden spoon to allow steam in the pastry to escape.

2 • Spoon the pastry into the bag, leaving enough space so you can
hold the bag securely.

3 • Close the bag by holding it at the top and giving it a quarter-turn,
making sure no air bubbles are trapped inside.
Pull lightly on the tip so the pastry can move down into it.

6 • Dip a fork in cold water and mark the top of each éclair
by running the tines down its length. Bake for 30–40 minutes until
risen, dry to the touch, and golden brown.

Filling Éclairs

Active time
15 minutes

Storage
Up to 2 days in the refrigerator

Equipment
Long pointed metal icing tip
Pastry bag fitted with a plain
⅓-in. (10-mm) tip

Ingredients
Éclairs (see technique p. 166)
Pastry cream (see technique p. 196)

1• Using the pointed tip, pierce 3 holes in the base of the baked and cooled éclairs, one at each end and one in the center.
This ensures the éclairs can be filled evenly with the pastry cream.

CHEFS' NOTES

• When filling choux puffs, pierce holes according to their size and shape. For religieuses, for example, a single hole in the center of the base of both the "head" (smaller puff) and the "body" (larger puff) are all that's needed.

• Before spooning the pastry cream into the bag, you can beat in a flavoring or extract of your choice.

2• Whisk or beat the cream until smooth. Spoon it into the pastry bag and pipe it into the éclairs through the holes. As the éclairs are filled you will feel them becoming heavier. Chill in the refrigerator until you are ready to ice them (see technique p. 169).

Icing Éclairs

Active time
15 minutes

Storage
Up to 2 days in the refrigerator

Equipment
Instant-read thermometer
Rack

Ingredients
Pouring fondant icing
Flavoring, such as chocolate, vanilla, or coffee
Coloring of your choice
Filled éclairs (see technique p. 168)

1 • Melt the pouring fondant over low heat in a saucepan. When the temperature reaches 95°F–99°F (35°C–37°C), remove from the heat and add the flavoring and coloring of your choice. Adjust the texture with syrup or water.

2 • Dip the tops of the éclairs in the fondant.

3 • Hold the éclairs upright so excess icing can drip back into the pan. ⊕

Icing Éclairs (continued)

4 • Lightly run your finger around the icing to neaten it.

5 • You can also ice the éclairs by letting the fondant run in a ribbon from a spatula over the tops of the éclairs until they are coated, removing any excess with your finger. Place the éclairs on a rack until the fondant has set.

CHEFS' NOTES

• It's important to heat the fondant to the correct temperature so the éclairs have a smooth, even layer of icing.

• You can choose how you decorate your iced éclairs, such as piping motifs with a paper cone **(see technique p. 598)** or adding chocolate shapes **(see techniques pp. 592–96)**. You can also top them with nuts, or dried, fresh, or candied fruit. Create your own ideas that will complement the flavor of the pastry cream filling.

• Reheat the pouring fondant and adjust the texture if necessary during its use.

LEVEL

1

COFFEE ÉCLAIRS

Éclair au Café

Makes 20

Active time
45 minutes

Cooking time
30–40 minutes

Storage
Up to 2 days in an airtight container in the refrigerator

Equipment
2 pastry bags fitted with plain ½-in. (15-mm) and ⅓-in. (10-mm) tips

Instant-read thermometer

Ingredients

CHOUX PASTRY
1 cup (250 ml) water
Heaping ½ tsp (3 g) salt
1 tsp (5 g) sugar
7 tbsp (3.5 oz./100 g) butter, diced, plus extra for greasing
1 cup plus 2 tbsp (5.25 oz./150 g) flour, sifted
1 cup (9 oz./250 g) lightly beaten egg (about 5 eggs), at room temperature
Clarified butter for brushing

COFFEE-FLAVORED PASTRY CREAM
4 cups (1 liter) whole milk
1 cup (7 oz./200 g) sugar
1 vanilla bean, split lengthwise and seeds scraped out
Scant 1 cup (7 oz./200 g) lightly beaten egg (about 4 eggs)
Or
½ cup plus 1 ½ tbsp (5.5 oz./160 g) egg yolk (about 8 yolks)
⅓ cup (1.75 oz./50 g) cornstarch
½ cup minus 1 tbsp (1.75 oz./50 g) flour
7 tbsp (3.5 oz./100 g) butter
1 tbsp (15 ml) coffee extract

COFFEE POURING FONDANT ICING
14 oz. (400 g) coffee-flavored pouring fondant icing

MAKING THE CHOUX PASTRY

Heat the water, salt, sugar, and butter in a pan and, when the butter is melted, bring to a fast boil. Remove from the heat and tip in all the flour, beating vigorously with a spatula until smooth. Return the saucepan to a low heat and stir constantly to dry out the mixture. Beat for 10 seconds or until the mixture is no longer sticking to the sides of the pan. Transfer it to a mixing bowl to prevent further cooking. Using a spatula, gradually mix in the beaten eggs, incorporating each addition before you add the next. Beat until the pastry is smooth and glossy. To check the consistency, draw a line through the pastry with the spatula and it should close up slowly. If necessary, beat in a little extra egg.

PIPING AND BAKING THE ÉCLAIRS

Preheat the oven to 350°F (180°C/Gas mark 4). Butter 2 baking sheets. Using the pastry bag fitted with the ½-in. (15-mm) tip, pipe 5-in. (12-cm) éclairs, brush them with a little clarified butter, and bake for 30–40 minutes, leaving the oven door slightly ajar after 15–20 minutes. When they are puffed, golden, and dry to the touch, transfer the éclairs to a rack to cool.

MAKING THE COFFEE-FLAVORED PASTRY CREAM

Using the ingredients listed, except the coffee extract, make the pastry cream (see technique p. 196). Remove from the heat and stir in the coffee extract.

PREPARING THE POURING FONDANT ICING

Heat the fondant in a saucepan over low heat to 98°F (37°C).

ASSEMBLING THE ÉCLAIRS

Pierce 3 small holes in the base of each éclair, one at each end and one in the center. Fill the éclairs with the coffee-flavored pastry cream using the pastry bag fitted with the ⅓-in. (10-mm) tip (see technique p. 168). Dip the tops of the éclairs in the icing, neatening the edges with your finger (see technique p. 169).

CHEFS' NOTES

You can replace the coffee extract in the pastry cream with finely ground instant coffee granules or powder, adding it with the other ingredients when you heat the milk.

LEVEL
2

CRISP-COATED LEMON ÉCLAIRS

Éclair au Citron Craquelin Croustillant

Makes 20

Active time
2 hours

Chilling time
2 hours

Cooking time
30–40 minutes

Storage
Up to 2 days in the refrigerator

Equipment
Stand mixer
2 pastry bags fitted
with plain ½-in. (15-mm)
and ⅓-in. (10-mm) tips

Instant-read thermometer
Fine-mesh conical sieve
Stick blender

Ingredients

CRISP COATING (CRAQUELIN)
¼ cup (1 oz./30 g) flour
3 ½ tbsp (1.75 oz./50 g) butter
3 ½ tbsp (0.75 oz./20 g)
almond flour
0.35 oz. (10 g) candied lemon zest
¼ cup (1.75 oz./50 g) light
brown sugar
Finely grated zest of 1 lemon

CHOUX PASTRY
1 cup (250 ml) water
Heaping ½ tsp (3 g) salt
1 tsp (5 g) sugar
7 tbsp (3.5 oz./100 g) butter,
diced, plus extra for greasing
1 cup plus 2 tbsp (5.25 oz./150 g)
flour, sifted
1 cup (9 oz./250 g) lightly
beaten egg (about 5 eggs),
at room temperature

LEMON CRÉMEUX
3 sheets (0.2 oz./6 g) gelatin
Scant 1 cup (7 oz./200 g) lightly
beaten egg (about 4 eggs)
½ cup (3.5 oz./100 g) sugar
1 oz. (30 g) finely grated
lemon zest
⅔ cup (170 ml) lemon juice
1 stick plus 2 tbsp (5.25 oz./150 g)
butter

LEMON POURING FONDANT ICING
14 oz. (400 g) pouring
fondant icing
2 ½ tbsp (40 ml) lemon juice
Finely grated zest of ½ lemon
⅔ tsp (3 g) yellow coloring

MAKING THE CRISP COATING CRAQUELIN
Fit the stand mixer with the paddle beater and beat all the ingredients together until they form a paste. Place between 2 sheets of parchment paper and roll the paste ⅛ in. (3 mm) thick. Place flat in the freezer, still between the sheets of parchment, until firmed up.

PIPING AND BAKING THE ÉCLAIRS
Using the ingredients listed, make the choux pastry (see technique p. 162). Preheat the oven to 350°F (180°C/Gas mark 4). Butter 2 baking sheets. Spoon the pastry into the pastry bag fitted with the ½-in. (15-mm) tip and pipe 5-in. (12-cm) éclairs onto the sheets. Cut the *craquelin* paste into 4 × ¾-in. (10 × 2-cm) rectangles and lay them carefully on top of the éclairs. Bake for 30–40 minutes.

MAKING THE LEMON CRÉMEUX
Soak the gelatin in a bowl of cold water. Put the eggs, sugar, lemon zest, and lemon juice in a pan and heat until the sugar dissolves and the temperature reaches 185°F (85°C). Strain through a fine-mesh sieve. Squeeze out the gelatin sheets and stir in until dissolved. Allow to cool to 140°F (60°C) and then stir in the butter. Process with the stick blender and then chill for at least 2 hours.

PREPARING THE LEMON POURING FONDANT ICING
Heat the fondant in a pan over low heat to 98°F (37°C). Stir in the lemon juice, lemon zest, and coloring. The icing should become very glossy but, if it is too thick, add a little plain sugar syrup.

ASSEMBLING THE ÉCLAIRS
Pierce 3 small holes in the base of each éclair, one at each end and one in the center. Fill the éclairs with the lemon crémeux using the pastry bag fitted with the ⅓-in. (10-mm) tip (see technique p. 168). Coat the tops of the éclairs with the icing, neatening the edges with your finger (see technique p. 169).

LEVEL

3

MASCARPONE COFFEE ÉCLAIRS

Éclair Café-Mascarpone

by Christophe Adam

BEST PASTRY CHEF OF THE YEAR, 2014 AND 2015

Makes 10

Active time
2 hours

Chilling time
13 hours

Cooking time
40 minutes

Equipment
Instant-read
thermometer
Stick blender
Pastry bag fitted
with a fluted
¾-in. (2-cm) tip
Pastry bag fitted
with a plain ½-in.
(15-mm) tip
Metal brush

Ingredients

MASCARPONE COFFEE CREAM
6 sheets (12 g) gelatin
2.5 oz. (70 g) sugar
1.5 oz. (45 g) butter
⅓ tsp (2 g) fleur de sel
6 tbsp (90 ml) hot strong
espresso coffee
6.5 oz. (190 g) mascarpone

CHOUX PASTRY
⅔ cup (150 ml) water
⅔ cup (150 ml) whole milk
¾ tsp (4 g) fleur de sel
1 ¼ tsp (5 g) sugar
5.5 oz. (160 g) butter, diced
2 tsp (10 ml) vanilla extract
5.5 oz. (160 g) flour
9.5 oz. (280 g) lightly beaten egg

CHOCOLATE GLAZE
10.5 oz. (300 g) bittersweet
couverture chocolate
10.5 oz. (300 g) Valrhona Dulcey
chocolate

——————— MAKING THE MASCARPONE COFFEE CREAM

A day ahead, soften the gelatin in cold water. Put the sugar in a small saucepan and cook until it melts and forms a caramel. Deglaze with the butter and then add the salt and hot coffee. Let the mixture cool to 122°F (50°C) and stir in the squeezed-out gelatin until dissolved. When the caramel cools to 113°F (45°C), pour it into a bowl, add the mascarpone, and blend until smooth with the stick blender. Chill in the refrigerator for 12 hours.

——————— MAKING THE CHOUX PASTRY

The next day, preheat the oven to 350°F (180°C/Gas mark 4) and make the choux pastry (see technique p. 162). When the dough is smooth and holds its shape, transfer it to the pastry bag fitted with the fluted tip and pipe 10 parallel strips of choux pastry onto a greased baking sheet, spaced slightly apart to allow the éclair shells room to expand during baking. Place in the oven and bake for 40 minutes. When the shells are well risen, prop open the oven door by about ½ in. (1 cm) to allow steam to escape and stop the éclairs from collapsing.

——————— ASSEMBLING THE ÉCLAIRS

Temper the bittersweet couverture chocolate and Dulcey chocolate separately (see techniques pp. 570 and 572) and set aside. To fill the éclair shells, pierce 2 small holes in the base of each one. Spoon the mascarpone cream into the pastry bag fitted with the plain tip and pipe it into the éclairs to fill them. Glaze by dipping the top of each éclair into the tempered bittersweet chocolate and chill for a few minutes or until the chocolate has almost set. Dip the same surface into the Dulcey chocolate and allow to cool for 1 hour. To decorate, carefully brush the surface of the Dulcey chocolate down the length of each éclair with the metal brush.

CHEFS' NOTES

To prevent the éclair shells from collapsing,
start by baking them with the oven door tightly shut
and then leave the door slightly ajar
when the shells have fully puffed up.

CHOCOLATE RELIGIEUSES

Religieuse au Chocolat

Makes 16

Active time
1 hour

Cooking time
30–45 minutes

Storage
Up to 2 days in the refrigerator

Equipment
2 pastry bags fitted
with plain ½-in. (15-mm)
and ⅓-in. (10-mm) tips

Instant-read thermometer
Marble slab

Ingredients

CHOUX PASTRY
1 cup (250 ml) water
Heaping ½ tsp (3 g) salt
1 tsp (5 g) sugar
7 tbsp (3.5 oz./100 g) butter,
diced, plus extra for greasing
1 cup plus 2 tbsp (5.25 oz./150 g)
flour, sifted
1 cup (9 oz./250 g) lightly
beaten egg (about 5 eggs),
at room temperature

Clarified butter for brushing

CHOCOLATE-FLAVORED PASTRY CREAM
4 cups (1 liter) whole milk
1 cup (7 oz./200 g) sugar
1 vanilla bean, split lengthwise
and seeds scraped out
½ cup plus 1 ½ tbsp (5.5 oz./160 g)
egg yolk (about 8 yolks)
Generous ¼ cup (1.5 oz./45 g)
cornstarch
⅓ cup (1.5 oz./45 g) flour
7 tbsp (3.5 oz./100 g) butter
3 oz. (90 g) chocolate,
50% cacao, chopped

CHOCOLATE POURING FONDANT ICING
10.5 oz. (300 g) chocolate
pouring fondant icing

CHOCOLATE SQUARES
1.75 oz. (50 g) chocolate,
50% cacao

MAKING THE CHOUX PASTRY
Heat the water, salt, sugar, and butter in a pan and, when the butter is melted, bring to a fast boil. Remove from the heat and tip in all the flour, beating vigorously with a spatula until smooth. Return the saucepan to a low heat and stir constantly to dry out the mixture. Beat for 10 seconds or until the mixture is no longer sticking to the sides of the pan. Transfer it to a mixing bowl to prevent further cooking. Using a spatula, gradually mix in the beaten eggs, incorporating each addition before you add the next. Beat until the pastry is smooth and glossy. To check the consistency, draw a line through the pastry with the spatula and it should close up slowly. If necessary, beat in a little extra egg.

PIPING AND BAKING THE RELIGIEUSES
Preheat the oven to 350°F (180°C/Gas mark 4). Butter 2 baking sheets. Using the pastry bag fitted with the ½-in. (15-mm) tip, pipe 16 × 2-in. (5-cm) choux puffs for the Religieuses' "bodies" and 16 × 1-in. (2.5-cm) puffs for the "heads." Brush the puffs with clarified butter. Bake for 35–40 minutes, leaving the oven door slightly ajar after 15–20 minutes. When they are well risen, golden, and dry to the touch, transfer the puffs to a rack to cool.

MAKING THE CHOCOLATE-FLAVORED PASTRY CREAM
Using the ingredients listed, except the chocolate, make the pastry cream (see technique p. 196). Remove the pan from the heat and stir in the chocolate until melted.

PREPARING THE CHOCOLATE POURING FONDANT ICING
Heat the icing over low heat until the temperature reaches 98°F (37°C).

MAKING THE CHOCOLATE SQUARES
Temper the chocolate (see techniques pp. 570 and 572). Spread it very thinly on a marble slab and leave until lightly set. Mark into 16 × 1 ¼-in. (3-cm) squares and leave until set hard before carefully lifting the squares off the slab.

ASSEMBLING THE RELIGIEUSES
Using the pastry bag fitted with the ⅓-in. (10-mm) tip, fill the choux puffs with the pastry cream (see technique p. 168). Dip the top of each puff in the chocolate fondant icing, neatening the edges of the icing with your finger (see technique p. 169). Place a chocolate square on each large puff and sit a small puff on top, fixing it in place with a dab of pastry cream.

CHEFS' NOTES

When the éclairs are half-baked,
open the oven door slightly to allow the steam to escape.

CARAMEL AND VANILLA RELIGIEUSES

Religieuse Caramel Vanille

Makes 12

Active time
2 hours

Cooking time
30–40 minutes

Storage
Up to 2 days in the refrigerator

Equipment
Stand mixer
4 pastry bags, 1 fitted
with a plain ½-in. (15-mm) tip
and 3 with plain ⅓-in. (10-mm) tips

Instant-read thermometer

Ingredients

CRISP COATING (CRAQUELIN)
¼ cup (1 oz./30 g) flour
3 ½ tbsp (1.75 oz./50 g) butter
3 ½ tbsp (0.75 oz./20 g)
almond flour
¼ cup (1.75 oz./50 g) light
brown sugar

CHOUX PASTRY
1 cup (250 ml) water
Heaping ½ tsp (3 g) salt
1 tsp (5 g) sugar
7 tbsp (3.5 oz./100 g) butter,
diced, plus extra for greasing
1 cup plus 2 tbsp (5.25 oz./150 g)
flour, sifted
1 cup (9 oz./250 g) lightly
beaten egg (about 5 eggs),
at room temperature

BASE CARAMEL
1 ½ cups (10.5 oz./300 g) sugar
1 ¼ cups (300 ml) whipping cream,
35% butterfat
1 ½ sticks (6.25 oz./180 g) lightly
salted butter

CARAMEL CRÉMEUX
1 sheet (2 g) gelatin
2 tsp (10 ml) cold water
12.5 oz. (350 g) base caramel
(see ingredients above)
1 cup (250 g) mascarpone

CARAMEL-FLAVORED PASTRY CREAM
1 ½ cups (350 g) milk
¼ cup (1.75 oz./50 g) sugar
3 tbsp (1.75 oz./50 g) egg yolk
(about 3 yolks)
1 tbsp plus 2 ½ tsp (0.75 oz./17 g)
custard powder or cornstarch
2 tbsp (0.75 oz./17 g) flour
12.5 oz. (350 g) base caramel
(see ingredients above)

CARAMEL POURING FONDANT ICING
Scant 1 cup (200 ml) whipping
cream, 35% butterfat
½ cup (3.5 oz./100 g) sugar
2 tbsp plus 1 tsp (1.75 oz./50 g)
glucose syrup
1 tbsp (0.5 oz./15 g) lightly
salted butter
14 oz. (400 g) pouring
fondant icing

VANILLA PASTRY CREAM
1 cup (250 ml) milk
3 tbsp (1.25 oz./35 g) sugar
1 vanilla bean, split lengthwise
and seeds scraped out
2 ½ tbsp (1.5 oz./40 g) egg yolk
(about 2 yolks)
2 ½ tbsp (1 oz./25 g) custard
powder or cornstarch
¾ sheet (1.5 g) gelatin
2 tbsp (1 oz./ 25 g) butter
½ cup (125 ml) heavy cream,
36% butterfat, whipped

TO DECORATE
Edible gold leaf (optional)
Chocolate ruffles, made with
12.7 oz. (360 g) bittersweet
chocolate, 58% cacao
(see technique p. 593)

MAKING THE CRISP COATING (CRAQUELIN)
Fit the stand mixer with the paddle beater and mix the ingredients together to make a paste. Roll out between 2 sheets of parchment paper until ⅛ in. (3 mm) thick and freeze flat, still between the sheets, until needed.

MAKING AND BAKING THE CHOUX PUFFS
Using the ingredients listed, make the choux pastry (see technique p. 162). Preheat the oven to 350°F (180°C/Gas mark 4). Butter 2 baking sheets and pipe 12 × 2-in. (5-cm) puffs for the "bodies" and 12 × 1-in. (2.5-cm) puffs for the "heads." Cut the *craquelin* paste into 2-in. (5-cm) and 1-in. (2.5-cm) diameter disks and lay them carefully on top of the choux puffs. Bake for 30–40 minutes. As soon as they are cooked, remove from the oven and allow to cool on a rack.

MAKING THE BASE CARAMEL
Melt the sugar in a heavy pan, without adding any water, over low heat and cook to a rich brown caramel. Meanwhile, bring the cream to a boil in another pan and, protecting your hand with an oven mitt, carefully pour it into the caramel. Stir in the butter and divide the mixture in half, one for the pastry cream and the other for the crémeux. Cool the crémeux half to 122°F (50°C).

MAKING THE CARAMEL CRÉMEUX
Soak the gelatin in cold water. When softened, squeeze out excess water and stir the gelatin into the base caramel half at 122°F (50°C). Whisk into the mascarpone until combined.

MAKING THE CARAMEL-FLAVORED PASTRY CREAM
Using the ingredients listed, make the pastry cream (see technique p. 196). Remove from the heat and stir in the remaining base caramel until combined.

MAKING THE CARAMEL POURING FONDANT ICING
Bring the cream to a boil in a small saucepan. In another pan, dissolve the sugar in the glucose syrup and boil to a rich caramel. Protecting your hand, carefully stir in the hot cream. Heat until the temperature reaches 228°F (109°C), then stir in the butter. Add the caramel mixture to the pouring fondant icing, stir well until smooth, and allow to cool.

MAKING THE VANILLA PASTRY CREAM
Using the ingredients listed, make the pastry cream (see technique p. 196).

ASSEMBLING THE RELIGIEUSES
Using the pastry bags fitted with the ⅓-in. (10-mm) tips, fill the large puffs with a little caramel crémeux and then the caramel pastry cream, and the small puffs with the vanilla pastry cream. Dip the tops of all the puffs in the fondant, neatening the edges with your finger (see technique p. 169). Before the icing sets, place the small puffs on the larger ones with a chocolate ruffle in between. Decorate with a little edible gold leaf, if you wish.

3

CARAMEL RELIGIEUSES

Religieuse Caramel

by Christophe Michalak
WORLD PASTRY CUP CHAMPION, 2005

Makes 15

Active time
2 hours

Freezing time
30 minutes

Chilling time
1 hour

Cooking time
25 minutes

Storage
Up to 24 hours
in the refrigerator

Equipment
Instant-read thermometer
Stand mixer with paddle beater
and dough hook attachments
Food processor
Stick blender
Food-safe acetate sheets
2 ½-in. (7-cm) round pastry
cutter
Striated relief mold
3 pastry bags, 2 fitted with
plain tips and 1 with a fluted
¼-in. (6-mm) tip

Ingredients
1 oz. (30 g) Valrhona Dulcey
chocolate, 32 % cacao

FUDGE
⅓ tsp (1.7 ml) maple syrup
0.7 oz. (17.7 g) light
brown sugar
⅓ tsp (1 g) flour
0.01 oz. (0.2 g) fresh
(compressed) yeast
1 tsp (4.4 g) butter
1 small pinch (0.1 g) salt
½ tbsp (8 ml) evaporated milk

CARAMEL CHANTILLY CREAM
0.03 oz. (0.6 g) Bourbon
vanilla bean
0.02 oz. (0.4 g) ready-to-infuse
vanilla (available in sachets)
⅓ tsp (1.6 ml) cold water
0.01 oz. (0.3 g) gelatin powder
⅓ cup (79.4 ml) whipping cream,
35% butterfat, well chilled
0.2 oz. (5.3 g) glucose syrup
1 pinch (0.2 g) salt
0.01 oz. (0.1 g) tonka bean
1 tbsp (13.2 g) superfine sugar

ALMOND PASTE DECORATION
¾ tsp (3.7 ml) glucose syrup
1 pinch (0.01 g) water-soluble
yellow food coloring
1 pinch (0.01 g) water-soluble
lemon-yellow food coloring
1 pinch (0.01 g) water-soluble
coffee-brown food coloring
8 oz. (225.9 g) white
almond paste
2 ½ tsp (11.3 g) cocoa butter,
melted
3 ½ tsp (9 g) invert sugar

CHOUX PASTRY
5 ½ tbsp (81.4 ml) water
5 ½ tbsp (81.4 ml) low-fat milk
¾ tsp (3.6 g) salt
1 tsp (3.6 g) superfine sugar
2.5 oz. (72.4 g) butter
3 oz. (90.5 g) flour
6 oz. (167.3 g) lightly beaten egg
Craquelin disks
(see 1st step, recipe p. 180)
Equal amounts of dextrose
and Mycryo cocoa butter,
mixed together, for dusting

VANILLA PASTE
0.04 oz. (0.8 g) vanilla mix
(see step for caramel chantilly cream)
⅓ tsp (1.6 ml) water
2 drops (0.1 ml)
Ballantine's whisky
2 drops (0.1 ml)
Saint James rum
2 drops (0.1 ml) glucose syrup

LIGHT CARAMEL CRÉMEUX
1 tbsp (14.4 ml) water
½ tsp (2.4 g) gelatin powder
6 oz. (169.9 g) superfine sugar
2 cups (492.6 ml) low-fat milk
½ tsp (2.4 g) vanilla paste
(see ingredients above)
2.75 oz. (75 g) egg yolk
1 oz. (25.5 g) sugar
1.5 oz. (38.2 g) cornstarch
½ tsp (2.4 g) salt
9.5 oz. (273.5 g) butter
4 ⅕ cups (984.8 ml) whipping
cream 35% butterfat, whipped

——— MAKING THE FUDGE
In a saucepan, combine all the ingredients and cook to 237°F (114°C). Transfer to the bowl of the stand mixer and beat with the paddle beater for 10 minutes to cool the mixture. Roll out between 2 sheets of parchment paper about ½ in. (1 cm) thick and cut into ¼-in. (5-mm) cubes.

——— MAKING THE CARAMEL CHANTILLY CREAM
Prepare the vanilla mix by freezing the vanilla bean and then grinding it in the food processor. Add the sacheted vanilla. Mix the water with the gelatin, set in the refrigerator, and then cut into cubes. Mix the cream, glucose, 0.01 oz. (0.2 g) of the vanilla mix (set aside the rest for the vanilla paste), salt, and grated tonka bean together. Bring to a boil and infuse for 10 minutes. Make a caramel with the sugar and then stop the cooking process with the hot cream. Bring the caramel cream to a boil, add the gelatin cubes, strain through a fine-mesh sieve, and blend. Set aside in the refrigerator.

——— MAKING THE ALMOND PASTE DECORATION
Warm the syrup to 59°F (15°C) and mix in the food colorings. Pour this coloring into the bowl of the stand mixer fitted with the dough hook and combine with the almond paste. Add the hot melted cocoa butter and invert sugar and mix well. Roll out between 2 sheets of acetate to a thickness of 1⁄16 in. (2 mm). Using the pastry cutter, cut out 15 disks. Press the disks into the relief mold to give them a ruffled shape.

——— MAKING THE CHOUX PASTRY
Preheat the oven to 425°F (220°C/Gas mark 7). Make the choux pastry (see technique p. 162). Using a pastry bag with a plain tip, pipe 15 large and 15 small puffs. Top the large ones with a *craquelin* disk and sprinkle the dextrose and cocoa butter mix over the small balls. Bake for about 20 minutes.

——— MAKING THE VANILLA PASTE
Blend all the ingredients until the mixture forms a smooth paste.

——— MAKING THE LIGHT CARAMEL CRÉMEUX
Mix the water with the gelatin, allow to set in the refrigerator , then cut into cubes. In a saucepan, make a dry caramel with the sugar. At the same time, heat the milk with the vanilla paste. Deglaze the caramel with the hot milk strained through a fine-mesh sieve. In a separate bowl, beat the egg yolks, sugar, and cornstarch until pale and thick. Whisk the caramel milk into the yolk mixture, pour back into the pan, and bring to a boil. Add the salt, stir in the gelatin, and lastly the butter. Cover in plastic wrap and cool quickly in a shallow container in the refrigerator. When chilled, whisk the caramel crémeux to soften it and then fold in the whipped cream.

——— ASSEMBLING THE RELIGIEUSES
Toast the small and large choux puffs for 2 minutes at 350°F (180°C/Gas mark 4) and cool on a rack. Using a pastry bag with a plain tip, fill all the puffs with caramel crémeux. Top the larger puffs with disks of almond paste, shaping them so they fit snugly over the puffs without misshaping them. Trim the rounded side of the small puffs and sit on top of the larger ones, sticking them in place with a little melted Dulcey chocolate. Whip the caramel Chantilly cream until stiff and, using the pastry bag with a fluted tip, pipe a rosette of cream on top of each puff. Decorate each one with a fudge cube.

PRALINE-FLAVORED CHOUX RING

Paris-Brest

Serves 8

Active time
1 ½ hours

Cooking time
45 minutes

Storage
Up to 2 days in the refrigerator

Equipment
2 pastry bags fitted
with a plain ⅓-in. (10-mm) tip
and a fluted ¾-in. (20-mm) tip

Electric hand beater

Ingredients

CHOUX PASTRY
1 cup (250 ml) water
Heaping ½ tsp (3 g) salt
1 tsp (5 g) sugar
7 tbsp (3.5 oz./100 g) butter,
diced, plus extra for greasing
1 cup plus 2 tbsp (5.25 oz./150 g)
flour, sifted
1 cup (9 oz./250 g) lightly
beaten egg (about 5 eggs),
at room temperature

EGG WASH
3 ½ tbsp (1.75 oz./50 g) lightly
beaten egg (about 1 egg)
3 tbsp (1.75 oz./50 g) egg yolk
(about 3 yolks)

PASTRY CREAM
1 cup plus scant ½ cup (350 ml)
whole milk
¼ cup (1.75 oz./50 g) sugar
¼ cup (2 oz./60 g) lightly
beaten egg (about 1 ½ eggs)
3 ½ tbsp (1.25 oz./35 g) custard
powder or cornstarch

PRALINE-FLAVORED MOUSSELINE CREAM
1 lb. 2 oz. (500 g) pastry cream
(see ingredients above)
1 stick plus 2 tbsp (5.25 oz./150 g)
butter, diced and softened
5.25 oz. (150 g) praline paste
1 oz. (25 g) hazelnut paste

Sliced almonds for sprinkling
Confectioners' sugar for dusting

MAKING AND BAKING THE CHOUX RINGS
Heat the water, salt, sugar, and butter in a pan and, when the butter is melted, bring to a fast boil. Remove from the heat and tip in all the flour, beating vigorously with a spatula until smooth. Return the saucepan to a low heat and stir constantly to dry out the mixture. Beat for 10 seconds or until the mixture is no longer sticking to the sides of the pan. Transfer it to a mixing bowl to prevent further cooking. Using a spatula, gradually mix in the beaten eggs, incorporating each addition before you add the next. Beat until the pastry is smooth and glossy. To check the consistency, draw a line through the pastry with the spatula and it should close up slowly. If necessary, beat in a little extra egg.
Preheat the oven to 350°F (180°C/Gas mark 4). Spoon the pastry into the bag with the plain tip and pipe 3 × 7 ½-in. (18-cm) rings, one on top of the other, on a nonstick baking sheet. Brush the rings with the egg wash, sprinkle with sliced almonds, and bake for about 45 minutes. Cool on a rack.

MAKING THE PASTRY CREAM
Using the ingredients listed, make the pastry cream (see technique p. 196). Cover a baking sheet with plastic wrap and spread the cream over it. Press another piece of plastic wrap over the surface of the cream. Allow to cool to room temperature.

MAKING THE PRALINE-FLAVORED MOUSSELINE CREAM
Whisk the pastry cream until smooth. Combine the butter with the praline and hazelnut pastes and mix into the pastry cream. Whisk with an electric hand beater until smooth.

ASSEMBLING THE CHOUX RING
Cut off the top third of the choux ring. This will be the "hat" and the deeper part the "base." Spoon the mousseline cream into the pastry bag fitted with the fluted tip and pipe it in a thick rope over the base. Place the "hat" on top and dust with confectioners' sugar.

PRALINE-FILLED CHOUX ROLL

Paris-Brest

Makes 20 slices

Active time
2 hours

Cooking time
3 ¼ hours

Chilling time
1 hour

Storage
Up to 2 days in the refrigerator

Equipment
Electric hand beater
16 × 24-in. (40 × 60-cm) cake frame on a silicone baking mat
Instant-read thermometer
Stick blender
2 pastry bags fitted with plain ⅓-in. (10-mm) tips

Ingredients
CHOUX SPONGE LAYER
½ cup plus 1 tbsp (140 ml) whole milk
7 tbsp (3.5 oz./100 g) butter, diced
1 cup plus 2 tbsp (5 oz./140 g) flour
⅔ cup (6 oz./170 g) egg yolk (about 9 yolks)
Scant ½ cup (3.5 oz./100 g) lightly beaten egg (about 2 eggs)
Finely grated zest of 2 lemons
1 cup plus 2 tbsp (9 oz./250 g) egg white (about 8 whites)
2 ½ tbsp (1 oz./30 g) superfine sugar

PRALINE CRÉMEUX
3 tbsp (50 ml) whole milk
1.75 oz. (50 g) almond-hazelnut praline paste
2 ¾ tsp (0.5 oz./15 g) egg yolk (about 1 yolk)
¼ cup (1.75 oz./50 g) superfine sugar
4 tbsp (2.25 oz./64 g) butter

FEUILLETINE PRALINE LAYER
0.5 oz. (15 g) milk chocolate
3.5 oz. (100 g) praline paste
0.75 oz. (20 g) *feuilletine* flakes (or use crushed wafers)

CHOUX PUFFS
½ cup (125 ml) water
⅛ tsp (1 g) salt
¾ tsp (3 g) sugar
3 tbsp (1.75 oz./50 g) butter
Scant ⅔ cup (2.75 oz./75 g) flour
½ cup (4.5 oz./125 g) lightly beaten egg (about 2 ½ eggs)
Light brown sugar for sprinkling

PRALINE MOUSSELINE CREAM
5.25 oz. (150 g) praline paste
1 oz. (25 g) hazelnut paste
1 stick plus 2 tbsp (5.25 oz./150 g) butter, diced and softened
1 lb. 2 oz. (500 g) pastry cream, at 64°F (18°C) (see technique p. 196)

LEMON MERINGUES
¼ cup (1.75 oz./50 g) egg white (about 1 ½ whites)
½ cup (3.5 oz./100 g) sugar
Very finely grated zest of 1 lemon

DECORATION
2 lemons
Edible gold leaf

MAKING THE CHOUX SPONGE LAYER
Preheat the oven to 325°F (170°C/Gas mark 3). Put the milk and butter in a large saucepan and bring to a boil. Add the flour, egg yolk, and egg and stir with a spatula over low heat until smooth. Stir in the lemon zest. In a mixing bowl, whisk the egg whites, gradually whisking in the sugar until soft peaks form. Lightly fold into the sponge batter until combined and then spread it evenly into the cake frame. Bake for about 30–35 minutes, with the door slightly ajar, until lightly golden.

MAKING THE PRALINE CRÉMEUX
Bring the milk to a boil in a saucepan and stir in the praline paste. Whisk the egg yolk with the sugar and pour over a little of the boiling milk mixture, stirring to combine. Pour the mixture back into the pan and stir constantly over low heat, as you would for a custard. Remove from the heat and cool to 104°F (40°C). Stir in the butter and process with a stick blender until smooth. Cover a baking sheet with plastic wrap, pour the praline crémeux over it, and press more wrap over the crémeux. Chill for 20–30 minutes.

MAKING THE FEUILLETINE PRALINE LAYER
Melt the chocolate in a bowl over a pan of hot water, pour it over the praline paste, and mix well. Stir in the *feuilletine*.

MAKING THE CHOUX PUFFS
Preheat the oven to 350°F (180°C/Gas mark 4). Using the ingredients listed, make the choux pastry (see technique p. 162) and pipe into 60 choux puffs, ¾ in. (2 cm) in diameter. Sprinkle the tops with the brown sugar and bake for 30–40 minutes.

MAKING THE PRALINE MOUSSELINE CREAM
Mix together the praline paste and hazelnut paste. Add to the butter and room-temperature pastry cream, whisking until evenly combined. Set aside.

MAKING THE LEMON MERINGUES
Using the ingredients listed, make a French meringue (see technique p. 234), adding the lemon zest to the whisked egg whites. Preheat the oven to 210°F (100°C/Gas mark ¼). Using a pastry bag fitted with a plain tip, pipe out about 30 small shells onto a silicone baking sheet and bake for about 2 hours.

ASSEMBLING THE CAKE
Spread the *feuilletine* praline very thinly over the sponge layer. Peel the lemons, remove the pith, and cut into segments between the membranes. Chop the segments into small dice and arrange over the praline layer. Spread the praline mousseline cream on top and roll up into a log, 2 ½ in. (6 cm) in diameter. Chill in the refrigerator for 30 minutes. Fill the choux puffs with the praline crémeux and fix them to the top of the roll with dabs of the crémeux. Cut into 1 ¼-in. (3-cm) slices and decorate with the meringues and edible gold leaf.

LEVEL

3

PISTACHOUX

by Philippe Conticini

BEST PASTRY CHEF OF THE YEAR, 1991

Makes 6

Active time
2 hours

Cooking time
1 ¼ hours

Storage
Up to 24 hours
in the refrigerator

Equipment
Stick blender
Silicone tray with
24 half-sphere molds
(smaller than the size
of the choux you make)

Food processor fitted
with the chopper blade

Stand mixer fitted
with the whisk attachment

Pastry bag fitted
with a plain ½-in. (15-mm) tip

Ingredients
LEMON CREAM LAYER
10.5 oz. (300 g) butter
1 lb. 1 oz. (480 g)
superfine sugar
1 ¼ lb. (600 g) lightly
beaten egg
1 ⅓ cups (320 ml)
fresh lemon juice
0.5 oz. (16 g) grated lime zest
1.25 oz. (36 g) bloomed
gelatin

CANDIED LEMON ZEST
3.5 oz. (100 g) lemons
1 cup (250 ml) lemon juice
5.25 oz. (150 g)
superfine sugar
0.5 oz. (12 g) lemon
verbena leaves

CHOCOLATE STREUSEL
6.75 oz. (195 g) flour
1 oz. (30 g) unsweetened
cocoa powder
8 oz. (223 g) toasted
ground almonds
8 oz. (223 g) brown sugar
⅓ tsp (4 g) fleur de sel
8 oz. (223 g) chilled butter,
diced

CRAQUELIN
2.75 oz. (80 g) butter,
softened
3.5 oz. (100 g) brown sugar
3.5 oz. (100 g) flour

CHOUX PASTRY
¾ cup (187 ml) low-fat milk
¾ cup (187 ml) water
5.75 oz. (165 g) butter
0.75 oz. (22 g) sugar
½ tsp (3 g) fleur de sel
7.5 oz. (214 g) flour
13 oz. (375 g) lightly
beaten egg

PISTACHIO PASTRY CREAM
1 ⅓ cups plus 1 ½ tbsp
(336 ml) low-fat milk
4 tbsp (60 ml) whipping
cream
2.5 oz. (74 g) sugar
2.75 oz. (80 g) egg yolk
1.25 oz. (36 g) cornstarch
6.6 oz. (186 g) butter, diced
1.75 oz. (50 g) bloomed
gelatin
7.5 oz. (214 g) pistachio paste

Confectioners' sugar
for dusting

--------- MAKING THE LEMON CREAM LAYER

Heat the butter and sugar and stir until smooth. Add the eggs, lemon juice, and grated lime zest. Place back over the heat, whisking constantly, until the mixture comes to a simmer. Remove from the heat, add the bloomed gelatin, and blend. Fill the half-sphere molds and allow to set in the refrigerator.

--------- MAKING THE CANDIED LEMON ZEST

Wash the lemons. Using a peeler, peel off the zest, removing as little as possible of the bitter white pith. Immerse the zests in a small saucepan half-filled with water and bring to a boil to blanch them. Drain and repeat the process twice more: this will ensure you retain the lemon flavor without any bitterness. Cook the zests with the lemon juice and sugar in a saucepan over medium heat for 40–50 minutes. When well reduced, add the verbena leaves and blend, while still hot, in the food processor. Use sparingly, as this tangy mixture has an intense, concentrated flavor. Spoon a little into the center of each lemon cream.

--------- MAKING THE CHOCOLATE STREUSEL

Preheat the oven to 300°F (150°C/Gas mark 2). Combine all the dry ingredients and rub in the butter until crumbly. Spread out thinly on a baking sheet lined with parchment paper and bake for 20 minutes.

--------- MAKING THE CRAQUELIN

Combine the ingredients to make a dough without incorporating any air. Roll out between 2 sheets of parchment paper to a thickness of ¹⁄₁₆ in. (2 mm). Freeze to harden and then cut out disks the same size as the choux puffs and keep in the freezer until ready to use.

--------- MAKING THE CHOUX PASTRY

Increase the oven temperature to 400°F (210°C/Gas mark 6). Bring the milk, water, butter, sugar, and salt to a boil in a saucepan. Remove from the heat, pour in all the sifted flour at once, and mix in using a spatula. Return to the heat and stir continuously for about 1 minute to dry out the mixture. Transfer to the stand mixer and whisk at medium speed to cool down the dough. When it stops steaming, beat in the egg, a little at a time, until fully incorporated and the dough is smooth. Spoon the dough into the pastry bag and pipe 6 rows of 4 choux puffs touching each other, and then top each one with a *craquelin* disk. Bake for 20–25 minutes.

--------- MAKING THE PISTACHIO PASTRY CREAM

Bring the milk and cream to a boil in a saucepan. Beat the sugar and egg yolks in a bowl until pale and thick and add the sifted cornstarch. Whisk the hot milk into the yolk mixture and then continue to cook as for a pastry cream (see technique p. 196). Stir in the butter, gelatin, and pistachio paste and mix well.

--------- ASSEMBLING THE PISTACHOUX

Cut each row of choux horizontally into 2 layers. Spoon a little streusel into the bottom of the puffs and then pipe a layer of pistachio cream. Place a half-sphere of lemon cream in the center of each puff, pipe the rest of the pistachio cream on top, and sprinkle with streusel. Carefully replace the choux lids and dust with confectioners' sugar.

CREAMS

CREAMS

STORING CREAMS

Whipped creams (such as Chantilly) do not keep as well as other creams. When beating air into cream, bacteria is incorporated as well, making spoilage more likely. They are sensitive to heat, so keep them in the refrigerator (40°F/4°C).

AIR: AN IMPORTANT INGREDIENT

The way creams are made—by beating in as much air as is needed to increase their volume—is crucial in determining their final texture. Some creams, like Chantilly, need a lot of air. Others, like almond cream, should be beaten as little as possible so they do not puff up during baking. The difference between folding or stirring in and whipping is all important.

PROPERLY COOKED

When all the ingredients have been mixed together, bring the cream to a boil and continue to boil it for 2–3 minutes to pasteurize it, as well as cook the cornstarch or flour completely.

WHICH STARCH?

Cornstarch or flour can be replaced by custard powder or potato starch.

COOL QUICKLY

A good way to cool cream quickly is to line a baking sheet with plastic wrap, spread the warm cream over it and press another piece of plastic wrap over the top. This has two advantages: it avoids conditions that favor microbial growth (and thus increases storage time) and prevents a skin from forming on the surface of the cream.

TO FREEZE OR NOT TO FREEZE?

Creams can be frozen as long as they contain a sufficiently high percentage of butterfat and are properly stored. It is preferable, however, to make these creams as and when you are going to use them.

A WORLD OF BUTTERCREAMS

There are many ways to make buttercream. Some people use sugar syrup boiled to 245°F (118°C), others use Italian meringue. In the United States, the standard recipe calls for just butter, sugar, and a little milk. Always check which type of buttercream is needed when you see it in a recipe.

AND ALCOHOL?

Before flavoring creams with alcohol, cool them to 160°F (70°C) or less. For a cream that is cold, ensure the alcohol is at room temperature before adding. If the cream is hot, the alcohol will evaporate but the aroma will remain.

BASIC CREAMS

PASTRY CREAM (see p. 196)	
Uses	Choux pastries (éclairs, cream puffs, religieuses), napoleons, frangipane, individual cakes and pastries, raisin swirls, Parisian flan pie, or base for other creams
Refrigerator storage time*	Up to 24 hours

FRENCH BUTTERCREAM (see p. 202)	
Uses	Entremets (opéra, mocha cake), mignardises, Yule logs, decoration
Refrigerator storage time*	Up to 5 days

CUSTARD (see p. 204)	
Uses	Bavarian cream, chocolate mousse, accompaniment to entremets and other desserts, base for making ice cream
Refrigerator storage time*	Up to 24 hours

CHANTILLY CREAM (see p. 201)	
Uses	Choux pastries, napoleons, decoration, accompaniment to ice cream, custard, and individual cakes and pastries
Refrigerator storage time*	Up to 24 hours

ALMOND CREAM (see p. 208)	
Uses	Tarts, bourdaloue pear tart, pithiviers, *galette des rois* (kings' cake), almond croissants
Refrigerator storage time*	Up to 2 days

*(40°F/4°C)

MIXED CREAMS

MOUSSELINE BUTTERCREAM	
Description	Pastry cream blended with butter (see p. 198)
Uses	Strawberry and raspberry mousse cakes, croquembouches
Refrigerator storage time*	Up to 2 days

DIPLOMAT CREAM	
Description	Pastry cream mixed with whipped cream and gelatin (see p. 200)
Uses	Entremets, individual cakes and pastries, tarts and tartlets
Refrigerator storage time*	Up to 24 hours

CRÈME PRINCESSE OR *CRÈME MADAME* (DIPLOMAT CREAM WITHOUT GELATIN)	
Description	Pastry cream mixed with whipped cream
Uses	Entremets, individual cakes and pastries, tarts and tartlets
Refrigerator storage time*	Up to 24 hours

CHIBOUST CREAM (ALSO KNOWN AS SAINT-HONORÉ CREAM)	
Description	Pastry cream mixed with Italian meringue (see p. 206)
Uses	Saint-Honoré cakes, choux pastries, napoleons, babas, tarts, individual cakes and pastries
Refrigerator storage time*	Up to 24 hours

FRANGIPANE	
Description	⅓ pastry cream and ⅔ almond cream
Uses	Tarts, bourdaloue pear tart, pithiviers, *galette des rois* (kings' cake), almond croissants
Refrigerator storage time*	Up to 2 days

*(40°F/4°C)

Pastry Cream

Crème Pâtissière

**Makes scant 3 ½ cups
(1 ¾ lb./ 800 g)**

Active time
15 minutes

Cooking time
2–3 minutes

Storage
Up to 24 hours
in the refrigerator

Ingredients
2 cups (500 ml) whole milk
½ cup (3.5 oz./100 g) sugar, divided
1 vanilla bean, split lengthwise
Scant ½ cup (3.5 oz./100 g) egg (about 2 eggs)
2 tbsp (1 oz./25 g) cornstarch
2 tbsp (1 oz./25 g) flour
3 ½ tbsp (1.75 oz./50 g) butter, diced, at room temperature

Flavorings
Coffee: Add 1–1 ½ tbsp (15–20 ml) coffee extract or 1 tbsp (0.5 oz./15 g) instant coffee to the milk, or steep ¾ cup (2.5 oz./70 g) ground coffee in the milk, and then strain.

Alcohols: When the cream is cold, mix in the equivalent of 2–3% of the total weight of the cream (about 1 tsp/5 g).

Chocolate: Mix ⅓ cup (1.5 oz./40 g) 100% pure cacao paste into the warm cream.

Uses
Choux pastries, napoleons, frangipane, various individual cakes and pastries, raisin swirls

1 • Combine the milk and half of the sugar in a saucepan. Scrape in the seeds of the vanilla bean and bring to a boil over medium heat.

4 • As soon as the milk comes to a boil, slowly pour it onto the egg and starch mixture, whisking constantly. This will loosen the mixture and heat it a little.

5 • Return to the saucepan and bring to a boil over medium heat, whisking vigorously. Continue to boil, still whisking, for 2–3 minutes.

For chocolate-flavored pastry cream the 100% pure cacao paste can be replaced with any chocolate of your choice, but you will need to reduce the amount of sugar in the recipe so that the cream is not too sweet.

2 • Meanwhile, whisk the egg with the remaining sugar in a mixing bowl until blended and slightly thickened.

3 • Sift the cornstarch and flour into the egg mixture and whisk until combined.

6 • Remove from the heat and stir in the diced butter until smooth.

7 • To cool the pastry cream quickly, line a baking sheet with plastic wrap and spread the cream over it. Press another piece of plastic wrap over the surface of the cream.

Mousseline Buttercream

Crème Mousseline

**Makes scant 4 cups
(2 lb./900 g)**

Active time
30 minutes

Cooking time
2–3 minutes

Storage
Up to 2 days
in the refrigerator

Equipment
Stand mixer
Instant-read thermometer

Ingredients
2 cups (500 ml) whole milk
Scant ⅔ cup (3.75 oz./110 g)
sugar, divided
½ vanilla bean, split lengthwise
⅓ cup (2.75 oz./80 g) egg yolk
(about 4 ½ yolks)
Scant 2 tbsp (1 oz./25 g) flour
2 tbsp (1 oz./30 g) cornstarch
7 tbsp (3.5 oz./100 g) butter,
diced, at room temperature
7 tbsp (3.5 oz./100 g) butter,
diced and softened

Uses
Napoleons, choux pastries,
various entremets (e.g., *fraisier*),
and individual cakes and pastries

1 • Combine the milk and half the sugar in a saucepan. Scrape in the seeds of the split vanilla bean and bring to a boil over low heat.

4 • Return to the saucepan and bring to a boil over low heat, whisking vigorously. Continue to boil, still whisking, for 2–3 minutes.

5 • Remove from the heat and stir in the room temperature butter until evenly incorporated. Line a baking sheet with plastic wrap, spread the cream over it and press another piece of plastic wrap over the surface of the cream. Cool to 65°F (18°C).

2 • Meanwhile, whisk the egg yolks with the remaining sugar in a mixing bowl until blended and slightly thickened. Sift in the flour and cornstarch, and whisk until smooth.

3 • As soon as the milk comes to a boil, slowly pour it onto the egg and starch mixture, whisking constantly. This will loosen the mixture and heat it a little.

6 • In the bowl of the stand mixer, fitted with a whisk, beat the cooled cream to loosen it. Gradually add the softened butter, beating on high speed to incorporate the butter and add volume to the cream.

CHEFS' NOTES

• Do not mix the softened butter with very cold cream as this will solidify the butter and the cream could separate.

• Mousseline buttercream can be frozen for up to 1 month.

• You can flavor the cold cream with alcohol, which has first been gently heated, adding the equivalent of 2–3% of the total weight of the cream (about 1 tbsp for this recipe). You can also add other flavorings of your choice.

Diplomat Cream

Crème Diplomate

**Makes 2 cups
(1 lb. 2 oz./500 g)**

Active time
20 minutes

Cooking time
2–3 minutes
(for the pastry cream)

Storage
Up to 24 hours
in the refrigerator

Uses
Entremets, individual cakes
and pastries, tarts and tartlets

Ingredients
1 cup (250 ml) whole milk
¼ cup (1.75 oz./50 g) sugar,
divided
1 vanilla bean, split lengthwise
and seeds scraped out
3 ½ tbsp (1.75 oz./50 g) egg
(about 1 egg)
1 tbsp (0.5 oz./15 g) custard
powder
2 tsp (0.35 oz./10 g) flour
2 tbsp (1 oz./25 g) butter,
at room temperature
1 ½ sheets (0.1 oz./3 g) gelatin
(optional) (see Chefs' Notes)
1 cup (250 ml) whipping cream,
35% butterfat, well chilled

CHEFS' NOTES

Adding gelatin will give the cream more body and help it hold its shape. Soak the gelatin sheets in cold water for 10 minutes and then drain and squeeze them to remove excess water. Stir into the warm pastry cream until dissolved.

1 • Make a vanilla-flavored pastry cream using the first 7 ingredients (see technique p. 196). If using gelatin, add it now (see Chef's Notes). Once the cream has cooled, stir it with a spatula to loosen it.

2 • Meanwhile, whisk the well-chilled cream until it holds medium peaks. Using the whisk, fold the whipped cream into the pastry cream in three equal amounts.

3 • Mix gently until the cream and pastry cream are evenly combined.

Chantilly Cream

Crème Chantilly

Makes 1 cup (9 oz./250 g)

Active time
10 minutes

Storage
Up to 24 hours
in the refrigerator

Equipment
Mixing bowl with a round base,
well chilled

Ingredients
1 cup (250 ml) whipping cream,
35% butterfat, well chilled
2 tbsp plus 1 tsp (0.75 oz./20 g)
confectioners' sugar
½ vanilla bean, split lengthwise,
or 1 tsp vanilla extract

Uses
Choux pastries, napoleons,
for decoration,
as an accompaniment
to ice cream, custards, and
individual cakes and pastries

CHEFS' NOTES

The amount of butterfat in the cream is very important when
making Chantilly cream—it must contain at least 35%.

1 • Combine the cream and confectioners' sugar in the chilled mixing bowl. Scrape in the vanilla bean seeds or add the vanilla extract.

2 • Whisk until the cream holds its shape.

3 • Avoid over-whisking, as the fats in the cream will clump together and it will develop a grainy appearance.

French Buttercream

Crème au Beurre

**Makes about 3 cups
(1 lb. 9 oz./700 g)**

Active time
30 minutes

Cooking time
5–6 minutes

Storage
Up to 5 days
in the refrigerator

Equipment
Stand mixer
Instant-read thermometer

Ingredients
1 ⅓ cups (9 oz./250 g) sugar
⅓ cup (90 ml) cold water
Scant ½ cup (3.5 oz./100 g)
egg (about 2 eggs), at room
temperature
3 sticks (12.5 oz./350 g) butter,
diced, at room temperature

Flavorings
A wide variety of flavorings
can be added to French
buttercream, such as coffee,
chocolate, pistachio paste,
or others of your choice.

You can also add liqueurs
like Grand Marnier or kirsch, and
essences like violet or rose.

Uses
Various entremets, individual
cakes and pastries, religieuses,
Yule logs, etc.

1 • Add the sugar to the water in a saucepan and
heat over medium heat until the sugar dissolves,
then boil the syrup to 245°F (118°C).

CHEFS' NOTES

• It is important to take care when whisking
the hot sugar syrup into the eggs. As soon as the syrup is ready,
slowly pour it down the inside of the mixing bowl rather
than directly onto the beaters of the whisk.

• French buttercream can be made using any
of the following combinations: egg yolks; egg yolks + whole eggs;
egg whites; custard + Italian meringue.

2 • Meanwhile, fit the stand mixer with the whisk and whisk the eggs until frothy. Gradually pour in the hot syrup, whisking constantly at medium-low speed (see Chefs' Notes).

3 • Continue beating at medium speed until the mixture cools to 75°F (25°C).

4 • Gradually add the butter and whisk until creamy. Finally, add flavoring, if using.

5 • Stir with a spatula until the ingredients and flavoring are evenly combined.

Custard

Crème Anglaise

**Makes 3 cups
(1 lb. 9 oz./700 g)**

Active time
20 minutes

Cooking time
3 minutes

Storage
Up to 2 days
in the refrigerator

Equipment
Instant-read thermometer

Uses
Bavarian cream, French
buttercream, chocolate mousse,
as a sauce for desserts

Ingredients
2 cups (500 ml) whole milk
½ cup (3.5 oz./100 g) sugar,
divided

1 vanilla bean, split lengthwise
Scant ½ cup (4.25 oz./120 g)
egg yolk (about 6 ½ yolks)

Flavorings
Coffee: Add 3–4 tsp (15–20 ml)
coffee extract or ⅔–1 tbsp
(0.35–0.5 oz./10–15 g) instant
coffee to the milk. Alternatively,
steep ½ cup (1.75 oz./50 g)
ground coffee in the milk
and then strain.

Alcohols: When the custard
is cold, mix in 1–2%
of the total weight of the
custard (about 1–2 tsp).

Chocolate: Mix 2.5 oz. (70 g)
100% pure cacao paste into
the warm custard.

1 • Combine the milk with half the sugar in a saucepan.
Scrape in the vanilla seeds, place over medium heat,
and bring to a boil.

4 • Pour the mixture back into the saucepan.
Stir constantly with a spatula until the temperature
of the custard reaches 180°F (83°C).

5 • Draw a line with your finger through the custard on the spatula
and if the line stays visible the custard is ready.

2 • Meanwhile, whisk the egg yolks with the remaining sugar in a mixing bowl until creamy and slightly thickened.

3 • When the milk comes to a boil, pour a little into the yolk mixture, whisking until combined.

6 • When the custard is cooked, strain it through a fine-mesh strainer into a small bowl.

7 • Stand the bowl of custard in a larger bowl filled with ice cubes and water and allow to cool, stirring occasionally to prevent a skin forming on top, before using.

Chiboust Cream

Crème Chiboust

**Makes scant 3 ½ cups
(1 ¾ lb./800 g)**

Active time
20 minutes

Cooking time
2–3 minutes

Storage
Up to 24 hours
in the refrigerator

Equipment
Instant-read thermometer
Stand mixer fitted
with the whisk attachment

Ingredients
Pastry cream
1 cup (250 ml) whole milk
¼ cup (1.75 oz./50 g) sugar
1 vanilla bean, split lengthwise
Scant ½ cup (4.25 oz./120 g)
egg yolk (about 6 ½ yolks)
2 tbsp (1 oz./25 g) custard
powder
4 sheets (0.25 oz./8 g) gelatin
Scant ¼ cup (50 ml) cold water

Reduced-sugar Italian meringue
1 ½ cups (10.5 oz./300 g) sugar
6 tbsp (90 ml) water
1 ¾ cups (14 oz./400 g) egg
white (about 13 whites)

Flavorings
Coffee: Add 1–2 tbsp
(20–30 ml) coffee extract
or ⅓ cup (0.7 oz./20 g) instant
coffee to the milk or steep ¾ cup
(2.5 oz./70 g) ground coffee
in the milk and then strain.

Chocolate: Mix ½ cup
(1.75 oz./50 g) 100% pure cacao
paste into the warm cream.
The 100% pure cacao paste can
be replaced by any chocolate
of your choice, but you will need
to reduce the amount of sugar
in the recipe so that the cream
is not too sweet.

Fruit purée: Use the fruit
purée of your choice in place
of the milk.

Uses
Various tarts, as well as
individual cakes and pastries

1• Make a pastry cream using the first 5 ingredients
(see technique p. 196). Meanwhile, soak the gelatin sheets in the
cold water for 10 minutes. Remove the cream from the heat.
Gently squeeze the gelatin sheets to remove excess water
and add to the warm cream, stirring until dissolved.

2 • To make the Italian meringue, dissolve the sugar in the water over medium heat, then boil to 245°F (119°C).

3 • Meanwhile, whisk the egg whites in the bowl of the stand mixer until stiff. Slowly add the hot syrup in a thin stream, whisking constantly (see technique, p. 233, step 3). Continue whisking until cold.

4 • Carefully fold the meringue into the warm (95°F–105°F/ 35°C–40°C) pastry cream until evenly combined.

5 • Once combined, the cream should be used straight away.

Almond Cream

Crème d'Amande

**Makes scant 1 cup
(7 oz./200 g)**

Active time
20 minutes

Storage
Up to 2 days
in the refrigerator

Ingredients
3 ½ tbsp (1.75 oz./50 g) butter,
diced, at room temperature

¼ cup (1.75 oz./50 g) sugar

3–3 ½ tbsp (1.5–1.75 oz./45–50 g)
egg (about 1 egg),
at room temperature

½ cup (1.75 oz./50 g)
almond flour

1 tsp (5 g) custard powder
(see Chefs' Notes)

1 vanilla bean, split lengthwise

½ tsp (2.5 ml) rum,
at room temperature

Uses
Frangipane, almond croissants,
filling for various tarts, tartlets,
and other pastries

1 • In a mixing bowl, work the butter with a spatula until
it is very soft and smooth.

4 • Add the almond flour and mix until the cream is smooth.
Avoid overbeating, as the extra air beaten in will make the cream
swell up during baking.

2 • Add the sugar and beat until light and creamy.

3 • Gradually add the egg, stirring until thoroughly incorporated.

5 • Add the custard powder, the seeds from the vanilla bean, and the rum, mixing well. Store covered in the refrigerator until ready to use.

CHEFS' NOTES

• The custard powder can be replaced by flour, cornstarch, or potato starch.

• When almond cream is used as a filling (for galettes, almond croissants, tarts, etc.), the baking time will need to be increased.

• Avoid excessive beating, as too much air will cause the almond cream to puff up during baking.

SPONGE
& MERINGUE
LAYERS

SPONGE AND MERINGUE LAYERS

Layers of sponge or meringue form the basis of many spectacular French cakes and desserts. These are known as *biscuits*, which means "cooked twice." In the past, when ovens were not as efficient as they are today, the thin layers were often baked for a second time to make them firmer.

With the exception of the genoise, these layers:
– require no heat during their preparation
– contain a high proportion of egg whites, making them light and airy

THE SECRET OF SUCCESS

For perfect layers, it is essential to:
– have all the ingredients at room temperature before you begin; take the eggs out of the refrigerator 2 hours ahead
– the egg whites must be thoroughly whisked, but not until they are very stiff and dry. They should hold their shape in peaks and have the consistency of shaving foam, so they can be folded easily into the batter. This ensures the sponge rises well in the oven and has a soft, light texture.

LADYFINGERS

Spoon or Pastry Bag?
Ladyfingers are called *biscuits à la cuillère* in French—*cuillère* meaning spoon, as in the past they were shaped with a spoon. The practice of piping them using a pastry bag only began in 1820.

Pale Yet Properly Baked
As ladyfingers are dusted generously with confectioners' sugar, it is not always easy to check the sponge is fully baked by just looking at the tops. The best way is to carefully lift the parchment and peep underneath. If the sponge is lovely and golden, it is ready. Take care not to overbake as the ladyfingers will quickly become crumbly.

DACQUOISE

A Cake or Meringue Layers?
Dacquois are residents of the town of Dax in southwest France and they've given their name to this classic cake, but dacquoise refers to the name of the base layers of nut meringue used to make the cake as well. The cake is also known as *Palois*, a reference to the inhabitants of the nearby city of Pau, in the same region. The meringue layers are sandwiched with buttercream and then dusted with confectioners' sugar.

How to Add Extra Flavor to a Dacquoise
For a fuller flavor, roast the ground nuts (hazelnuts or almonds) before folding them into the batter.

GENOISE

You can bake genoise sponge batter on a parchment-lined baking sheet, or alternatively in a round cake pan and cut it into thin layers once it has cooled. The latter is especially useful if your batter is too runny to spread over a baking sheet.

Cool Completely
If baking your genoise on a lined baking sheet, as soon as it is ready, slide it carefully onto a wire rack, still on the parchment, and let it cool completely. This will make the sponge easier to handle and to peel off the paper, without damaging its thin, golden crust.

Super Glue
Parchment paper used to line a baking sheet can blow around in the oven so needs sticking to the sheet to hold it in place. The easiest way is to dab a little batter at each corner of the parchment and place it upside down on the sheet—the batter will act as the ideal glue and it's food-safe and heatproof!

TYPE OF SPONGE	USES	STORAGE	ADVANTAGES
Joconde sponge	Layered desserts, Yule logs and other rolled cakes, opéra	Covered in plastic wrap. 2 days in the refrigerator. 2 weeks in the freezer.	Good for imprinting with decorative patterns
Genoise	Rolled cakes, strawberry layer cake, mocha layer cake, etc.	Covered in plastic wrap. 2 days in the refrigerator. 2 weeks in the freezer.	Easy to make Suitable for drizzling with syrup
Ladyfingers	Charlottes, tiramisu, strawberry layer cake, etc.	Covered in plastic wrap. 1–2 days in an airtight container (preferably a tin).	Soft texture Good for moistening with syrup
Dacquoise	Layered desserts, Yule logs and other rolled cakes, etc.	Covered in plastic wrap. 2–3 days in the refrigerator. 2 weeks in the freezer.	Gluten-free. Slightly crunchy texture. Can be made using any nuts (walnuts, pistachios, etc.)
Flourless chocolate sponge	Jelly rolls, Yule logs, layered desserts, etc.	Covered in plastic wrap. 2 days in the refrigerator. 2 weeks in the freezer.	Gluten-free

Sacher Torte Sponge

Biscuit Sacher

Serves 4

Active time
20 minutes

Cooking time
18 minutes

Storage
Up to 3 days in the refrigerator
or 2 weeks in the freezer,
well wrapped

Equipment
7-in. (18-cm) round cake pan
or ring, 1.5 in. (4 cm) deep,
brushed with melted butter
and dusted with flour

Instant-read thermometer

Ingredients
5 oz. (140 g) almond paste,
chopped and softened in the
microwave for 20 seconds

¼ cup (2.5 oz./70 g) egg yolk
(about 4 yolks)

3 ½ tbsp (1.75 oz./50 g) whole
egg (about 1 egg)

3 ½ tbsp (1 oz./30 g) flour,
plus extra for the pan

2 tbsp plus ½ tsp (0.5 oz./15 g)
unsweetened cocoa powder

1.25 oz. (35 g) bittersweet
couverture chocolate

2 tbsp plus 1 tsp (1.25 oz./35 g)
butter, plus extra for the pan

⅓ cup (2.75 oz./80 g) egg white
(about 2 ½ whites)

Scant ¼ cup (1.5 oz./45 g) sugar

1• Preheat the oven to 350°F (180°C/Gas mark 4). In a mixing bowl,
beat the almond paste with the egg yolks until smooth.

CHEFS' NOTES

Stirring a spoonful of the whisked egg whites
into the melted chocolate and butter first softens the mixture
and makes it easier to gently fold in the rest of the whites.

2· Add the whole egg and whisk until the mixture reaches the ribbon stage. Sift the flour and cocoa powder together and set aside.

3· Melt the chocolate and butter in a bowl over a pan of hot water. When the temperature reaches 122°F–131°F (50°C–55°C), remove from the heat.

4· Whisk the egg whites, gradually adding the sugar, until the mixture holds soft peaks. Stir a large spoonful into the melted chocolate and butter until mixed in.

5· Pour the melted chocolate mixture into the rest of the whisked egg whites and carefully fold in until evenly combined. ⊙

Sacher Torte Sponge (continued)

6 • Add the almond paste and egg mix, followed by the flour and cocoa powder, and fold everything together.

7 • Pour the batter into the prepared cake pan and bake for 18 minutes.

8 • Run a knife around the rim of the pan to make it easier to turn the cake out.

Joconde Sponge

Biscuit Joconde

Makes 12 oz. (350 g)

Active time
30 minutes

Cooking time
8–10 minutes

Storage
Up to 2 days in the refrigerator
or 2 weeks in the freezer,
well wrapped

Equipment
Stand mixer with paddle
beater and whisk

Angled spatula
Silicone baking mat

Ingredients
¾ cup (2.75 oz./75 g) almond
flour

Generous ½ cup (2.75 oz./75 g)
confectioners' sugar

2 ½ tbsp (0.75 oz./20 g) flour

Scant ½ cup (3.5 oz./100 g)
lightly beaten egg
(about 2 eggs)

1 tbsp (0.5 oz./15 g) butter,
melted and cooled

Scant ⅓ cup (2.5 oz./70 g) egg
white (about 2 ½ whites)

2 ½ tsp (0.35 oz./10 g) sugar

1• Preheat the oven to 450°F (230°C/Gas mark 8). Fit the stand
mixer with the paddle beater and add the almond flour and
confectioners' sugar.

2• Mix them together and stir in the flour. Add the whole eggs
in 3 equal quantities and beat at medium speed for 5 minutes
until the mixture is smooth, creamy, and light. ⊕

Joconde Sponge (continued)

3 • Transfer the batter to a mixing bowl.

4 • Mix in the melted butter

7 • Lay the silicone baking mat on a baking sheet and spread the batter over it using the angled spatula.

8 • Wipe the edges of the baking mat clean with your finger to neaten them. Bake for 8–10 minutes.

5 • Wash the stand mixer bowl and dry it. Fit the whisk and beat the egg whites, gradually adding the sugar and whisking constantly, until the whites are standing in firm peaks.

6 • Using a spatula, gently fold the batter into the whisked whites, until evenly combined and light.

CHEFS' NOTES

• Removing the baking mat from the baked sponge as soon as it comes out of the oven prevents the sponge becoming dry, as it would continue to cook if left on the hot mat.

• A Joconde sponge can be wrapped around a layered dessert. It can also be baked on a silicone mat with a raised relief pattern, or colored the shade of your choice.

9 • When you remove the sponge from the oven, turn it over carefully and, with the help of a wire rack, peel the baking mat away.

Genoise

Serves 4–6

Active time
40 minutes

Cooking time
20 minutes

Storage
Up to 2 days in the refrigerator
or 2 weeks in the freezer,
well wrapped

Equipment
6-in. (16-cm) round cake pan
Instant-read thermometer

Ingredients
1 ½ tbsp (0.75 oz./20 g)
clarified butter for the pan

Generous ⅓ cup
(5.5 oz./160 g) lightly beaten
egg (about 3 ½ eggs)

Scant ½ cup (3.25 oz./95 g)
sugar

1 ½ tbsp (0.75 oz./20 g) butter,
melted and cooled

⅔ cup plus 1 tbsp (3 oz./90 g)
flour, plus extra for the pan

Flavorings
Coffee genoise: Add 2 ½ tsp
(0.5 oz./12 g) instant coffee
powder to the eggs.

Chocolate genoise: Replace
1 tbsp–1 tbsp plus 1 tsp (15–20 g)
of the flour with unsweetened
cocoa powder.

1 • Preheat the oven to 350°F (180°C/Gas mark 4).
Brush the base and sides of the cake pan with the clarified butter.
Cool and then dust with flour.

4 • Mix in the melted butter.

5 • Sift in the flour and fold in gently using a spatula.

CHEFS' NOTES

- A genoise baked on a sheet can be used to make a rolled cake with a filling, as layers separating the filling of a dessert, and for making small, cut-out cakes moistened with a syrup or liqueur of your choice.

- A genoise baked in a cake pan is done when it feels springy to the touch and it pulls away from the sides of the pan.

- You can make the batter using an electric hand beater, if you prefer.

2 • Whisk the eggs and sugar in a bowl over a pan of hot water until thickened, without letting the temperature rise above 113°F (45°C).

3 • Continue whisking until the ribbon stage is reached.

6 • Pour the batter into the prepared cake pan and bake for 20 minutes.

Ladyfingers

Biscuit à la Cuillère

Makes 20

Active time
30 minutes

Cooking time
6–8 minutes

Storage
Up to 2 days in an airtight container

Equipment
Pastry bag fitted with a plain ½-in. (10-mm) tip

Uses
Layered desserts such as charlottes

Can be served on their own as cookies

Ingredients
Scant ½ cup (3.5 oz./100 g) egg white (about 3 ½ whites)

½ cup (3.5 oz./100 g) superfine sugar

¼ cup (2.75 oz./75 g) beaten egg yolk (about 4 yolks)

⅓ cup (1.5 oz./45 g) flour

Generous ¼ cup (1.5 oz./45 g) cornstarch

Confectioners' sugar for dusting

Flavorings
Chocolate ladyfingers: Replace 2 tsp (10 g) of the flour with unsweetened cocoa powder.

Vanilla ladyfingers: Add ½ tsp (2.5 ml) vanilla extract.

Coffee ladyfingers: Add 2 tsp (10 g) instant coffee granules.

Pink ladyfingers: Add scant ¼ tsp (1 g) natural red food coloring.

1 • Preheat the oven to 400°F (200°C/Gas mark 6). Line a baking sheet with parchment paper. Whisk the egg whites, adding the sugar in 4 or 5 equal quantities, until the meringue is stiff and glossy.

4 • Fold in the sifted flour and cornstarch, taking care not to deflate the mixture. For the chocolate variation, mix the cocoa with the flour; for the vanilla and coffee, dissolve the extract or granules in a little water before adding; for the pink, add the color after the whites have been whisked.

5 • Using the pastry bag, pipe out logs about 5 in. (12 cm) long onto the lined baking sheet.

For a firmer consistency, add a small amount of powdered egg white
before you begin whisking the egg whites.

2 • Using a spatula, fold a large spoonful of the whites into the egg yolks until smooth.

3 • Pour the egg yolk mixture into the remaining meringue and fold in until evenly combined.

6 • Dust the logs twice with a fine layer of confectioners' sugar just before they go into the oven and bake for 6–8 minutes. The ladyfingers should be soft and not dried out.

Walnut Dacquoise

Dacquoises aux Noix

Makes 12

Active time
30 minutes

Cooking time
20–25 minutes

Storage
Up to 2 days in the refrigerator
or 2 weeks in the freezer,
well wrapped

Equipment
Pastry bag fitted with
a plain ⅓-in. (10-mm) tip
Silicone baking mat

Ingredients
Scant ½ cup (3.5 oz./100 g)
egg white (about 3 ½ whites)

½ tbsp (0.25 oz./8 g)
superfine sugar

6 tbsp (2.75 oz./80 g)
confectioners' sugar

Scant 1 cup (2.75 oz./80 g)
almond flour

⅜ cup (1.5 oz./40 g) finely
chopped walnuts

Confectioners' sugar for dusting

1 • Preheat the oven to 350°F (180°C/Gas mark 4).
Line a baking sheet with the silicone mat.
Whisk the egg whites, gradually adding the superfine sugar.

4 • Fill the pastry bag with the meringue.

5 • Pipe 12 spirals onto the lined baking sheet,
starting to pipe at the center of each and working outward,
or pipe the meringue into a silicone mold.

This meringue can be piped onto lined baking sheets into 2 spirals,
each about 7 in. (18 cm) in diameter and ¾ in. (1.5 cm) deep.
Bake at 350°F (180°C/Gas mark 4) for 25–30 minutes.

2 • Mix the confectioners' sugar with the almond flour.

3 • Using a spatula, carefully fold the sugar and almond flour mixture into the beaten whites with the chopped walnuts, until the ingredients are evenly combined.

6 • Dust with confectioners' sugar just before they go into the oven and bake for 20–25 minutes.

Flourless Chocolate Sponge

Biscuit sans Farine au Chocolat

Makes 12 oz. (350 g)

Active time
20 minutes

Cooking time
7–8 minutes

Storage
Up to 2 days in the refrigerator
or 2 weeks in the freezer,
well wrapped

Equipment
12 × 16-in. (30 × 40-cm)
baking sheet
Silicone baking mat
Instant-read thermometer
Angled spatula

Ingredients
3.5 oz. (100 g) bittersweet
couverture chocolate,
50% cacao, chopped

2 tbsp (1 oz./30 g) butter, diced

1.75 oz. (50 g) almond paste,
50% almonds

1 ½ tbsp (1 oz./25 g) egg yolk
(about 1 ½ yolks)

½ cup (4.5 oz./125 g) egg white
(about 4 whites)

Scant ¼ cup (1.5 oz./45 g) sugar

1 • Preheat the oven to 350°F (180°C/Gas mark 4). Line the baking
sheet with the silicone baking mat. Melt the chocolate and butter
in a bowl over a pan of hot water until the temperature reaches
122°F–131°F (50°C–55°C). Remove from the heat.

4 • In a round-based mixing bowl, whisk the egg whites until firm,
gradually adding the sugar. With a spatula, lightly fold the
two mixtures together until evenly combined.

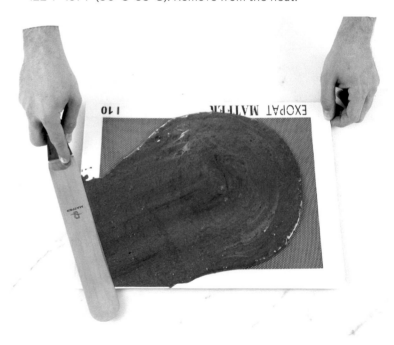

5 • Pour onto the silicone mat, spreading evenly to the edges
of the mat with the angled spatula.

• The egg whites can be whisked
using an electric hand beater, if you prefer.

• When mixing the almond paste and egg yolks, ensure no lumps
remain before adding the melted chocolate and butter.

2 • Soften the almond paste in the microwave for 20 seconds
at medium power. Mix with a spatula and gradually incorporate
the egg yolk.

3 • When smooth, stir in the melted chocolate and butter.

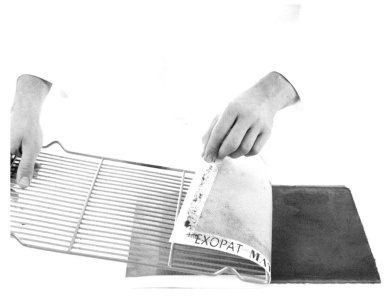

6 • Using your finger, clean the edges of the mat to neaten them.
Bake for 7–8 minutes.

7 • As soon as you take the sponge out of the oven,
carefully turn it over and, using a wire rack to help you,
peel away the silicone mat.

MERINGUES

MERINGUES

Egg whites and sugar are the two ingredients needed to make three types of meringue. French meringue, Italian meringue, and Swiss meringue are prepared using different techniques, two of which require heat, and each meringue is used in a different way.

NO TRACE OF FAT

The smallest amount of fat will prevent the whites from whipping up, so make sure the eggs are cleanly separated, with no flecks of yolk in the whites. And, of course, the mixing bowl and the whisk must be completely clean and dry as well.

AT ROOM TEMPERATURE

Egg whites whip up far more easily at room temperature rather than being taken straight from the refrigerator, so remember to get them out at least 2 hours before making your meringue.

WHICH SUGAR IS BEST?

The egg whites should be whisked with superfine sugar rather than confectioners' sugar, as the latter contains starch, which will prevent the whites from whisking up properly. Sugars with larger crystals are not suitable, as they will not dissolve as well as superfine sugar when whisked with the egg whites.

WHY ADD VINEGAR OR CREAM OF TARTAR TO FRENCH MERINGUE?

Adding a few drops of white vinegar, lemon juice, or a pinch of cream of tartar to the meringue mixture results in a smoother texture and stops the whipped whites becoming granular and losing bulk. Adding one of these is strongly recommended if you are making a large quantity of mixture or large meringues.

NO LINGERING, PLEASE

Like time, meringues wait for no one, so shape and bake the mixture as soon as you have made it.

USE AND STORAGE (AFTER BAKING)

TYPE OF MERINGUE	USES	STORAGE
French meringue	Base for iced desserts, individual pastries, petits fours	Several weeks in an airtight container, protected from moisture
Italian meringue	Decorating layered desserts and small pastries, *polonaises* (Polish brioches), baked Alaska, mousses	24 hours in the refrigerator, well covered in plastic wrap.
Swiss meringue	Individual pastries and decorations	Several weeks, well covered in plastic wrap, in an airtight container and protected from moisture

A BRIEF HISTORY OF THE MERINGUE

The word "meringue" can be traced back to the late 17th century, when it first appeared in François Massaliot's Nouvelle Instruction pour les Confitures, les Liqueurs et les Fruits (New Methods for Making Jams, Liqueurs, and Fruits). Macarons and meringues were also included in the same chapter. One theory is that meringues were first made in Switzerland, in particular in the town of Meiringen. Another claims they were based on Italian biscotti (meaning baked twice), which were cooked in a very low oven and are mentioned in even earlier pastry books dating from the start of the 17th century. Queen Marie Antoinette adored meringues, and is even said to have participated in making them at the Petit Trianon, her own private château at Versailles. Originally meringues were shaped using spoons until Antonin Carême began piping them using a pastry bag with a tip. Meringues can be eaten on their own, sandwiched with cream, used to decorate tarts (such as lemon meringue tart), or as the base for cakes like Pavlova or the chestnut cream–filled Mont Blanc.

Italian Meringue

Makes about 10 oz. (300 g)

Active time
15 minutes

Cooking time
10–15 minutes

Storage
Up to 24 hours
in the refrigerator,
well wrapped

Equipment
Stand mixer fitted
with the whisk
Pastry bag fitted
with a tip of your choice
Instant-read thermometer

Ingredients
1 cup (7 oz./ 200 g)
superfine sugar
⅓ cup (80 ml) water
Scant ½ cup (3.5 oz./100 g)
egg white (about 3 ½ whites)

Uses
Decorating desserts
and small cakes, *polonaises*
(Polish brioches), baked Alaska,
adding to flavored mousses

1• Dissolve the sugar in the water and boil to 240°F–250°F (116°C–121°C)—the exact temperature
will depend on the type of meringue you need.

For this method, the meringue is cooked by incorporating cooked sugar,
followed by a few minutes in the oven to lightly brown it.

2 • When the temperature of the syrup reaches 230°F (110°C), begin whisking the egg whites in the stand mixer at high speed.

3 • When the required temperature of the syrup is reached, very carefully pour it over the partially whisked egg whites in a thin, steady stream, taking care not to let it touch the beaters and whisking continuously. Reduce to medium speed after 2 minutes.

4 • Whisk until the mixture has cooled completely.

CHEFS' NOTES

• The egg whites must be whisked until they are frothy so as to produce a smooth, glossy meringue.

• If the meringue is to be incorporated into a mousse, the required temperature depends on how fragile the mousse ingredients are. For a chocolate mousse, it should be between 113°F and 122°F (45°C and 50°C) and for a fruit mousse, between 95°F and 100°F (35°C and 40°C).

• For creamy mixtures being "lightened" with meringue, incorporate the meringue at 75°F (25°C), particularly if the mixture contains butter, such as a praline buttercream.

French Meringue

Makes about 10 oz. (300 g)

Active time
15 minutes

Cooking time
2–4 hours, depending
on the size of the meringues

Storage
Up to several weeks,
well wrapped and stored
in an airtight container

Equipment
Silicone baking mat
Stand mixer fitted
with the whisk
Pastry bag fitted with a plain
tip of your choice, depending
on the desired size
and shape of the meringues

Ingredients
Scant ½ cup (3.5 oz./100 g)
egg white (about 3 ½ whites)
1 tsp (5 ml) white vinegar
1 pinch of salt
Scant 1 cup (6 oz./175 g)
superfine sugar
2 tbsp (1 oz./25 g)
confectioners' sugar, sifted

Uses
As a base for iced, layered
desserts, individual meringues,
petits fours

1• Preheat the oven to 200°F–225°F (95°C–105°C/Gas mark ¼).
Line a baking sheet with the silicone baking mat and place it on another baking sheet.
Whisk the egg whites, vinegar, and salt in the stand mixer at medium-high speed until firm and frothy.
Whisk in the superfine sugar gradually so the whites do not deflate.

CHEFS' NOTES

• The "magic" pinch of salt also helps to ensure the egg whites are smooth, which makes them easier to whisk up.

• Fresh egg whites have two different textures: a thick portion surrounding the yolk and a thinner portion around the outside. Mix them gently before whisking to ensure they are smooth.

2 • Keep whisking until the sugar has dissolved completely and the whites are stiff and shiny. When you lift the whisk, the mixture should hold firm peaks.

3 • Quickly and carefully fold in the confectioners' sugar using a flexible spatula, taking care not to deflate the meringue.

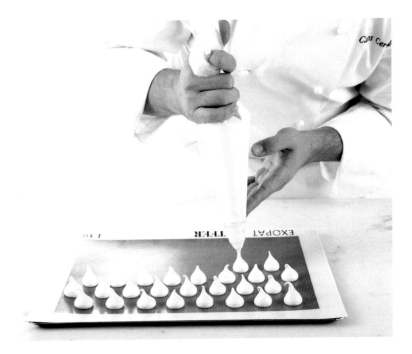

4 • Spoon the meringue into the pastry bag fitted with the tip of your choice (see technique p. 30).

5 • Pipe the desired shapes onto the lined baking sheet and bake for 2–4 hours, depending on the size of the meringues.

Swiss Meringue

Makes about 10 oz. (300 g)

Active time
15 minutes

Cooking time
1–1 ½ hours

Storage
Up to several weeks,
well wrapped and stored
in an airtight container

Equipment
Silicone baking mat
Stand mixer fitted
with the whisk attachment
Instant-read thermometer
Pastry bag fitted
with a plain tip of your choice

Ingredients
Scant ½ cup (3.5 oz. oz./100 g)
egg whites (about 3 ½ whites)
1 cup (7 oz./200 g)
superfine sugar
Confectioners' sugar
for dusting

Uses
Small meringues,
decorations

1• Preheat the oven to its lowest setting, ideally 175°F/80°C/Gas mark ¼ (see Chefs' Notes).
Line a baking sheet with the silicone baking mat. Place the egg whites in the mixing bowl of the stand
mixer. Set it over a pan of hot water and add the sugar, stirring continuously and vigorously
so the egg whites do not cook. Heat the mixture to 113°F–122°F (45°C–50°C).

2 • Transfer the bowl to the stand mixer and whisk at high speed until the mixture is standing in firm peaks.

3 • Using the pastry bag fitted with the tip of your choice (see technique p. 30), pipe meringues onto the lined baking sheet.

CHEFS' NOTES

You can vary your meringues according to the temperature at which you bake them. With your oven set to its lowest temperature, the meringues will remain white and firm.

4 • Dust with confectioners' sugar and bake for 1–1 ½ hours, depending on the size of the meringues.

MACARONS

MACARONS

A BRIEF HISTORY OF THE MACARON

The first reference to macarons was in the 16th century by François Rabelais in his classic Gargantua and Pantagruel. *Ever since, the word has referred to a small pastry made with almonds, sugar, and egg whites but not all macarons are the same. Differing techniques and quantities of the base ingredients have produced many variations, ranging from moist to dry and from smooth to cracked. Numerous cities across France claim the macaron as a specialty, including Amiens, Boulay, Nancy, Saint-Jean-de-Luz, and Saint Émilion.*

In 1830, the Parisian pastry chef Claude Gerbet invented a smooth macaron that was smaller than the one from Nancy and he gave it his name. But it was Pierre Desfontaines, the grandson of the famous pastry chef Ladurée, who came up with the idea in the early 20th century of sandwiching two macarons together—and the rest is history! The range of fillings for these Parisian macarons has grown to include jams, marmalades, candied fruits, creams, and much more. Today, the macaron is an iconic symbol of French pâtisserie, being made in an array of colors and flavors to suit every whim.

WAYS TO MAKE MACARON SHELLS

There are different ways to make macaron shells but most recipes use either French meringue or Italian meringue. The main difference lies in the way the meringue is prepared. French meringue is uncooked as the sugar is whisked directly into the egg whites, while Italian meringue is made with hot sugar syrup, which cooks the egg whites, making the meringue more stable. Currently, the Italian meringue method is the most widely used.

WHY USE ITALIAN MERINGUE?

Although French meringue makes macaron shells that are beautifully crisp and melt in the mouth, moisture in the meringue can make the shells crack as they bake. Italian meringue shells are made with hot sugar syrup and so are less fragile.

PERFECT EGG WHITES

To ensure success when making macarons, it is best to use egg whites separated from the yolks 4 or 5 days ahead. Newly separated whites whisk up well to begin with but then have a tendency to look "grainy" and start to separate. They are less stable and will lose bulk during baking. Chilled whites, from the refrigerator or freezer, will be more liquid, will remain glossy, and won't spread in the oven. Be sure to bring your egg whites to room temperature before using them to make macarons.

SHOULD MACARON SHELLS REST BEFORE BAKING?

Depending on the weather, room temperature, and humidity, it may be necessary to leave the macaron shells to rest for 1 hour—or longer—after they have been piped onto the baking sheet. This ensures they form a thin crust and helps them produce the distinctive "small collar" when baked.

DIFFERENT FILLINGS

The choice of fillings for macarons is many and varied but remember that the filling will determine their keeping time. The most popular are buttercream (see technique p. 202), ganache, or jam (see techniques pp. 552–62), almond paste whipped with butter, jelled fruit purées, a crémeux, but there are many more. You can also combine several fillings, such as a thin layer of jelled fruit purée with a layer of ganache. For the perfect balance, allow about 0.5 oz. (15 g) of filling per macaron.

MATURING AND STORING

Once filled, macarons improve by being rested in the refrigerator. Place them on a rack, without covering them, and chill for a minimum of 2 hours. Remove and pack in airtight plastic containers. They can then be stored in the refrigerator for 3–4 days.

FREEZING FILLED MACARONS

Filled macarons freeze well, if properly stored. Chill the macarons uncovered in the refrigerator for 2 hours before packing them in airtight plastic containers. Cover the containers with plastic wrap and freeze at 0°F (-18°C) for up to 1 month. Defrost in the refrigerator for 6 hours before serving.

COLOR IS FIRST AND FOREMOST!

The current success of the macaron owes much to the fact that it can be any color thanks to its neutral, light-colored shell (see recipes on the following pages). The colors of the fillings can match or complement the color of the shell, meaning the potential range of macaron shades is almost infinite. Pastry chefs can take inspiration from the seasons or from current trends, or adapt their creations to mirror the theme or style of a buffet or other occasion. In France, pyramids made of macarons have become just as popular at celebrations as the croquembouche, the traditional puff pastry tower.

THE FERRANDI PARIS COLOR PALETTE

Unlike other chapters, this one does not follow the 1-2-3 levels of difficulty for making the recipes. Instead, it is arranged by color, which is better suited to the unique nature of the macaron. This makes it possible to better explore the wide range of possible flavors and, of course, colors. For each color on the Ferrandi palette, you can make two different macarons at two levels of difficulty: one is a classic and the other offers something more original.

Macaron Shells

**Makes about 24 shells,
for 12 macarons**

Active time
1 hour

Baking time
15 minutes

Storage
Up to 10 days,
at room temperature

Equipment
Food processor
Candy thermometer
Stick blender
Pastry bag fitted with
a plain ½-in. (10-mm) tip
Silicone baking mat

Ingredients
1 cup (3.5 oz./100 g)
almond flour

¾ cup (3.5 oz./100 g)
confectioners' sugar

3 tbsp (1.5 oz./40 g)
egg white (about 1 ½ whites),
at room temperature

Water-soluble powdered
food coloring (optional)
(see Chefs' Notes)

Italian meringue
½ cup (3.5 oz./100 g)
superfine sugar

2 tbsp (30 ml) water

3 tbsp (1.5 oz./40 g)
egg white (about 1 ½ whites),
at room temperature

1 • Whisk the almond flour and confectioners' sugar together
in a bowl. Preheat the oven to 300°F (150°C/Gas mark 2).

2 • Transfer the almond flour and sugar to the bowl of the food
processor. Pulse until a flour-like consistency, being careful
not to overwork and heat the ingredients.

3 • If using food coloring, add it to the 3 tbsp (1.5 oz./40 g)
of egg white. ⊕

Macaron Shells (continued)

4 • Beat with the stick blender until the color (if using) is evenly mixed in, taking care not to whisk up the egg whites.

5 • Prepare the Italian meringue using the quantities listed (see technique p. 232). When the meringue has cooled to about 122°F (50°C), fold in the almond flour and sugar mixture with a spatula.

8 • Continue folding until the meringue has deflated slightly and you have a smooth mixture that falls off the spatula in thick ribbons (see Chefs' Notes).

9 • Line a baking sheet (at room temperature) with the silicone mat. Spoon the mixture into the pastry bag and pipe macaron shells approximately 1 in. (2.5 cm) in diameter onto the mat.

• Letting the mixture deflate after folding in the meringue gives the piped shells a glossy sheen.

• Powdered food coloring is recommended for macarons as it adds no extra liquid to the mixture and is easy to blend with the egg whites.

6 • Pour in the colored egg whites.

7 • Begin to fold the mixtures together with a spatula.

10 • Carefully lift up the baking sheet slightly and gently drop it back onto the work surface to make the tops of the macarons smooth. Bake for 15 minutes.

VANILLA MACARONS

Macarons Vanille

Makes 12

Active time
2 hours

Infusing time
20 minutes–12 hours (overnight)

Chilling time
3 hours

Storage
Up to 4 days in the refrigerator

Equipment
Instant-read thermometer
Stick blender
Stand mixer
Pastry bag fitted
with a plain ⅓-in. or ½-in.
(8-mm or 10-mm) tip

Ingredients
24 macaron shells
(see technique p. 243 and method)

WHIPPED GANACHE
1 sheet (2 g) gelatin
⅓ cup (75 ml) whole milk
½ vanilla bean, split lenghtwise
and seeds scraped out
2.25 oz. (65 g) white chocolate,
finely chopped
Scant ½ cup (100 ml) whipping
cream, 35% butterfat

MAKING THE MACARON SHELLS
Prepare the macaron shells (see technique p. 243).

MAKING THE WHIPPED GANACHE
Soak the gelatin in a bowl of cold water. Meanwhile, bring the milk, vanilla bean, and seeds to a boil in a saucepan over medium heat. Take off the heat and remove the vanilla bean. Squeeze out the gelatin and stir it into the hot milk until dissolved. Place the chocolate in a bowl, pour over the hot milk and process with the stick blender to make a smooth ganache. Once the ganache has cooled to about 140°F (60°C), mix in the cream until combined. Line a baking sheet with plastic wrap, spread the ganache over it and press another sheet of plastic wrap over the surface. Chill for at least 1 hour. Lightly whisk the cold ganache in the stand mixer to soften it.

ASSEMBLING THE MACARONS
Spoon the ganache into the pastry bag, pipe the filling over the flat side of half the shells and lightly press the other shells on top so the filling reaches the edges. Chill for at least 2 hours before serving.

CHEFS' NOTES

• For a stronger vanilla flavor, leave the vanilla bean and seeds in the milk to infuse overnight in the refrigerator.

• Whisking the ganache makes it softer and easier to pipe.

COCONUT MOCHA MACARONS

Macarons Café-Noix de Coco

MAKING THE MACARON SHELLS
Prepare the macaron shells (see technique p. 243), sprinkling the tops with grated coconut before baking.

MAKING THE COCONUT MOCHA CRÉMEUX
Infuse the coffee beans in the cold milk for at least 20 minutes or, if possible, chill overnight. Soak the gelatin in a bowl of cold water. Strain the milk and stir in half the coconut purée. Bring to a boil over medium heat. Whisk the egg, egg yolk, and sugar together until pale and thick. Stir the rest of the coconut purée and mix in the hot milk, whisking constantly. Pour the mixture into a saucepan and heat over medium heat to 180°F (82°C), stirring constantly. Squeeze out the gelatin to remove excess water and stir it into the hot custard until dissolved. Once the custard cools to 95°F-104°F (35°C-40°C), add the butter and process with the stick blender until smooth. Press plastic wrap over the surface and chill until firm enough to pipe.

ASSEMBLING THE MACARONS
Spoon the crémeux into the pastry bag, pipe it over the flat side of half the shells, and lightly press the others on top so the filling reaches the edges. Chill for at least 2 hours before serving.

CHEFS' NOTES

• Weigh or measure the milk after straining out the coffee beans and top up with more milk to the 4 tsp (20 ml) needed for the recipe, as the coffee beans will have absorbed some of the milk.

• To speed up the infusion, crush the coffee beans before adding them to the milk.

Makes 12

Active time
1¾ hours

Infusing time
20 minutes–12 hours (overnight)

Chilling time
3 hours

Storage
Up to 4 days in the refrigerator

Equipment
Instant-read thermometer
Stick blender
Pastry bag fitted
with a plain ⅓-in. or ½-in.
(8-mm or 10-mm) tip

Ingredients
24 macaron shells
(see technique p. 243 and method)
Grated coconut for sprinkling

COCONUT MOCHA CRÉMEUX
0.2 oz. (5 g) coffee beans
4 tsp (20 ml) whole milk
1 sheet (2 g) gelatin
Scant ⅓ cup (2.75 oz./80 g)
coconut purée
Scant ¼ cup (1.75 oz./50 g)
lightly beaten egg (about 1 egg)
Scant 2 tbsp (1 oz./30 g) egg yolk
(about 1 ½ yolks)
3 tbsp (1.25 oz./35 g) sugar
4 tbsp (2 oz./60 g) butter,
preferably 84% butterfat, diced,
at room temperature

1

ORANGE MACARONS

Macarons Orange

Makes 12

Active time
1 ¾ hours

Chilling time
3 hours

Storage
Up to 4 days in the refrigerator

Equipment
Food processor
Instant-read thermometer
Stick blender
Pastry bag fitted
with a plain ⅓-in. or ½-in.
(8-mm or 10-mm) tip

Ingredients
24 macaron shells
(see technique p. 243 and method)
Heaping ⅛ tsp (0.6 g)
water-soluble powdered orange
food coloring

CANDIED ORANGE FILLING
8 oz. (220 g) whole oranges
4 ½ tsp (0.7 oz./18 g)
superfine sugar
1 ¼ tsp (5 g) pectin NH

MAKING THE MACARON SHELLS
Prepare the macaron shells (see technique p. 243), adding
the orange food coloring at step 3.

MAKING THE CANDIED ORANGE FILLING
Wash the oranges, place in a saucepan, cover with
cold water, bring to a boil, and blanch for 30 seconds.
Drain and repeat the blanching process 2 or 3 times.
Quarter the oranges, remove the seeds and reduce
the pulp and peel to a purée in the food processor.
Transfer the purée to a saucepan and heat slowly to
113°F (45°C). Mix the sugar and pectin together and
gradually whisk into the hot orange purée. Bring the
mixture to a boil, still whisking constantly, and cook
for a few minutes until the purée thickens. To cool the
filling, line a baking sheet with plastic wrap, spread it
over the sheet and press another piece of plastic wrap
over the surface. Chill for at least 1 hour.

ASSEMBLING THE MACARONS
Transfer the candied orange filling to a bowl and process with the stick blender until smooth. Spoon the
filling into the pastry bag, pipe it over the flat side of
half the shells, and lightly press the remaining shells on
top so the filling reaches the edges. Chill for at least
2 hours before serving.

CHEFS' NOTES

To enhance the flavor of the orange filling,
the seeds from ½ vanilla bean can be stirred
into the purée before heating.

MANGO AND PASSION FRUIT MACARONS

Macarons Mangue-Passion

MAKING THE MACARON SHELLS

Prepare the macaron shells (see technique p. 243), adding the orange food coloring at step 3. Once the shells are baked and cooled, use the spray gun to mist the tops with the green-colored kirsch to create a shadow effect.

MAKING THE MANGO-PASSION FRUIT GANACHE

Melt the chocolate in a bowl over a pan of hot water to 95°F–104°F (35°C–40°C). Heat the cream and the fruit purées to 104°F (40°C) in another saucepan, then gradually pour over the melted chocolate, stirring until the chocolate has melted. Whisk in the lemon juice, using the stick blender, and then strain through a fine-mesh strainer to make a smooth ganache. To cool the filling, line a baking sheet with plastic wrap, spread the filling over the sheet and press another piece of plastic wrap over the surface. Chill for at least 1 hour.

ASSEMBLING THE MACARONS

Spoon the ganache into the pastry bag, pipe it over the flat side of half the shells and lightly press the others on top so the filling reaches the edges. Chill for at least 2 hours before serving.

Makes 12

Active time
1 ¾ hours

Chilling time
3 hours

Cooking time
10–15 minutes

Storage
Up to 4 days in the refrigerator

Equipment
Spray gun
Stick blender
Instant-read thermometer
Pastry bag fitted
with a plain ⅓-in. or ½-in.
(8-mm or 10-mm) tip

Ingredients
24 macaron shells
(see technique p. 243 and method)
¼ tsp (0.8 g) water-soluble powdered orange food coloring
¼ tsp (0.8 g) water-soluble powdered green food coloring, diluted in a little kirsch, for spraying

MANGO-PASSION FRUIT GANACHE
5 oz. (140 g) white chocolate, finely chopped
⅓ cup (75 ml) whipping cream, 35% butterfat
5 tsp (1 oz./25 g) mango purée
5 tsp (1 oz./25 g) passion fruit purée
Scant ½ tsp (2 ml) lemon juice

RASPBERRY MACARONS

Macarons Framboise

Makes 12

Active time
1 ¾ hours

Chilling time
3 hours

Storage
Up to 4 days in the refrigerator

Equipment
Instant-read thermometer
Stick blender
Pastry bag fitted
with a plain ⅓-in. or ½-in.
(8-mm or 10-mm) tip

Ingredients
24 macaron shells
(see technique p. 243 and method)
Heaping ⅛ tsp (0.6 g)
water-soluble powdered pink
food coloring

CANDIED RASPBERRY FILLING
1 cup (9 oz./250 g)
raspberry purée
½ cup (3.5 oz./100 g)
superfine sugar
1 ¼ tsp (5 g) pectin NH

MAKING THE MACARON SHELLS
Prepare the macaron shells (see technique p. 243), adding the pink food coloring at step 3.

MAKING THE CANDIED RASPBERRY FILLING
Heat the raspberry purée to 113°F (45°C) in a saucepan over low heat. Mix the sugar and pectin together and gradually add to the raspberry purée, whisking constantly. Bring the mixture to a boil, still whisking all the time, and cook for a few minutes until the purée thickens. Line a baking sheet with plastic wrap, spread the purée over it and press another piece of plastic wrap over the surface. Chill for at least 1 hour.

ASSEMBLING THE MACARONS
Blend the raspberry filling with the stick blender until smooth. Spoon it into the pastry bag, pipe it over the flat side of half the shells and lightly press the others on top so the filling reaches the edges. Chill for at least 2 hours before serving.

ROSE-LYCHEE MACARONS

Macarons Rose-Litchi

MAKING THE MACARON SHELLS
Prepare the macaron shells (see technique p. 243), adding the pink food coloring at step 3.

MAKING THE ROSE-LYCHEE MARSHMALLOW FILLING
Soak the gelatin in a bowl of cold water. Add the sugar and about 2 tbsp (1.5 oz./45 g) of the invert sugar to the water in a medium saucepan and cook over medium heat until the sugar dissolves and the temperature of the syrup reaches 230°F (110°C). Squeeze out the gelatin and melt it in a bowl over a pan of hot water. Fit the stand mixer with the whisk and put the remaining invert sugar (2.25 oz./65 g) in the bowl. Carefully pour in the hot syrup and melted gelatin and whisk until the mixture is mousse-like. Cool to lukewarm and then fold in the lychee purée and rose water using a spatula.

ASSEMBLING THE MACARONS
Spoon the filling into the pastry bag, pipe it over the flat side of half the shells and lightly press the others on top so the filling reaches the edges. Chill for at least 2 hours before serving, topping each one with a rose petal.

CHEFS' NOTES

• These macarons are best made a day ahead and stored at room temperature.

• Fill the macarons while the marshmallow filling is still warm so it does not set too quickly.

Makes 12

Active time
1 ¾ hours

Chilling time
3 hours

Storage
Up to 4 days in the refrigerator

Equipment
Instant-read thermometer
Stand mixer
Stick blender
Pastry bag fitted
with a plain ⅓-in. or ½-in.
(8-mm or 10-mm) tip

Ingredients
24 macaron shells (see technique p. 243 and method)
¼ tsp (0.8 g) water-soluble powdered pink food coloring

ROSE-LYCHEE MARSHMALLOW FILLING
6 sheets (0.4 oz./12 g) gelatin
½ cup plus 3 tbsp
(4.5 oz./130 g) superfine sugar
¼ cup plus 2 tsp (3.75 oz./110 g) invert sugar, divided
3 tbsp plus 1 tsp (50 ml) water
3 ½ tbsp (1.75 oz./55 g) lychee purée
Scant ½ tsp (2 ml) rose water

12 organic rose petals

LEVEL

1

STRAWBERRY MACARONS

Macarons Fraise

Makes 12

Active time
1 ¾ hours

Chilling time
3 hours

Storage
Up to 4 days in the refrigerator

Equipment
Instant-read thermometer
Pastry bag fitted
with a plain ⅓-in. or ½-in.
(8-mm or 10-mm) tip

Ingredients
24 macaron shells
(see technique p. 243 and method)
Heaping ⅛ tsp (0.6 g)
water-soluble powdered red
food coloring

STRAWBERRY GANACHE
¼ cup plus 2 tsp (70 ml)
whipping cream, 35% butterfat
¼ cup (2.25 oz./65 g)
strawberry purée
4.5 oz. (130 g) white chocolate,
finely chopped

MAKING THE MACARON SHELLS
Prepare the macaron shells (see technique p. 243), adding
the red food coloring at step 3.

MAKING THE STRAWBERRY GANACHE
Heat the cream and strawberry purée in a saucepan
over medium heat until the temperature reaches 95°F
(35°C). Meanwhile, melt the white chocolate to 95°F
(35°C) in a bowl over a saucepan of hot water. Slowly
pour the hot strawberry cream over the melted chocolate and stir with a spatula until you have a smooth,
creamy ganache. To cool the ganache, line a baking
sheet with plastic wrap, spread the ganache over it, and
press another piece of plastic wrap over the surface.
Refrigerate for at least 1 hour.

ASSEMBLING THE MACARONS
Spoon the strawberry filling into the pastry bag, pipe
it over the flat side of half the shells, and lightly press
the others on top so the filling reaches the edges. Chill
for at least 2 hours before serving.

CHEFS' NOTES

• Add a pinch of black pepper
to the strawberry ganache for a spicy kick.

• Go for ripe, full-flavored strawberries,
using a mix of different varieties if you wish.

RED BELL PEPPER, RASPBERRY, AND CHOCOLATE MACARONS

Macarons Poivron, Framboise & Chocolat

MAKING THE MACARON SHELLS
Prepare the macaron shells (see technique p. 243), adding the red food coloring at step 3.

MAKING THE VELVET SPRAY
Once the shells are baked and cooled, prepare the spray. Place the cocoa butter and white chocolate in separate bowls over saucepans of hot water, melt both to 95°F (35°C) and then mix together. Gradually stir in the red food coloring until you obtain the shade you want and then blend with the stick blender until smooth. Stand the bowl back over a pan of hot water and heat to 122°F (50°C). Strain through a fine-mesh strainer and pour into the spray gun. Spray the tops of the cooled macaron shells for a velvet-like sheen.

MAKING THE CRÉMEUX
Heat the raspberry and red bell pepper purées in a saucepan over low heat to 140°F (60°C). Meanwhile, melt the bittersweet chocolate in a bowl over a saucepan of hot water. Mix the sorbitol powder and glucose syrup together and stir into the purées. Carefully pour the purée mixture over the melted chocolate and stir with a spatula until well blended. Once the mixture

CHEFS' NOTES

To make your own red bell pepper purée, roast then peel them, and purée the flesh in a blender.

cools to 95°F–104°F (35°C–40°C), add the butter and blend until smooth. Cover the surface of the crémeux with plastic wrap and refrigerate for 30–40 minutes, until the crémeux is cool and thick enough to be piped.

ASSEMBLING
Spoon the filling into the pastry bag, pipe it over the flat side of half the shells, and lightly press the others on top so the filling reaches the edges. Chill for at least 2 hours before serving.

Makes 12

Active time
1 ¾ hours

Chilling time
3 hours

Storage
Up to 4 days in the refrigerator

Equipment
Instant-read thermometer
Stick blender
Spray gun
Pastry bag fitted
with a plain ⅓-in. or ½-in.
(8-mm or 10-mm) tip

Ingredients
24 macaron shells
(see technique p. 243 and method)
Heaping ⅛ tsp (0.6 g)
water-soluble powdered red
food coloring

VELVET SPRAY
1.75 oz. (50 g) cocoa butter
1.75 oz. (50 g) white chocolate,
finely chopped
2 ½ tsp (0.3 oz./8 g) fat-soluble
powdered red food coloring

CRÉMEUX
3 tbsp (1.75 oz./50 g)
raspberry purée
4 tsp (0.75 oz./20 g)
red bell pepper purée
(see Chefs' Notes)
5.5 oz. (160 g) bittersweet
chocolate, 60% cacao, finely
chopped
2 ¼ tsp (0.25 oz./7 g) sorbitol
powder
2 tsp (0.5 oz./16 g) glucose syrup
3 tbsp (1.5 oz./45 g) butter,
diced, at room temperature

1

BLACK CURRANT MACARONS

Macarons Cassis

Makes 12

Active time
1 ¾ hours

Chilling time
3 hours

Storage
Up to 4 days in the refrigerator

Equipment
Instant-read thermometer
Stick blender
Pastry bag fitted
with a plain ⅓-in. or ½-in.
(8-mm or 10-mm) tip

Ingredients
24 macaron shells
(see technique p. 243 and method)
Heaping ⅛ tsp (0.6 g)
water-soluble powdered purple
food coloring

CANDIED BLACK CURRANT FILLING
¾ cup (7 oz./200 g)
black currant purée
3 tbsp plus 1 tsp (50 ml)
pear juice
½ cup minus 1 tbsp
(2.75 oz./80 g) superfine sugar
1 ¼ tsp (0.2 oz./5 g)
pectin NH

MAKING THE MACARON SHELLS
Prepare the macaron shells (see technique p. 243), adding the purple food coloring at step 3.

MAKING THE CANDIED BLACK CURRANT FILLING
Heat the black currant purée and pear juice in a saucepan over low heat to 113°F (45°C). Mix the sugar and pectin together and gradually whisk into the purée. Bring the mixture to a boil, whisking all the time, and cook for a few minutes until the purée thickens. Line a baking sheet with plastic wrap, spread the purée over it and press another piece of plastic wrap over the surface. Refrigerate for 1 hour.

ASSEMBLING THE MACARONS
Blend the candied black currant filling with the stick blender until smooth. Spoon it into the pastry bag, pipe it over the flat side of half the shells, and lightly press the others on top so the filling reaches the edges. Chill for at least 2 hours before serving.

VIOLET MACARONS

Macarons à la Violette

MAKING THE MACARON SHELLS
Prepare the macaron shells (see technique p. 243), adding the purple food coloring at step 3.

MAKING THE VIOLET GANACHE
Heat the cream in a saucepan to 95°F (35°C) over medium heat. Meanwhile, melt the white chocolate in a bowl over a pan of hot water to 95°F (35°C). Stir the cream into the melted chocolate using a spatula, add the violet extract, and stir in. Line a baking sheet with plastic wrap, spread the ganache over it, and press another piece of plastic wrap over the surface. Refrigerate for 1 hour.

ASSEMBLING THE MACARONS
Spoon the violet ganache into the pastry bag, pipe it over the flat side of the half shells, and lightly press the others on top so the filling reaches the edges. Chill for at least 2 hours before serving.

Makes 12

Active time
1 ¾ hours

Chilling time
3 hours

Storage
Up to 4 days in the refrigerator

Equipment
Instant-read thermometer
Pastry bag fitted
with a plain ⅓-in. or ½-in.
(8-mm or 10-mm) tip

Ingredients
24 macaron shells
(see technique p. 243 and method)
¼ tsp (0.8 g) water-soluble
powdered purple food coloring

VIOLET GANACHE
½ cup minus 2 tsp (115 ml)
whipping cream, 35% butterfat
4 oz. (115 g) white chocolate,
finely chopped
4 drops of natural violet extract

BLUEBERRY MACARONS

Macarons Myrtille

Makes 12

Active time
2 hours

Chilling time
3 hours

Storage
Up to 4 days in the refrigerator

Equipment
Instant-read thermometer
Stick blender
Pastry bag fitted
with a plain ⅓-in. or ½-in.
(8-mm or 10-mm) tip

Ingredients
24 macaron shells
(see technique p. 243 and method)
Heaping ⅛ tsp (0.6 g) water-
soluble powdered blue food
coloring

CANDIED BLUEBERRY FILLING
¾ cup (7 oz./200 g)
blueberry purée
4 tsp (0.5 oz./15 g)
superfine sugar
1 tsp (4 g) pectin NH

MAKING THE MACARON SHELLS
Prepare the macaron shells (see technique p. 243), adding
the blue food coloring at step 3.

MAKING THE CANDIED BLUEBERRY FILLING
Heat the blueberry purée to 113°F (45°C) in a saucepan
over low heat. Mix the sugar and pectin together and
gradually whisk into the purée. Bring the mixture to a
boil, whisking all the time, and cook for a few minutes
until the purée thickens. Line a baking sheet with plastic wrap, spread the purée over it, and press another
piece of plastic wrap over the surface. Refrigerate for
at least 1 hour.

ASSEMBLING THE MACARONS
Transfer the blueberry filling to a bowl and blend until
smooth. Spoon the filling into the pastry bag, pipe it
over the flat side of half the shells, and lightly press the
others on top so the filling reaches the edges. Chill for
at least 2 hours before serving.

CHEFS' NOTES

You can replace the candied blueberry filling
with set blueberry or blackberry jam.

ALMOND AND BLACKBERRY MACARONS

Macarons Mûre-Amande

MAKING THE MACARON SHELLS

Prepare the macaron shells (see technique p. 243), adding the blue food coloring at step 3.

MAKING THE BLACKBERRY ALMOND FILLING

Heat the blackberry purée and lemon juice in a saucepan over a low heat to 113°F (45°C). Meanwhile, melt the cocoa butter in a bowl over a saucepan of hot water to 113°F–122°F (45°C–50°C). Using the hand beater, beat the almond paste in a large bowl until smooth and then gradually whisk in the hot blackberry purée to make a paste. Gradually pour in the melted cocoa butter, mixing until smooth. Chill for 2–3 hours. Remove the filling from the refrigerator and whisk until it is light and has a pipe-able texture.

ASSEMBLING THE MACARONS

Spoon the filling into the pastry bag, pipe it over the flat side of half the shells, and lightly press the others on top so the filling reaches the edges. Allow the macarons to stand at room temperature (60°F–70°F/15°C–20°C) for 24 hours, so the flavors have time to develop.

CHEFS' NOTES

• Choose a good-quality almond paste with a high percentage of almonds as it will contain less sugar and have a stronger almond flavor.

• Warm the almond paste briefly so it softens and is easier to mix with the other ingredients.

Makes 12

Active time
2 hours

Chilling time
3 hours

Resting time
24 hours

Storage
Up to 4 days in the refrigerator

Equipment
Instant-read thermometer
Electric hand beater
Pastry bag fitted
with a plain ⅓-in. or ½-in.
(8-mm or 10-mm) tip

Ingredients
24 macaron shells
(see technique p. 243 and method)
¼ tsp (0.8 g) water-soluble
powdered blue food coloring

BLACKBERRY ALMOND FILLING
2 ½ tbsp (1.5 oz./40 g)
blackberry purée
1 tsp (5 ml) lemon juice
1 oz. (25 g) cocoa butter
9 oz. (250 g) almond paste,
55% almonds

PISTACHIO MACARONS

Macarons Pistache

Makes 12

Active time
1 ¾ hours

Chilling time
3 hours

Storage
Up to 4 days in the refrigerator

Equipment
Instant-read thermometer
Stick blender
Pastry bag fitted
with a plain ⅓-in. or ½-in.
(8-mm or 10-mm) tip

Ingredients
24 macaron shells
(see technique p. 243 and method)
Heaping ⅛ tsp (0.6 g)
water-soluble powdered pistachio
green food coloring

PISTACHIO GANACHE
½ cup minus 2 tsp (115 ml)
whipping cream, 35% butterfat
Heaping 1 tbsp (0.75 oz./20 g)
pistachio paste
4 oz. (115 g) white chocolate,
finely chopped

MAKING THE MACARON SHELLS
Prepare the macaron shells (see technique p. 243), adding the green food coloring at step 3.

MAKING THE PISTACHIO GANACHE
Heat the cream and pistachio paste in a saucepan over medium heat to 95°F (35°C), stirring frequently. Meanwhile, melt the white chocolate in a bowl over a pan of hot water to 95°F (35°C). Pour the pistachio cream over the melted chocolate and stir it in using a spatula to make a smooth ganache. Line a baking sheet with plastic wrap, spread the ganache over it, and press another piece of plastic wrap over the surface. Refrigerate until completely cooled.

ASSEMBLING THE MACARONS
Transfer the pistachio ganache to a bowl and blend until smooth. Spoon into the pastry bag, pipe it over the flat side of half the shells, and lightly press the others on top so the filling reaches the edges. Chill for at least 2 hours before serving.

CHEFS' NOTES

As orange blossom water pairs well with pistachio, a few drops can be added to the ganache to enhance the flavor of the macarons.

BLACKBERRY AND AVOCADO MACARONS

Macarons Avocat-Mûre

MAKING THE MACARON SHELLS
Prepare the macaron shells (see technique p. 243), adding the pistachio food coloring at step 3.

MAKING THE EMERALD TOPPING
Put the cocoa butter and white chocolate in separate bowls, set the bowls over pans of hot water, and melt both to 95°F (35°C). Mix the two together. Add the food coloring little by little until you get the shade you require. Beat with the stick blender until smooth. When the baked macaron shells have cooled, dip the tops of half the shells in the emerald topping.

MAKING THE AVOCADO CREAM
Bring the milk to a boil in a saucepan over medium heat. Add the avocado flesh and lemon juice and mix until evenly blended. In another bowl, whisk the egg yolk and custard powder with the electric beater until pale and thickened. Slowly pour the warm milk and avocado mixture into the egg yolk, whisking constantly. Return to the saucepan and bring to a boil over medium heat, whisking constantly. When the temperature reaches 95°F–104°F (35°C–40°C), remove from the heat and stir in the butter. Blend until smooth. Line a baking sheet with plastic wrap, spread the cream over it, and press another piece of plastic wrap over the surface. Chill for at least 1 hour.

MAKING THE BLACKBERRY JELLY
Heat the blackberry purée in a saucepan over low heat to 113°F (45°C). Mix the sugar and pectin together and whisk gradually into the purée. Bring to a boil, whisking constantly, and cook for a few minutes until the purée thickens. To cool the jelly, line a baking sheet with plastic wrap, spread the jelly over it and press another piece of plastic wrap over the surface. Chill for at least 1 hour.

ASSEMBLING THE MACARONS
Transfer the blackberry jelly to a bowl and beat it with the stick blender until smooth. Spoon it into the pastry bag with the ⅓-in. or ½-in. (8-mm or 10-mm) tip. Spoon the avocado cream into the pastry bag with the ¼-in. (6-mm) tip. Pipe a ring of avocado cream around the edge of the flat side of half the shells, leaving a narrow border between the ring and the edge. Fill the centers with blackberry jelly and lightly press the remaining shells on top so the filling reaches the edges. Chill for at least 2 hours before serving.

Makes 12

Active time
2 hours

Chilling time
4 hours

Storage
Up to 4 days in the refrigerator

Equipment
Instant-read thermometer
Stick blender
Electric hand beater
Pastry bag fitted
with a plain ⅓-in. or ½-in.
(8-mm or 10-mm) tip
Pastry bag fitted
with a ¼-in. (6-mm) tip

Ingredients
24 macaron shells
(see technique p. 243 and method)
Heaping ⅛ tsp (0.6 g)
water-soluble powdered pistachio
green food coloring

EMERALD TOPPING
1.75 oz. (50 g) cocoa butter
1.75 oz. (50 g) white chocolate,
finely chopped
2 ½ tsp (8 g) fat-soluble
powdered green food coloring

AVOCADO CREAM
2 tbsp (30 ml) milk
3.75 oz. (110 g) avocado flesh
1 tsp (5 ml) lemon juice
1 tbsp (0.75 oz./20 g)
egg yolk (about 1 yolk)
1 tsp (3 g) custard powder
5 tbsp (2.75 oz./75 g) butter,
diced

BLACKBERRY JELLY
6 tbsp (3.5 oz./100 g)
blackberry purée
2 tsp (0.3 oz./8 g)
superfine sugar
½ tsp (2 g) pectin NH

LEMON MACARONS

Macarons Citron

Makes 12

Active time
1 ¾ hours

Infusing time
20 minutes or longer

Chilling time
3 hours

Storage
Up to 4 days in the refrigerator

Equipment
Instant-read thermometer
Stick blender
Pastry bag fitted
with a plain ⅓-in. or ½-in.
(8-mm or 10-mm) tip

Ingredients
24 macaron shells
(see technique p. 243 and method)
Heaping ⅛ tsp (0.6 g)
water-soluble powdered yellow
food coloring

LEMON CREAM
¼ cup (60 ml) whipping cream,
35% butterfat
Strips of zest from 1 lemon
4 tsp (20 ml) water
5 tsp (25 ml) lemon juice
Scant ¼ cup (1.5 oz./40 g)
superfine sugar
⅓ cup (2.75 oz./75 g) lightly
beaten egg (about 1 ½ eggs)
1 sheet (2 g) gelatin

MAKING THE MACARON SHELLS
Prepare the macaron shells (see technique p. 243), adding
the yellow food coloring at step 3.

MAKING THE LEMON CREAM
Heat the cream with the lemon zest in a saucepan.
Remove from the heat and let infuse. In another saucepan, heat the water and lemon juice and bring just to
a boil. Meanwhile, whisk the sugar and eggs in a bowl
until pale and thick. Slowly pour the hot lemon juice
and water over the mixture, whisking constantly, and
then strain in the lemon-infused cream to remove the
zest, whisking all the time. Soak the gelatin in a bowl of
cold water. Pour the cream mixture into a saucepan and
heat to 181°F (83°C). Remove from the heat, squeeze
excess water from the gelatin, and stir in until dissolved.
To cool the cream, line a baking sheet with plastic wrap,
spread the cream over it, and press another piece of
plastic wrap over the surface. Chill for at least 1 hour
before using.

CHEFS' NOTES

• Infuse the lemon zest in the cream
for at least 20 minutes while the cream cools,
for an enhanced aromatic flavor.

• Try replacing the lemon with lime,
bergamot orange, or other citrus fruits.

ASSEMBLING THE MACARONS
Transfer the lemon cream to a bowl and blend with the
stick blender until smooth. Spoon into the pastry bag,
pipe it over the flat side of half the shells, and lightly
press the other shells on top so the filling reaches the
edges. Chill for at least 2 hours before serving.

TEA AND HONEY MACARONS

Macarons Thé au Miel

MAKING THE MACARON SHELLS

Prepare the macaron shells (see technique p. 243), adding the yellow food coloring at step 3. Before baking the shells, sprinkle them with loose Earl Grey tea.

MAKING THE WHITE TEA INFUSION

Heat the cream in a saucepan over low heat. Remove from the heat and add the white tea. Once the cream has cooled, allow it to infuse in the refrigerator for 24 hours. The next day, heat the infused cream in a saucepan over medium heat to 122°F (50°C). Strain through a fine-mesh strainer and top up with extra cream to ⅔ cup (150 ml), as the tea will have absorbed some of the cream.

MAKING THE TEA AND HONEY GANACHE

Put the cocoa butter and white chocolate in separate bowls and set each over a pan of hot water. Melt both to 95°F (35°C) and then mix them together. In another saucepan, combine the honey and infused cream and heat them together, before pouring onto the chocolate and cocoa butter, mixing with a spatula to make a glossy ganache. Cool the ganache to 95°F (35°C),

CHEFS' NOTES

It is best to avoid making the ganache with black tea, as it will impart a smoky flavor—unless that's what you want! Earl Grey tea remains top choice.

add the butter, and blend until smooth. Line a baking sheet with plastic wrap, spread the ganache over it, and press another piece of plastic wrap over the surface. Chill for at least 1 hour.

ASSEMBLING THE MACARONS

Spoon the ganache into the pastry bag, pipe it over the flat side of half the shells, and lightly press the remaining shells on top so the filling reaches the edges. Chill for several hours, ideally 24, before serving.

Makes 12

Active time
2 hours

Infusing time
24 hours

Chilling time
3 hours

Resting time
24 hours

Storage
Up to 4 days in the refrigerator

Equipment
Instant-read thermometer
Stick blender
Pastry bag fitted
with a plain ⅓-in. or ½-in.
(8-mm or 10-mm) tip

Ingredients
24 macaron shells
(see technique p. 243 and method)
Heaping ⅛ tsp (0.6 g)
water-soluble powdered yellow
food coloring
Loose Earl Grey tea, for sprinkling

WHITE TEA INFUSION
⅔ cup (150 ml) whipping cream,
35% butterfat, plus a little extra
0.35 oz. (10 g) loose white tea

TEA AND HONEY GANACHE
1 oz. (25 g) cocoa butter
8.5 oz. (340 g) white chocolate,
finely chopped
3 ½ tsp (1 oz./25 g) honey
⅔ cup (150 ml) white tea infusion
(see ingredients above)
6 tbsp (3 oz./85 g) butter, diced,
at room temperature

LEVEL

SALTED CARAMEL MACARONS

Macarons Caramel Beurre Salé

Makes 12

Active time
1 ¾ hours

Chilling time
3 hours

Storage
Up to 4 days in the refrigerator

Equipment
Instant-read thermometer
Stick blender
Pastry bag fitted
with a plain ⅓-in. or ½-in.
(8-mm or 10-mm) tip

Ingredients
24 macaron shells
(see technique p. 243 and method)
Heaping ⅛ tsp (0.6 g)
water-soluble powdered brown
food coloring

SALTED BUTTER CARAMEL
¼ cup (1.75 oz./50 g)
superfine sugar
5 ½ tsp (1.5 oz./40 g)
glucose syrup
Scant ¼ cup (55 ml) whipping
cream, 35% butterfat
2 tbsp (1 oz./28 g) evaporated milk
5 tbsp (2.75 oz./75 g) butter,
diced, at room temperature
1 pinch (0.02 oz./0.5 g) fleur de sel

MAKING THE MACARON SHELLS
Prepare the macaron shells (see technique p. 243), adding
the brown food coloring at step 3.

MAKING THE SALTED CARAMEL
Heat the sugar and glucose syrup in a saucepan over
medium heat until the sugar dissolves and the syrup has
caramelized. Remove the pan from the heat. In another
saucepan, bring the cream and evaporated milk to a boil
and very carefully pour it into the caramelized syrup,
stirring until combined. Weigh the caramel and mix in
enough cold water so the total weight is 5 oz. (140 g).
Cool the caramel to 95°F–104°F (35°C–40°C), add
the butter and the fleur de sel, and blend with the stick
blender until smooth. Line a baking sheet with plastic
wrap, spread the caramel over it, and press another
piece of plastic wrap over the surface. Refrigerate for
at least 1 hour.

ASSEMBLING THE MACARONS
Spoon the salted caramel into the pastry bag, pipe it
over the flat side of half the shells, and lightly press the
remaining shells on top so the filling reaches the edges.
Chill for at least 2 hours before serving.

CHEFS' NOTES

• It is best to make these macarons a day ahead
and store them at room temperature.

• Boil the syrup a little longer for a richer
caramel flavor and deeper color, but avoid cooking
for too long or the caramel will turn bitter.

• The butter must be added at 95°F–104°F
(35°C–40°C) to ensure it remains stable
in the prepared mixture.

SALTED CARAMEL, MACADAMIA, AND BANANA MACARONS

Macarons Caramel, Noix de Macadamia & Banane

MAKING THE MACARON SHELLS
Prepare the macaron shells (see technique p. 243), adding the brown food coloring at step 3.

FOR THE MARBLING
Put the white chocolate and milk chocolate in separate bowls and stand each over a pan of hot water. Melt the white chocolate to 95°F (35°C) and the milk chocolate to 104°F (40°C). Pour a little milk chocolate into the white chocolate and with the tip of a knife stir just enough to marble the two together. Once the shells have cooled, dip the top of half of them into the marbled chocolate, rotating to create a spiral design.

MAKING THE SALTED CARAMEL
Heat the sugar and glucose syrup in a saucepan over medium heat until the sugar dissolves and the syrup is caramelized. Remove the pan from the heat. In another saucepan, bring the cream and evaporated milk to a boil and carefully pour into the caramel, stirring until blended. Weigh the caramel and mix in enough water to make the total weight 5 oz. (140 g). When the caramel has cooled to 95°F–104°F (35°C–40°C), add the butter and the fleur de sel. Beat with the stick blender until smooth. Line a baking sheet with plastic wrap, spread the caramel over it, and press another piece of plastic over the surface. Chill for at least 1 hour.

ROASTING THE MACADAMIAS
Preheat the oven to 325°F (170°C/Gas mark 3). Finely chop the nuts and spread over a baking sheet lined with parchment paper. Roast until golden, checking frequently as they will burn quickly. Let cool.

MAKING THE BANANA CRÉMEUX
Soak the gelatin in a bowl of cold water. In a saucepan, bring half the banana purée to a boil, stirring frequently. In another bowl, whisk the egg yolk, egg, and sugar together until pale and thickened. Whisk in the remaining banana purée and a little of the hot purée to loosen the mixture. Pour into the saucepan with the hot purée and whisk to blend. Stirring constantly, heat the mixture to 180°F (82°C). Squeeze excess water from the gelatin and stir into the hot crémeux until dissolved. Cool it to 95°F–104°F (35°C–40°C), add the butter, and blend until smooth. Cover the surface of the crémeux with plastic wrap and chill for at least 1 hour.

ASSEMBLING THE MACARONS
Spoon the crémeux into the pastry bag and pipe a ring around the edge of the flat side of half the shells, leaving a narrow border. Fill the centers of the rings with chopped nuts and salted caramel and lightly press the remaining shells on top so the filling reaches the edges. Chill for at least 2 hours before serving.

Makes 12

Active time
1 ¾ hours

Chilling time
4 hours

Storage
Up to 4 days in the refrigerator

Equipment
Instant-read thermometer
Stick blender
Pastry bag fitted
with a plain ¼-in. (6-mm) tip

Ingredients
24 macaron shells
(see technique p. 243 and method)
¼ tsp (0.8 g) water-soluble
powdered brown food coloring

MARBLING
White chocolate
Milk chocolate

SALTED CARAMEL
¼ cup (1.75 oz./50 g)
superfine sugar
5 ½ tsp (1.5 oz./40 g)
glucose syrup
Scant ¼ cup (55 ml) whipping
cream, 35% butterfat
2 tbsp (1 oz./28 g) evaporated milk
5 tbsp (2.75 oz./75 g) butter,
diced, at room temperature
0.02 oz. (0.5 g) fleur de sel

ROASTED MACADAMIA NIBS
2 oz. (60 g) macadamia nuts

BANANA CRÉMEUX
1 sheet (2 g) gelatin
6 tbsp (3.5 oz./100 g)
banana purée, divided
Scant 2 tbsp (1 oz./30 g) egg yolk
(about 1 ½ yolks)
Scant ¼ cup (1.75 oz./50 g)
lightly beaten egg (about 1 egg)
2 ½ tbsp (1 oz./30 g) sugar
4 tbsp (2 oz./60 g) butter

MILK CHOCOLATE MACARONS

Macarons Chocolat au Lait

Makes 12

Active time
1 ¾ hours

Chilling time
3 hours

Storage
Up to 4 days in the refrigerator

Equipment
Instant-read thermometer
Pastry bag fitted
with a plain ⅓-in. or ½-in.
(8-mm or 10-mm) tip

Ingredients
24 macaron shells
(see technique p. 243 and method)
Heaping ⅛ tsp (0.6 g)
water-soluble powdered brown
food coloring

Feuilletine flakes
(or use crushed wafers)
for sprinkling

MILK CHOCOLATE GANACHE
6 tbsp (90 ml) whipping cream,
35% butterfat
2 tsp (0.5 oz./15 g) glucose syrup
5 oz. (140 g) milk couverture
chocolate, 35% cacao,
finely chopped

MAKING THE MACARON SHELLS
Prepare the macaron shells (see technique p. 243), adding the brown food coloring at step 3. Before baking, sprinkle the tops with crushed *feuilletine* flakes.

MAKING THE MILK CHOCOLATE GANACHE
Heat the cream and glucose syrup in a saucepan over medium heat until the temperature reaches 95°F (35°C). Meanwhile, melt the milk chocolate in a bowl over a pan of hot water to 95°F (35°C). Pour the hot cream over the melted chocolate, stirring with a spatula to make a smooth ganache. Line a baking sheet with plastic wrap, spread the ganache over it, and press another piece of plastic wrap over the surface. Chill for at least 1 hour.

ASSEMBLING THE MACARONS
Spoon the ganache into the pastry bag, pipe it over the flat side of half the shells, and lightly press the remaining shells on top so the filling reaches the edges. Chill for at least 2 hours before serving.

CHESTNUT AND MANDARIN MACARONS

Macarons Marron-Mandarine

MAKING THE MACARON SHELLS

Prepare the macaron shells (see technique p. 243), adding the brown food coloring at step 3.

MAKING THE CHESTNUT CREAM

Bring the milk to a boil in a saucepan over medium heat and then stir in the chestnut spread. Whisk the egg yolk and custard powder using the electric beater until pale and thick. Pour the warm milk mixture over the egg yolk mixture, whisking continuously, then return it to the saucepan and heat to 95°F–104°F (35°C–40°C), stirring constantly. Remove from the heat and stir in the butter until smooth. To cool the cream, line a baking sheet with plastic wrap, spread it over the sheet, and press another piece of plastic wrap over the surface. Chill for at least 1 hour.

MAKING THE CANDIED MANDARIN FILLING

Heat the mandarin purée in a saucepan to 113°F (45°C) over low heat. Mix the sugar and pectin together and gradually whisk into the purée. Bring to a boil, whisking all the time, and cook for a few minutes, until the purée thickens. Line a baking sheet with plastic wrap, spread the filling over it, and press another piece of plastic wrap over the surface. Chill for at least 1 hour.

MAKING THE CHOCOLATE DISKS

Temper the milk chocolate (see techniques pp. 570 and 572). Lay the stencil on the baking mat. When the tempered chocolate has cooled to 86°F (30°C), pour it over the stencil to fill the circles. Remove excess chocolate with a spatula and allow the disks to set for 5 minutes.

ASSEMBLING THE MACARONS

Blend the mandarin filling with the stick blender until smooth and spoon into the pastry bag with the ⅓-in. or ½-in. (8-mm or 10-mm) tip. Spoon the chestnut cream into the pastry bag with the ¼-in. (6-mm) tip. Pipe a ring of chestnut cream around the edge of the flat side of half the shells, leaving a narrow border. Fill the centers of the rings with the mandarin filling. Lightly press the remaining shells on top so the filling reaches the edges. Decorate each macaron with a chocolate disk, using a little melted chocolate to hold the disk in place. Chill for at least 2 hours before serving.

CHEFS' NOTES

Instead of making chocolate disks, dip the tops of the macarons in the tempered milk chocolate.

Makes 12

Active time
2 hours 20 minutes

Setting time
5 minutes

Chilling time
3 hours

Storage
Up to 4 days in the refrigerator

Equipment
Electric hand beater
Instant-read thermometer
Silicone baking mat
2 pastry bags fitted
with plain ⅓-in. or ½-in. (8-mm or 10-mm) and ¼-in. (6-mm) tips

Chablon stencil mat
with 1 ½-in. (4-cm) diameter circles, for the chocolate disks

Stick blender

Ingredients
24 macaron shells
(see technique p. 243 and method)
Heaping ⅛ tsp (0.6 g) water-soluble powdered brown food coloring

CHESTNUT CREAM
2 tbsp (30 ml) milk
3.75 oz. (110 g) chestnut spread (*crème de marrons*)
1 tbsp (0.75 oz./20 g) egg yolk (about 1 yolk)
1 tsp (3 g) custard powder
5 tbsp (2.75 oz./75 g) butter, diced, at room temperature

CANDIED MANDARIN FILLING
6 tbsp (3.5 oz./100 g) mandarin purée
2 tsp (0.3 oz./8 g) superfine sugar
½ tsp (2 g) pectin NH

CHOCOLATE DISKS
9 oz. (250 g) milk couverture chocolate, finely chopped

BITTERSWEET CHOCOLATE MACARONS

Macarons Chocolat Noir

Makes 12

Active time
2 hours 10 minutes

Setting time
5 minutes

Chilling time
3 hours

Storage
Up to 4 days in the refrigerator

Equipment
Instand-read thermometer
Chablon stencil mat
with 1 ½-in. (4-cm) diameter
circles, for the chocolate disks

Silicone baking mat
Pastry bag fitted
with a plain ⅓-in. or ½-in.
(8-mm or 10-mm) tip

Ingredients
24 macaron shells
(see technique p. 243 and method)
Heaping ⅛ tsp (0.6 g)
water-soluble powdered brown
food coloring

BITTERSWEET CHOCOLATE GANACHE
½ cup minus 2 tsp (115 ml)
whipping cream, 35% butterfat
1 ¾ tsp (0.5 oz./12 g) honey
4 oz. (115 g) bittersweet
couverture chocolate,
65% cacao, finely chopped

CHOCOLATE DISKS
9 oz. (250 g) bittersweet
couverture chocolate,
65% cacao, finely chopped

MAKING THE MACARON SHELLS
Prepare the macaron shells (see technique p. 243), adding the brown food coloring at step 3.

MAKING THE BITTERSWEET CHOCOLATE GANACHE
Heat the cream and honey in a saucepan until the temperature reaches 95°F (35°C). Meanwhile, melt the bittersweet chocolate in a bowl over a pan of hot water to 95°F (35°C). Pour the cream over the melted chocolate and stir gently with a spatula to make a smooth ganache. Line a baking sheet with plastic wrap, spread the ganache over it, and press another piece of plastic wrap over the surface. Chill for 30–40 minutes.

MAKING THE CHOCOLATE DISKS
Temper the bittersweet chocolate (see techniques pp. 570 and 572). Lay the stencil on the baking mat. Once the tempered chocolate cools to 86°F (30°C), pour it over the stencil so it fills the circles. Remove excess chocolate with a spatula and allow the disks to set for 5 minutes.

ASSEMBLING THE MACARONS
Spoon the ganache into the pastry bag, pipe it over the flat side of half the shells, and lightly press the remaining shells on top so the filling reaches the edges. Decorate each macaron with a chocolate disk, fixing it in place with a little melted chocolate. Chill for at least 2 hours before serving.

CHOCOLATE AND PEACH PRALINE MACARONS

Macarons Praliné, Pêche & Chocolat

MAKING THE MACARON SHELLS

Prepare the macaron shells (see technique p. 243), adding the brown food coloring at step 3.

MAKING THE CANDIED PEACH FILLING

Heat the peach purée in a saucepan over low heat to 113°F (45°C). Mix the sugar and pectin together and gradually whisk into the purée. Bring to a boil, whisking constantly, and cook for a few minutes, until the purée thickens. Line a baking sheet with plastic wrap, spread the purée over it, and press another piece of plastic wrap over the surface. Chill for 1 hour.

MAKING THE CHOCOLATE PRALINE GANACHE

Heat the cream and praline paste in a saucepan over medium heat until the temperature reaches 95°F (35°C), stirring occasionally. Meanwhile, melt the white chocolate in a bowl over a pan of hot water to 95°F (35°C). Pour the praline cream over the melted chocolate and stir gently with a spatula to make a smooth ganache. Line a baking sheet with plastic wrap, spread the ganache over it, and press another piece of plastic wrap over the surface. Chill for at least 1 hour.

ASSEMBLING THE MACARONS

Fill the pastry bag with the chocolate praline ganache and pipe a ring of ganache around the edge of the flat side of half the shells, leaving a slight border between the ring and the edge. Fill the centers of the rings with the candied peach filling. Lightly press the remaining shells on top so the filling reaches the edges and dust the tops with cocoa powder, using a sifter. Chill for at least 2 hours before serving.

Makes 12

Active time
1 ¾ hours

Chilling time
3 hours

Storage
Up to 4 days in the refrigerator

Equipment
Instant-read thermometer
Stick blender
Pastry bag fitted
with a plain ⅓-in. or ½-in.
(8-mm or 10-mm) tip

Ingredients
24 macaron shells
(see technique p. 243 and method)
¼ tsp (0.8 g) water-soluble
powdered brown food coloring

CANDIED PEACH FILLING
¾ cup (7 oz./200 g)
peach purée

4 tsp (0.5 oz./15 g)
superfine sugar

1 tsp (4 g) pectin NH

CHOCOLATE PRALINE GANACHE
½ cup minus 2 tsp (115 ml)
whipping cream, 35% butterfat

1.5 oz. (40 g) praline paste
3.5 oz. (100 g) white chocolate,
finely chopped

Cocoa powder for dusting

267

BLACK LICORICE MACARONS

Macarons Réglisse

Makes 12

Active time
1 ¾ hours

Chilling time
3 hours

Storage
Up to 4 days in the refrigerator

Equipment
Small paintbrush
Instant-read thermometer
Pastry bag fitted
with a plain ⅓-in. or ½-in.
(8-mm or 10-mm) tip

Ingredients
24 macaron shells
(see technique p. 243 and method)
Heaping ⅛ tsp (0.6 g)
water-soluble powdered
black food coloring

DECORATION
Scant ½ cup (100 ml) kirsch
Heaping ⅛ tsp (0.6 g)
water-soluble powdered
black food coloring

LICORICE CRÉMEUX
Scant ½ cup (100 ml) whipping
cream, 35% butterfat
0.75 oz. (20 g) black licorice paste
4 oz. (115 g) white chocolate,
finely chopped

MAKING AND DECORATING THE MACARON SHELLS
Prepare the macaron shells (see technique p. 243), adding the black food coloring at step 3. For the decoration, mix the kirsch with the black food coloring and, when the shells are baked and cooled, use a paintbrush to mark a stripe of kirsch over the tops.

MAKING THE LICORICE CRÉMEUX
Heat the cream and licorice paste in a saucepan over medium heat until the temperature reaches 95°F (35°C). Meanwhile, melt the white chocolate in a bowl over a pan of hot water to 95°F (35°C). Pour the licorice cream over the melted chocolate and gently stir with a spatula until well blended. Cover the surface of the crémeux with plastic wrap and refrigerate until it is firm enough to be piped.

ASSEMBLING THE MACARONS
Spoon the crémeux into the pastry bag, pipe it over the flat side of half the shells, and lightly press the remaining shells on top so the filling reaches the edges. Chill for at least 2 hours before serving.

CHEFS' NOTES

Licorice powder can be used
instead of licorice paste, if you prefer.

BLACK TRUFFLE MACARONS

Macarons Truffe Noire

MAKING AND SPRAYING THE MACARON SHELLS
Prepare the macaron shells (see technique p. 243), adding the black food coloring at step 3. For the spray, dilute the food coloring in the kirsch and spoon into the spray gun. Once the shells are baked and cooled, spray the tops for a velvet-like sheen.

MAKING THE TRUFFLE CHANTILLY CREAM
Mince the truffle and add to the cream. Cover, chill, and allow to infuse, preferably overnight, and then strain through a fine-mesh strainer, reserving the chopped truffle. Soften the mascarpone by stirring in a little of the infused cream (reserve the rest for another use). Whisk with the electric beater until soft peaks form. Add the truffle and mix gently using a spatula so as not to deflate the mixture.

ASSEMBLING THE MACARONS
Spoon the truffle cream into the pastry bag, pipe it over the flat side of half the shells, and lightly press the remaining shells on top so the filling reaches the edges. Chill for at least 2 hours before serving, topping each macaron with a little edible gold leaf.

CHEFS' NOTES

• You can add a little truffle oil to the cream for a more intense truffle flavor.

• Try putting the eggs to make the macaron shells in an airtight container with the truffle a week ahead, so the truffle can impart its flavor to the eggs!

Makes 12

Active time
1 ¾ hours

Infusing time
20 minutes–12 hours
(overnight)

Chilling time
2 hours

Storage
Up to 4 days in the refrigerator

Equipment
Spray gun
Electric hand beater
Pastry bag fitted
with a plain ⅓-in. or ½-in.
(8-mm or 10-mm) tip

Ingredients
24 macaron shells
(see technique p. 243 and method)
Heaping ⅛ tsp (0.6 g)
water-soluble powdered black
food coloring

SPRAY
Scant ¼ cup (55 ml) water-soluble
liquid black food coloring
2 tsp (10 ml) kirsch

TRUFFLE CHANTILLY CREAM
0.35 oz. (10 g) fresh black truffle
Scant ½ cup (100 ml) whipping
cream, 35% butterfat
1 oz. (30 g) mascarpone

Edible gold leaf

SIMPLE CAKES
& DESSERTS

EVERYDAY CAKES, PETIT FOUR COOKIES, AND SIMPLE DESSERTS

Providing a tasty quick snack or enjoyed at the end of a family meal, these cakes and desserts are simple to make but still require as much care and attention to detail to ensure success every time.

EVERYDAY CAKES AND SIMPLE DESSERTS

CAKES ON THE MOVE

Elaborate cakes containing cream are not just difficult to transport, but they also have to be kept chilled, which is why French chefs created gâteaux de voyage: literally, cakes for traveling. Most of these plainer cakes can be kept at room temperature and carried easily from one place to another. One of the earliest was the financier, created in 1890 by the pastry chef Lasne, but there are many others such as madeleines, spiced loaf, marble cake, and pound cake.

EGGS AT ROOM TEMPERATURE

It can't be said often enough: cakes and pastries cannot be made with eggs straight from the refrigerator! So, get into the routine of taking your eggs out of the refrigerator at least 2 hours before you need them. When making everyday cakes, eggs at room temperature can be beaten in perfectly, without firming up the butter or making the batter curdle. For mousses and other simple desserts that contain egg whites, the whites will whisk up more easily and the sugar will dissolve better.

WELL BEATEN

For light, well-risen cakes, beating the butter and sugar together correctly is essential. This incorporates air bubbles, which are produced as the butter rubs against the sugar crystals, aerating the batter. Beat for 3–4 minutes to reach the right consistency, keeping the ingredients in contact with the whisk all the time and regularly stopping and scraping down the sides of the bowl with a spatula to ensure the batter remains smooth.

WHY SIFT?

Sifting dry ingredients together distributes the raising agent evenly throughout the flour so both can be incorporated without overworking the dough or batter. This limits the development of the gluten and air bubbles remain in the batter, which is important for ensuring soft cakes.

STRAIGHT INTO THE OVEN

Cake batters that contain baking powder must be baked immediately, as the raising agent begins to act and produce carbon dioxide as soon as it is added. For maximum rise, bake your cakes as soon as you've made the batter.

AN EVEN BAKE

Carefully buttering the cake pan is important, but it's even better if done with clarified butter. There is no danger of this burning and the sides of your cake will color evenly without darkening too much.

A HINT OF HAZELNUT

Some recipes, such as financiers and madeleines, are made with melted butter, but for added flavor, continue cooking the melted butter until it turns golden brown—*beurre noisette* (hazelnut butter) in French. Strain the butter, add it according to your recipe, and it will give the cake a lovely nutty flavor.

WHY USE INVERT SUGAR?

Invert sugar keeps cakes moist and extends their storage time. It's sufficient to simply replace a small amount of the sugar with invert sugar. Honey and maple syrup also make cakes softer, moister, and less likely to dry out.

WELL RISEN

For an even rise and a distinctive crack on top, run a well-buttered knife down the center of the cake 10 minutes before the end of the cooking time. Or fill a paper cone with softened butter and pipe it down the cake before it goes into the oven. However, if the ingredients are weighed accurately (be careful not to use too much baking powder!), the cake should rise and crack naturally.

SOFT OR CRISP?

To guarantee a super soft cake, cover it in plastic wrap while it is still hot so the steam stays inside—when you eat the cake it will melt in the mouth. If you prefer a crisp crust, unmold the cake onto a rack and cool completely before wrapping.

STORAGE

Plain cakes, whether large or small, tend to dry out quite quickly, so prolong their storage time by covering them tightly in plastic wrap.

WHAT ABOUT FREEZING?

Uncooked cake batter cannot be frozen. Once baked, on the other hand, cakes can be sliced, carefully wrapped in plastic wrap, and frozen for up to 2 months. Defrost in the refrigerator for 6–8 hours and serve at room temperature.

PETIT FOUR COOKIES (*FOURS SECS*)

WHY USE BAKING POWDER?

Certain crumbly cookies—such as shortbread and chocolate chip—contain baking powder, not to make them rise but to improve their texture. The dough spreads more as it bakes, helping the sugar to caramelize. This results in cookies that are thinner and more golden in color, with a more pronounced caramel flavor.

WHICH SUGAR FOR WHICH TEXTURE?

The type of sugar used affects the texture of a cookie. White sugar melts when baked, but re-crystallizes quickly, making a cookie crisp. In contrast, brown sugars that contain molasses are moist, so a cookie will spread more and have a softer, chewier texture. You can try mixing sugars to experiment with different textures.

CORRECTLY STORED

Moisture is the arch enemy of crisp cookies, as it makes them go soft. To preserve their crispness, store them in an airtight tin, separating the layers with sheets of parchment paper.

READY TO BAKE

Certain cookies, such as chocolate chip and sparkling shortbread, can be frozen before baking. Once the dough has been shaped into a log, cover it tightly in plastic wrap and freeze for up to 2 months. Defrost for 6–8 hours in the refrigerator, before slicing and baking as normal.

WHAT ARE PETITS FOURS?
In the days of wood-burning ovens, once the bread and large cakes had been baked in the initial fierce heat, smaller, more delicate items were baked as the oven cooled down. These were said to have been cooked à petit four—in a small oven—which is the name these little cakes and pastries are still known by. The recipes in this chapter are for small plain cookies, known in French as fours secs.

Financiers

Serves 10

Active time
20 minutes

Chilling time
2 hours

Cooking time
About 20 minutes for 2–3-in.
(4–8-cm) individual cakes

Storage
Up to 2 days in the refrigerator
before piping
Up to 2 days in the refrigerator,
baked and covered
in plastic wrap
Up to 3 months in the freezer

Equipment
Instant-read thermometer
Pastry bag fitted with a plain
½-in. (10-mm) tip
Financier pan

Ingredients
7 tbsp (3.5 oz./100 g) butter
Scant ½ tsp (2 g) salt
2 tbsp plus 1 tsp
(1.75 oz./50 g) honey
¾ cup (5.25 oz./160 g)
egg white (about 5 ½ whites)
½ cup (2.5 oz./70 g)
confectioners' sugar
Finely grated zest of 1 orange
½ cup (1.75 oz./50 g)
almond flour
½ cup minus 1 tbsp
(1.75 oz./50 g) flour

Uses
Individual cakes or as the base
for layered desserts

1• Heat the butter in a saucepan until it browns and has
a nutty aroma (*beurre noisette*). Stir in the salt and strain
through a fine-mesh sieve.

CHEFS' NOTES

• Avoid overbaking the financiers
as they will not keep as long.

• It's not essential to whisk the egg whites
but it gives the financiers a lighter texture.

• Instead of orange zest, the financiers
can be flavored with vanilla extract.

• For pistachio-flavored financiers,
replace half the almond flour with pistachio flour.

• For chocolate-flavored financiers,
replace 1 tbsp (0.25 oz./10 g) of the flour with unsweetened
cocoa powder and sprinkle with small pieces of chocolate.

2 • Stir in the honey to prevent the butter cooking any more. Allow to cool to 95°F–104°F (35°C–40°C).

3 • Whisk the egg whites until frothy and then lightly fold in the confectioners' sugar until combined.

4 • Add the orange zest, almond flour, and flour, followed by the butter, and lightly fold everything together. Chill for 2 hours to make the batter easier to pipe.

5 • Preheat the oven to 425°F (220°C/Gas mark 7). Pipe the batter into the pans and bake for 15 minutes. Reduce the oven to 400°F (200°C/Gas mark 6) and then 375°F (190°C/Gas mark 5) until the financiers are golden around the edges—about 20 minutes in total.

Pound Cake

Quatre-Quarts

Serves 8

Active time
30 minutes

Cooking time
45 minutes–1 hour
(for large cakes)

Storage
Up to 1 week in an airtight
container, well covered
in plastic wrap, or up
to 3 months in the freezer

Equipment
Pastry bag without a tip
2 × 5 ½ × 3-in. (14 × 7.3-cm) loaf
pans, 2 ¾ in. (7 cm) deep
Parchment paper cone
(see technique p. 598)

Ingredients
1 stick plus 2 tbsp
(5.25 oz./150 g) butter,
softened, plus extra for greasing

1 cup (5 oz./140 g)
confectioners' sugar

1 ¾ tsp (0.4 oz./12 g)
invert sugar

⅔ cup (5.25 oz./150 g)
lightly beaten egg
(about 3 eggs),
at room temperature

Scant ½ tsp (2 ml) vanilla extract
1 pinch of salt
1 cup plus 2 tbsp
(5.25 oz./150 g) flour,
plus extra for dusting

1 tsp (4 g) baking powder
Softened butter to pipe
over the unbaked batter

Uses
Large cakes to be sliced
or individual cakes

1 • Preheat the oven to 375°F (190°C/Gas mark 5). Butter the pans
and dust them with flour. In a mixing bowl, whisk together
the butter, sugar, and invert sugar and then add the eggs, vanilla,
and salt, beating until evenly combined.

CHEFS' NOTES

• The piped softened butter helps the cake to rise evenly
and crack on top as it bakes, without having to cut it.

• To ensure the cakes remain moist, unmold them
as soon as they come out of the oven and cover them
with plastic wrap.

3 • Spoon the batter into the pastry bag, snip off the point,
and pipe into the pans, filling them by three-quarters.

2 • Sift in the flour with the baking powder and fold in.

4 • Spoon the softened butter into the paper cone and pipe a line of butter down the center of the batter. Bake for 20 minutes, reduce the oven temperature to 350°F (180°C/Gas mark 4) and bake for an additional 40 minutes.

To test for doneness, insert a cake tester or the tip of a knife into the center of the cake; it should come out clean.

Fruit Loaf Cake

Cake aux Fruits Confits

Serves 4–6

Active time
30 minutes

Cooking time
45 minutes

Storage
Up to 1 week in a dry place,
well covered in plastic wrap,
or up to 3 months in the freezer

Equipment
5 ½ × 3-in. (14 × 7.3-cm) loaf pan,
2 ¾ in. (7 cm) deep
Pastry bag without a tip
Parchment paper cone
(see technique p. 598)

Ingredients
1.75 oz. (50 g) assorted
candied fruit
0.75 oz. (20 g) candied
red cherries
1 tsp (5 ml) rum
0.75 oz. (20 g) raisins
¾ stick (3 oz./85 g) butter,
softened, plus extra for greasing
Scant ½ cup (3 oz./85 g)
superfine sugar
¾ tsp (0.2 oz./5 g) honey
6 tbsp (3 oz./85 g) egg
(about 2 eggs),
at room temperature
¼ tsp (1 g) vanilla extract
¼ tsp (1 g) salt
¾ cup (3.25 oz./95 g) flour,
divided, plus extra for dusting
¾ tsp (3 g) baking powder
Sliced almonds for sprinkling
1 tbsp (15 ml) syrup
½ tsp (2 g) softened butter,
to pipe on the batter

Use for
Large cakes to be sliced
or individual cakes

1 • Preheat the oven to 350°F (180°C/Gas mark 4). Butter
the pan and dust with flour. Drain and rinse the candied fruit
and cherries under running water. Soak them in the rum
and plump the raisins in a little boiling water.

4 • Coat the fruit with 2 tablespoons of the flour. Sift the remaining
flour with the baking powder and add to the batter.

CHEFS' NOTES

Dusting the candied fruits in flour prevents them
sinking to the bottom during baking.

2 • Whisk together the butter, sugar, and honey.
Add the egg, a little at a time, followed by the vanilla and salt.
Mix until all the ingredients form a smooth batter.

3 • Drain the candied fruit and raisins, reserving the rum
to spoon over the baked cake.

5 • Fold in the flour-coated fruit with a spatula.

6 • Arrange sliced almonds evenly around the sides and over
the base of the pan. Spoon the batter into the pastry bag, snip off
the point, and pipe into the pan until it is three-quarters full. ⊕

281

Fruit Loaf Cake (continued)

7 • Fill the paper cone with the softened butter. Mark a line down the center of the loaf and pipe the butter into it so the loaf rises evenly and cracks on top as it bakes.

8 • Sprinkle with more sliced almonds and bake for about 45 minutes. To test for doneness, insert a cake tester or the tip of a knife into the center of the loaf; it should have no batter sticking to it when it comes out.

9 • As soon as the loaf comes out of the oven, brush the syrup and reserved rum over it. Allow to cool on a rack.

Spiced Loaf Cake

Pain d'Épice

Serves 4–6

Active time
1 hour

Chilling time
15 minutes

Cooking time
30–40 minutes

Resting time
24 hours

Storage
Up to 6 days in a dry place, well covered in plastic wrap

Equipment
5 ½ × 3-in. (14 × 7.3-cm) loaf pan, 2 ¾ in. (7 cm) deep
Parchment paper cone
(see technique p. 598)

Ingredients
⅓ cup (3.5 oz./100 g) orange flower honey
2 tbsp (30 ml) whole milk, heated
¼ tsp (1 g) ground cinnamon
¼ tsp (1 g) ground nutmeg
¼ tsp (1 g) ground star anise
¼ tsp (1 ml) vanilla extract
½ tsp (2 g) finely grated lemon zest
½ tsp (2 g) finely grated orange zest
¾ cup (2.5 oz./70 g) rye flour
⅓ cup (1 oz./30 g) flour
2 tsp (0.25 oz./7 g) baking powder
1 ¾ tbsp (0.75 oz./20 g) superfine sugar
⅓ cup (2.75 oz./70 g) lightly beaten egg (about 1 ½ eggs)
½ tsp (2 g) softened butter, to pipe on the batter

1 • Line the loaf pan with parchment paper. Stand the opened jar of honey in a pan of hot water to melt the honey.

CHEFS' NOTES

• Leave the loaf for 24 hours before serving to give the flavors time to develop.

• You can brush the top of the loaf with jam and decorate it with cinnamon sticks, whole star anise, and pieces of candied citrus zest.

• You can also spoon a light syrup flavored with orange zest over the loaf as soon as it comes out of the oven.

2 • Infuse the milk in a pan with the spices, vanilla, and citrus zests. ➔

Spiced Loaf Cake (continued)

3 • Cover the pan with plastic wrap and chill for about 15 minutes.

4 • Preheat the oven to 300°F (150°C/Gas mark 2). Sift together the flours and baking powder.

6 • Add the spice-infused milk, the warm honey, and the dry ingredients, and stir with a spatula until evenly mixed.

7 • Pour the batter into the loaf pan, filling it three-quarters full.

5 • In a mixing bowl, whisk the sugar and eggs until pale and thick.

8 • Fill the paper cone with the softened butter and pipe a line of butter down the center of the loaf. Bake for 30–40 minutes. To test for doneness, insert a cake tester or the tip of a knife into the center of the cake; it should come out clean.

Marble Loaf Cake

Cake Marbré

Serves 4–6

Active time
1 hour

Cooking time
35–40 minutes

Storage
Up to 1 week in a dry place,
well covered in plastic wrap,
or up to 2 months in the freezer

Equipment
5 ½ × 3-in. (14 × 7.3-cm) loaf pan,
2 ¾ in. (7 cm) deep
Stand mixer fitted
with the paddle beater
Disposable pastry bags

Ingredients
¾ stick (2.75 oz./80 g) butter,
softened
⅔ cup (3 oz./90 g)
confectioners' sugar
1 tsp (8 g) invert sugar
Scant ½ cup (3.5 oz./100 g)
lightly beaten egg
(about 2 eggs),
at room temperature

¼ tsp (1 ml) vanilla extract
1 pinch of salt
¾ cup plus 2 tbsp
(3.5 oz./100 g) flour
¼ tsp (1 g) baking powder
1 tbsp (0.25 oz./8 g)
unsweetened cocoa powder,
sifted

1 • Line the loaf pan with parchment paper. Beat the butter, confectioners' sugar, and invert sugar in the stand mixer until combined and then beat in the eggs, vanilla, and salt. Continue beating until smooth.

3 • Divide the batter equally between 2 bowls and stir the cocoa powder into one using a spatula.

4 • Spoon the batters into separate pastry bags, snip off the points, and pipe alternate layers of chocolate and plain batter into the loaf pan, until it is three-quarters full.

2 • Sift the flour with the baking powder and beat into the mixture. Preheat the oven to 400°F (200°C/Gas mark 6).

5 • Using the tip of a knife or a toothpick, marble the two mixtures together by making zigzag patterns. Bake for 15 minutes and then lower the oven temperature to 325°F (160°C/Gas mark 3) and bake for an additional 20–25 minutes.

Lemon Loaf Cake

Cake au Citron

Serves 8

Active time
15 minutes

Cooking time
30 minutes

Storage
Up to 5 days in a dry place,
well covered in plastic wrap

Equipment
Stand mixer
2 × 5 ½ × 3-in. (14 × 7.3-cm) loaf
pans, 2 ¾ in. (7 cm) deep

Ingredients
½ oz. (13 g) Earl Grey tea
1 ½ tbsp (25 ml) hot water
⅓ cup (1.75 oz./55 g) sugar
1.5 oz. (45 g) almond paste,
50% almonds, softened
Finely grated zest of 1 lemon
Finely grated zest of 1 lime
1 ½ tbsp (1.25 oz./35 g) acacia
honey (or multi-floral honey)
Generous ½ cup
(4.75 oz./135 g) lightly beaten
egg (about 3 eggs)
¾ cup plus 2 tbsp
(3.5 oz./100 g) flour,
plus extra for dusting
¾ tsp (3 g) baking powder
Scant 1 stick (3.75 oz./110 g)
butter, melted to lukewarm,
plus extra for greasing

1 • Preheat the oven to 325°F (160°C/Gas mark 3).
Infuse the tea in the hot water.

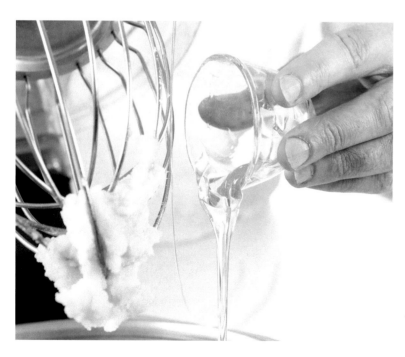

3 • Swap the beater for the whisk and gradually beat in the honey,
tea, and eggs until smooth and creamy.

4 • Sift the flour with the baking powder, add the butter,
and mix in until the batter is smooth.

2 • Meanwhile, fit the stand mixer with the paddle beater and beat the sugar, almond paste, and grated zests together.

5 • Grease the pans with butter and dust them lightly with flour. Pour the batter into the pans and bake for about 30 minutes, or until a cake tester or the tip of a knife inserted into the center comes out clean. Allow to cool in the pans before unmolding onto a rack.

Chocolate and Nut Loaf Cake

Cake au Chocolat

Serves 4–6

Active time
25 minutes

Cooking time
50 minutes

Storage
Up to 3 days in a dry place, well covered in plastic wrap

Equipment
5 ½ × 3-in. (14 × 7.3-cm) loaf pan, 2 ¾ in. (7 cm) deep
Stand mixer
Parchment paper cone
(see technique p. 598)

Ingredients
2.5 oz. (70 g) almond paste, 50% almonds

Scant ½ cup (3 oz./85 g) superfine sugar

Scant ½ cup (3.5 oz./100 g) egg (about 2 eggs)

Scant 1 cup (3 oz. /90 g) flour, plus extra for dusting

2 tbsp (0.5 oz./15 g) unsweetened cocoa powder

¾ tsp (3 g) baking powder

⅓ cup (75 ml) whole milk

¾ stick (3 oz./85 g) butter, melted to lukewarm, plus extra for greasing

½ tsp (2 g) softened butter, to pipe on the batter

Filling
⅓ cup (1.5 oz./50 g) whole hazelnuts

Scant ¼ cup (1 oz./25 g) whole unsalted pistachios

1 oz. (25 g) candied orange peel

1 • Grease the loaf pan with butter and dust it with flour. Soften the almond paste with a spatula.

4 • Sift together the flour, cocoa powder, and baking powder.

5 • Add the milk to the almond paste mixture and then fold in half the sifted dry ingredients. Preheat the oven to 300°F (150°C/Gas mark 2).

2 • Fit the stand mixer with the whisk, mix the almond paste with the sugar, and then beat in the eggs, one at a time.

3 • When combined, beat with a spatula for 10 minutes to make the mixture light and airy.

6 • Spread out the hazelnuts on a baking sheet and roast for 15 minutes. Cool and then chop. Increase the oven temperature to 400°F (200°C/Gas mark 6).

7 • Coarsely chop the pistachios and finely dice the candied orange peel. ⊕

Chocolate and Nut Loaf Cake (continued)

8 • Coat the nuts and diced orange peel in the remaining sifted dry ingredients and mix into the batter.

9 • Fold in the melted butter. Pour the batter into the pan, filling it three-quarters full. Place in the oven for 10 minutes.

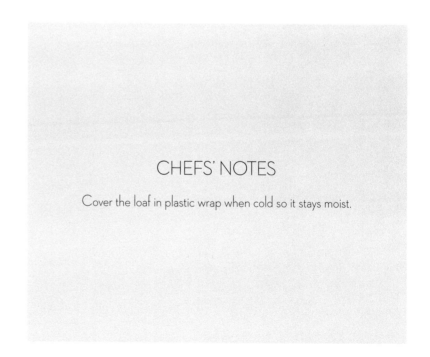

CHEFS' NOTES

Cover the loaf in plastic wrap when cold so it stays moist.

10 • Remove from the oven, make an incision on the top of the cake lengthwise, fill the paper cone with the softened butter and pipe a line of butter in the incision. Place back in the oven, reduce the temperature to 325°F (160°C/Gas mark 3), and bake for 30–35 minutes. Cool in the pan before unmolding onto a rack.

Pistachio and Raspberry Loaf Cake

Cake à la Pistache et Framboise

Serves 4–6

Active time
30 minutes

Cooking time
45–50 minutes (plus making
the raspberry concentrate)

Storage
Up to 3 days in a dry place,
well covered in plastic wrap

Equipment
5 ½ × 3-in. (14 × 7.3-cm) loaf pan,
2 ¾ in. (7 cm) deep

Parchment paper cone
(see technique p. 598)

Ingredients
Raspberry concentrate
9 oz. (250 g) raspberries

Batter
Scant ⅓ cup (2.75 oz./80 g)
egg yolk (about 4 ½ yolks)
⅔ cup (4.25 oz./120 g) sugar
4 tbsp (60 ml) full fat crème
fraîche or heavy cream
Scant 1 cup (3.25oz./95 g) flour
½ tsp (2 g) baking powder
½ tsp (2 g) finely grated lime
zest
3 ¾ tbsp (1.5 oz./40 g) butter,
melted and cooled
0.5 oz. (15 g) pistachio paste
½ tsp (2 g) softened butter
to pipe on the batter

1 • Make the raspberry concentrate by cooking the raspberries
in a pan over low heat until reduced to a pulp weighing 3.5 oz.
(100 g). Line the loaf pan with parchment paper.

4 • Layer the two mixtures alternately in the loaf pan.
Preheat the oven to 325°F (155°C/Gas mark 3).

5 • Using the tip of a knife or a toothpick, marble the two mixtures
together by making zigzag patterns.

2 • Whisk the egg yolks and sugar in a bowl until pale and thick, and then whisk in the cream. Sift in the flour and baking powder, add the lime zest, and mix together. Finally, incorporate the melted butter.

3 • Divide the batter between 2 bowls, putting one-third in one and two-thirds in the other. Color the one-third red with the raspberry concentrate, and the two-thirds green with the pistachio paste.

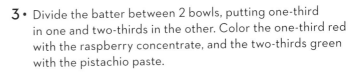

6 • Fill the paper cone with the softened butter and pipe a line of butter down the center of the cake. Bake for about 15 minutes and then lower the temperature to 300°F (145°C/Gas mark 2) and bake for 25–30 minutes.

Chestnut Loaf Cake

Cake aux Marrons

Serves 8

Active time
30 minutes

Resting time
40 minutes

Cooking time
30–40 minutes

Storage
Up to 2 weeks in a dry place, well covered in plastic wrap (undecorated cakes); up to 2 days in the refrigerator (decorated)

Equipment
Stand mixer
2 × 5 ½ × 3-in. (14 × 7.3-cm) loaf pans, 2 ¾ in. (7 cm) deep
2 baking sheets
1 large (or 2 smaller) silicone baking mats
2 pastry bags fitted with a plain ½-in. (10-mm) tip and a vermicelli tip

Ingredients
Cake batter
½ cup (4.25 oz./120 g) egg white (about 4 whites), divided
1 cup (2.75 oz./75 g) confectioners' sugar, sifted
⅔ cup (1.75 oz./55 g) almond flour
½ cup (1.75 oz./50 g) flour, sifted
½ stick (1.75 oz./50 g) butter, melted, browned, and cooled, plus extra for greasing
1 ¼ tbsp (0.5 oz./15 g) sugar
1.5 oz. (40 g) red currants
1.5 oz. (40 g) candied chestnut pieces

Red currant cream
3.5 oz. (100 g) red currant purée
⅓ cup (3 oz./90 g) egg (about 2 eggs)
Scant ½ cup (2.75 oz./80 g) sugar
Scant 1 tsp (4 g) powdered gelatin
1 ½ tbsp (25 ml) water
3 tbsp (1.5 oz./40 g) butter, softened

Chestnut cream
3 oz. (85 g) chestnut spread (*crème de marrons*)
1 ½ tbsp (25 ml) whole milk
1 tbsp (0.75 oz./20 g) egg yolk (about 1 yolk)
1 tsp (3 g) custard powder (or cornstarch)
½ tsp (3 ml) rum
⅔ stick (2 oz./60 g) butter, softened

Decoration
Confectioners' sugar
Candied chestnut pieces
Small sprigs of red currants

1 • Butter the loaf pans. Fit the stand mixer with the paddle beater and beat half the egg whites with the confectioners' sugar, almond flour, and flour. When combined, beat in the browned butter and transfer the batter to a mixing bowl.

4 • Pour the batter into the loaf pans. Lay the silicone mat on a baking sheet, stand the pans on it, fold the mat over them (or use a second mat) and place the second baking sheet on top. Bake for 30–40 minutes.

2 • Fit the stand mixer with the whisk and whisk the remaining egg whites with the sugar to firm peaks. Fold into the batter, taking care not to deflate the whisked whites.

3 • Fold in the red currants and candied chestnut pieces. Preheat the oven to 325°F (160°C/Gas mark 3).

5 • To make the red currant cream, bring the red currant purée to a boil. Whisk the egg and sugar until pale and thick. Soak the gelatin in the water to soften it.

6 • Whisk a little of the hot red currant purée into the egg mixture, pour the mixture back into the pan, and bring to a boil, whisking constantly. ⊕

Chestnut Loaf Cake (continued)

7 • Stir in the butter and gelatin. Transfer to a mixing bowl, cool, and then chill until needed.

8 • Heat the chestnut spread with the milk. Whisk the egg yolks and custard powder together in a bowl. Whisk in a little of the hot chestnut milk, and pour the mixture back into the pan.

11 • When the cakes are cool, spoon the red currant cream into the pastry bag with the plain tip and pipe it over the tops of the cakes.

12 • Spoon the chestnut cream into the pastry bag fitted with the vermicelli tip and pipe it generously over the red currant cream.

9 • Continue as for a pastry cream (see technique p. 196, step 5). Remove from the heat, stir in the rum, and cool for about 20 minutes.

10 • In a bowl and using a spatula, stir in the softened butter.

13 • Dust with confectioners' sugar and decorate with candied chestnut pieces and small sprigs of red currants.

Madeleines

Makes 12

Active time
15 minutes

Chilling time
1 ½ hours

Cooking time
10–12 minutes

Storage
Up to 1 week in a dry place,
well covered in plastic wrap,
or 3 months in the freezer

Equipment
Instant-read thermometer
Madeleine pan
Pastry bag fitted with a plain
½-in. (10-mm) tip

Ingredients
Scant ½ cup (3.5 oz./100 g)
lightly beaten egg
(about 2 eggs)

1 cup plus 1 tbsp
(4 oz./115 g) sugar

2 tsp (0.5 oz./15 g) honey

⅓ cup (80 ml) milk,
warmed to 68°F (20°C)

1 ½ cups (6.25 oz./180 g)
flour, plus extra for dusting

1 ½ tsp (6 g) baking powder

9 oz. (250 g) butter, melted, plus
extra for greasing

1 tsp vanilla extract
Finely grated zest of ⅓ lemon

1• Whisk the eggs, sugar, and honey together.

CHEFS' NOTES

• The batter needs to be chilled before being piped into the pan.
This gives the flour time to absorb moisture and the batter to thicken,
so the baked madeleines have their distinctive bump.

• Instead of chilling, you can pipe the batter into the pan
and freeze it briefly until just firm. This also helps
the madeleines rise and develop a better bump.

3• Whisk in the lemon zest and then chill for 1 ½ hours.
Grease the madeleine pan with butter and dust lightly with flour.
Preheat the oven to 375°F (190°C/Gas mark 5).

2 • Add the warm milk and then sift in the flour with the baking powder. Whisk until combined and then mix in the melted butter and vanilla.

4 • Spoon the batter into the pastry bag and pipe into the madeleine pan, filling each cavity two-thirds full. Bake for 10–12 minutes. Unmold as soon as they come out of the oven and cover in plastic wrap.

Genoa Bread

Pain de Gênes

Serves 6

Active time
1 hour

Cooking time
35–40 minutes

Storage
3–4 days in a dry place,
well covered in plastic wrap

Equipment
Stand mixer
8-in. (20-cm) round cake pan

Ingredients
5.25 oz. (150 g) almond paste,
50% almonds
2 ½ tbsp (1.5 oz./40 g)
egg yolk (about 2 yolks)
⅔ cup (5.25 oz. /150 g) lightly
beaten egg (about 3 eggs)
½ tsp (2 ml) vanilla extract
½ tsp (0.1 oz./2.5 g)
baking powder
3 tbsp (1 oz./30 g) cornstarch
Scant ½ stick (1.75 oz./50 g)
butter, melted and cooled,
plus extra for greasing
1 oz. (30 g) sliced almonds

1• Microwave the almond paste briefly to soften it slightly.
Fit the stand mixer with the paddle beater and beat the almond
paste with the egg yolks.

CHEFS' NOTES

Just before unmolding the baked cake,
you can spoon a light syrup flavored with orange zest over it.
Wrap the still-warm cake in plastic wrap
so it stays moist for longer.

4• Butter the cake pan and arrange the sliced almonds
evenly over the base and up the sides.
Preheat the oven to 400°F (200°C/Gas mark 6).

2 • Change to the whisk attachment, add the eggs and vanilla and whisk for 10 minutes at medium speed. Sift in the baking powder with the cornstarch and fold in with a spatula.

3 • Gradually drizzle in the melted butter and fold it in gently.

5 • Carefully pour the batter into the pan and place in the oven. Reduce the temperature immediately to 350°F (180°C/Gas mark 4) and bake for 35–40 minutes.

Bordeaux Rum and Vanilla Cakes

Canelés

Makes 12

Active time
15 minutes

Chilling time
24 hours

Cooking time
45 minutes

Storage
24 hours

Equipment
Copper canelé molds, 2 ¼ in.
(5.5 cm) in diameter
Instant-read thermometer

Ingredients
2 cups (500 ml) whole milk,
divided

1 vanilla bean, split lengthwise
and seeds scraped out

Scant ½ stick
(1.75 oz./50 g) butter

Melted vegetable wax
or beeswax, for greasing

1 ¼ cups (9 oz./250 g)
confectioners' sugar

¾ cup plus 2 tbsp
(3.5 oz./100 g) flour

Scant ½ cup (3.5 oz./100 g)
lightly beaten egg
(about 2 eggs)

2 ½ tbsp (1.5 oz./40 g)
egg yolk (about 2 yolks)

3 tbsp (40 ml) rum

1 • Bring three-quarters of the milk to a boil with the vanilla bean
and seeds. Stir in the butter and allow it to melt.

4 • Sift the sugar and flour together into a bowl.
Pour over the remaining cold milk and whisk to combine.
Then pour over the warm vanilla-infused milk.

5 • Whisk in the beaten eggs and egg yolks, and then the rum.
Continue whisking until the mixture is smooth with no lumps.
Cover with plastic wrap flush with the surface and chill
for 24 hours.

CHEFS' NOTES

The temperature of the milk is crucial when making canelé batter: it should never exceed 175°F (80°C)
when it is added to the other ingredients, so check the temperature with a thermometer.

2 • Remove from the heat, cover with plastic wrap, and allow to cool
to below 175°F (80°C). Remove the vanilla bean.

3 • Using a pastry brush, lightly brush the insides of the molds
with the wax (or you can do this the next day).

6 • Preheat the oven to 425°F (220°C–230°C/Gas mark 7).
Whisk the chilled batter well to make it easier to pour,
then pour it into the prepared molds: fill them to within ¼ in.
(5 mm) of the top. Bake for about 45 minutes.
Unmold onto a rack as soon as they are taken out of the oven.

Brownies

Serves 4

Active time
30 minutes

Cooking time
25–30 minutes

Storage
3–4 days in a dry place,
well covered in plastic wrap

Equipment
Stand mixer
Instant-read thermometer
7-in. (18-cm) shallow square pan

Ingredients
7 tbsp (3.5 oz./100 g) butter,
diced, plus extra for greasing

4.25 oz. (120 g) bittersweet
chocolate, chopped

Scant ½ cup (3.5 oz./100 g)
lightly beaten egg
(about 2 eggs)

Scant ⅓ cup (2 oz./60 g) sugar

⅓ cup (1.5 oz./40 g) flour,
sifted, plus extra for dusting

Generous ¼ cup (1 oz./30 g)
walnut halves

1 • Preheat the oven to 325°F (160°C/Gas mark 3).
Butter the pan and dust it with flour. Melt the chocolate
and butter in a bowl over a pan of hot water.

3 • When the temperature of the melted chocolate reaches
113°F (45°C), whisk into the egg mixture, one-third at a time,
at medium speed, ensuring it retains its volume
and does not deflate.

4 • Using a spatula, gradually fold in the flour and walnuts.

CHEFS' NOTES

You can serve the brownies with pouring custard, Chantilly cream, or vanilla ice cream.
Pecans or macadamia nuts can replace the walnuts and you can also add small chunks of white or milk chocolate.

2 • Fit the stand mixer with the whisk attachment and whisk the eggs and sugar together for at least 7 minutes, until pale and thick.

5 • Pour the batter into the prepared pan and bake for 25–30 minutes.

6 • Allow to cool before cutting into squares.

Basque Cake

Gâteau Basque

Serves 6–8

Active time
30 minutes

Chilling time
15 minutes

Cooking time
45 minutes

Storage
Up to 3 days in the refrigerator

Equipment
Nonstick baking sheet
Pastry bag fitted with a plain
¾-in. (1.5-cm) tip
7-in. (18-cm) cake ring

Ingredients
Pastry layers
1 ⅔ cups (7 oz./200 g) flour
1 tbsp (0.5 oz./12 g)
baking powder
Generous ⅔ cup
(4.5 oz./130 g) superfine sugar
1 stick plus 2 tbsp
(5 oz./140 g) butter, diced
¼ cup (2.5 oz./70 g)
egg yolk (about 4 yolks)
¼ tsp (1 g) salt
Finely grated zest of ½ lemon

Pastry cream
1 cup (250 ml) whole milk
3 ½ tbsp (1.5 oz./40 g) sugar
½ vanilla bean, split lengthwise
and seeds scraped out
Scant ⅓ cup (2.75 oz./80 g)
egg yolk (about 4 ½ yolks)
1 ½ tbsp (0.5 oz./15 g) cornstarch
1 heaping tbsp
(0.35 oz./10 g) flour
1 tbsp plus 1 tsp (0.75 oz./20 g)
butter

Egg wash
1 ½ tbsp (1 oz./25 g) lightly
beaten egg (about ½ egg)
1 tbsp (0.75 oz./20 g)
egg yolk (about 1 yolk)
1 ½ tbsp (25 ml) whole milk

1 • To make the pastry, sift the flour and baking powder onto a work surface and make a well in the center. Put the sugar and butter in the well.

4 • Using a scraper, begin mixing everything together.

2 • Work the ingredients together with your fingers until crumbly.

3 • Form another well and add the egg yolks, salt, and lemon zest.

5 • Knead the dough lightly with your hand until smooth. Cover with plastic wrap and chill for 15 minutes.

6 • Roll into 2 × 8-in. (20-cm) disks, ¼ in. (6 mm) thick and place one on the baking sheet. ⊕

Basque Cake (continued)

7 • Using the ingredients listed, make the pastry cream (see technique p. 196). Spoon about 12 oz. (350 g) into the pastry bag and pipe a spiral on the pastry, starting in the center and finishing about ¾ in. (2 cm) from the edge.

8 • Brush egg wash over the pastry border. Preheat the oven to 350°F (180°C/Gas mark 4).

9 • Lift the other pastry disk on top of the pastry cream and, using the cake ring, trim away the excess dough around the sides so the 2 layers can be sealed. Leave the cake ring in place.

10 • Brush the top with egg wash. Dip a fork in water and mark lines around the edge. Bake for about 45 minutes until golden.

Almond Tuiles

Tuiles aux Amandes

Makes about 50

Active time
30 minutes

Chilling time
20 minutes

Cooking time
12 minutes

Storage
Up to 2 weeks
in an airtight container

Equipment
Nonstick baking sheets
Curved mold or rolling pin
for shaping

Ingredients
Scant 1 cup (7.5 oz./210 g)
egg white (about 7 whites)
Scant 1 cup (6 oz./170 g)
superfine sugar
6 tbsp (3 oz./85 g) butter,
melted and cooled,
plus extra for greasing
⅓ cup (1.5 oz./40 g) flour, sifted
½ cup (1.75 oz./50 g) sliced
almonds

1 • Preheat the oven to 350°F (180°C/Gas mark 4).
Generously butter the baking sheets. In a mixing bowl,
lightly whisk the egg whites with the sugar.

3 • Place small amounts of the mixture onto the baking sheets
and spread with the back of a fork. Bake for about 12 minutes
until lightly golden.

4 • Remove from the baking sheets and immediately
shape the tuiles in the curved mold. Allow to cool.

CHEFS' NOTES

• The baking sheets need to be well buttered.

• As the tuiles need to be shaped as soon as they come out of the oven, it's practical to bake them in batches.

2 • Stir in the melted, cooled butter. Add the flour and sliced almonds, stirring until evenly combined. Chill for 20 minutes.

5 • You can also drape the tuiles over a rolling pin so they cool in the traditional curved shape.

Cigarette Cookies

Cigarettes

Makes about 50

Active time
30 minutes

Cooking time
8 minutes

Storage
Up to 2 weeks
in an airtight container

Equipment
Nonstick baking sheets
Pastry bag fitted
with a plain ⅓-in. (10-mm) tip
Honing steel
or other small cylinder

Ingredients
5 tbsp (2.75 oz./80 g) butter,
softened, plus extra for greasing
⅔ cup (2.75 oz./80 g)
confectioners' sugar
⅓ cup (2.75 oz./80 g)
egg white (about 2 ½ whites)
⅔ cup (2.75 oz./80 g) flour,
sifted

1 • Preheat the oven to 350°F (180°C/Gas mark 4).
Grease the baking sheets with butter. Beat the softened butter
with the confectioners' sugar in a mixing bowl, and then stir
in half the egg whites until a smooth mixture is obtained.

3 • Spoon the mixture into the pastry bag and pipe the batter
onto the prepared baking sheets.

4 • Lightly tap the baking sheets underneath so the batter
spreads evenly. Bake for about 8 minutes, until the edges
are lightly colored.

It's important not to make the mixture too far in advance before baking.

2 • Whisk in the flour and the other half of the egg whites until smooth.

5 • As soon as they come out of the oven, roll the cookies around the honing steel to form cigarette shapes.

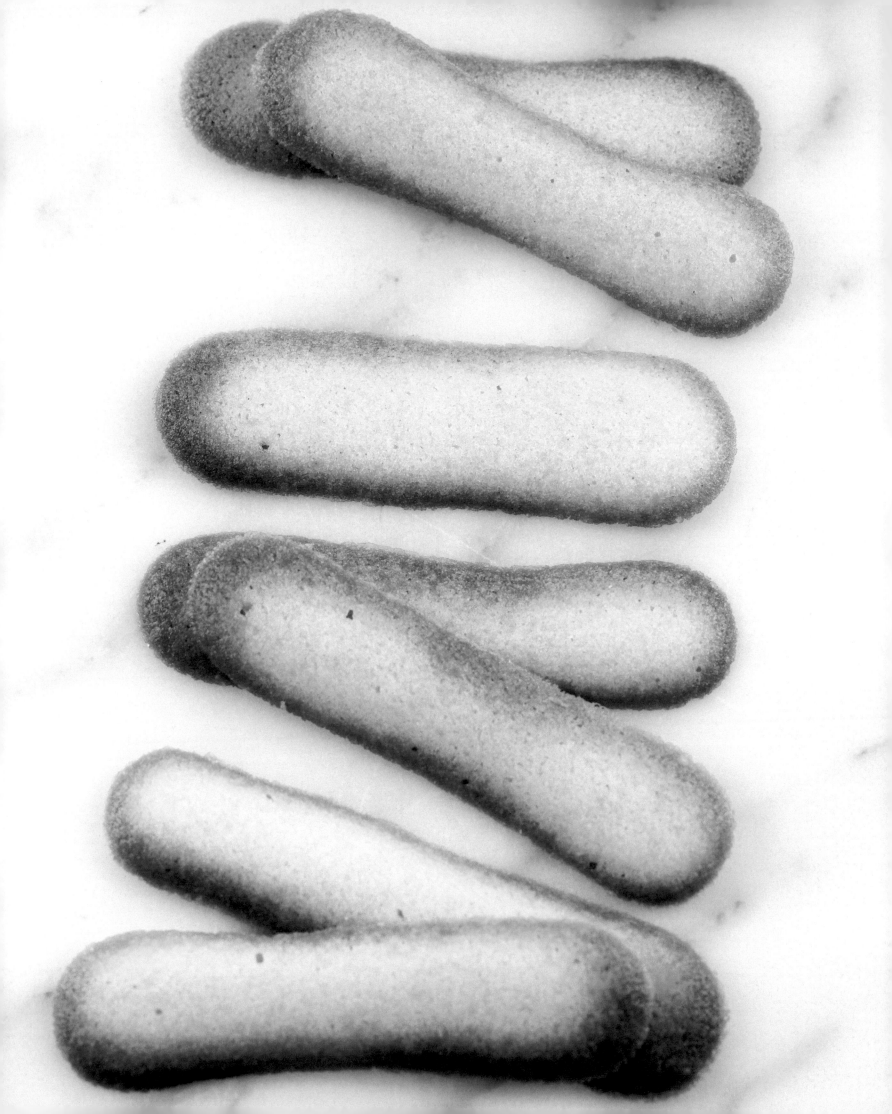

Cat's Tongue Cookies

Langues de Chat

Makes about 50

Active time
30 minutes

Cooking time
10 minutes

Storage
Up to 2 weeks in an airtight container

Equipment
Nonstick baking sheets
Pastry bag fitted with a plain
⅓-in. (10-mm) tip

Ingredients
4 tbsp (2 oz./60 g) butter, softened, plus extra for greasing

Scant ½ cup (2 oz./60 g) confectioners' sugar

¼ cup (2 oz./60 g) egg white (about 2 whites), at room temperature

⅔ cup (2.75 oz./75 g) flour, sifted

1 • Preheat the oven to 350°F (180°F/Gas mark 4). Grease the baking sheets with butter. Beat the butter, confectioners' sugar, and egg whites together briefly in a mixing bowl, until just smooth.

2 • Fold in the flour until evenly combined.

3 • Spoon into the pastry bag and pipe the mixture into short lengths on the baking sheets. Bake for 8–10 minutes until golden.

Sparkling Shortbread Cookies

Sablés Diamants

Makes about 50

Active time
30 minutes

Chilling time
2 hours minimum

Cooking time
12–15 minutes

Storage
Up to 2 weeks
in an airtight container

Equipment
Baking sheets lined with
silicone baking mats

Ingredients
1 ¾ sticks (6.5 oz./190 g) butter,
softened
Scant ⅔ cup (3 oz./90 g)
confectioners' sugar
1 tbsp (0.75 oz./20 g)
egg yolk (about 1 yolk)
1 vanilla bean, split lengthwise
and seeds scraped out
2 ¼ cups (9.5 oz./275 g) flour
1 ¼ cups (9 oz./250 g)
granulated sugar

1 • Beat the butter and confectioners' sugar together
in a mixing bowl using a spatula, and then beat in the egg yolk
and vanilla seeds.

3 • Divide the dough in half and shape into 2 logs, 12 in. (30 cm) long
and each weighing 10 oz. (280 g). Cover in plastic wrap and chill
for at least 2 hours.

4 • Preheat the oven to 350°F (180°C/Gas mark 4).
Sprinkle the granulated sugar on a work surface and roll
the logs over it until coated. Cut into ½-in. (1-cm) slices.

CHEFS' NOTES

The logs must be chilled thoroughly before being sliced.

2 • Sift in the flour and stir to make a smooth dough.

5 • Lay the slices on the baking mats and bake for 12–15 minutes until golden. Transfer to a rack to cool.

Piped Shortbread Cookies

Sablés Poche

Makes 15

Active time
30 minutes

Resting time
2–3 hours

Cooking time
10 minutes

Storage
Up to 2 weeks
in an airtight container

Equipment
Pastry bag fitted
with a fluted ¾-in. (2-cm) tip
(see Chefs' Notes)

Baking sheet lined
with a silicone baking mat

Ingredients
1 stick plus 2 tsp (4.5 oz./125 g)
butter, at room temperature

¾ cup (3.5 oz./100 g)
confectioners' sugar

3 ½ tbsp (1.75 oz./50 g) lightly
beaten egg (about 1 egg)

½ vanilla bean, split lengthwise
and seeds scraped out

Finely grated zest of ½ lime

2 cups (9 oz./250 g) flour, sifted

1 ¼ tsp (5 g) baking powder

15 blanched almonds

1 • Beat the butter in a mixing bowl with a spatula until it is softened.

3 • Add the grated lime zest, flour, and baking powder and stir until the ingredients are combined—do this lightly so you don't beat in too much air.

4 • Spoon the mixture into the pastry bag and pipe 1 ¼-in. (3-cm) rosettes on the baking mat.

CHEFS' NOTES

As the cookie mix is quite firm, use a cloth pastry bag rather than a disposable one.

2 • Beat in the confectioners' sugar, followed by the egg and vanilla seeds.

5 • Top each rosette with an almond. Allow to stand at cool room temperature for 2–3 hours, so a crust forms on the surface. Preheat the oven to 425°F (220°C/Gas mark 7) and bake for 10 minutes, until a light golden color. Transfer to a rack and allow to cool.

Nantes Shortbread Cookies

Sablés Nantais

Makes 12

Active time
20 minutes

Chilling time
1 hour

Cooking time
12–15 minutes

Storage
Up to 2 weeks
in an airtight container

Equipment
Baking sheet
3 ½-in. (8-cm) round
cookie cutter

Ingredients
1 stick plus 2 tsp (4.5 oz./125 g)
butter, softened, plus extra
for greasing

Scant 1 cup (4.5 oz./125 g)
confectioners' sugar

Scant ½ tsp (2 g) salt

3 ½ tbsp (1.75 oz./50 g) lightly
beaten egg (about 1 egg)

1 vanilla bean, split lengthwise
and seeds scraped out

2 cups (9 oz./250 g) flour, sifted

1 ¼ tsp (5 g) baking powder

Egg wash
2 tbsp (1 oz./30 g) lightly beaten
egg (about 1 egg)

1 tsp (5 ml) coffee extract

Uses
Lunettes (cookies sandwiched
in pairs with 2 peepholes
like reading glasses),
sweet petits fours

1 • Beat the butter and sugar together in a mixing bowl
with a spatula until smooth and creamy.

4 • Knead the dough gently on a work surface using the palm
of your hand. Cover in plastic wrap and chill for 1 hour.

5 • Preheat the oven to 350°F (180°C/Gas mark 4) and grease
the baking sheet with butter. Roll out the dough to a thickness
of ⅛ in. (4 mm) and stamp out rounds with the cutter.

2 • Dissolve the salt in the beaten egg and then stir in the vanilla seeds.

3 • Add the egg gradually to the creamed mixture, beating until smooth. Stir in the flour and baking powder until evenly combined.

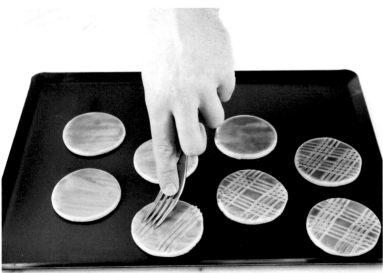

6 • Lay the rounds on the prepared baking sheet, leaving space between them for the heat to circulate. Brush the tops with egg wash and mark decorative lines with a fork. Bake for 12–15 minutes, until golden brown.

Buckwheat and Flaxseed Cookies

Sablés Céréales

Makes 12

Active time
1 hour

Cooking time
10–12 minutes

Storage
Up to 3 days
in an airtight container

Equipment
Baking sheet lined
with parchment paper

Ingredients
1 ½ cups (6.25 oz./180 g) flour
Scant ½ cup (2 oz./50 g)
buckwheat flour
1 ½ tsp (6 g) baking powder
1 stick plus 2 tbsp
(5.25 oz./150 g) butter,
diced and softened
⅓ cup (3 oz./85 g) light
brown sugar
¼ tsp (2 g) fleur de sel
3 ½ tbsp (1.5 oz./40 g) flaxseeds

Egg wash
1 ½ tbsp (1 oz./25 g) lightly
beaten egg (about ½ egg)
1 tbsp (0.75 oz./20 g) egg yolk
(about 1 yolk)
1 ½ tbsp (25 ml) whole milk

1 • Preheat the oven to 325°F (160°C/Gas mark 3).
Sift the flours and baking powder onto a work surface,
add the butter, and work lightly into the dry ingredients.

4 • Add the flaxseeds.

5 • Knead the dough with the palm of your hand until smooth.

2 • Add the brown sugar and fleur de sel.

3 • Rub the ingredients together with your hands until the mixture resembles fine bread crumbs.

6 • Shape the dough into a cylinder, 7 in. (18 cm) long, and cut into ¾-in. (1.5-cm) slices. Lay the slices on the baking sheet and brush with the egg wash.
Bake for about 10–12 minutes, until firm at the edges.

Coconut Pyramids

Rochers Coco

Makes 6

Active time
20 minutes

Cooking time
8 minutes

Storage
Up to 4 days in an airtight container

Equipment
Baking sheet lined with a silicone baking mat
Pastry bag fitted with a fluted ¾-in. (1.8-cm) tip

Ingredients
2 tbsp (1 oz./30 g) egg white (about 1 white)
Scant ⅓ cup (2 oz./60 g) superfine sugar
¾ cup (2 oz./60 g) unsweetened shredded coconut
2 tsp (8 g) applesauce

CHEFS' NOTES

After cooling, you can dip the top half of the pyramids in melted bittersweet chocolate.

1 • Preheat the oven to 450°F (230°C/Gas mark 8). Mix all the ingredients together in a bowl.

2 • Spoon the mixture into the pastry bag and pipe small mounds onto the silicone mat.

3 • Dampen your fingers with cold water and neaten into pyramid shapes. Bake for 8 minutes, until a crust forms on the outside of the pyramids.

Chocolate-Coated Hazelnut Cookies

Biarritz

Makes 35

Active time
45 minutes

Cooking time
10–12 minutes

Storage
Up to 4 days
in an airtight container

Equipment
2 baking sheets lined
with silicone baking mats
Drum sifter
Pastry bag fitted
with a plain ½-in. (10-mm) tip
Pastry bag without a tip

Ingredients
2 cups plus 1 tbsp (6 oz./175 g)
finely ground hazelnuts
Scant 1 cup (4.5 oz./125 g)
confectioners' sugar
½ cup plus 1 tbsp
(2.5 oz./70 g) flour
Finely grated zest of 1 orange
Scant ½ cup (100 ml) whole milk
⅔ cup (5.25 oz./150 g) egg
whites (about 5 whites)
5 tbsp (2.75 oz./80 g) butter
10.5 oz. (300 g) bittersweet
couverture chocolate,
68% cacao, tempered
(see techniques pp. 570 and 572)

1 • Preheat the oven to 350°F (180°C/Gas mark 4).
Sift the dry ingredients together.

4 • Melt the butter, add a little of the hazelnut batter, and stir in.
Pour back into the mixing bowl and fold in until combined.

5 • Spoon the batter into the pastry bag with a plain tip and pipe
small mounds like flattened choux puffs onto the silicone mats.
Bake for 10–12 minutes. Cool on a rack.

2 · Put them into a mixing bowl, add the grated zest and milk, and mix with a spatula until smooth.

3 · Whisk the egg whites until frothy. Stir about one-third into the hazelnut mixture to loosen it and then lightly fold in the rest until evenly combined.

6 · Spoon the tempered chocolate into the piping bag without a tip and snip off the point. Pipe small rounds of chocolate onto parchment paper and place the cookies, smooth side down, on top. Allow to set before removing.

Double Chocolate Chip Cookies

Cookies

Makes 25

Active time
30 minutes

Chilling time
30–40 minutes

Cooking time
12–15 minutes

Storage
Up to 2 weeks
in an airtight container

Ingredients
1 stick plus 3 tbsp
(5.5 oz./160 g) butter, softened

1 cup minus 3 tbsp
(5.5 oz./160 g) light brown sugar

3 ½ tbsp (1.75 oz./50 g)
lightly beaten egg (about 1 egg),
at room temperature

1 vanilla bean, split lengthwise
and seeds scraped out

2 cups (9 oz./250 g) flour

¾ tsp (3 g) baking powder

1.5 oz. (40 g) bittersweet
chocolate chips

4.25 oz. (120 g) white
chocolate chips

3 ½ tbsp (1 oz./25 g)
sliced almonds

1 • Using a spatula, mix the butter and sugar together.
Beat in the egg and vanilla seeds.

3 • Shape the dough into logs, 6 in. (15 cm) long, 2 in. (5 cm)
in diameter.

4 • Cover with plastic wrap and chill for 30–40 minutes.
Preheat the oven to 350°F (180°C/Gas mark 4).

2 • Sift the flour with the baking powder and fold in. When just combined, stir in the chocolate chips and sliced almonds.

5 • Line a baking sheet with parchment paper. Remove the plastic wrap and cut the dough into ½-in. (1-cm) slices. Place on the baking sheet, leaving room for the cookies to spread, and bake for 12–15 minutes.

Checkerboard Cookies

Damiers or *Sablés Hollandais*

Makes 20

Active time
45 minutes

Chilling time
1 hour 10 minutes

Cooking time
12 minutes

Storage
Up to 5 days in an airtight container

Equipment
Baking sheet lined with parchment paper

Ingredients
Vanilla short pastry
4 tbsp (2 oz./60 g) butter, diced
⅓ cup (1.5 oz./40 g) confectioners' sugar
½ tsp (2.5 ml) vanilla extract
¼ tsp (1 g) salt
1 tbsp (0.75 oz./20 g) lightly beaten egg (about ½ egg)
¼ cup (0.75 oz./20 g) almond flour
¾ cup plus 2 tbsp (3.5 oz./100 g) flour, sifted

Chocolate short pastry
4 tbsp (2 oz./60 g) butter, diced
⅓ cup (1.5 oz./40 g) confectioners' sugar
½ tsp vanilla extract
¼ tsp (1 g) salt
1 tbsp (0.75 oz./20 g) lightly beaten egg (about ½ egg)
¼ cup (0.75 oz./20 g) almond flour
¾ cup plus 2 tbsp (3.5 oz./100 g) flour, sifted
1 ½ tbsp (0.35 oz./10 g) unsweetened cocoa powder, sifted

Egg wash
1 ½ tbsp (1 oz./25 g) lightly beaten egg (about ½ egg)
1 ½ tbsp (1 oz./25 g) egg yolk (about 1 ½ yolks)
1 ½ tbsp (25 ml) whole milk

1 • Make the vanilla pastry by rubbing the butter and sugar together until it resembles fine bread crumbs.

4 • Make the chocolate pastry in the same way, adding the cocoa powder with the flour at step 2.

5 • Roll out both doughs into 3 × 8-in. (8 × 20-cm) rectangles, ¼ in. (7 mm) thick.

Chilling the dough well ensures that the checkerboard pattern
does not become misshapen when the cookies are baked.

2 • Add the vanilla and salt and then work in the egg, almond flour, and flour.

3 • Shape the dough into a ball, cover with plastic wrap, and chill for 20 minutes.

6 • Cut ½-in. (1-cm) wide strips: 5 from the vanilla dough and 4 from the chocolate dough. Set aside the rest of the doughs.

7 • Place 2 vanilla strips side by side with a chocolate strip between them. Brush with egg wash so the strips stick together. ⊙

Checkerboard Cookies (continued)

8 • Add 2 more layers, alternating the colored dough strips to create a checkerboard effect and sticking them together with egg wash. Chill for about 30 minutes.

9 • Roll the remaining chocolate dough into a 3 × 8-in. (8 × 20-cm) rectangle, about ⅛ in. (3 mm) thick. Brush with egg wash.

10 • Wrap the dough neatly around the strips to enclose them, sealing the edges.

11 • Preheat the oven to 400°F (200°C/Gas mark 6). Cut the dough into ¼-in. (5–7-mm) slices, lay them on the baking sheet, and bake for 10–12 minutes, ensuring the vanilla pastry doesn't color too much.

Crêpes

Makes 10

Active time
45 minutes

Chilling time
2 hours minimum

Cooking time
3 minutes per crêpe

Storage
Serve as soon as possible
after making

Equipment
Crêpe pan

Ingredients

Scant ½ cup (3.5 oz./100 g)
lightly beaten egg
(about 2 eggs)

2 ½ tbsp (1 oz./30 g)
superfine sugar

2 cups minus 1 ½ tbsp
(6 oz./170 g) flour

2 cups (500 ml) whole milk,
divided

Zest of 1 orange
(about 0.35 oz./10 g)

3 tbsp (1.75 oz./50 g) butter,
melted and cooled

2 tbsp (30 ml) brandy,
or another liquor of your choice

2 tbsp (30 ml) oil for the pan

1 · Whisk together the eggs, sugar, flour, and a little
of the milk—just a little to begin with, to make a firm batter
and prevent lumps forming.

4 · Lightly oil a crêpe pan and, when hot, use a small ladle
to add enough batter to thinly coat the base of the pan.

5 · When the crêpe is lightly browned underneath, turn it over to
cook the other side. Once cooked, slide the crêpe onto a plate.

• The batter is best if made the day
before you need it.

• Before you start cooking, first season the pan.
Pour in no more than ¼ in. (5 mm) oil, heat the pan, and then pour out the oil.
This ensures the crêpes cook to a good color without drying out.

2 • Whisk in the remaining milk in several additions.

3 • Grate in the orange zest, whisk in the melted butter
and the brandy or other liquor. Stir until smooth and then chill
for at least 2 hours.

6 • Layer the crêpes on the plate as they cook.
Cover with plastic wrap until you are ready to serve them.

Waffles

Gaufres

Makes 8–10

Preparation time
35 minutes

Chilling time
1 hour

Cooking time
3 minutes per batch

Storage
Serve immediately

Equipment
Electric waffle maker

Ingredients
3 ¾ tsp (0.5 oz./15 g) sugar
(see Chefs' Notes)
¼ tsp (1 g) salt
2 cups (9 oz./250 g) flour
1 ½ cups plus 3 tbsp (400 ml)
whole milk (see Chefs' Notes)
⅓ cup (2.75 oz./75 g)
butter, melted
⅛ tsp (1 ml) vanilla extract
Scant ½ cup (3 oz./90 g)
egg white (about 3 whites)
Confectioners' sugar
for dusting

CHEFS' NOTES

Using whole milk will result in a fluffier waffle.
You can also use vanilla-flavored sugar for a stronger flavor.

1 • Whisk the sugar, salt, flour, milk, and butter together in a mixing bowl. Stir in the vanilla extract and then chill the batter for 1 hour before using.

3 • Using a spatula, lightly fold the egg whites into the batter until evenly combined.

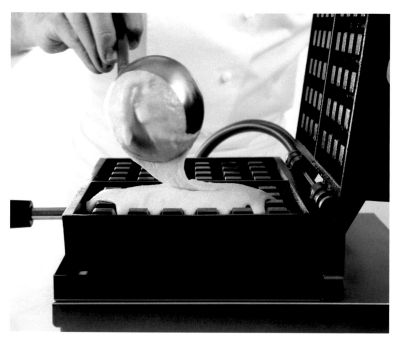

4 • Heat the waffle maker to 430°F (220°C). Spoon a ladleful of batter into each side, close the lid, and cook for about 3 minutes, until golden.

2 • In another bowl, whisk the egg whites until they hold soft peaks.

5 • Carefully remove the waffles and cook the rest of the batter in the same way.

6 • Dust the waffles with confectioners' sugar and serve immediately.

Fritters

Pâte à Frire

Makes 20

Active time
20 minutes

Cooking time
2 minutes per batch

Storage
Serve immediately

Equipment
Deep fryer

Ingredients
1 ⅔ cups (7 oz./200 g) flour
1 ½ tsp (6 g) baking powder
1 tbsp plus 2 tsp (0.75 oz./20 g)
superfine sugar
2 ½ tbsp (1.5 oz./40 g)
egg yolk (about 2 yolks)
Scant 1 cup (200 ml) whole milk
Scant ½ cup (3.5 oz./100 g)
egg white (about 3 ½ whites)
Fruit of your choice, prepared
as necessary
Oil for deep-frying
Confectioners' sugar
for dusting

1 • Sift the flour and baking powder together into a mixing bowl and stir in the sugar. Make a well in the center, pour in the egg yolks, and whisk to combine.

4 • Drain any juice from the fruit or pat dry. Using a fork, dip the fruit into the batter until coated.

5 • Heat the oil to 340°F (170°C). Lower the fruit carefully into the oil and fry for about 40 seconds on each side.

CHEFS' NOTES

• Make the fritters with fruit that has firm flesh, such as apple rings.

• Use grapeseed oil for deep-frying as it has a neutral flavor.

2 • Whisk in the milk, continuing until the batter is smooth.

3 • In another bowl, whisk the egg whites until frothy. Lightly fold into the yolk mixture with a spatula.

6 • Lift out the fritters using a slotted spoon or skimmer and drain on paper towel.

7 • Dust the fritters with confectioners' sugar and serve immediately.

French Toast

Pain Perdu

Serves 6

Active time
30 minutes

Cooking time
15 minutes

Storage
Serve immediately

Equipment
Baking sheet lined
with a silicone baking mat
or parchment paper

Ingredients
6 slices of bread, ¾ in. (1.5 cm)
thick

Scant 1 cup (200 ml) whole milk

¼ cup (2 oz./60 g) lightly beaten
egg (about 1 ½ eggs)

1 tbsp plus 1 tsp (0.75 oz./20 g)
butter

2 ½ tbsp (1 oz./30 g) sugar

CHEFS' NOTES

You can add a vanilla bean or extract to the milk,
or soak the bread in custard flavored with vanilla or another extract,
before baking in the oven.

1 • Preheat the oven to 325°F (170°C/Gas mark 3).
Soak the bread slices first in the milk and then in the beaten egg.

3 • Sprinkle over the sugar.

4 • Cook until the bread caramelizes.

CHEFS' NOTES

• Use leftover brioche or spice bread (don't waste it!) instead of plain bread, but reduce the quantity of sugar as these will be sweet already.

• You can toast the bread, brioche, or whatever you use, before preparing the French toast.

2 • Melt the butter in a large skillet and, when foaming, add the soaked bread slices.

5 • Transfer the hot slices to the baking sheet and finish cooking them in the oven for 6–8 minutes.

Bittersweet Chocolate Mousse

Mousse au Chocolat Noir 70%

Serves 4

Active time
30 minutes

Cooking time
10 minutes

Chilling time
6 hours minimum

Storage
Up to 24 hours
in the refrigerator

Equipment
Instant-read thermometer
Pastry bag fitted with a fluted
⅓-in. (10-mm) tip
4 glass serving dishes

Ingredients
5.25 oz. (150 g) bittersweet
chocolate, 70% cacao, chopped
⅓ cup (75 ml) whipping cream,
35 % butterfat
Scant ½ cup (3.5 oz./100 g)
egg white (about 3 ½ whites)
1 tbsp plus 2 tsp (0.75 oz./20 g)
sugar
1 ½ tbsp (1 oz./ 25 g) egg yolk
(about 1 ½ yolks)

1• Melt the chocolate in a bowl over a pan of hot water.

4 • Gradually pour the hot cream onto the melted chocolate
and stir with a spatula, starting in the center of the bowl
and working toward the outside, so the two are evenly
combined and the mixture is glossy and smooth.

5 • Stir in the egg yolk.

CHEFS' NOTES

- Getting the chocolate to the right temperature is important to avoid having any lumps of chocolate in the mousse.

- Whisk the egg whites gradually, starting on low speed and then increasing it, to prevent the whites developing a dull, grainy texture.

- Leave the mousse to set in the refrigerator for at least 6 hours.

2 • Bring the cream to a boil in a saucepan.

3 • Whisk the egg whites with the sugar until holding soft peaks.

6 • Allow the chocolate mixture to cool to 113°F–122°F (45°C–50°C) and then gradually fold in the egg whites gently, taking care not to deflate the mixture.

7 • Spoon the chocolate mousse into the pastry bag, pipe it into the serving dishes, and chill for 6 hours. Serve at room temperature.

White Chocolate Mousse

Mousse au Chocolat Blanc

Serves 4

Active time
30 minutes

Cooking time
10 minutes

Chilling time
6 hours

Storage
Up to 24 hours
in the refrigerator

Equipment
Instant-read thermometer
Pastry bag fitted
with a plain ⅓-in. (10-mm) tip
4 serving dishes

Ingredients
1 ½ sheets (0.1 oz./3 g) gelatin
6.75 oz. (195 g) white chocolate, chopped
⅓ cup (75 ml) whipping cream, 35% butterfat
Scant ½ cup (3.5 oz./100 g) egg white (about 3 ½ whites)
1 tbsp plus 2 tsp (0.75 oz./20 g) sugar
1 ½ tbsp (1 oz./25 g) egg yolk (about 1 ½ yolks)
Chocolate pearls for decoration (optional)

1· Soak the gelatin in a bowl of cold water until softened. Melt the white chocolate in a bowl over a pan of hot water.

4· Gradually pour the hot cream onto the melted chocolate and stir with a spatula, starting in the center of the bowl and working toward the outside, so the two are evenly combined and the mixture is glossy and smooth.

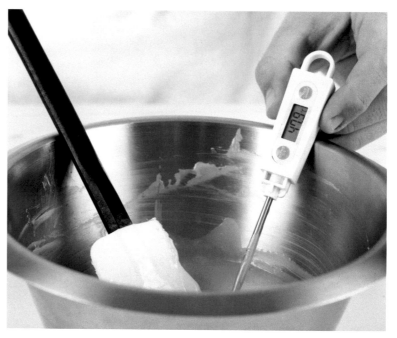

5· Stir in the egg yolk and continue stirring until the mixture cools to 113°F–122°F (45°C–50°C).

2 • Bring the cream to a boil in a saucepan. Squeeze the excess water from the gelatin and stir it into the cream until it melts.

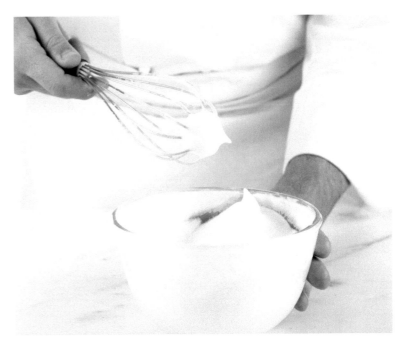

3 • Whisk the egg whites with the sugar until holding soft peaks.

6 • Gradually fold in the egg whites gently, taking care not to deflate the mixture.

7 • Spoon the mousse into the pastry bag, pipe it into the serving dishes, and chill for 6 hours. Serve at room temperature, decorated with chocolate pearls, if you wish.

Cream Caramel

Crème au Caramel

Serves 6

Active time
20 minutes

Cooking time
35 minutes

Storage
Up to 2 days
in the refrigerator

Equipment
6 × 3 ½-in. (9-cm) ramekins

Ingredients
Caramel
2 tsp (10 ml) water
½ cup (3.5 oz./100 g)
superfine sugar

Cream
2 cups (500 ml) whole milk
½ vanilla bean, split lengthwise
⅔ cup (5.25 oz./150 g) lightly
beaten egg (about 3 eggs)
½ cup (3.5 oz./100 g)
superfine sugar

1 • Preheat the oven to 275°F (140°C/Gas mark 1).
Heat the water and sugar in a saucepan and, when the sugar
has dissolved, bring to a boil. Take the pan off the heat
as soon as the syrup becomes a rich brown caramel.

3 • Bring the milk to a boil in a saucepan. Add the vanilla bean
and allow to infuse for a few minutes. Take the pan off the heat
and allow to cool a little.

4 • In a mixing bowl, whisk the eggs with the sugar until pale
and thick. Gradually pour in the warm milk through a strainer,
whisking until incorporated into the egg mixture.

CHEFS' NOTES

- Do not let the caramel become too dark or it could develop a bitter taste.

- You can flavor cream caramel and cream brûlée with finely grated citrus zest.

2 • Pour the caramel into the ramekins straight away, coating the base and sides evenly or just pouring it over the base.

5 • Pour the mixture into the ramekins, over the caramel, and bake in a water bath for 30 minutes until set. Turn out when cold.

Cream Brûlée

Crème Brûlée

Serves 4

Active time
1 hour

Cooking time
50 minutes

Freezing time
20 minutes

Storage
Up to 3 days in the refrigerator

Equipment
4 × 4 ¾-in. (12-cm) ramekins
Kitchen torch

Ingredients
1 cup (250 ml) whipping cream, 35% butterfat
3 tbsp (1.75 oz./50 g) egg yolk (about 3 yolks)
3 tbsp (1.5 oz./40 g) sugar
3 ½ tbsp (1 oz./25 g) powdered whole milk
Brown sugar, for the caramel crust

1• Preheat the oven to 225°F (100°C/Gas mark ¼). Using the first four ingredients, prepare a custard (see technique p. 204). Pour into the ramekins and bake for 50 minutes.

2• Cool and then place the creams in the freezer for 20 minutes, so they are well chilled before caramelizing the tops. Sprinkle a layer of brown sugar on top of each cream.

3• Caramelize the sugar with a kitchen torch.

CHEFS' NOTES

White sugar can be used in place of brown to caramelize the tops of the creams.
After caramelizing, chill the creams in the refrigerator so the topping firms up and it becomes crisp,
while the cream underneath stays cool and silky smooth.

Rice Pudding

Riz au Lait

Serves 6

Active time
40 minutes

Cooking time
40 minutes

Storage
Up to 6 days
(or 3 days if eggs are used),
in the refrigerator

Equipment
6 individual ramekins

Ingredients
1 heaping cup (7 oz./200 g)
round grain rice
4 ¼ cups (1 liter) whole milk
2 vanilla beans, split lengthwise
and seeds scraped out
Scant ⅔ cup (4.25 oz./120 g)
sugar
⅛ tsp (1 g) salt

CHEFS' NOTES

You can flavor the milk with finely grated citrus zest
or dissolve instant coffee in the milk:
allow 2.75 oz. (80 g) coffee granules to 4 ¼ cups (1 liter) of milk.

1• Bring 2 cups (500 ml) water to a boil in a large pan. Add the rice, cook for a few seconds to burst the starch grains, and then drain.

2• In another large pan, bring the milk to a boil with the vanilla beans, seeds, and the sugar.

3• Add the rice, stir in the salt, and cook over low heat, stirring regularly, until all the milk has been absorbed by the rice. Divide between the ramekins, cool, and chill before serving.

CHEFS' NOTES

• For a richer, softer pudding, stir in 2 egg yolks
and a scant ½ cup (100 ml) of whipping cream
when the rice is cooked.

• If you prefer, bake the rice pudding
in a 350°F (180°C/Gas mark 4) oven for 20 minutes.

• Accompany the rice pudding with homemade caramel sauce,
a fruit coulis, or Chantilly cream.

Cheesecake

Serves 6

Active time
20 minutes

Chilling time
20 minutes

Cooking time
35 minutes

Storage
Up to 3 days
in the refrigerator

Equipment
7-in. (18-cm)
diameter cake ring
or spring form pan,
2 in. (4 cm) deep

Food processor

Ingredients
Sweet short pastry
7 tbsp (3.5 oz./100 g)
butter
⅔ cup (2.75 oz./80 g)
confectioners' sugar
2 tbsp (1 oz./30 g)
lightly beaten egg
(about 1 egg)
½ tsp (2 ml) vanilla
extract
1 ¼ cups
(5.5 oz./160 g) flour
Scant ½ cup
(1.5 oz./40 g) almond
flour

Cheesecake filling
2 cups (1 lb.
2 oz./500 g) cream
cheese (Philadelphia
or similar)

⅓ cup (2.75 oz./75 g)
sugar
½ cup plus 2 tsp
(5 oz./150 g) egg
yolk (about 8 yolks)
¼ tsp (1.5 g) salt
1 vanilla bean,
split lengthwise and
seeds scraped out
¾ cup (180 ml)
crème fraîche
or heavy cream
½ cup (125 ml)
whipping cream,
35% butterfat
¼ tsp (1.5 ml) lemon
juice

Egg wash
1 egg, lightly beaten

1 • Using the ingredients listed, prepare the sweet short pastry using the creaming method (see technique p. 60). Roll out the dough ⅛ in. (3 mm) thick into a round at least 5 in. (13 cm) larger than the pan (see technique pp. 26–28, steps 1–10).

4 • For the filling, mix the cream cheese, sugar, egg yolks, salt, and vanilla seeds together in the food processor.

5 • Add the crème fraîche or heavy cream, whipping cream, and lemon juice and process until smooth.

2 • Lift the dough into the pan, pressing it down over the base with your fingers and then up the sides.

3 • Roll a rolling pin over the top to trim away the overhanging dough. Prick the base of the dough several times with a fork and chill for 20 minutes. Preheat the oven to 350°F (180°C/Gas mark 4) and blind bake for 15 minutes.

6 • Pour the filling into the crust. Brush with the egg wash and bake for 15–20 minutes, depending on your oven. Allow to cool before unmolding.

Tiramisu

Serves 8

Active time
1 hour

Chilling time
1 hour

Cooking time
10 minutes

Storage
Up to 3 days in the refrigerator

Equipment
Cookie cutter the same size
as the serving glasses
Stand mixer
Instant-read thermometer
Pastry bag without a tip
8 serving glasses

Ingredients
5 oz. (150 g) ladyfinger sponge
cooked on a baking sheet
(see technique p. 222)

Coffee syrup
¼ cup (1.75 oz./50 g) sugar
1 tsp (5 ml) rum
½ tsp (2.5 ml) coffee liqueur
Scant ½ cup (100 ml) strong
black coffee

Tiramisu cream
2 sheets (0.12 oz./4 g) gelatin
Sugar syrup made with ⅓ cup
(2.5 oz./70 g) sugar
and 2 tbsp (30 ml) water,
cooked to 230°F (110°C)

2 ½ tbsp (1.5 oz./40 g) egg yolk
(about 2 yolks), well beaten
½ cup (4.5 oz./125 g)
mascarpone
⅔ cup (150 ml) whipping cream,
35% butterfat
1 ½ tbsp (25 ml) amaretto

7 tbsp (1.75 oz./50 g)
unsweetened cocoa powder,
for dusting

1• Using the cookie cutter, cut out 16 disks of ladyfinger sponge.

4• Transfer the *pâte à bombe* to the stand mixer and continue
whisking until the mixture is frothy and has cooled completely.
Squeeze out the gelatin and heat to 104°F (40°C) until melted.
Stir into the *pâte à bombe*.

2• Heat all the ingredients for the coffee syrup in a pan until the sugar dissolves. Allow to cool and then dip the sponge disks in the syrup. Drain on a rack. Soak the gelatin in a bowl of cold water.

3• In the bowl of the stand mixer, prepare a *pâte à bombe* by gradually pouring the sugar syrup cooked to the pearl stage (230°F/110°C) into the beaten egg yolks in a thin stream, whisking constantly.

5• In a mixing bowl, whisk the mascarpone and cream together. Whisk in the amaretto.

6• Whisk in the *pâte à bombe*, which should now be at 68°F (20°C), and spoon into a pastry bag. ⊕

Tiramisu (continued)

7 • Snip off the point of the bag and pipe the tiramisu cream into the serving glasses so they are one-quarter full.

8 • Place a moistened disk of ladyfinger sponge on top, pressing it down lightly to remove any air bubbles. Repeat the layers, finishing with a layer of cream.

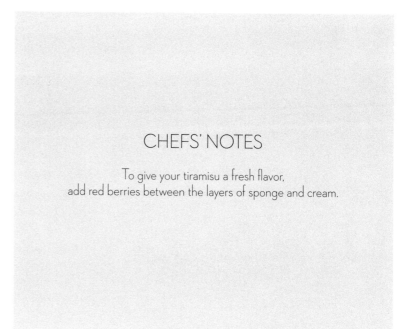

CHEFS' NOTES

To give your tiramisu a fresh flavor,
add red berries between the layers of sponge and cream.

9 • Chill for 1 hour. Fifteen minutes before serving, remove from the refrigerator and dust the tops with the cocoa powder.

Molten Chocolate Cakes

Moelleux au Chocolat

Serves 6–8

Active time
15 minutes

Freezing time
1 hour

Cooking time
7–10 minutes

Storage
Serve immediately

Equipment
3-in. (7-cm) cake rings
or other molds
Pastry bag without a tip
Silicone baking mat

Ingredients
3.5 oz. (100 g) semisweet
chocolate, 65% cacao, chopped
7 tbsp (3.5 oz./100 g) butter,
diced and softened,
plus extra for greasing
1 cup (8.5 oz./240 g) lightly
beaten egg (about 5 eggs)
Scant ½ cup (4.75 oz./130 g)
egg yolk (about 7 yolks)
4 tbsp (1.75 oz./55 g) sugar
¾ cup (2.75 oz./75 g) flour

1 • Grease the cake rings with butter and chill them
in the refrigerator while you prepare the mixture.
Melt the chocolate in a bowl over a pan of hot water.

3 • In another bowl, mix the eggs, egg yolks, and sugar together
with a spatula, and then stir into the melted chocolate and butter.

4 • Whisk in the flour until combined. Spoon the mixture into
the pastry bag and place the cake rings on the baking mat.

CHEFS' NOTES

• The uncooked mixture freezes very well.

• A small piece of chocolate can be tucked into the center of each cake before baking.

2 • Remove from the heat and stir in the butter.

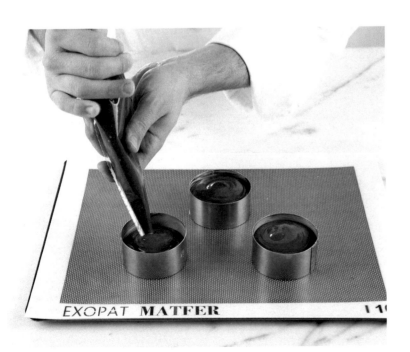

EXOPAT MATFER

5 • Snip off the point of the pastry bag and pipe the mixture into the rings. Freeze for 1 hour. Preheat the oven to 400°F (200°C/Gas mark 6). Bake from frozen for 7–10 minutes, until the tops feel firm. Allow to cool a little before unmolding while still lukewarm.

Cherry Clafoutis Tart

Clafoutis aux Cerises

Serves 6

Active time
30 minutes

Chilling time
1 hour

Cooking time
1 hour

Storage
Up to 3 days in the refrigerator

Equipment
9-in. (23-cm) round tart ring
or pan

Ingredients
9 oz. (250 g) sweet short pastry
or leftover puff pastry
(see techniques pp. 62 or 66)

Clafoutis filling
⅓ cup (2.75 oz./75 g) lightly
beaten egg (about 1 ½ eggs)
1 tbsp (0.75 oz./20 g)
egg yolk (about 1 yolk)
Scant ⅓ cup (2 oz./60 g) sugar
1 heaping tbsp (0.35 oz./10 g)
flour
½ cup (125 ml) milk
½ cup (125 ml) cream
10.5 oz. (300 g) cherries, pitted
Confectioners' sugar
for dusting

1• Line the ring with the pastry (see technique p. 26), trimming so it
stands ½ in. (1 cm) above the ring. Chill for 1 hour.
Preheat the oven to 325°F (170°C/Gas mark 3) and blind bake
the pastry crust for 15–20 minutes.

CHEFS' NOTES

When blind baking, line the pastry crust with parchment paper,
or heatproof plastic wrap designed for oven use, and fill with rice
or dried beans so the crust keeps its shape during baking.

3• Arrange the cherries over the base of the prebaked crust.

2 • Increase the oven temperature to 350°F (180°C/Gas mark 4). Whisk together the eggs, egg yolk, and sugar. Add the flour, then the milk, and finally the cream, whisking until combined.

4 • Pour the batter over the cherries and bake for 40 minutes. Carefully remove the ring and serve warm or cold, dusted with confectioners' sugar.

Parisian Custard Tart

Flan

Serves 6

Active time
30 minutes

Freezing time
10 minutes

Cooking time
30 minutes

Storage
Up to 24 hours
in the refrigerator

Equipment
7-in. (18-cm) tart ring or pan,
1 ¼ in. (3 cm) deep
Dough docker (see Chefs' Notes)

Ingredients
9 oz. (250 g) puff pastry
(see technique p. 66)

Custard filling
2 cups (500 ml) whole milk
½ cup (3.5 oz./100 g)
sugar, divided
1 vanilla bean, split lengthwise
and seeds scraped out
Scant ½ cup (3.5 oz./100 g)
lightly beaten egg
(about 2 eggs)
⅓ cup (1.75 oz./50 g) custard
powder (or cornstarch)
3 tbsp (1.75 oz./50 g) butter,
diced, at room temperature

Egg wash
1 egg, lightly beaten

1• Roll out the puff pastry to a thickness of ¾ in. (1.5 cm)
into a round larger than the tart ring. Roll the dough docker
over the pastry to mark it with small holes.

4• Raise the border with your fingers.
Place in the freezer while you prepare the custard filling.

2 • Line the tart ring (see techniques pp. 26–29) and press the pastry together around the top edge to make a border that stands about ¼ in. (5 mm) above the ring.

3 • Push a rolling pin across the top to remove the overhanging dough.

5 • Make a pastry cream (see technique p. 196) by heating the milk with half the sugar and the vanilla seeds. Whisk the eggs with the rest of the sugar until pale and thick.

6 • Whisk a little of the hot milk into the egg mixture and then pour the mixture back into the saucepan. ⊙

Parisian Custard Tart (continued)

7 • Whisk in the custard powder and allow to thicken without letting the mixture come to a boil. Remove from the heat and whisk in the butter.

8 • Preheat the oven to 375°F (190°C/Gas mark 5). Pour the custard filling into the chilled tart crust.

9 • Brush the filling with the egg wash and bake for 30 minutes.

Pavlova

Serves 4

Active time
2 hours

Cooking time
1 ½ hours

Storage
Up to 24 hours

Equipment
Stand mixer
3 pastry bags, fitted
with a plain ½-in. (10-mm) tip,
a closed fluted ½-in. (10-mm) tip,
and an open fluted ½-in.
(10-mm) tip

Pastry bag without a tip
Instant-read thermometer

Ingredients
Swiss meringue
3 tbsp (1.75 oz./50 g)
egg white (about 1 ½ whites)
⅓ cup (2.75 oz./75 g)
sugar, divided
½ tsp (2 g) cornstarch
¼ tsp (1 ml) white vinegar
Confectioners' sugar for dusting

Raspberry sauce
3.5 oz. (100 g) raspberry purée
⅓ cup (2.5 oz./70 g) sugar
0.25 oz. (8 g) pectin NH
1 ¾ tsp (8 ml) lemon juice

Mascarpone cream
½ cup (125 ml) whipping cream,
35% butterfat, well chilled
1 ½ tbsp (1 oz./25 g)
mascarpone, well chilled
1 ¾ tbsp (0.75 oz./20 g) sugar
1 vanilla bean, split lengthwise

Red fruits for decoration

1· Line a baking sheet with parchment paper and, using a cake ring as a guide, draw a circle on it about 7 in. (18 cm) in diameter.

2· Whisk the egg whites with 4 tbsp (2 oz./60 g) of the sugar in the bowl of the stand mixer set over a pan of hot water. Heat to 113°F (45°C), whisking continuously, then transfer to the stand mixer and whisk at high speed until the mixture has completely cooled.

3· Mix the remaining sugar with the cornstarch and add to the whites, followed by the vinegar. Gently fold everything together with a spatula. ↪

Pavlova (continued)

4 • Preheat the oven to 225°F (110°C/Gas mark ¼).
Spoon half the meringue into the pastry bag with the plain tip
and, starting in the center, pipe a spiral on the parchment
to fill the drawn circle.

5 • Spoon the remaining meringue into the pastry bag
with the closed fluted tip and pipe rosettes around the edge.
Dust with confectioners' sugar and bake for 1 ½ hours.
Store in a dry place.

8 • Spoon the raspberry sauce into the pastry bag without a tip,
snip off the point of the bag, and pipe a thin layer of sauce over
the meringue.

9 • Spoon the mascarpone cream into the pastry bag fitted
with the open fluted tip and pipe swirls of cream over the top.

CHEFS' NOTES

Hold the parchment in place on the baking sheet
with 4 small magnets or a tiny dot of meringue mixture in each corner.

6 • Heat the raspberry purée to 105°F (40°C).
Mix the sugar with the pectin and add. Bring to a boil,
add the lemon juice, and then allow to cool.

7 • For the cream, whisk together the whipping cream,
mascarpone, sugar, and vanilla seeds on low speed.
Increase the speed to medium and whisk until the mixture
holds its shape.

10 • Decorate with red fruits, prepared as necessary.
Dust with confectioners' sugar.

Soufflé

Serves 8

Active time
45 minutes

Cooking time
20–25 minutes

Storage
Serve immediately

Equipment
Instant-read
thermometer

Stand mixer fitted
with the whisk
attachment
(or use a hand whisk)

8 × 3 ½-in. (9-cm)
ramekins, 1 ¾ in.
(4.5 cm) deep

Ingredients
Basic soufflé mixture
1 lb. 7 oz. (650 g)
pastry cream
(see technique p. 196)

1 tsp (5 ml) vanilla
extract

1 ⅓ cups
(10.5 oz./300 g)
egg white
(about 10 whites)

½ cup (3.5 oz./100 g)
sugar

Just-melted butter
for greasing

Superfine sugar
for sprinkling

Confectioners' sugar
for dusting

Flavorings
Coffee:
1 tbsp plus 1 tsp
(0.75 oz./20 g) coffee
extract, or ⅓ cup
(0.75 oz./20 g) instant
coffee granules
dissolved in the milk,
or 3.5 oz. (100 g)
ground coffee infused
in the warmed milk
and then strained.

Various liqueurs:
2–3% of the weight
of the pastry cream.

Chocolate:
3–3.5 oz. (80–100 g)
cacao paste melted
in the hot
pastry cream.

1 • Preheat the oven to 400°F (200°C/Gas mark 6).
Brush the ramekins with melted butter and sprinkle
with superfine sugar.

4 • Gradually fold the meringue into the pastry cream using
a spatula, mixing the two together thoroughly
(any lumps of meringue will prevent the soufflés rising evenly)
but taking care not to deflate the mixture.

5 • Fill the ramekins with the soufflé mixture, smooth the tops,
and dust with confectioners' sugar.

2 • Warm the pastry cream to 95°F–105°F (35°C–40°C), beat with a whisk to lighten the texture, and then add the vanilla.

3 • Whisk the egg whites until standing in soft peaks. Gradually whisk in the sugar to make a glossy meringue.

6 • Run a finger around the edge of each ramekin to remove any excess mixture. Bake for about 20 minutes, until nicely risen and slightly browned on top, without opening the oven door as this will keep the steam in the oven and ensure they rise fully. Serve immediately.

Breton Custard and Prune Tart

Far Breton

Serves 10

Active time
20 minutes

Cooking time
40 minutes

Storage
Up to 2 days in the refrigerator

Equipment
8-in. (20-cm) round deep tart pan or ovenproof dish

Ingredients
1 cup (9 oz./250 g) egg (about 5 eggs)
¾ cup (5.25 oz./150 g) sugar
1 stick plus 2 tbsp (5.25 oz./150 g) butter, melted and cooled to lukewarm
1 cup (4.25 oz./120 g) flour, sifted
2 cups (500 ml) whole milk, infused with 1 vanilla bean
3 tbsp (50 ml) rum
7 oz. (200 g) prunes, pitted

1• Whisk the eggs and sugar together in a mixing bowl until pale and thick. Whisk in the melted, cooled butter.

CHEFS' NOTES

• You can replace some of the whole egg with egg yolks, in which case reduce the quantity of flour so the filling is not too stiff.

• Before making the tart, you can macerate the prunes in tea or a liquor, if you wish.

• You can also use salted butter.

3• Arrange the prunes in the tart pan or dish.

2 • Add the flour and whisk until the mixture is smooth.
Pour in the vanilla-infused milk (removing the vanilla bean first),
whisking constantly, and then the rum.

4 • Preheat the oven to 400°F–425°F (200°C–220°C).
Pour the mixture over the prunes and bake for 40 minutes
until set and golden brown on top.

Floating Islands

Île Flottante or *Œufs à la Neige*

Serves 10–12

Active time
30 minutes

Cooking time
2–3 minutes for each batch

Storage
Up to 2 days in the refrigerator

Equipment
Stand mixer
Pastry bag fitted
with a plain ⅓-in. (10-mm) tip
Ladle, lightly greased with oil
Serving bowls

Ingredients
Custard
2 cups (500 ml) whole milk
½ cup (3.5 oz./100 g) sugar,
divided
1 vanilla bean, split lengthwise
and seeds scraped out
Scant ½ cup (4.25 oz./120 g)
egg yolk (about 6 ½ yolks)

Meringue
¾ cup (6.25 oz./180 g) egg white
(about 6 whites)
1 pinch of salt
Scant ½ cup (3 oz./90 g) sugar
Milk or water for poaching
the meringues

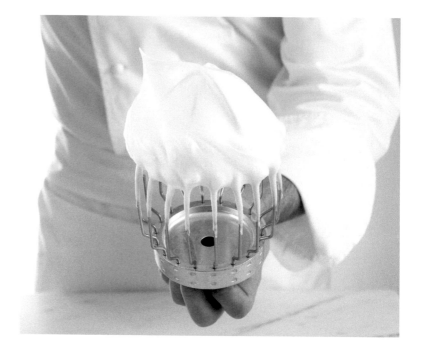

1 • Prepare the custard (see technique p. 204) using the quantities listed.
Let cool and then chill until needed. Whisk the egg whites
with the salt in the stand mixer until soft peaks form. Gradually
add the sugar, whisking until the meringue is stiff and glossy.

4 • Drain the meringue into a shallow dish lined with paper towels.
Cook the rest of the mixture in the same way.
Cover with plastic wrap and chill until needed.

5 • Pour the chilled custard into individual bowls
and place a poached meringue into each one.

2 • Bring milk or water to a simmer in a large saucepan. Spoon the meringue into the pastry bag and pipe some into the ladle to shape it into a round.

3 • Slide the meringue out of the ladle into the simmering water or milk and poach for 1 minute. Turn it over and poach for an additional minute.

6 • If you wish, pipe a little salted butter caramel spread over each meringue (see technique p. 524).

CHEFS' NOTES

• Poaching the meringues in milk
(you can make the meringues first and then use the milk for the custard)
makes them thicker but it's a more delicate operation than using water.

• You can top the meringues with caramel,
or add a flavoring to the custard or egg whites.

• Instead of poaching, the meringues can be baked in the microwave.
Pipe the mixture onto greased parchment paper or into
very lightly oiled ramekins. Alternatively, bake them in lightly oiled
soufflé dishes in a 275°F (140°C/Gas mark 1) oven,
using the convection setting, for 10 minutes.

Polish Brioches

Polonaise

Makes 6

Active time
1 ½ hours (plus time for making the brioche, pastry, pastry cream, and meringue)

Cooking time
About 40 minutes

Freezing time
1 hour

Storage
Up to 2 days

Equipment
6 × individual brioche molds
3 ½-in. (8-cm) plain round dough cutter
6 × 3-in. (7-cm) tartlet pans
Instant-read thermometer
Pastry bag without a tip

Ingredients
Brioche
1 quantity brioche dough
(see technique p. 130)

Sweet short pastry
2 quantities sweet short pastry dough
(see technique p. 60)

Syrup
4 cups (1 liter) water
2 ⅔ cups
(1 lb. 2 oz./500 g) sugar
Orange zest to flavor
Scant ½ cup (100 ml) kirsch

Pastry cream
½ quantity pastry cream, cooled
(see technique p. 196)

Italian meringue
1 quantity Italian meringue
(see technique p. 232)

Filling and decoration
6 tbsp (2 oz./50 g)
candied fruit, or raisins soaked in rum and drained

Sliced almonds
Confectioners' sugar
for dusting

1 • Divide the brioche dough into 6 and place in the brioche molds. Bake at 400°F (200°C/Gas mark 6) for about 15–20 minutes, until golden. Cool and then cut horizontally into 4 slices. Reduce the oven temperature to 350°F (180°C/Gas mark 4).

4 • Spoon the cooled pastry cream into the pastry bag and pipe it into the prebaked tartlet crusts.

2 • Roll out the pastry to a thickness of ⅛ in. (3 mm) and cut out 6 disks using the dough cutter. Line the tartlet pans with the pastry and blind bake for 20 minutes. Set aside.

3 • Make a syrup using the water, sugar, and orange zest. Remove from the heat and stir in the kirsch. When the syrup has cooled to 140°F (60°C), briefly soak the brioche slices in it and drain on a rack.

5 • Arrange some of the candied fruit or raisins over the pastry cream.

6 • Place a drained brioche slice in each crust over the pastry cream. Pipe more pastry cream over the brioche slice and sprinkle with more fruit. ⊕

Polish Brioches (continued)

7 • Make another layer of brioche, pastry cream, and fruit, finishing with the tops of the brioche buns. Place in the freezer for 1 hour.

8 • Place the Italian meringue in a mixing bowl. Spear the base of each tartlet with the tip of a knife and dip the brioche layers into the meringue until evenly coated.

9 • Dip the tartlets so the brioche layers are completely covered but the pastry crusts remain visible.

10 • Scatter almond slices over the meringue.

CHEFS' NOTES

You can replace the candied fruit or raisins with fresh orange segments, if you prefer.

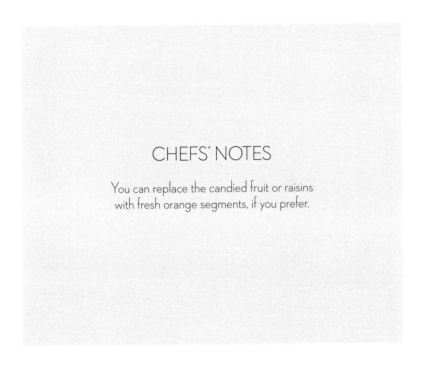

11 • Preheat the oven to 450°F (240°C/Gas mark 8). Dust with confectioners' sugar and bake for a few minutes until the meringue is lightly golden.

Lemon and Lime Creams

Yaourts

Serves 6

Active time
15 minutes

Cooking time
6–8 minutes

Storage
Up to 2 days in the refrigerator

Equipment
Instant-read thermometer
6 glass bowls or glasses

Ingredients
1 cup (250 ml) whipping cream, 35% butterfat
1 ½ tbsp (0.75 oz./20 g) sugar
1 tsp (5 g) lime zest
1 ½ tbsp (20 ml) lemon juice

1 • Heat the cream, sugar, and lime zest in a saucepan to 175°F (80°C).

3 • Divide the mixture immediately between the bowls or glasses. Once the creams have set, chill in the refrigerator until ready to serve.

2 • Strain into a jug through a fine-mesh sieve to remove the lime zest and immediately stir in the lemon juice.

4 • Serve topped with a fruit coulis or fresh fruit of your choice.

ENTREMETS

LAYERED DESSERTS
& GÂTEAUX

ENTREMETS: LAYERED DESSERTS AND GÂTEAUX

Entremets are the classic gâteaux the French often serve as desserts. These elegant centerpieces—made by layering sponges or sweet yeast cakes with creamy fillings, providing a combination of different textures and tastes—require organization and the mastery of special techniques to achieve perfect results.

A BRIEF HISTORY OF GREAT FRENCH GÂTEAUX
Saint-Honoré

Created by the pastry chef Chiboust around 1850, the Saint-Honoré was named for the patron saint of bakers and was also the address of Chiboust's pastry store, on Rue Saint-Honoré in Paris. Originally a large brioche filled with pastry cream, it now consists of a plain tart pastry base, decorated with caramel-glazed choux puffs filled with Chiboust cream.

Baba

First mentioned at King Stanislas Leszczynski's court in the 18th century, it is believed this was originally a stale kugelhopf soaked with sweet wine. Another theory holds that the name derives from babka, a Polish brioche, which inspired Parisian pastry chef Stohre, whose Paris store, founded in 1730, is still renowned today for its pastries and decor.

Opéra

Two celebrated pastry stores claim to have created this rich chocolate and coffee cake: the Maison Dalloyau in 1955, and the equally renowned Gaston Lenôtre. Flat and quite shallow, it is said to represent the stage of the original Paris opera house, the Palais Garnier, which gave the cake its name.

WHAT SIZE FOR THE NUMBER OF GUESTS?

In France, cake rings 1 ¾ in. (4.5 cm) high rather than pans are used. For every 2 additional servings add 1 in. (2 cm) to the diameter of the ring.

Number of servings	4–6 SERVINGS	8 SERVINGS	10 SERVINGS
Cake ring size	5 or 6-in. (14 or 16-cm) diameter	7-in. (18-cm) diameter	8-in. (20-cm) diameter

MAKE SPACE IN THE FREEZER

Some entremets require layers that need time in the freezer to make them easier to assemble and glaze. Before starting, check there is sufficient space in your freezer to position things correctly.

THE INDISPENSABLE SERRATED KNIFE

To cut a sponge cake, such as for a *fraisier* (strawberry layer cake), into even layers or neaten the edges after it has been assembled, use a thin, serrated knife so that fragile sponges can be sliced without their delicate crumb tearing.

FRUITS AND GELATIN

To set fruit-based mixtures like mousses and jellies, gelatin is often added. But beware! Some fruits contain proteolytic enzymes and these react against the proteins in gelatin, preventing a set. Pineapple, kiwi, guava, prickly pear, fig, and honeydew melon cannot be used with gelatin. The gelatin must be replaced by agar-agar or the fruit first boiled to a pulp.

PERFECT GANACHE

Chocolate ganache is often used for decorating entremets. Hot cream is poured over chopped chocolate, the heat melting the chocolate so the two can be mixed together. For a perfectly smooth result, stir briskly from the center outward using circular movements—a bit like making mayonnaise.

PRICKING ALL OVER

To rise evenly, puff pastry for napoleons (millefeuilles) must be pricked all over. Pastry chefs use a pastry docker to make holes at regular intervals. If you do not have one, simply use two forks to prick the dough.

A SOLID BASE

To make sure the sponge stays firm when cut into portions, the base of certain moistened cakes, such as Opéra, is brushed with a thin layer of chocolate. This adds crispness and also ensures the soft, filled cake layers keep their shape when the cake is sliced.

Mont-Blanc
This chestnut-flavored cake
was mainly inspired by
an Alsatian specialty:
the torche aux marrons.
It is thought to have been
created in 1903 in the Paris
tearoom Rumpelmayer,
now called Angelina, where
it is still a signature cake.

INNOVATIONS
Pastry chefs justifiably
consider that they are
the bearers of a fine tradition,
but this does not stop them
from revisiting the classics.
So, while the classic Opéra
is traditionally square
or rectangular, it could be
rearranged to fit into glasses;
a classic napoleon might
be served on its side; exotic
fruits can enhance
a Saint-Honoré and modern
decorations may be added.
Textures, too, are changing.
A crémeux may top a jelled
or frozen layer, known in
French as an insert:
a surprising addition whose
shape and flavor can
be hidden from view.

TAKE CARE WHEN UNMOLDING

For some entremets, the sides of the ring are lined with food-safe acetate to help with unmolding. Make sure the strip is ¾ in. (2 cm) taller than the cake so the ring can be lifted off easily. Freezing the entremets allows the acetate to be removed neatly.

THE RIGHT ORDER WHEN MAKING A SYRUP

For a syrup to moisten a sponge, pour the water into the pan first and then add the sugar. This allows the sugar to dissolve more easily and prevents it caramelizing on the bottom of the pan.

AN ALMOND PASTE THAT IS EASY TO WORK WITH

Almond paste, whether added to a sponge batter or used as decoration, is difficult to work with when it is too firm. Simply microwave it for 10–20 seconds to soften it and make it easier to handle. Always use a good quality almond paste.

DIFFERENT GRADES OF ALMOND PASTE

The quality of almond paste depends on the percentage of almonds it contains: the higher the percentage, the better it will be. Standard almond paste is usually made from two parts ground almonds to one part sugar but superior brands contain 65–67% almonds, meaning they are less sweet and have a crumblier texture. Marzipan differs from almond paste in that it is made with equal quantities of almonds and sugar, plus a little corn syrup and sometimes egg white. Sweeter, softer, and more pliable, it is used for modeling cake decorations or eaten as candies.

AN EASY CARAMEL GLAZE

Crisp choux puffs for Saint-Honoré are glazed with caramel. Adding glucose syrup to the sugar and water prevents the sugar from recrystallizing as the syrup caramelizes and limits the absorption of moisture by the caramel.

COVERING AN ENTREMETS WITH ALMOND PASTE

A quick and easy way to decorate an entremets is with colored almond paste. Roll out the paste between 2 acetate sheets, slightly larger than the diameter of the cake. Peel off the top sheet of acetate and turn the paste over onto the cake (still in its ring) so it sticks to the cream covering the top. Remove the other sheet of acetate and run a rolling pin over the almond paste to trim it to the exact size of the cake (this will ensure a neat fit), before carefully lifting off the ring.

LEVEL

1

OPÉRA

Serves 6–8

Active time
2 hours

Cooking time
8 minutes

Chilling time
1 hour

Storage
Up to 3 days in the refrigerator

Equipment
Stand mixer
16 × 24-in. (40 × 60-cm) baking sheet lined with parchment paper
Instant-read thermometer
Stick blender
5-in. (12-cm) square cake frame, 1 in. (2.5 cm) high

Ingredients

JOCONDE SPONGE
⅔ cup (5.25 oz./150 g) lightly beaten egg (about 3 eggs)
1 cup minus 1 ½ tbsp (4 oz./115 g) confectioners' sugar
1 heaping cup (4 oz./115 g) almond flour
3 tbsp (1.5 oz./45 g) melted butter
¼ cup (1 oz./30 g) flour
Scant ½ cup (3.5 oz./105 g) egg white (about 3 ½ whites)
1 heaping tbsp (0.5 oz./15 g) sugar

BUTTERCREAM
½ cup (3.5 oz./100 g) sugar
Scant ½ cup (100 ml) water
½ cup (4.5 oz./125 g) egg white (about 4 whites)
2 sticks plus 6 tbsp (11.5 oz./325 g) butter, diced, at room temperature
Coffee flavoring to taste

GANACHE
⅔ cup (160 ml) whole milk
2 tbsp plus 1 tsp (35 ml) whipping cream, 35% butterfat
4.5 oz. (125 g) bittersweet chocolate, 64% cacao, chopped
4 tbsp plus 1 tsp (2.25 oz./65 g) butter, diced, at room temperature

COFFEE-FLAVORED SYRUP
Scant ⅓ cup (2 oz./60 g) sugar
3 cups (750 ml) water
2 oz. (60 g) instant espresso coffee granules

GLAZE
3.5 oz. (100 g) *pâte à glacer brune* (brown glazing paste)
3.5 oz. (100 g) bittersweet chocolate, 58% cacao
3 tbsp (1.75 oz./50 g) grape-seed oil

A little melted chocolate for the cake base

MAKING THE JOCONDE SPONGE
Preheat the oven to 425°F (220°C/Gas mark 7). Whisk the eggs, confectioners' sugar, almond flour, melted butter, and flour at high speed for 5 minutes in the stand mixer. Transfer the mixture to a bowl. Wash and dry the bowl of the stand mixer and whisk the egg whites, gradually adding the sugar, until firm and glossy. Gently fold the first mixture into the meringue, spread over the baking sheet, and bake for 5–8 minutes. The sponge should be springy to the touch but not dry.

MAKING THE BUTTERCREAM
Dissolve the sugar in the water in a pan and boil to 243°F (117°C). Meanwhile, whisk the egg whites in the stand mixer and then slowly drizzle in the hot syrup, whisking constantly at medium speed until the whites cool to between 68°F–77°F (20°C–25°C). Whisk in the butter until the mixture is creamy and then the coffee flavoring. Chill until needed.

MAKING THE GANACHE
Bring the milk and cream to a boil in a pan, pour over the chocolate, and stir until melted. Add the butter and blend with the stick blender until smooth.

MAKING THE COFFEE-FLAVORED SYRUP
Dissolve the sugar in the water in a saucepan and bring to a boil. Remove from the heat and stir in the espresso granules until dissolved. Allow to cool.

ASSEMBLING THE CAKE
Cut the sponge layer into 3 × 5-in. (12-cm) squares. Brush a little melted chocolate on the underside of one square, place it in the cake frame and allow to set. Moisten the sponge with syrup and spread with buttercream. Moisten the second sponge with syrup on both sides and place on top. Spread over the ganache. Moisten the last square on both sides, place on the ganache and spread with buttercream. Chill for 1 hour until firm. Melt the glazing paste and chocolate over a pan of hot water or in the microwave oven and stir in the oil. When the cake is well chilled, coat with the glaze.

LEVEL

2

OPÉRA

Serves 8

Active time
1 hour

Cooking time
10 minutes

Chilling time
1 hour

Storage
Up to 24 hours in the refrigerator

Equipment
Instant-read thermometer
Electric hand beater
16 × 24-in. (40 × 60-cm) baking
sheet lined with parchment paper
3 pastry bags fitted
with plain ½-in. (10-mm) tips
Stick blender
8 shot glasses, 4 in. (10 cm) deep
and 1 ½ in. (4 cm) in diameter

Ingredients

FLOURLESS SPONGE
1 tbsp (0.5 oz./15 g) butter
1.75 oz. (50 g) semisweet
chocolate, 70% cacao
2 ½ tbsp (0.5 oz./15 g)
almond flour
¼ cup (1.75 oz./50 g) sugar,
divided
2 ¾ tsp (0.5 oz./15 g) egg yolk
(about 1 yolk)
¼ cup (2 oz./60 g) egg white
(about 2 whites)

GANACHE
Scant 1 cup (200 ml) whole milk
Scant 1 cup (200 ml) whipping
cream, 35% butterfat
14 oz. (400 g) bittersweet
chocolate, 50% cacao, chopped
7 tbsp (3.5 oz./100 g) butter,
diced, at room temperature

COFFEE MOUSSE
1 ⅔ cups (400 ml) whipping cream,
35% butterfat, divided
2 tbsp (0.25 oz./7 g) instant coffee
granules
7 oz. (200 g) milk chocolate,
chopped

FOAM TOPPING (OPTIONAL)
3.5 oz. (100 g) bittersweet
chocolate, 70% cacao
Scant ½ cup (100 ml) whole milk
Gold leaf

MAKING THE SPONGE
Preheat the oven to 400°F (210°C/Gas mark 6). Melt the butter and chocolate in a bowl over a pan of hot water and heat to 122°F (50°C). Lightly mix the almond flour with 3 ½ tbsp (1.5 oz./40 g) of the sugar and the egg yolk, taking care not to beat in any air. Whisk the egg whites with the electric beater, gradually adding the remaining sugar until they hold firm peaks. Stir the melted chocolate and butter into the egg yolk mixture and then lightly fold in the whisked whites until combined. Spoon into a pastry bag and pipe 8 × 1 ¾-in. (4-cm) disks on the baking sheet. Bake for 10 minutes.

MAKING THE GANACHE
Bring the milk and cream to a boil, pour over the chocolate and stir until smooth. Cool to lukewarm and stir in the butter until just combined. Allow to cool.

MAKING THE COFFEE MOUSSE
Bring a scant ½ cup (100 ml) of the cream and the coffee to a boil, pour over the milk chocolate and stir until smooth. Using the electric beater, whisk the remaining cream until it holds soft peaks. Fold into the mousse.

MAKING THE FOAM TOPPING
Melt the chocolate with the milk in a pan. Cool and chill for about 1 hour. Just before serving, process with the stick blender until very foamy.

ASSEMBLING THE INDIVIDUAL LAYERS
Place a sponge disk in the base of each glass. Spoon the coffee mousse into the second pastry bag and pipe a layer, just under ½ in. (1 cm) deep, over the sponge disks. Chill for a few minutes. Pipe a layer of ganache, the same depth as the mousse, using the third pastry bag. Repeat the layers, finishing with a layer of sponge. When ready to serve, spoon over the foam topping and top with a little gold leaf.

CHEFS' NOTES

For best results, assemble the layers in the glasses a day ahead
but only add the foam topping just before serving.

LEVEL

3

A TALE OF THE OPÉRA

Il Était une Fois L'Opéra

by Angelo Musa

MEILLEUR OUVRIER DE FRANCE, PÂTISSIER, 2007

Makes about 10

Active time
2 ½ hours

Infusing time
24 hours

Cooking time
15 minutes

Chilling time
3 hours

Storage
Up to 24 hours
in the refrigerator

Equipment
Stand mixer with whisk
attachment
Silicone baking mat
2 ½-in. (7-cm) round
cookie cutter
Instant-read thermometer
Acetate sheets
Stick blender
10 × 3-in. and 4-in.
(7-cm and 8-cm) tartlet rings,
1 in. (3 cm) deep
Pastry bags fitted with plain tips

Ingredients
HAZELNUT SPONGE
2.25 oz. (65 g) freshly ground
coffee
1 ¾ cups (440 ml) cold water
5.5 oz. (160 g) egg
1.75 oz. (50 g) egg yolk
5.25 oz. (155 g)
confectioners' sugar
5.25 oz. (155 g) ground toasted
hazelnuts
5 oz. (140 g) egg white
0.75 oz. (20 g) brown sugar
1 oz. (25 g) hazelnut paste
1 ¾ tbsp (25 ml) grape seed oil
1.25 oz. (35 g) flour
2 ½ tsp (8 g) cornstarch

MOCHA PRALINE CRISP
1 oz. (25 g) milk couverture
chocolate, chopped
8.5 oz. (240 g) almond praline
1.5 oz. (40 g) coffee paste
0.75 oz. (20 g) *feuilletine*
flakes (or use crushed wafers)
½ tsp (2.5 g) fleur de sel
4.5 oz. (130 g) caramelized
almonds, chopped

OPERA GANACHE
5 ¾ tbsp. (85 ml) whipping
cream, 35% butterfat
1 oz. (25 g) dextrose
1 ½ tsp (5 g) sorbitol powder
3 oz. (90 g) bittersweet
couverture chocolate,
62% cacao, chopped

MOCHA BUTTERCREAM
⅔ cup (150 ml) whole milk
1.5 oz. (45 g) sidamo coffee,
freshly ground
1.75 oz. (50 g) egg
1 oz. (30 g) egg yolk
2 oz. (60 g) superfine sugar
10.5 oz. (295 g) butter
½ tbsp (6 g) coffee paste

MERINGUE FOR BUTTERCREAM
1 oz. (30 g) invert sugar
1 oz. (30 g) glucose syrup
1.5 oz. (40 g) egg white

MILK MOUSSE
2 tbsp (30 ml) whole milk
1 tsp (4 g) Louis François
Gallimousse expansion agent
1 oz. (25 g) Louis François
Chantifix whipped cream
stabilizer

GLAZE
1 ¼ lb. (600 g) bittersweet
couverture chocolate,
70% cacao
2.5 oz. (70 g) milk couverture
chocolate, 40% cacao
⅓ cup (80 ml) grape seed oil

COFFEE JELLY
1 ¼ cups (115 g) green coffee
beans
2 cups (500 ml) water
1 ¼ tbsp (17.5 g) gelatin powder
7 tsp (3.5 ml) water
4 tsp (16 g) sugar

DECORATION
Toasted hazelnuts
Edible gold leaf

——— THE DAY BEFORE
Infuse the coffee for the sponge in the cold water overnight. Infuse the coffee for
the buttercream in the cold milk for 24 hours. Roast the beans for the jelly at 450°F
(230°C/Gas mark 8) for 10 minutes, then soak in the cold water for 24 hours.

——— MAKING THE HAZELNUT SPONGE
Preheat the oven to 350°F (180°C/Gas mark 4). Whisk the eggs with the yolks,
confectioners' sugar, and ground hazelnuts. Whisk the whites with the brown sugar
to soft peaks. Stir the hazelnut paste and oil into the egg mixture, then fold in the
whisked whites and finally the sifted flour and cornstarch. Spread about 1 lb. 9 oz.
(700 g) over the silicone mat and bake for 8–10 minutes. Remove from the oven and
let cool. Cut out 30 sponge disks using the cookie cutter. Strain the coffee-infused
water and use it to moisten the sponges (about ½ tbsp/8 ml per sponge).

MAKING THE MOCHA PRALINE CRISP
Melt the chocolate to 104°F (40°C) over a bain-marie. Mix the other ingredients
together, stir into the melted chocolate, and quickly spread thinly over an acetate
sheet on a baking sheet. Allow to set and then use the cookie cutter to cut out 10 disks.

——— MAKING THE OPERA GANACHE
Heat the cream, dextrose, and sorbitol. Melt the chocolate, pour over the hot cream,
mix well, and then process with the stick blender until smooth and glossy.

——— MAKING THE MOCHA BUTTERCREAM
Strain the coffee-infused milk and bring ⅓ cup (75 ml) to a boil. Whisk the egg, yolk,
and sugar together until pale, then whisk in the coffee-infused milk as for a custard.
When it cools to 104°F (40°C), whisk in the butter and then add the coffee paste.

——— MAKING THE MERINGUE FOR THE BUTTERCREAM
In a saucepan, heat the invert sugar and glucose until melted. Pour over the egg whites
in the stand mixer, whisking until stiff. Cool completely and fold into the buttercream.

——— MAKING THE MILK MOUSSE
Whisk all the ingredients together until frothy and fold into the buttercream.

——— MAKING THE GLAZE
Melt all the ingredients together over a bain-marie.

——— MAKING THE COFFEE JELLY
Strain the coffee-bean infusion: you need a scant 1 cup (200 ml). Soak the gelatin in
the cold water. Heat one-third of the infusion and stir in the gelatin and sugar until
dissolved. Remove from the heat, stir in the remaining infusion, and pour into the
3-in. (7-cm) tartlet rings. Place in the refrigerator to set, then cut into small cubes.

——— ASSEMBLING
Pipe 4 tsp (20 g) of coffee cream into each 4-in. (8-cm) ring and top with a disk of
moistened sponge. Pipe ganache on top and add a second layer of sponge. Pipe
over about 2 tsp (10 g) of coffee cream, and finish with the praline crisp stuck to the
remaining sponge layer. Chill until firm. Unmold and use the glaze at 104°F (40°C)
to coat the cakes completely. Decorate with a few chopped toasted hazelnuts, 4 or
5 cubes of coffee jelly, and gold leaf.

LEVEL

1

BLACK FOREST GÂTEAU

Forêt Noire

Serves 6–8

Active time
1 ½ hours

Cooking time
20 minutes

Chilling time
30 minutes

Storage
Up to 24 hours in the refrigerator

Equipment
7-in. (18-cm) round cake pan, greased
Stand mixer
Pastry bag fitted
with a plain ½-in. (10-mm) tip

Ingredients

CHOCOLATE GENOISE
Scant ½ cup (3.5 oz./100 g)
lightly beaten egg (about 2 eggs)
Scant ⅓ cup (2 oz./60 g) sugar
½ cup minus 1 tbsp
(1.75 oz./50 g) flour
2 tsp (0.2 oz./6 g) cornstarch
2 ½ tsp (0.2 oz./6 g) unsweetened
cocoa powder

CHERRY-FLAVORED SYRUP
3 tbsp (50 ml) water
¼ cup (1.75 oz./50 g) sugar
3 tbsp (50 ml) juice
from Morello cherries in kirsch
1 ½ tbsp (25 ml) mineral water

WHIPPED GANACHE
Generous ⅓ cup (90 ml) whipping
cream, 35% butterfat, divided
0.3 oz. (8 g) invert sugar
1 oz. (30 g) bittersweet couverture
chocolate, 58% cacao, chopped

CHANTILLY CREAM
1 ¼ cups (300 ml) whipping cream,
35% butterfat, divided, chilled
Scant ¼ cup (1 oz./30 g)
confectioners' sugar
Scant ½ tsp (2 ml) vanilla extract

FILLING AND DECORATION
5.25 oz. (150 g) Morello cherries
in kirsch
Chocolate shavings

MAKING THE GENOISE
Preheat the oven to 350°F (180°C/Gas mark 4). Using the ingredients listed, make the sponge batter (see technique p. 220), pour it into the cake pan, and bake for 20 minutes.

MAKING THE SYRUP
Combine all the ingredients in a saucepan. Heat until the sugar dissolves and then bring to a boil. Allow to cool.

MAKING THE WHIPPED GANACHE
Heat 2 tbsp (30 ml) of the cream with the invert sugar in a pan. Stir in the couverture chocolate and, when melted, blend until smooth. Allow to cool. Whisk the ganache with the remaining chilled cream in the stand mixer until it is smooth and silky.

MAKING THE CHANTILLY CREAM
Wash and dry the stand mixer bowl and whisk all the ingredients together in it until light and airy.

ASSEMBLING THE CAKE
Cut the sponge into 3 equal layers. Brush 1 layer with syrup and spread the ganache over it with a spatula. Arrange the cherries on top. Place a second layer of sponge on the cherries and brush with syrup. Spread a layer of cream over it and top with the final layer. Brush with syrup and cover the cake with cream. Chill for 30 minutes before serving, decorated with chocolate shavings.

LEVEL

2

WHITE FOREST GÂTEAU

Forêt Blanche

Serves 6–8

Active time
2 hours

Cooking time
8–10 minutes

Chilling time
2 hours

Storage
Up to 24 hours in the refrigerator

Equipment
Stand mixer
3 pastry bags fitted with plain
¼-in. (6-mm) tips
16 × 24-in. (40 × 60-cm) baking
sheet lined with parchment paper
Strips of food-safe acetate
Curved tuile mold or rolling pin
6-in. (16-cm) cake ring,
1 ½ in. (3.5 cm) high

Ingredients

CHOCOLATE LADYFINGER SPONGE
⅓ cup (2.75 oz./75 g)
egg white (about 2 ½ whites)
Generous ⅓ cup
(2.75 oz./75 g) sugar
3 tbsp (1.75 oz./55 g) egg yolk
(about 3 yolks)
Generous ¼ cup
(1.25 oz./35 g) flour
2 tbsp plus 2 ½ tsp
(1.25 oz./35 g) cornstarch
2 tsp (0.2 oz./5 g)
unsweetened cocoa powder

KIRSCH-MARASCHINO SYRUP
½ cup (125 ml) cold simple syrup
(made of equal parts water and sugar)
1 ½ tbsp (25 ml) kirsch
1 ½ tbsp (25 ml) maraschino
1 ½ tbsp (25 ml) water

LIGHT VANILLA CREAM
1 ½ sheets (0.1 oz/3 g) gelatin
⅓ cup (75 ml) whole milk
2 tsp (10 ml) whipping cream,
35% butterfat
1 ½ tbsp (1 oz./25 g) egg yolk
(about 1 ½ yolks)
1 heaping tbsp (0.5 oz./15 g) sugar
Seeds from 1 vanilla bean
1 tbsp plus 1 tsp (20 ml) water
1 cup (250 ml) whipping cream,
35% butterfat, whipped

WHIPPED GANACHE
Generous ⅓ cup (90 ml)
whipping cream, 35% butterfat,
divided, chilled

0.3 oz. (8 g) invert sugar
1 oz. (30 g) bittersweet couverture
chocolate, 58% cacao

CHANTILLY CREAM
1 tbsp plus 2 tsp
(0.75 oz./20 g) sugar
1 cup (250 ml) whipping cream,
35% butterfat
½ tsp (3 ml) vanilla extract

WHITE CHOCOLATE PETALS
5.25 oz. (150 g) white couverture
chocolate

3.5 oz. (100 g) Morello cherries
in kirsch

MAKING THE SPONGE
Preheat the oven to 400°F (200°C/Gas mark 6). Whisk the egg whites and sugar in the stand mixer. Beat in the egg yolks and then the flour, cornstarch, and cocoa powder. When combined, transfer to a pastry bag and pipe 2 × 6-in. (16-cm) disks, ⅔ in. (16 mm) thick, onto the baking sheet. Bake for 8–10 minutes and then cool on a rack.

MAKING THE KIRSCH-MARASCHINO SYRUP
Combine the syrup with the kirsch, maraschino, and water.

MAKING THE LIGHT VANILLA CREAM
Soak the gelatin in cold water. Bring the milk and cream to a boil. Whisk the egg yolk with the sugar and vanilla seeds until pale. When the milk is hot, whisk a little into the yolk mixture. Return it to the saucepan and stir constantly over the heat until it has a custard consistency. Squeeze the water from the gelatin and stir in until dissolved. Remove the cream from the heat, cool, and then fold in the whipped cream. Chill in the refrigerator.

MAKING THE WHIPPED GANACHE
Bring one-third of the cream and the invert sugar to a boil in a pan. Stir in the chocolate until melted and smooth. Allow to cool. Pour the ganache and remaining cream into the bowl of the stand mixer and whisk until creamy.

MAKING THE CHANTILLY CREAM
Wash and dry the bowl of the stand mixer and whisk all the ingredients until light and holding soft peaks.

MAKING THE WHITE CHOCOLATE PETALS
Temper the chocolate (see techniques pp. 570 and 572) and spoon into the second pastry bag. Pipe small amounts onto strips of acetate, leaving space for them to spread. Lightly press another strip of acetate on top to form the chocolate into disks. Carefully peel away the top strips and lay the chocolate, still on the bottom strips of acetate, over a tuile mold or rolling pin so the disks set in a curved shape. Once set, carefully remove them.

ASSEMBLING THE CAKE
Place a sponge layer in the base of the cake ring. Brush with syrup and pipe a layer of vanilla cream over it. Arrange the cherries evenly over the cream. Place the second sponge layer on top, brush with syrup and spread a layer of whipped ganache over it right to the edge of the ring. Chill for 1 ½ hours before carefully removing the ring. Coat the cake completely with the Chantilly cream, smoothing it evenly with a spatula. Arrange the chocolate petals attractively on top.

LEVEL

3

BLACK FOREST YULE LOG

Bûche Forêt Noire

by Nicolas Boussin

MEILLEUR OUVRIER DE FRANCE, PÂTISSIER, 2000

Makes 6

Active time
2 hours

Cooking time
30 minutes

Macerating time
Overnight

Storage
Up to 24 hours
in the refrigerator

Equipment
Stand mixer fitted
with the paddle beater
14 × 22-in. (36 × 56-cm)
cake frame
Instant-read thermometer
Stick blender
Acetate sheets
Christmas tree-shaped
cookie cutter
Chocolate relief mat
6 × 22 × 3-in. (57 × 7-cm) Yule
log molds, 2 in. (5 cm) deep
2 pastry bags fitted
with plain tips
Velvet spray gun

Ingredients
MACERATED SOUR CHERRIES
3 lb. (1.3 kg) frozen sour cherries
7.5 oz. (215 g) sugar
5.25 oz. (150 g) sour cherry purée
⅔ cup (150 ml) kirsch (optional)

SACHER SPONGE
8 oz. (230 g) raw almond paste,
50% almonds
8.25 oz. (235 g) superfine sugar,
divided
5.5 oz (160 g) egg
6.5 oz. (185 g) egg yolk
10.25 oz. (290 g) egg white
3.75 oz. (110 g) flour
2.75 oz. (75 g) unsweetened
cocoa powder
2 ⅔ tsp (10 g) baking powder
2.75 oz. (75 g) butter, melted

SOUR CHERRY JELLY
3 ¾ cups (900 ml) juice
from macerated cherries
(see above)
1 ⅔ tbsp (22 g) gelatin powder
½ cup (132 ml) water
0.75 oz. (21 g) pectin NH
4.25 oz. (120 g) sugar, divided
1 tsp (4.5 ml) citric acid solution

**BITTERSWEET
CHOCOLATE CRÉMEUX**
1 ¼ cups (300 ml) whole milk
13.75 oz. (390 g) bittersweet
couverture chocolate,
63% cacao, melted
0.5 oz. (15 g) glucose syrup
½ tbsp (8 g) gelatin powder
3 ¼ tbsp (48 ml) water
to soak the gelatin
2 ½ cups (600 ml) whipping
cream, 35% butterfat

VANILLA CREAM
Seeds from 3 vanilla beans
4 ½ cups (1.1 liters) whipping
cream, 35% butterfat
3.75 oz. (110 g) glucose syrup
1 lb. 10 oz. (740 g) white
chocolate, 33% cacao
2 tbsp (27 g) powdered
gelatin 200 bloom
¾ cup (162 ml) water
to soak the gelatin
½ cup (110 ml) kirsch
7 ⅓ cups (1.75 liters) whipping
cream, 35% butterfat, whipped

SUBLIME CREAM
2 cups (500 ml) sublime cream,
with mascarpone
1.5 oz. (40 g) sugar
Seeds from ½ vanilla bean
2 tsp (10 ml) kirsch

TO FINISH
Tempered bittersweet
couverture chocolate
Red velvet chocolate spray
Red jelly glaze

——— MACERATING THE SOUR CHERRIES (1 DAY AHEAD)
Defrost the cherries, put their juice in a saucepan, add the sugar and cherry purée and bring to a simmer. Add the kirsch and cherries, and let macerate, if possible, overnight.

——— MAKING THE SACHER SPONGE
Preheat the oven to 400°F (200°C/Gas mark 6). Beat the almond paste with 1.75 oz. (50 g) of the sugar in the stand mixer. Gradually beat in the eggs and egg yolks. Meanwhile, whisk the egg whites with the remaining 6.75 oz. (185 g) of the sugar. Fold the sifted dry ingredients (flour, cocoa, baking powder) into the first mixture, then add the melted butter and whisked whites. Pour into the frame and bake for 25 minutes.

——— MAKING THE SOUR CHERRY JELLY
Drain the macerated cherries and put their juice in a saucepan. Soak the gelatin in the water. Heat the cherry juice to 104°F (40°C), mix the pectin with 2 oz. (60 g) of the sugar, and stir in. Bring to a boil and stir in the rest of the sugar, citric acid, and bloomed gelatin until dissolved. Finally add the cherries.

——— MAKING THE BITTERSWEET CHOCOLATE CRÉMEUX
Bring the milk to a boil and pour it over the melted chocolate and glucose. Add the bloomed gelatin and whipping cream and blend until smooth with the stick blender.

——— MAKING THE VANILLA CREAM
Infuse the vanilla seeds in the cream. Add the glucose, bring to a boil, and pour over the white chocolate. Add the soaked gelatin and kirsch and blend until smooth. When the temperature cools to 82°F (28°C), fold in the whipped cream.

——— MAKING THE SUBLIME CREAM
Whip all the ingredients together until stiff.

——— MAKING THE CHOCOLATE DECORATIONS
Pour tempered bittersweet chocolate between 2 acetate sheets. When set, cut out shapes with the Christmas tree cutter. Spread more tempered bittersweet chocolate over the relief mat and, when set, cut 12 × 2 ½ × 1 ½-in. (6 × 4-cm) rectangles.

——— ASSEMBLING THE YULE LOGS
Coat the sponge with melted bittersweet couverture chocolate and turn it over. Spread the sponge with a layer of the cherry jelly before it sets and chill. When set, cover the jelly with a layer of the bittersweet chocolate crémeux and place in the freezer. Cut the layered sponge into 2 ½-in. (6-cm) wide strips the same length as the molds. Assemble the logs upside down. Pipe 1 ¼ lb. (600 g) of the vanilla cream into the log molds and smooth the surface. Place the layered sponges on top and freeze. When firm, unmold and, using the spray gun, coat the logs with red velvet chocolate. Pipe small mounds of sublime cream on top and arrange the chocolate trees between them. Add dots of red jelly glaze and finish by placing the chocolate rectangles at each end of the logs.

LEVEL

1

STRAWBERRY LAYER CAKE

Fraisier

Serves 8

Active time
1 ½ hours

Cooking time
20 minutes

Chilling time
1 hour

Storage
Up to 2 days in the refrigerator

Equipment
Electric hand beater
Instant-read thermometer
6-in. (16-cm) cake ring, 1 ¾ in.
(4.5 cm) high, on a baking sheet
7-in. (18-cm) cake ring, 1 ¾ in.
(4.5 cm) high, on a baking sheet
Rolling pin embossed
with a basket-weave pattern

Ingredients

GENOISE
Scant ½ cup (3.5 oz./100 g)
lightly beaten egg (about 2 eggs),
divided

Scant ⅓ cup (2 oz./60 g) sugar
½ cup minus 1 tbsp
(1.75 oz./50 g) flour
1 tbsp plus 1 scant tsp
(0.35 oz./12 g) cornstarch

KIRSCH-SCENTED SYRUP
¾ cup (5 oz./140 g) sugar
½ cup plus 1 tbsp (140 ml) water
1 ½ tsp (8 ml) kirsch

MOUSSELINE CREAM
1 cup (250 ml) whole milk
3 ½ tbsp (1.75 oz./50 g) lightly
beaten egg (about 1 egg)
⅓ cup (2.25 oz./65 g) sugar
2 ½ tbsp (1 oz./25 g) custard
powder or cornstarch
1 stick plus 2 tsp (4.5 oz./125 g)
butter, divided

DECORATION
10.5 oz. (300 g) strawberries
2.75 oz. (80 g) almond paste

MAKING THE GENOISE
Preheat the oven to 350°F (180°C/Gas mark 4). Using the electric beater, whisk the eggs and sugar in a bowl over a pan of hot water until the temperature reaches 113°F (45°C). Remove from the heat and continue whisking until the mixture cools completely. Sift the flour and cornstarch together and fold in. Pour into the smaller cake ring and bake for 17–20 minutes, with the oven door ajar.

MAKING THE SYRUP
Dissolve the sugar in the water in a pan and bring to a boil, skimming the surface and brushing any crystals from the sides of the pan. Allow to cool and stir in the kirsch.

MAKING THE MOUSSELINE CREAM
Bring the milk to a boil. Whisk the egg and sugar on high speed in a mixing bowl and then whisk in the custard powder. Whisk in a little of the hot milk, pour back into the saucepan and bring to a boil, stirring constantly. Simmer for 3 minutes, stirring all the time. Allow to cool to room temperature before whisking in 1 tbsp plus 2 tsp (1 oz./25 g) of the butter until smooth. Soften the remaining butter and whisk it in, until the cream is light and airy.

ASSEMBLING THE CAKE
Slice the genoise in half horizontally to make 2 equal layers. Place 1 layer in the larger cake ring and brush with syrup. Reserve a few strawberries for decoration and halve the rest lengthwise. Place upright strawberry halves around the sides of the ring and the rest over the sponge. Cover with mousseline cream, filling the gaps between the strawberry halves. Place the second layer of genoise on top and brush with syrup. Spread over more mousseline cream, smoothing it with a spatula so it is level with the cake ring. Place in the refrigerator for 1 hour to set. Roll the almond paste into a 7-in. (18-cm) disk, ¹⁄₁₆ in. (2 mm) thick. Roll the embossed pin over it and carefully lift the almond paste over the cake. Decorate with the reserved strawberries. If you wish, add almond paste flowers or wavy lines of tempered chocolate (see techniques pp. 570 and 572) piped with a paper cone (see technique p. 598).

LEVEL

2

STRAWBERRY LAYER CAKE

Fraisier

Serves 6–8

Active time
2 hours

Cooking time
20 minutes

Chilling time
1 hour

Storage
Up to 2 days in the refrigerator

Equipment
12 × 16-in. (30 × 40-cm) rimmed baking sheet lined with parchment paper

11 × 15-in. (28.5 × 37.5-cm) cake frame, 2 in. (5 cm) high, on a baking sheet

Kitchen torch
Pastry bag fitted with a plain ¼-in. (6-mm) tip

Ingredients

GENOISE
1.75 oz. (50 g) almond paste
Scant ⅓ cup (2 oz./60 g) sugar
Scant ⅔ cup (5 oz./140 g) lightly beaten egg (about 3 eggs)
⅔ cup (2.75 oz./80 g) flour
¼ tsp (1 ml) vanilla extract
2 tbsp (1 oz./30 g) butter, melted

VANILLA-KIRSCH MOUSSELINE CREAM
1 lb. 10 oz. (725 g) pastry cream (see technique p. 196), at room temperature
2 sticks (8.5 oz./240 g) butter, softened
4.25 oz. (120 g) Italian meringue (see technique p. 232)
2 ½ tsp (12 ml) kirsch
1 vanilla bean, split lengthwise and seeds scraped out

LIGHT KIRSCH SYRUP
1 ½ cups (375 ml) cold simple syrup (made of equal parts water and sugar)
2 tbsp plus 2 tsp (40 ml) water
1 ½ tbsp (25 ml) kirsch

FILLING AND DECORATION
9 oz. (250 g) strawberries
3.5 oz. (100 g) clear neutral glaze

MAKING THE GENOISE
Preheat the oven to 350°F (180°C/Gas mark 4). Mix the almond paste and sugar with a little of the egg to obtain a coarse sandy mixture. Gradually whisk in the remaining eggs. Combine the flour, vanilla extract, and melted butter and whisk in. Spread over the baking sheet and bake for 17 minutes.

MAKING THE MOUSSELINE CREAM
Combine the pastry cream with the butter and then lightly fold in the Italian meringue. Fold in the kirsch and vanilla seeds until combined.

MAKING THE KIRSCH SYRUP
Bring the syrup and water to a boil in a saucepan. Allow to cool before adding the kirsch.

ASSEMBLING THE CAKE
Cut the genoise into 2 rectangles to fit the cake frame. Place 1 in the bottom of the frame and brush with the syrup. Spread a generous layer of mousseline cream over it. Cut some of the strawberries in half and arrange these around the sides of the frame. Fill the center with whole strawberries, packing them tightly together and reserving a few for decoration. Spread with another layer of cream so the strawberries are covered, and top with the second layer of sponge. Brush with syrup and place in the refrigerator for 1 hour to set. Using the kitchen torch, lightly scorch the top of the genoise. Brush with a thin layer of neutral glaze and decorate with the remaining strawberries. Pipe the rest of the cream in small shells on top.

LEVEL

3

THE STRAWBERRY LAYER CAKE

Le Fraisier

by Arnaud Larher

MEILLEUR OUVRIER DE FRANCE, PÂTISSIER, 2007

Makes 3

Active time
1 ½ hours

Cooking time
10 minutes

Storage time
Up to 24 hours
in the refrigerator

Equipment
Baking sheet lined
with a silicone baking mat
Instant-read thermometer
3 × 7-in. (18-cm) cake rings
Stand mixer fitted
with the whisk attachment
Kitchen torch

Ingredients

ALMOND GENOISE
4.5 oz. (130 g) almond paste
5.5 oz. (160 g) sugar
13.25 oz. (380 g) egg
0.5 oz. (15 g) emulsifier
3 oz. (90 g) butter
1 tbsp (10 g) sorbitol powder
7.75 oz./220 g) flour

RASPBERRY SYRUP
Generous ½ cup (138 ml)
water
3 oz. (84 g) sugar
2 ¼ tbsp (33 ml) crème
de framboise
(raspberry liqueur)
3 tbsp (44 ml) kirsch

PASTRY CREAM
½ cup (125 ml) whole milk
1 oz. (24 g) sugar, divided
½ vanilla bean, split and
seeds scraped out
1 oz. (30 g) egg yolk
0.5 oz. (12 g) custard powder
1 ¼ tsp (6 g) butter, diced

BUTTERCREAM
9.5 oz. (270 g) sugar
4.75 oz. (134 g) egg
1 ¼ lb. (595 g) butter

ITALIAN MERINGUE
½ cup (120 ml) water
10.5 oz. (300 g) sugar
5.25 oz. (150 g) egg white

FILLING AND DECORATION
White chocolate, melted
Strawberries
Kirsch
Superfine sugar
Clear neutral glaze

——————— MAKING THE ALMOND GENOISE

Preheat the oven to 350°F (180°C/Gas mark 4). Beat together the almond paste, sugar and eggs until combined. Beat in the emulsifier, a little at a time, whisking to the ribbon stage. Melt the butter with the sorbitol, lightly fold into the batter, and then fold in the sifted flour. Spread the batter over the silicone mat and bake for 8–10 minutes.

——————— MAKING THE RASPBERRY SYRUP

Bring the water and sugar to a boil in a saucepan, add the crème de framboise and kirsch. Use cold.

——————— MAKING THE PASTRY CREAM

Bring the milk, 1 tbsp (12 g) of the sugar, and the vanilla bean and seeds to a boil in a saucepan. Whisk the egg yolks with the remaining sugar and custard powder until pale and thick. Pour over a little of the hot milk, stirring constantly, return to the saucepan, and simmer gently for 3 minutes, stirring continuously, to cook the cream. Take the pan off the heat, add the butter, and stir in until melted. Remove the vanilla bean and allow to cool.

——————— MAKING THE BUTTERCREAM

Whisk all the ingredients together and then fold in the cooled pastry cream.

——————— MAKING THE ITALIAN MERINGUE

In a saucepan, heat the water and sugar to 250°F (120°C). Whisk the egg whites to soft peak stage in the stand mixer and slowly drizzle in the hot syrup, whisking constantly to make a stiff meringue. Cool slightly.

——————— ASSEMBLING THE CAKES

Cut out 2 disks of sponge for each cake, 7 in. (18 cm) in diameter. Moisten half the disks with syrup, coat with a thin layer of white chocolate, and place in the rings. Cover with a thin layer of buttercream, arrange strawberry halves upright around the sides of the rings, cut sides out, and fill the centers with whole strawberries. Drizzle the strawberries with kirsch, dust with sugar, and then cover with buttercream. Moisten the remaining sponge layers with syrup and place on top. Spread over a thin layer of warm meringue and caramelize with the kitchen torch. Glaze with clear neutral glaze and decorate as you wish.

LEVEL

1

NAPOLEON

Millefeuille

Serves 6–8

Active time
4 hours

Chilling time
2 ½ hours

Cooking time
50 minutes

Storage
Up to 2 days in the refrigerator

Equipment
Baking sheet lined
with plastic wrap
Pastry bag with a plain ½-in.
(10-mm) tip

Ingredients

PUFF PASTRY
2 cups (9 oz./250 g) flour, sifted,
plus extra for dusting
1 tsp (5 g) salt
½ cup (125 ml) water
2 tbsp (1 oz./25 g) chilled butter,
diced
1 ¾ sticks (6.5 oz./190 g) butter,
preferably 84% butterfat, chilled

PASTRY CREAM
1 cup (250 ml) whole milk
¼ cup (1.75 oz./50 g) sugar,
divided
1 vanilla bean, split lengthwise
and seeds scraped out
2 ½ tbsp (1.5 oz./40 g) egg yolk
(about 2 yolks)
2 ½ tbsp (0.5 oz./15 g) custard
powder or cornstarch
1 heaping tbsp (0.35 oz./10 g)
flour, sifted
2 tbsp (1 oz./25 g) softened butter

DECORATION
White pouring fondant icing
Tempered bittersweet couverture
chocolate, 66% cacao

MAKING THE PUFF PASTRY
Put the flour on a work surface and make a well in the center. Dissolve the salt in the water and pour into the well. Add the smaller quantity of butter and work the ingredients together into a dough. Shape into a flattened disk and chill for 30 minutes. Dust the work surface with flour and roll out the dough. With the larger amount of butter, begin to fold and turn. Make 1 double turn and 1 single (see techniques pp. 70–71, steps 4–6, and p. 69, step 10). Chill for 45 minutes, make another double turn and another single and chill for another 45 minutes. Preheat the oven to 425°F (220°C/Gas mark 7). Roll the dough into 3 × 8-in. (20-cm) disks, ⅛ in. (5 mm) thick. Bake for 10 minutes, reduce the temperature to 375°F (190°C/Gas mark 5) and bake until golden (about 40 minutes). Carefully remove from the baking sheet and allow to cool.

MAKING THE PASTRY CREAM
Heat the milk with half the sugar, the vanilla bean, and seeds in a pan. Meanwhile, whisk the egg yolks with the remaining sugar until thick. Whisk in the custard powder and flour, whisk in a little of the hot milk and then return to the pan. Bring to a simmer and simmer for 2 minutes, stirring constantly. Take off the heat, remove the vanilla bean and stir in the butter until melted. Spread over the baking sheet lined with plastic wrap and press another piece of plastic wrap over the surface. Chill in the refrigerator.

PREPARING THE DECORATIONS
Prepare the fondant icing (see technique p. 169). Make a paper cone (see technique p. 598) and fill it with tempered chocolate (see techniques pp. 570 and 572).

ASSEMBLING THE NAPOLEON
Using a paring knife, cut the puff pastry into 3 × 7-in. (18-cm) disks. Pipe half the pastry cream over 1 disk. Place a second disk on top and pipe the remaining pastry cream over it. Top with the third disk and pour over the fondant, smoothing it with a spatula. Pipe a spiral of chocolate from the paper cone, starting at the center and working outward. Draw a small knife through the fondant to create a feathered pattern, alternating the direction of the knife each time. Remove any excess fondant from the edges, crush the leftover puff pastry and press the crumbs around the sides of the napoleon.

CHEFS' NOTES

If you do not have a large enough baking sheet, use 2 sheets, baking two-thirds of the pastry on one and one-third on the other.

LEVEL

2

NAPOLEON

Millefeuille

Serves 6

Active time
4 hours

Chilling time
3 hours

Cooking time
50 minutes

Storage
Up to 2 days in the refrigerator

Equipment
12 × 16-in. (30 × 40-cm)
baking sheet
Baking sheet lined
with plastic wrap
Electric hand beater
2 pastry bags fitted
with a plain ½-in. (10-mm) tip
and a Saint-Honoré tip
Long, thin, serrated knife

Ingredients

INVERSE PUFF PASTRY
Beurre manié
¾ cup plus 2 tbsp
(3.5 oz./100 g) flour
1 ¾ sticks (7 oz./200 g) butter,
preferably 84% butterfat,
well chilled

Water dough
1 cup plus 2 tbsp
(5.25 oz./150 g) flour
1 tsp (5 g) salt
⅓ cup (90 ml) water

MOUSSELINE CREAM
1 cup (250 ml) whole milk
¼ cup (1.75 oz./50 g) sugar,
divided
1 vanilla bean, split lengthwise
and seeds scraped out
2 ½ tbsp (1.5 oz./40 g)
egg yolk (about 2 yolks)
2 ½ tbsp (0.5 oz./15 g)
custard powder or cornstarch
4 tbsp (2 oz./60 g) butter, diced
4 tbsp plus 1 tsp (2.25 oz./65 g)
butter, softened

CHANTILLY CREAM
Scant ½ cup (100 ml) whipping
cream, 35% butterfat
2 ½ tsp (0.35 oz./10 g) sugar
Seeds from 2 vanilla beans

Edible silver leaf

MAKING THE INVERSE PUFF PASTRY

Using the quantities listed, make the pastry (see technique p. 72). Roll the dough to the dimensions of the baking sheet, ⅛ in. (3 mm) thick. Chill for 30 minutes. Preheat the oven to 425°F (220°C/Gas mark 7) and bake for 10 minutes. Reduce the temperature to 375°F (190°C/Gas mark 5) and bake until golden (about 40 minutes). Carefully remove from the baking sheet and allow to cool.

MAKING THE MOUSSELINE CREAM

Heat the milk with half the sugar, the vanilla bean, and seeds in a pan. Meanwhile, whisk the egg yolks with the remaining sugar until thick. Sift in the custard powder or cornstarch and whisk in. Whisk in a little of the hot milk, return to the pan and bring to a simmer, stirring constantly. Simmer for 2 minutes over low heat, stirring all the time. Take off the heat, remove the vanilla bean and stir in the 4 tbsp (2 oz./60 g) diced butter. Spread the pastry cream over the baking sheet lined with plastic wrap and press another piece of plastic wrap over the surface. Chill in the refrigerator and then, using the electric beater, whisk in the softened butter.

MAKING THE CHANTILLY CREAM

Using the electric beater, whisk the cream until it starts to thicken. Gradually whisk in the sugar and vanilla seeds until the cream holds fairly firm peaks.

ASSEMBLING THE NAPOLEON

Using the serrated knife, cut the puff pastry into 3 equal strips. Soften the mousseline cream with a spatula, spoon it into the pastry bag fitted with the plain tip and pipe a line of cream over one strip of pastry. Lay a second strip on top and pipe more cream over that. Place the third strip on top and chill for about 30 minutes until set. Using the serrated knife, cut the napoleon into 6 equal portions. Place each one on its side and, using the pastry bag fitted with the Saint-Honoré tip, decorate with piped waves of Chantilly cream and a little silver leaf.

VANILLA NAPOLEONS

Millefeuille

by Yann Couvreur
FORMER FERRANDI PARIS STUDENT

Serves 6

Active time
1 hour

Freezing time
30 minutes

Chilling time
3 hours

Infusing time
30 minutes

Drying time
2 hours

Storage
Up to 24 hours
in the refrigerator

Equipment
Stand mixer fitted
with the whisk attachment
Food processor fitted
with the chopper blade
Panini press
Pastry bag fitted
with a plain tip

Ingredients
KOUIGN AMANN
(BRETON PASTRY)
1 lb. 3 oz. (550 g) flour
1 tbsp (17 g) fleur de sel
0.5 oz. (10 g) fresh
(compressed) yeast
1 lb. 2 oz. (500 g) butter,
preferably 84% butterfat
1 ⅛ cups (280 ml) water
12.5 oz. (350 g)
superfine sugar
3.5 oz. (100 g) brown sugar

LIGHT PASTRY CREAM
2 cups (500 ml) whole milk
4 Madagascan vanilla beans,
split lengthwise
and seeds scraped out
4 Comorian vanilla beans,
split lengthwise and seeds
scraped out
4.25 oz. (120 g) egg yolk
3.5 oz. (100 g) superfine
sugar
1 oz. (25 g) flour
1 tbsp (10 g) custard powder
Generous ½ cup (140 ml)
whipping cream,
35% butterfat, whipped

Confectioners' sugar
for dusting

———— MAKING THE KOUIGN AMANN (BRETON PASTRY)
Put the flour, fleur de sel, yeast, butter, and water in the stand mixer and whisk at high speed for about 6 minutes. Remove the dough from the bowl and shape it into a square. Cover in plastic wrap, freeze for 30 minutes, and then let rest in the refrigerator for 1 hour to make it easier to handle. Blend the white and brown sugars together in the food processor until combined and fine. Give the dough 2 single turns (roll out the dough and fold the top third down and the bottom third up), allowing 1 hour between each turn. Give the dough two more single turns, sprinkling the blended sugars over the layers as you roll and setting aside a little of the sugar mixture. Roll out the dough to a thickness of ½ in. (1 cm), sprinkle with the reserved sugar mixture, and roll up tightly like a jelly roll. Freeze the tube of dough until firm and then cut it into 30 thin oval slices, ⅛ in. (3 mm) thick, of 5 different sizes. Place the slices between 2 sheets of parchment paper and cook in the panini press at 375°F (190°C) for about 1 minute or until crisp and golden.

———— MAKING THE LIGHT PASTRY CREAM
Bring the milk and vanilla beans and seeds to a boil in a saucepan and infuse for 30 minutes. Once infused, remove the beans and set aside. Whisk the egg yolks with the sugar until pale and thick. Fold in the sifted flour and custard powder. Bring the infused milk back to a boil and add it to the mixture, stirring constantly. Pour it back into the pan, bring to a boil, and simmer for 2 minutes, stirring constantly until thick and smooth. Remove from the heat and let cool. When cool, fold the whipped cream into 2 cups (500 ml) of the pastry cream.

———— MAKING THE VANILLA POWDER
Dry the vanilla beans used for the pastry cream in an *étuve* (drying oven) at 104°F (40°C) for about 2 hours. Grind the beans to a powder and then sift through a fine-mesh sieve.

———— ASSEMBLING THE NAPOLEONS
Pipe 3 lines of pastry cream side by side in the center of 6 dessert plates and carefully place the smallest of the wafers on top. Repeat the layers using more pastry cream, adding 3 more wafers in ascending size and then finish with the fifth and largest. Dust with confectioners' sugar and lightly sprinkle the tops and the plates with vanilla powder.

LEVEL

1

CHOCOLATE MOUSSE CAKE

Royal Chocolat

Serves 8–10

Active time
2 hours

Cooking time
10–12 minutes

Freezing time
1 ½ hours

Storage
Up to 3 days in the refrigerator

Equipment
Stand mixer
12 × 16-in. (30 × 40-cm) nonstick baking sheet
Instant-read thermometer
Spray gun
8-in. (20-cm) cake ring on a baking sheet
Angled spatula
Pastry bag fitted with a plain ⅛-in. (3-mm) tip

Ingredients

ALMOND DACQUOISE
Scant 1 cup (4.5 oz./125 g) confectioners' sugar
1 ¼ cups (4.5 oz./125 g) almond flour
2 ½ tbsp (1 oz./25 g) cornstarch
⅔ cup (5.25 oz./150 g) egg white (about 5 whites)
Generous ⅓ cup (2.75 oz./75 g) sugar
2 tbsp (1 oz./25 g) light brown sugar

FEUILLETINE
1.5 oz. (40 g) milk couverture chocolate
1.75 oz. (50 g) hazelnut (or almond) praline paste
1.75 oz. (50 g) *feuilletine* flakes (or use crushed wafers)

CHOCOLATE MOUSSE
Custard base
1 cup plus 3 tbsp (160 ml) whole milk
2 ½ tbsp (1 oz./30 g) sugar
3 tbsp (1.75 oz./50 g) egg yolk (about 3 yolks)
6.5 oz. (190 g) bittersweet couverture chocolate, 58% cacao, chopped
1 ¼ cups (300 ml) whipping cream, 35% butterfat

VELVET SPRAY
1.75 oz. (50 g) cocoa butter
1.75 oz. (50 g) milk couverture chocolate, 58% cacao

MAKING THE ALMOND DACQUOISE
Preheat the oven to 400°F (210°C/Gas mark 6). Sift the confectioners' sugar, almond flour, and cornstarch together. Fit the stand mixer with the whisk and whisk the egg whites until holding soft peaks. Gradually whisk in the sugar and light brown sugar until stiff and glossy. Lightly fold in the dry ingredients with a spatula until combined. Spread half the batter evenly over the baking sheet and bake for 10–12 minutes, reserving the rest for another use.

MAKING THE FEUILLETINE
Melt the milk couverture chocolate and then gently combine with the other ingredients.

MAKING THE CHOCOLATE MOUSSE
Make a custard using the custard base ingredients (see technique p. 204). Strain through a fine-mesh sieve over the couverture chocolate, stirring until the chocolate melts. Cool to 104°F (40°C). Whip the cream until it holds soft peaks and fold it into the chocolate custard.

MAKING THE VELVET SPRAY
Melt the cocoa butter and the chocolate in separate bowls over pans of hot water, heating both to 95°F (35°C). Mix the two together and heat to 122°F (50°C). Wash the fine-mesh sieve, strain the mixture, and then pour into the spray gun.

ASSEMBLING THE CAKE
Cut the dacquoise into 2 × 7-in. (18-cm) disks. Place 1 in the cake ring and spread enough chocolate mousse over it to fill the ring by about one-third. Smooth with the angled spatula to burst any air bubbles and level the surface. Spread a layer of *feuilletine* over the second disk and place it on the chocolate mousse. Spread more chocolate mousse over the second dacquoise, smoothing it with the spatula. Freeze for 1 ½ hours. Spoon the remaining mousse into the pastry bag and pipe decorative threads down one side, preferably while the cake is still frozen. Spray the cake to give it a velvety sheen.

LEVEL

2

CHOCOLATE MOUSSE CAKE

Royal II

Serves 8

Active time
3 hours

Chilling time
20 minutes

Cooking time
25–30 minutes

Storage
Up to 2 days in the refrigerator

Equipment
Stand mixer
Instant-read thermometer
Electric hand beater
2 × 7-in. (18-cm) cake rings
on baking sheets
Stick blender
6-in. (16-cm) cake ring
on a baking sheet

Ingredients

CHOCOLATE CRUST
7 tbsp (3.5 oz./100 g) butter, softened
Scant ½ cup (2 oz./60 g) confectioners' sugar
1 cup plus 1 tbsp (4.75 oz. /135 g) flour
2 tbsp plus 2 tsp (0.5 oz./15 g) unsweetened cocoa powder
3 tbsp (0.5 oz./15 g) almond flour
2 tbsp (1 oz./30 g) lightly beaten egg (about 1 egg)

CHOCOLATE SPONGE
1.5 oz. (45 g) bittersweet couverture chocolate, 70% cacao
⅓ cup plus 1 tbsp (3 oz./90 g) egg white (about 3 whites)
⅓ cup (2.5 oz./70 g) sugar, divided
Scant ¼ cup (2 oz./60 g) egg yolk (about 3 ½ yolks)

HAZELNUT CRÉMEUX
Scant 1 tsp (4 g) gelatin powder
⅔ cup (160 ml) whipping cream, 35% butterfat
2 ½ tbsp (1.5 oz./40 g) egg yolk (about 2 yolks)
2 ½ tbsp (1 oz./30 g) sugar
1 oz. (25 g) hazelnut paste

HAZELNUT PRALINE LAYER
1.5 oz. (45 g) milk couverture chocolate
1.75 oz. (50 g) hazelnut praline paste
1 oz. (30 g) baked chocolate crust (see ingredients above)
0.75 oz. (20 g) puffed rice
¼ tsp (1 g) fleur de sel sea salt

BITTERSWEET CHOCOLATE MOUSSE
⅔ cup (150 ml) whole milk
3 tbsp (1.75 oz./50 g) egg yolk (about 3 yolks)
2 ½ tbsp (1 oz./30 g) sugar
5.5 oz. (160 g) bittersweet couverture chocolate, 64% cacao
Scant 1 cup (220 ml) whipping cream, 35% butterfat, whipped

CHOCOLATE GLAZE
2 tsp (3.5 oz./10 g) gelatin powder
¾ cup (5.25 oz./150 g) sugar
½ cup plus 1 tbsp (135 ml) water, divided
½ cup minus 1 tbsp (5.25 oz./150 g) glucose syrup
½ cup minus 1 ½ tbsp (3.5 oz./100 g) sweetened condensed milk
5.25 oz. (150 g) bittersweet chocolate, 60% cacao, chopped

DECORATION
Tempered chocolate in the shapes of your choice

MAKING THE CHOCOLATE CRUST
Cream the butter and sugar together in the stand mixer fitted with the paddle beater. Sift the flour with the cocoa and then the almond flour. Beat the egg into the creamed mixture and stir in the dry ingredients in two amounts. Chill for 20 minutes. Preheat the oven to 325°F (160°C/Gas mark 3). Roll out the dough ⅛ in. (3 mm) thick and bake on a baking sheet for 15 minutes.

MAKING THE CHOCOLATE SPONGE
Increase the oven to 350°F (180°C/Gas mark 4). Melt the chocolate in a bowl over a pan of hot water to 122°F (50°C). Using the electric beater, whisk the egg whites with three-quarters of the sugar. Whisk the yolks with the remaining sugar until thick. Lightly fold the egg mixtures together. Fold in the melted chocolate. Pour into a 7-in. (18-cm) cake ring and bake for 10 minutes.

MAKING THE HAZELNUT CRÉMEUX
Dissolve the gelatin powder in a little cold water. In a saucepan, make a custard using the cream, egg yolks, and sugar (see technique p. 204). Remove from the heat and stir in the gelatin and hazelnut paste. Using the stick blender, process until smooth. Pour into the 6-in. (16-cm) ring and chill well.

MAKING THE HAZELNUT PRALINE LAYER
Melt the chocolate in a bowl over a pan of hot water to 113°F (45°C) and stir in the hazelnut praline paste. Chop 1 oz. (30 g) of the chocolate crust and stir in with the puffed rice until coated. Stir in the fleur de sel and spread over the hazelnut crémeux.

MAKING THE BITTERSWEET CHOCOLATE MOUSSE
Make a custard using the milk, egg yolks, and sugar (see technique p. 204). Meanwhile, melt the chocolate in a bowl over a pan of hot water. Strain the custard through a fine-mesh sieve, add to the melted chocolate and process until smooth. Fold in the whipped cream and chill in the refrigerator.

MAKING THE CHOCOLATE GLAZE
Dissolve the gelatin powder in ¼ cup (60 ml) cold water. Heat the sugar, the rest of the water, and glucose syrup in a pan to 221°F (105°C). Stir into the condensed milk and then the dissolved gelatin. Pour over the chocolate and process with the stick blender while still hot.

ASSEMBLING THE CAKE
Cut a 7-in. (18-cm) disk of chocolate crust and place in a 7-in. (18-cm) cake ring. Spread a layer of chocolate mousse, just under ½ in. (1 cm) thick, over the chocolate crust and top with the hazelnut crémeux and the praline. Spread another layer of mousse, the same thickness, on top. Place the chocolate sponge over the mousse and lift off the ring. Spread the sides with a smooth layer of mousse. Heat the glaze to 95°F (35°C), pour it over the cake and add decorations of your choice (see techniques pp. 592 and 598).

LEVEL

3

CHOCOLATE MOUSSE CAKE

Le Royal

by Pierre Marcolini

PÂTISSERIE WORLD CHAMPION, 1995

Serves 6

Active time
1 ½ hours

Chilling time
2 hours

Storage
Up to 24 hours
in the refrigerator

Equipment
2 × 12-in. (30-cm) square cake
frames, on baking sheets
Electric hand beater
Instant-read thermometer
Sheet of food-safe acetate

Ingredients

MILK CHOCOLATE PRALINE
2.75 oz. (80 g) milk chocolate
1.5 oz. (45 g) cocoa butter
4.5 oz. (125 g) *feuilletine*
flakes (or use crushed
wafers)
4.25 oz. (120 g) hazelnut
praline paste
4.25 oz. (120 g) almond
praline paste

CHOCOLATE MOUSSE
¾ tsp (3.5 g) gold grade
gelatin
1 tbsp plus 1 tsp (20 ml)
water, for the gelatin
6 oz. (170 g) crème fraîche,
35% butterfat, or heavy
cream, divided
2 oz. (60 g) superfine sugar
1 tbsp plus 1 tsp (20 ml)
water, for the *pâte à bombe*
1.75 oz. (55 g) egg yolk
1.75 oz. (50 g) lightly
beaten egg
7 oz. (200 g) bittersweet
chocolate, 64% cacao,
chopped

CHOCOLATE SQUARES
2.75 oz. (80 g) bittersweet
couverture chocolate,
64% cacao

Scant ¼ cup (50 ml)
whipping cream,
35% butterfat

——————— MAKING THE MILK CHOCOLATE PRALINE

Chop the milk chocolate with a knife and melt it in a bowl over a pan of hot water. Meanwhile, melt the cocoa butter in a saucepan. Mix the chocolate with the cocoa butter and stir in the *feuilletine* flakes, followed by the hazelnut and almond pastes. Spread in the base of one of the frames and chill in the refrigerator. When set, cut into 2-in. (5-cm) squares.

——————— MAKING THE CHOCOLATE MOUSSE

Soak the gelatin in the water and then dissolve it. Lightly whip half the cream until it holds very soft peaks. Dissolve the sugar in the water for the *pâte à bombe* and heat to 250°F (121°C). Pour the syrup over the egg yolks and egg and whisk to make a *pâte à bombe*. Heat the remaining cream, stir in the dissolved gelatin, and pour over the chopped chocolate to make a ganache. Fold in the whipped cream in two equal amounts, and then the *pâte à bombe*. Spread evenly into the other frame and chill in the refrigerator. Cut it into 2-in. (5-cm) squares.

——————— MAKING THE CHOCOLATE SQUARES

Melt the chocolate and cream in a bowl over a pan of hot water. Spread the mixture thinly over a sheet of food-safe acetate. As soon as it begins to firm up, cut into 2 ½-in. (6.5-cm) squares and leave to set completely.

——————— TO ASSEMBLE

Place a square of praline on a square of chocolate. Set another square of chocolate over the praline and then a square of mousse in the center. Top with a third square of chocolate.

LEVEL

1

GÂTEAU SAINT-HONORÉ

Serves 6

Active time
1 ½ hours

Cooking time
30 minutes

Storage
Up to 24 hours in the refrigerator

Equipment
2 pastry bags fitted
with a plain ½-in. (10-mm) tip
and a fluted ½-in. (10-mm) tip

Instant-read thermometer
Electric hand beater

Ingredients

PASTRY BASE
½ cup (2 oz./60 g) flour
2 tbsp (1 oz./30 g) butter
1 tbsp plus 2 tsp (1 oz./25 g) lightly beaten egg (about ½ egg)
¼ tsp (1 g) salt
¾ tsp (3 g) sugar

CHOUX PASTRY
½ cup (125 ml) water
¼ tsp (1 g) salt
3 ½ tbsp (1.75 oz./50 g) butter, diced
Scant ⅔ cup (2.75 oz./75 g) flour
½ cup (4.5 oz./125 g) lightly beaten egg (about 2 ½ eggs)

EGG WASH
2 tsp (0.35 oz./10 g) lightly beaten egg (about ¼ egg)
1 ¾ tsp (0.35 oz./10 g) egg yolk (about ½ yolk)
2 tsp (10 ml) whole milk

CARAMEL
1 ¼ cups (9 oz./250 g) sugar
⅓ cup (75 ml) water
1 ½ tbsp (1 oz./30 g) glucose syrup
2 tsp (0.35 oz./10 g) melted butter
1 pinch of salt

CHANTILLY CREAM
1 cup (250 ml) whipping cream, 35% butterfat
3 tbsp (1 oz./25 g) confectioners' sugar
Seeds from 1 vanilla bean

MAKING THE PASTRY BASE
Crumble the flour and butter together on a work surface and make a well in the center. Combine the egg with the salt and sugar and pour into the well. Work the ingredients together, kneading with the palm of your hand until just combined. Weigh out 3 ½ oz. (100 g) of the dough and roll into a 7-in. (18-cm) disk, just under ⅛ in. (2.5 mm) thick. Prick the dough with a fork.

MAKING THE CHOUX PASTRY
Bring the water, salt, and butter to a boil. Remove from the heat and add all of the flour. Beat until the mixture is smooth. Return to low heat to dry the mixture out, stirring constantly until it pulls away from the sides of the pan—this should take about 10 seconds. Transfer to a bowl to prevent the pastry from cooking further. Gradually beat in the eggs until smooth and glossy.

ASSEMBLING AND BAKING THE PASTRY BASE
Preheat the oven to 350°F (180°C/Gas mark 4). Dampen a baking sheet, place the pastry base on it and brush with the egg wash. Transfer the choux pastry to the pastry bag with a plain tip and pipe a ring around the edge of the pastry base. Pipe small choux puffs to decorate the Saint-Honoré onto the baking sheet and bake for 30 minutes.

MAKING THE CARAMEL
Dissolve the sugar in the water in a saucepan and bring to a boil. Skim off any foam and brush crystals from the sides of the pan. Add the glucose syrup and heat to 333°F–340°F (167°C–170°C) so the syrup is a rich caramel color. To prevent further cooking, dip the base of the pan in cold water. Stir in the melted butter off the heat, followed by the salt.

MAKING THE CHANTILLY CREAM
Whip the cream with the electric beater in a chilled mixing bowl. Whisk in the confectioners' sugar and vanilla seeds.

ASSEMBLING THE SAINT-HONORÉ
Dip the tops of the choux puffs into the caramel and allow them to cool. Using more caramel, stick them around the edge of the pastry base. Split the choux puffs horizontally and set aside the "hats." Spoon the Chantilly cream into the pastry bag with the fluted tip and pipe swirls of cream over the base. Fill the choux puffs with more cream and sit their "hats" on top.

LEVEL

2

PINEAPPLE AND LIME SAINT-HONORÉ

Saint-Honoré Ananas-Citron Vert

Serves 6–8

Active time
3 hours

Chilling time
At least 2 hours

Cooking time
45 minutes

Storage
Up to 24 hours in the refrigerator

Equipment
3 pastry bags, 2 fitted with plain ½-in. (10-mm) tips and 1 fitted with a Saint-Honoré tip

Instant-read thermometer
Stand mixer

Ingredients

PUFF PASTRY
½ tsp (2.5 g) salt
Scant ⅓ cup (65–70 ml) water
1 cup (4.5 oz./125 g) flour
1 tbsp (0.5 oz./15 g) butter
5 tbsp (2.75 oz./75 g) butter, preferably 84% butterfat
Confectioners' sugar for dusting

CHOUX PASTRY
½ cup (125 ml) water
¼ tsp (1 g) salt
3 ½ tbsp (1.75 oz./50 g) butter, diced
Scant ⅔ cup (2.75 oz./75 g) flour
½ cup (4.5 oz./125 g) lightly beaten egg (about 2 ½ eggs)

GOLDEN LIGHT CARAMEL
Scant ¼ cup (50 ml) water
1 cup (7 oz./200 g) sugar
2 tbsp plus 1 tsp (1.75 oz./50 g) glucose syrup
A little yellow food coloring
A little edible gold dust

PINEAPPLE PASTRY CREAM
3 tbsp (1.75 oz./50 g) egg yolk (about 3 yolks)
½ cup (3.5 oz./100 g) superfine sugar
¼ cup (1.5 oz./40 g) custard powder or cornstarch
1 lb. 2 oz. (500 g) pineapple purée
Finely grated zest and juice of 1 lime

PINEAPPLE MARMALADE
10.5 oz. (300 g) peeled and cored pineapple
⅓ cup (1.75 oz./50 g) brown sugar
Seeds from 1 vanilla bean
Ground Timut pepper (or Sichuan pepper) to taste
1.5 oz. (40 g) passion fruit seeds
Juice of 1 lime

LIME-FLAVORED CHANTILLY CREAM
1 ¼ cups (300 ml) whipping cream, 35% butterfat
3 ½ tbsp (1.5 oz./40 g) superfine sugar
Finely grated zest of ½ lime

MAKING THE PUFF PASTRY
Using the quantities listed, make a 5-turn puff pastry (see technique p. 66). Preheat the oven to 400°F (200°C/Gas mark 6). Roll the dough to a 12-in. (30-cm) square, place between 2 baking sheets to keep it flat and bake for 25 minutes. Allow to cool and then trim to an 8-in. (20-cm) square. Reduce the oven temperature to 375°F (190°C/Gas mark 5) to bake the choux puffs.

MAKING THE CHOUX PASTRY
Line a baking sheet with parchment paper. Bring the water, salt, and butter to a boil. Remove from the heat and add all of the flour. Beat until the mixture is smooth. Return to low heat to dry the mixture out, stirring constantly until it pulls away from the sides of the pan—this should take about 10 seconds. Transfer to a bowl to prevent the pastry from cooking further. Gradually beat in the eggs until smooth and glossy. Transfer the pastry to a pastry bag with a plain tip and pipe about 20 choux puffs of equal size on the baking sheet. Bake with the door slightly ajar for about 20 minutes, until puffed, golden, and crisp.

MAKING THE GOLDEN LIGHT CARAMEL
Heat the water, sugar, and glucose syrup in a pan until the sugar dissolves and cook to 340°F (170°C). Stir in the yellow food coloring and gold dust off the heat.

MAKING THE PINEAPPLE PASTRY CREAM
Beat the egg yolk, sugar, and custard powder together in a bowl until pale. Bring the pineapple purée to a boil in a saucepan, whisk a little into the egg yolk mixture and then pour it back into the saucepan. Whisking constantly, continue to cook until the mixture thickens (about 3 minutes). Allow to cool before stirring in the lime zest and juice.

MAKING THE PINEAPPLE MARMALADE
Cut the pineapple into very small dice. Caramelize the sugar in a skillet, stir in the pineapple, vanilla seeds, and Timut pepper and deglaze with the passion fruit and lime juice.

MAKING THE LIME-FLAVORED CHANTILLY CREAM
Chill the bowl of the stand mixer, fit it with the whisk, and whip the cream. Add the sugar, whip to almost firm peak stage, and then whisk in the lime zest. Chill in the refrigerator.

ASSEMBLING THE SAINT-HONORÉ
Using a pastry bag fitted with a plain tip, fill the choux puffs with pineapple pastry cream. Dip the base of the puffs in the caramel and stick them around the pastry square. Pipe more pastry cream into the center and spoon the marmalade over it. Using the pastry bag fitted with the Saint-Honoré tip, pipe the lime-flavored Chantilly cream in the center and between the choux puffs.

CITRUS SAINT-HONORÉ

Saint-Honoré Agrumes

by Nicolas Bernardé

MEILLEUR OUVRIER DE FRANCE, PÂTISSIER, 2004, AND FORMER FERRANDI PARIS STUDENT

Serves 6–8

Active time
2 hours

Cooking time
1 hour 50 minutes

Chilling time
2 hours and overnight

Storage
Up to 24 hours
in the refrigerator

Equipment
2 pastry bags fitted
with a plain ½-in. (15-mm) tip
and a Saint-Honoré tip

6-in. (16-cm) cutter
Crystallizing tray
Stand mixer fitted
with the whisk attachment
6-in. (16-cm) charlotte mold

Ingredients
CHOUX PASTRY
½ cup (125 ml) water
½ cup (125 ml) whole milk
1 ¼ tsp (5 g) sugar
1 tsp (5 g) salt
4.25 oz. (120 g) butter
4.5 oz. (125 g) flour
4 eggs

SWEET PASTRY
3.5 oz. (100 g)
confectioners' sugar
3.5 oz. (100 g) butter,
softened
1 oz. (30 g) egg yolk
7 oz. (200 g) flour
1.75 oz. (50 g) almond flour
¾ tsp (4 g) salt

CANDIED CITRUS FRUITS
5 citrus fruits of your choice
Sugar
Butter

CITRUS COULIS
7 oz. (200 g) pear purée
1 ¼ cups (300 ml)
citrus juices
2 oz. (60 g) superfine sugar
0.2 oz. (6 g) pectin NH
1.75 oz. (50 g) glucose syrup
1 oz. (25 g) invert sugar

LIGHT MASCARPONE CREAM
1 ¾ cups (400 ml) whipping
cream, 35% butterfat, chilled
7 oz. (200 g) mascarpone
2 oz. (60 g)
confectioners' sugar
Seeds from 1 vanilla bean

VANILLA AND ORANGE
CUSTARD CREAM
1 cup (250 ml) whole milk
1 cup (250 ml) whipping
cream, 35% butterfat
3.5 oz. (100 g)
superfine sugar
1 vanilla bean,
split lengthwise
and seeds scrapped out
Grated orange zest
5 oz. (140 g) egg yolk

DECORATION
Edible gold leaf
Marbled white
chocolate thins
Caramel

————— MAKING THE CHOUX PASTRY

Preheat the oven to 350°F (180°C/Gas mark 4). Make the choux pastry (see technique p. 162). Spoon it into the pastry bag with the plain tip and pipe 15 small choux buns onto a baking sheet. Bake for 25–30 minutes.

————— MAKING THE SWEET PASTRY

Cream the sugar and butter together in a mixing bowl with a wooden spoon until smooth and light. Beat in the egg yolks and then gradually stir in the sifted flour, almond flour, and salt. Lightly knead with the palm of your hand to make a dough. Shape into a ball, cover with plastic wrap, and chill for 2 hours. Preheat the oven to 350°F (180°C/Gas mark 4). Roll out the dough thinly, cut out a circle 6 in. (16 cm) in diameter, and bake for about 10 minutes.

————— MAKING THE CANDIED CITRUS FRUITS

Peel and segment the citrus fruits and then cut the segments into small slices. Place in a bowl and sprinkle with sugar, mixing well. Let stand for 15 minutes. Preheat the oven on convection setting to 400°F (200°C/Gas mark 6). Spread out the fruit in the crystallizing tray, dot with cubes of butter, and bake for 10 minutes. Remove from the oven, cover with plastic wrap, and let cool.

————— MAKING THE CITRUS COULIS

Put the pear purée and citrus juices in a saucepan. Combine the sugar and pectin, stir in, and bring to a boil. Heat the glucose syrup and invert sugar and stir them into the hot mixture. Bring back to a boil, remove from the heat, and transfer to a bowl. Press plastic wrap over the surface of the coulis and set aside in the refrigerator. When ready to use, carefully fold in the candied citrus fruits.

————— MAKING THE LIGHT MASCARPONE CREAM

Whip the chilled cream, mascarpone, confectioners' sugar, and vanilla seeds in the stand mixer until stiff. Chill in the refrigerator.

————— MAKING THE VANILLA AND ORANGE CUSTARD CREAM

Bring the milk, cream, sugar, vanilla bean and seeds, and orange zest to a boil in a saucepan. As soon as the mixture boils, remove from the heat, cover with plastic wrap, and let infuse for 10 minutes. Pour the infused milk mixture over the egg yolks, whisking constantly, strain through a fine-mesh sieve, and pour into the charlotte mold. Lift into a pan lined with sheets of newspaper and filled with water—the newspaper prevents the water from getting into the charlotte mold. Preheat the oven on the convection setting to 250°F (120°C/Gas mark ½) and bake the custard cream in the bain-marie for about 1 hour. Let chill in the refrigerator overnight. The next day, unmold onto a flat or shallow plate.

————— ASSEMBLING THE SAINT-HONORÉ

Dip the choux puffs in the caramel (see technique p. 169) and fill with mascarpone cream (see technique p. 168). Use dots of caramel to stick the puffs around the sweet pastry crust in the form of a crown. Carefully place the vanilla and orange cream in the center and cover with a layer of coulis. Pipe cream in a wavy pattern on top using the pastry bag with the Saint-Honoré tip and arrange the citrus slices among the waves. Decorate with gold leaf and chocolate thins.

LEVEL

1

FRUIT BABAS

Savarin aux Fruits

Makes 15

Active time
1 hour

Rising time
45 minutes

Cooking time
30 minutes

Storage
Up to 2 days in the refrigerator

Equipment
15 × 3-in. (8-cm) baba molds
Instant-read thermometer
Pastry bag fitted with a fluted
½-in. (10-mm) tip

Ingredients

BABA DOUGH
0.5 oz. (15 g) fresh yeast
Scant ½ cup (100 ml) lukewarm water (about 77°F/25°C)
⅔ cup (5.25 oz./150 g) lightly beaten egg (about 3 eggs)
2 ¾ cups (9 oz./250 g) flour
1 ¼ tsp (5 g) salt
1 heaping tbsp (0.5 oz./15 g) sugar
4 tbsp (2 oz./60 g) butter, melted, divided

SYRUP
2 ¼–2 ½ cups (1 lb.–1 lb. 2 oz./450–500 g) sugar
4 cups (1 liter) water

DECORATION
9 oz. (250 g) Chantilly cream (see technique p. 201)
Fresh fruit of your choice, such as pineapple, raspberries, etc., prepared as necessary

MAKING THE BABA DOUGH
In a mixing bowl, dissolve the yeast in the water and whisk in the eggs. Add the remaining ingredients, except the butter, and work them together with your hands, kneading well. Knead in 3 tbsp (1.5 oz./45 g) of the melted butter and then allow the dough to rise (see Chefs' Notes). Lightly grease the molds with the remaining butter. Knead the dough again and divide it between the molds, filling each one, and then allow to rise in a warm place until doubled in volume. Preheat the oven to 400°F (210°C/Gas mark 6). Place the babas in the oven and bake for 10 minutes, then lower the temperature to 325°F (160°C/Gas mark 3) and bake for an additional 15 minutes or until well risen and golden. Turn out of the molds immediately.

MAKING THE SYRUP
In a saucepan, dissolve the sugar in the water and bring to a boil. Remove from the heat.

TO FINISH
Allow the syrup to cool to 140°F (60°C). Soak the babas well in the syrup. Spoon the cream into the pastry bag fitted with a fluted tip and pipe rosettes on top of the babas. Decorate with fresh fruit.

CHEFS' NOTES

• Leave the baba dough to rise in a warm place or a cool étuve oven (75°F/25°C) with a bowl of boiling water.

• Do not butter the molds too generously or small holes will appear in the baba crust.

• If the baked babas are too dry, soak them in boiling syrup rather than cooled syrup.

• If you wish, you can flavor the syrup with a liqueur or fruit purée of your choice.

LEVEL

2

CHOCOLATE BABAS

Savarin au Chocolat

Makes 15

Active time
1 ½ hours

Rising time
45 minutes

Cooking time
30 minutes

Chilling time
3–12 hours

Storage
Up to 2 days in the refrigerator

Equipment
15 × 3-in. (8-cm) baba molds
Electric hand beater
Pastry bag fitted with a fluted
½-in. (10-mm) tip

Ingredients

BABA DOUGH
0.5 oz. (15 g) fresh yeast
Scant ½ cup (100 ml) lukewarm
water (about 77°F/25°C)
⅔ cup (5.25 oz./150 g) lightly
beaten egg (about 3 eggs)
2 ¾ cups (9 oz./250 g) flour
1 ¼ tsp (5 g) salt
1 heaping tbsp (0.5 oz./15 g) sugar
4 tbsp (2 oz./60 g) butter, melted

CHOCOLATE SYRUP
2 ¼ cups (1 lb./450 g) sugar
Generous ½ cup (2.25 oz./65 g)
unsweetened cocoa powder
4 cups (1 liter) water
1 orange
Orange liqueur to taste (optional)

MILK CHOCOLATE WHIPPED GANACHE
1 ¾ cups (450 ml) whipping cream,
35% butterfat, divided
0.5 oz. (15 g) invert sugar
2 tsp (0.5 oz./15 g) glucose syrup
Seeds from ½ vanilla bean
3.75 oz. (110 g) almond paste,
50% almonds, chopped
2.75 oz. (80 g) milk couverture
chocolate, 41% cacao, chopped

DECORATION
Clear neutral glaze
1–2 oranges, depending on size
3 ½ oz. (100 g) bittersweet
couverture chocolate,
64% cacao, shaped into
decorations of your choice
(see techniques pp. 570, 572, and 592–97)

MAKING THE BABA DOUGH
In a mixing bowl, dissolve the yeast in the lukewarm water and whisk in the eggs. Add the remaining ingredients, except the butter, and work them together with your hands, kneading well. Knead in 3 tbsp (1.5 oz./45 g) of the melted butter and then allow the dough to rise in a warm place, or in a cool *étuve* oven (75°F/25°C) with a bowl of boiling water. Lightly grease the molds with the remaining butter. Knead the dough again and divide it between the molds, filling each one, and then leave to rise in a warm place until doubled in volume. Preheat the oven to 400°F (210°C/Gas mark 6). Place the babas in the oven and bake for 10 minutes, then lower the temperature to 325°F (160°C/Gas mark 3) and bake for an additional 15 minutes or until well risen and golden. Turn out of the molds immediately.

MAKING THE CHOCOLATE SYRUP
Dissolve the sugar and cocoa powder in the water and bring to a boil. Shave off strips of zest from the orange using a vegetable peeler and add them to the syrup. Cover the pan and allow to infuse for a few minutes before straining through a fine-mesh sieve.

MAKING THE MILK CHOCOLATE WHIPPED GANACHE
In a saucepan, bring ⅔ cup (160 ml) of the whipping cream, the invert sugar, and glucose syrup to a boil. Reduce the heat to low, add the vanilla seeds, and simmer for 2–3 minutes to infuse. Gradually stir in the almond paste. Pour the hot mixture over the chocolate, stirring until it melts. Stir in the remaining cream until smooth and chill in the refrigerator for 3–12 hours. Whip the ganache with the electric beater to aerate it.

ASSEMBLING THE BABAS
Soak the babas in the syrup so they are very moist but still hold their shape. Stand them on a rack over a shallow dish. If you are using orange liqueur, add it to the remaining syrup and pour it over the babas. Place in the refrigerator and when the babas are well chilled, cover them in the clear neutral glaze. Spoon the ganache into the pastry bag and pipe two rosettes, one on top of the other, on each baba. Peel, segment, and chop the oranges and arrange attractively around the savarins. Top with chocolate decorations of your choice.

BABA ISPAHAN

by Pierre Hermé
BEST PASTRY CHEF IN THE WORLD, 2016

Serves 6–8

Active time
2 hours

Rising time
45 minutes

Cooking time
25 minutes

Standing time
48 hours

Chilling time
2 hours and overnight

Storage
Up to 24 hours
in the refrigerator

Equipment
Stand mixer fitted
with dough hook
and whisk attachments

Instant-read thermometer
7-in. (18-cm) savarin mold
or Bundt pan

Nonstick cooking spray
Stick blender
Glucose decorating bag
2 pastry bags fitted
with a plain ½-in. (14-mm) tip
and a Saint-Honoré tip

2 × 8-in. (21-cm) crimped
disposable gold plates

Ingredients
BABA DOUGH
0.75 oz. (20 g) fresh
(compressed) yeast

3.5 oz. (100 g) pasteurized
whole egg

4 oz. (120 g) fine-milled
soft wheat flour

1 oz. (30 g) superfine sugar

2.5 oz. (70 g) best-quality
butter

¼ tsp (2 g) Guérande salt

ROSE-FLAVORED
MASCARPONE CREAM
⅔ tsp (3 g) fish gelatin
powder 200 bloom

4 ¼ tsp (21 ml) cold mineral
water

1.25 oz. (35 g) pasteurized
egg yolk

1.5 oz. (40 g) superfine sugar

⅔ cup (150 ml) whipping
cream, 35% butterfat

5.75 oz. (165 g) mascarpone

4 tsp (20 ml) rose syrup

⅓ tsp (2 ml) rose petal
extract

RASPBERRY AND ROSE BABA
STEEPING SYRUP
2 ½ cups (600 ml)
mineral water

9 oz. (250 g) superfine sugar

Scant ½ cup (100 g)
raspberry purée

Scant ½ cup (100 ml)
rose syrup

⅔ tsp (3 ml) rose petal
extract

Scant ¼ cup (50 ml)
raspberry eau de vie

STEEPING THE BABA
Steeping syrup (see above)
2 tbsp (30 ml) raspberry
eau de vie

DECORATION
2.75 oz. (75 g) pieces
of lychee

14 oz. (400 g) rose-flavored
mascarpone (see above)

7 tsp (35 ml) raspberry
eau de vie

Clear neutral glaze
4.25 oz. (120 g) raspberries
10 rose petals

——————— MAKING THE BABA DOUGH

Dilute the yeast in three-quarters of the egg in the bowl of the stand mixer and add the flour and sugar. Mix at low speed to make a smooth dough. Increase the speed to medium for 5 minutes and add the remaining egg. Continue to mix until the dough begins to pull away from the sides of the bowl and reaches a temperature of 77°F (25°C). Add the butter and salt and mix at medium speed until the dough pulls away from the bowl again and slaps against the sides (79°F/26°C). Grease the mold with the nonstick spray. Shape 9 oz. (250 g) of dough by hand, making a hole in the center, and place it in the mold. Tap the mold on a work surface a few times to remove any air bubbles. Cover, and let rise at 90°F (32°C) for about 45 minutes. Preheat the oven on convection setting to 325°F (170°C/Gas mark 3) and bake for 20 minutes. Unmold and put the baba back in the oven for 5 minutes. Remove and let it dry out for 2 days at room temperature. Store in an airtight container.

——————— MAKING THE ROSE-FLAVORED MASCARPONE CREAM

A day ahead, soak the gelatin in the water for at least 20 minutes. Whisk the egg yolk with the sugar until pale and thick. Bring the cream to a boil and gradually whisk it into the yolk mixture. Pour back into the pan and heat to 185°F (85°C), as for making a custard. Squeeze excess water from the gelatin and add, along with the mascarpone, rose syrup, and rose extract. Blend until smooth. Press a piece of plastic wrap over the surface of the cream and keep in an airtight container in the refrigerator overnight.

——————— MAKING THE RASPBERRY AND ROSE BABA STEEPING SYRUP

Bring the water, sugar, and raspberry purée to a boil. Add the rose syrup, extract, and raspberry eau de vie. Remove from the heat and allow to cool. Use at 122°F (50°C) or set aside in the refrigerator.

——————— STEEPING THE BABA

In a large saucepan, heat the steeping syrup to 122°F (50°C). Immerse the baba in the syrup, turning it over and basting with syrup from time to time. Once the baba is thoroughly soaked, lift it from the pan with a skimmer and place on a wire rack over a baking sheet. Baste it generously with the raspberry eau de vie. Let drain and chill for 2 hours.

——————— ASSEMBLING THE BABA

Drain the lychee pieces thoroughly in a fine-mesh sieve. In the bowl of the stand mixer fitted with the whisk, beat the rose mascarpone cream until stiff. Stick the 2 plates together using glucose from the decorating bag. Baste the baba generously with the raspberry eau de vie and chill. Brush the chilled baba with warm glaze, ensuring it is not too hot or the glaze will not be absorbed. Divide the mascarpone cream between the 2 pastry bags. Place the baba on the gold plates and using the pastry bag with the plain tip, pipe mascarpone cream halfway up the inside of the cake. Sprinkle the chopped lychees and whole fresh raspberries generously over the cream. Cover the fruit with cream, creating a slight dome shape. Using the bag with the Saint-Honoré tip, pipe flame shapes on the baba in a circular pattern, working from the outside toward the center of the cake. Arrange the rose petals attractively around the piped cream, and place a fresh raspberry in the center.

LEVEL

1

RASPBERRY AND STRAWBERRY CHARLOTTE

Charlotte Vanille-Fruits Rouges

Serves 6

Active time
1 ½ hours

Cooking time
12 minutes

Chilling time
3 hours (plus several hours
for the Bavarian cream)

Storage
Up to 3 days in the refrigerator

Equipment
Pastry bag fitted
with a plain ½-in. (10-mm) tip
Instant-read thermometer
7-in. (18-cm) cake ring
on a baking sheet
Roll of food-safe acetate

Ingredients

LADYFINGER SPONGE
¾ cup (6.25 oz./180 g)
egg white (about 6 whites)
¾ cup (5.25 oz./150 g) sugar
Scant ½ cup (4.25 oz./120 g)
egg yolk (about 6 ½ egg yolks)
3 ½ tbsp (1.75 oz./50 g)
lightly beaten egg (about 1 egg)
1 cup plus 2 tbsp
(5.25 oz./150 g) flour
Confectioners' sugar for dusting

VANILLA SYRUP
Scant ¼ cup (1.5 oz./45 g)
sugar
⅔ cup (150 ml) water
½ vanilla bean, split lengthwise
and seeds scraped out

VANILLA BAVARIAN CREAM
½ cup (125 ml) milk
½ vanilla bean, split lengthwise
and seeds scraped out
Scant 2 tbsp (1 oz./30 g)
egg yolk (about 1 ½ yolks)
2 tbsp (1 oz./25 g) sugar
1 ½ sheets (0.1 oz./3 g) gelatin
¾ cup (175 ml) whipping cream,
35% butterfat

DECORATION
3.5 oz. (100 g) strawberries
3.5 oz. (100 g) raspberries
Confectioners' sugar for dusting
Apple blossoms

MAKING THE LADYFINGER SPONGE
Using the ingredients listed, prepare the ladyfinger batter (see technique p. 222). Preheat the oven to 400°F (200°C/Gas mark 6). Line a baking sheet with parchment paper. Spoon the batter into the pastry bag and pipe 2×6-in. (16-cm) disks, a 2 ½×16-in. (6×40-cm) strip, and a 6-in. (16-cm) rosette with a 3-in. (8-cm) hole in the center (as shown in the picture) onto the baking sheet. Dust with confectioners' sugar and bake for 12 minutes. Transfer to a rack and allow to cool.

MAKING THE VANILLA SYRUP
Dissolve the sugar in the water with the vanilla bean and seeds and bring to a boil. Remove from the heat and allow to cool.

MAKING THE BAVARIAN CREAM
Make a custard (see technique p. 204) using the milk, vanilla, egg yolks, and sugar, heating it to 181° F (83°C) until it coats the back of a spoon. Chill for several hours to give the flavors time to develop. Soak the gelatin in a bowl of cold water until softened. Reheat the custard to 113°F (45°C), squeeze out the gelatin sheets and stir in until melted. Whip the cream until it holds soft peaks. When the custard has cooled to 77°F (25°C), lightly fold in the whipped cream. It is now ready to use and must not set before you assemble the charlotte.

ASSEMBLING AND DECORATING THE CHARLOTTE
Line the sides of the cake ring with a strip of acetate. Brush the strip of ladyfinger sponge with the vanilla syrup and fit it around the sides of the ring against the acetate. Brush one of the sponge disks with syrup, place in the ring and pour in half the Bavarian cream. Brush the second disk of sponge with syrup and place over the cream. Pour in the remaining cream, smoothing the top. Chill in the refrigerator for at least 2–3 hours. Top with the sponge rosette, fill the center with berries, dust with confectioners' sugar, and decorate with apple blossoms.

CHEFS' NOTES

• Serve with a fruit coulis or flavored custard.

• Use apple blossoms that have not been sprayed with pesticides.

COCONUT AND PASSION FRUIT CHARLOTTE

Charlotte Coco-Passion

Serves 6

Active time
2 hours

Cooking time
12 minutes

Freezing time
3 hours

Chilling time
40 minutes

Storage
Up to 3 days in the refrigerator

Equipment
Pastry bag fitted
with a plain ½-in. (10-mm) tip
Stick blender
5 ½-in. (14-cm) diameter silicone
mold, ½ in. (1 cm) high
Instant-read thermometer
Sheet and roll of food-safe
acetate
7-in. (18-cm) cake ring, 1 ¾ in.
(4.5 cm) high

Ingredients

LADYFINGER SPONGE
⅓ cup plus 1 tbsp (3 oz./90 g) egg
white (about 3 whites)
Generous ⅓ cup (2.75 oz./75 g)
sugar
¼ cup (2 oz./60 g) egg yolk
(about 3 ½ yolks)
1 tbsp plus 2 tsp (1 oz./25 g)
lightly beaten egg (about ½ egg)
Scant ⅔ cup (2.75 oz./75 g) flour
Confectioners' sugar for dusting

**JELLED PASSION FRUIT
AND COCONUT LAYER**
2.75 oz. (75 g) passion fruit purée
2 oz. (60 g) coconut purée
1 tbsp (0.5 oz./12 g) superfine
sugar
1 tsp (2 g) agar-agar

**PASSION FRUIT
AND LEMON GRASS SYRUP**
¼ cup (60 ml) water
0.35 oz. (10 g) lemon grass stalk,
thinly sliced
3 tbsp (1.25 oz./35 g) sugar
1 tbsp plus 1 tsp (20 ml) fresh
lime juice
2.75 oz. (75 g) passion fruit purée

COCONUT MOUSSE
2 ½ sheets (0.15 oz./5 g) gelatin
9 oz. (250 g) coconut purée
3 tbsp (1.5 oz./ 40 g) egg white
(about 1 ½ whites)
¼ cup (1.75 oz./50 g) sugar
½ cup (130 ml) whipping cream,
35% butterfat, whipped

DECORATION
3.5 oz. (100 g) clear neutral glaze
3 pineapple cubes
Fruit of your choice

MAKING THE LADYFINGER SPONGE
Using the ingredients listed, prepare the ladyfinger batter (see technique p. 222). Preheat the oven to 400°F (200°C/Gas mark 6). Line a baking sheet with parchment paper. Spoon the batter into the pastry bag and pipe 2 × 6-in. (16-cm) disks and 2 × 2 ½ × 24-in. (6 × 60-cm) strips onto the sheet. Dust with confectioners' sugar and bake for 12 minutes. Transfer to a rack and allow to cool.

MAKING THE JELLED COCONUT-PASSION FRUIT LAYER
In a saucepan, heat the passion fruit and coconut purées. Combine the sugar and agar-agar and stir in. Allow to boil for 2 minutes, remove from the heat, and cool. Blend at low speed, pour into the silicone mold, and freeze for 1 hour.

MAKING THE PASSION FRUIT AND LEMON GRASS SYRUP
In a saucepan, bring the water to a boil. Add the lemon grass and allow to infuse for 20 minutes. Process with the stick blender and strain through a fine-mesh sieve. Pour into a measuring cup and top up with water to ¼ cup (60 ml) to replace any that has evaporated. Add the sugar, heat until it dissolves, and bring to a boil. Pour into a bowl, stir in the lime juice and passion fruit purée, and chill for about 40 minutes.

MAKING THE COCONUT MOUSSE
Soften the gelatin sheets in a bowl of cold water. In a saucepan, heat one-third of the coconut purée to 122°F (50°C), squeeze excess water from the gelatin and stir into the purée until melted. Stir in the remaining cold purée. Whisk the egg whites to soft peak stage and gradually whisk in the sugar to make a meringue. Lightly fold the meringue into the coconut until combined and then fold in the whipped cream.

ASSEMBLING THE CHARLOTTE
Line a baking sheet with the sheet of acetate (or use plastic wrap) and place the cake ring on it. Line the sides of the ring with a strip of acetate. Unmold the coconut-passion fruit layer into the ring so it is slightly off-center and spread a layer of coconut mousse over it just under ½ in. (1 cm) deep. Freeze for 1 hour. Brush the strip of sponge with syrup and fit it around the sides of the ring against the acetate. Fill with the remaining coconut mousse, brush the second disk of sponge with syrup and place over the mousse layer. Freeze for at least 1 hour. Upturn the charlotte onto a serving plate and lift off the cake ring. Brush with neutral glaze and decorate with the pineapple cubes and fruit of your choice.

LEVEL

3

CANDIED CLEMENTINE AND CHESTNUT CHARLOTTE

Charlotte aux Marrons et Clémentines Confites

by Gilles Marchal

BEST PASTRY CHEF OF THE YEAR, 2004

Makes 15 mini-charlottes

Active time
2 hours

Chilling time
2 hours

Cooking time
4 minutes

Storage
24 hours in the refrigerator

Equipment
2 pastry bags fitted with plain ⅓-in. (8-mm) and ½-in. (12-mm) tips

Instant-read thermometer

Stainless steel piping syringe or pastry bag fitted with a vermicelli tip

Stand mixer fitted with the whisk attachment

15 × 3-in. (8-cm) individual charlotte molds

Ingredients

LADYFINGER SPONGE
3 oz. (90 g) egg yolk
8 oz. (220 g) egg white
9 oz. (250 g) superfine sugar
9 oz. (250 g) cake flour, sifted

AGED DARK RUM PUNCH
¾ cup (200 ml) mineral water

1 oz. (30 g) confectioners' sugar

2 tsp (10 ml) aged dark rum

CANDIED CHESTNUT MOUSSE
4.25 oz. (120 g) egg yolk
½ cup (125 ml) 30° Baumé syrup (equal parts sugar and water)
12.5 oz. (350 g) chestnut paste
2.75 oz. (80 g) chestnut spread
4 ½ sheets (10 g) gelatin
¾ tbsp (12 ml) aged dark rum
1 ⅔ cups (380 ml) whipping cream, 35% butterfat, whipped
5.25 oz. (150 g) chestnut pieces, drained and finely chopped

CHESTNUT VERMICELLI
9 oz. (250 g) chestnut spread
1.5 oz. (40 g) butter, room temperature

BOURBON VANILLA CHANTILLY CREAM
1 cup (250 ml) whipping cream, 35% butterfat
0.75 oz. (20 g) superfine sugar
Seeds from ½ Madagascan Bourbon vanilla bean

DECORATION
Candied clementine pieces
Caramelized hazelnuts
Confectioners' sugar for dusting
Edible gold leaf

——— MAKING THE LADYFINGER SPONGE
Preheat the oven to 400°F (210°C/Gas mark 6). Lightly whisk the egg yolks until pale. Whisk the egg whites to soft peak stage, gradually whisking in the sugar until stiff. Gently fold in the egg yolks and then the flour. Spoon the batter into the piping bag with the plain ⅓-in. (8-mm) tip and pipe 30 × 2-in. (5-cm) disks onto a baking sheet lined with parchment paper. Bake immediately for about 3–4 minutes.

——— MAKING THE AGED DARK RUM PUNCH
Mix all the ingredients together.

——— MAKING THE CANDIED CHESTNUT MOUSSE
Whisk the egg yolks until pale. Heat the syrup to 250°F (121°C) and gradually whisk it into the egg yolks. Let cool completely and then use to thin the chestnut spread and paste. Soften the gelatin in water. Warm the rum, squeeze excess water from the gelatin, and dissolve it in the rum. Fold into the chestnut sabayon, followed by the whipped cream and then the chestnuts pieces. Spoon into the pastry bag with the plain ½-in. (12-mm) tip.

——— MAKING THE CHESTNUT VERMICELLI
Combine the ingredients to make a smooth paste. Transfer to the piping syringe or pastry bag fitted with the vermicelli tip.

——— MAKING THE BOURBON VANILLA CHANTILLY CREAM
In the stand mixer, whisk the well-chilled cream, sugar, and vanilla seeds until a smooth and glossy Chantilly cream is obtained. Chill in the refrigerator until needed.

——— ASSEMBLING THE CHARLOTTES
Chop the candied clementines and a few caramelized hazelnuts into small pieces. Dip the sponge disks in the syrup and place one in the base of each charlotte mold. Pipe in enough chestnut mousse to come halfway up the sides of the molds. Sprinkle with a few chopped clementines and hazelnuts and place a second layer of moistened sponge on top. Chill in the refrigerator for 2 hours until firm. Unmold the charlottes and coat with the cream, shaping it into a dome on top. Pipe over the chestnut vermicelli so the cream is completely covered. Decorate each one with a candied chestnut, candied clementine, caramelized hazelnut, a dusting of confectioners' sugar, and a little gold leaf.

LEVEL

1

CHESTNUT MERINGUE CAKE

Mont-Blanc

Serves 6

Active time
1 hour

Cooking time
3 hours

Freezing time
20 minutes

Storage
Up to 2 days in the refrigerator

Equipment
Stand mixer
6-in. (16-cm) cake ring
on a baking sheet lined
with parchment paper

3 pastry bags fitted with
a plain ½-in. (15-mm) tip,
a plain ¼-in. (6-mm) tip, and
a small fluted or Mont-Blanc tip

5 ½-in. (14-cm) cake ring
on a baking sheet

Ingredients

FRENCH MERINGUE
½ cup plus 2 tsp (4.25 oz./120 g)
egg white (about 4 whites)
½ cup (3.5 oz./100 g) sugar
¾ cup (3.5 oz./100 g)
confectioners' sugar
Butter, for greasing

CHANTILLY CREAM
1 ¼ cups (300 ml) whipping cream,
35% butterfat
3 tbsp (1 oz./25 g) confectioners'
sugar
Seeds from 1 vanilla bean

CHESTNUT CREAM
10.5 oz. (300 g) chestnut paste
(*pâte de marrons*) (see Chefs' Notes)
Scant ½ cup (3.5 oz./100 g)
whipping cream, 35% butterfat
10.5 oz. (300 g) chestnut spread
(*crème de marrons*) (see Chefs' Notes)

Edible gold leaf for decoration

MAKING THE FRENCH MERINGUE
Preheat the oven to 175°F (80°C/Gas mark ¼). Use the ingredients listed to make a French meringue (see technique p. 234). Lightly butter the 6-in. (16-cm) cake ring on the lined baking sheet. Using the pastry bag fitted with the plain ½-in. (15-mm) tip, pipe a meringue base into the ring, just under ½ in. (1 cm) deep. Spread the meringue right up to the sides the ring, smoothing the top and neatening the edges. Pipe a few meringue sticks on the baking sheet, using the pastry bag fitted with the ¼-in. (6-mm) tip, as decorations. Carefully remove the ring and bake the meringue for about 3 hours.

MAKING THE CHANTILLY CREAM
Fit the stand mixer with the whisk attachment and whip the cream with the sugar and vanilla seeds until the cream holds its shape.

MAKING THE CHESTNUT CREAM
In a mixing bowl, beat the chestnut paste with the whipping cream until smooth, and then beat in the chestnut spread.

ASSEMBLING THE CAKE
Pipe a mound of Chantilly cream in the center of the meringue. Using the pastry bag fitted with the small fluted or Mont-Blanc tip, pipe a generous amount of chestnut cream strings close together over a sheet of parchment paper (or instead of piping, you could force the cream through a potato ricer) and freeze for about 20 minutes. Using the smaller cake ring as a guide, cut a neat disk of chestnut strings and place it on top of the Chantilly cream. Decorate with the meringue sticks and a little edible gold leaf.

CHEFS' NOTES

• Chestnut paste (pâte de marrons) is made from chestnuts,
sugar, glucose syrup, and vanilla extract.

• Chestnut spread (crème de marrons) is made from chestnuts,
sugar, crushed candied chestnuts, glucose syrup,
a very small amount of water, and vanilla extract.

LEVEL

2

RHUBARB AND CHESTNUT LAYER CAKE

Mont-Blanc Rhubarbe-Marron

Serves 6

Active time
2 hours

Chilling time
2 hours

Cooking time
3 ½ hours

Storage
Up to 2 days in the refrigerator

Equipment
6-in. (16-cm) cake ring on a baking sheet lined with parchment paper

Instant-read thermometer
5 ½-in. (14-cm) cake ring, 1 ¾ in. (4 cm) high, on a baking sheet lined with parchment paper

3 pastry bags fitted
with a plain ½-in. (15-mm) tip,
a plain ¼-in. (6-mm) tip, and
a small fluted Mont-Blanc tip

Stand mixer

Ingredients

SWEET HAZELNUT PASTRY CRUST
5 tbsp (2.75 oz./75 g) butter
⅓ cup (1.75 oz./50 g) confectioners' sugar
3 tbsp (0.5 oz./15 g) finely ground hazelnuts
1 tbsp plus 1 tsp (0.75 oz./20 g) lightly beaten egg (about ½ egg)
1 knifepoint ground vanilla bean
1 cup (4.5 oz./125 g) flour

RHUBARB JELLY LAYER
1 ¼ sheets (2.5 g) gelatin
4.5 oz. (125 g) rhubarb purée
1 ¾ tsp (0.25 oz./7 g) sugar
½ tsp (3 ml) lemon juice

LADYFINGER SPONGE
1 tbsp plus 2 tsp (1 oz./25 g) egg white (about 1 white)
1 heaping tbsp (0.5 oz./15 g) sugar
2 ¾ tsp (0.5 oz./15 g) egg yolk (about 1 yolk)

1 heaping tbsp (0.35 oz./10 g) flour
1 tbsp (0.35 oz./10 g) cornstarch

RHUBARB SYRUP
3 tbsp (45 ml) water
1.5 oz. (45 g) rhubarb purée
Scant ¼ cup (1.5 oz./45 g) sugar
½ vanilla bean, split lengthwise and seeds scraped out

SET CUSTARD
Heaping ½ tsp (3 g) gelatin powder
1 tbsp plus 1 tsp (18 ml) water
¾ cup (190 ml) whipping cream, 35% butterfat
Scant ¼ cup (1.5 oz./45 g) sugar
1 vanilla bean, split lengthwise and seeds scraped out
2 ½ tbsp (1.5 oz./40 g) egg yolk (about 2 yolks)

VANILLA-FLAVORED MASCARPONE CREAM
4 oz. (115 g) mascarpone
6 oz. (170 g) set custard
(see ingredients above)

CHESTNUT CREAM
3 oz. (85 g) chestnut paste (*pâte de marrons*)
(see Chefs' Notes p. 136)
½ tsp (2 ml) rum
¾ tsp (0.2 oz./5 g) honey
3 oz. (85 g) chestnut spread (*crème de marrons*)
(see Chefs' Notes p. 436)
3 tbsp (1.5 oz./40 g) butter, softened

FRENCH MERINGUE
Scant ½ cup (3.5 oz./100 g) egg white (about 3 ½ whites)
½ cup (3.5 oz./100 g) sugar
¾ cup (3.5 oz./100 g) confectioners' sugar

MAKING THE SWEET HAZELNUT PASTRY CRUST
Make the crust with the ingredients listed (see technique p. 60). Cover in plastic wrap and chill for about 30 minutes. Preheat the oven to 350°F (180°C/Gas mark 4). Roll out and line the larger cake ring and bake for about 12 minutes.

MAKING THE RHUBARB JELLY LAYER
Soften the gelatin in a bowl of cold water. In a saucepan, heat the rhubarb purée to 122°F (50°C) and stir in the sugar and lemon juice, making sure the sugar is completely dissolved. Squeeze the water from the gelatin and stir in until melted. Pour into the smaller cake ring and chill for 1 hour.

MAKING THE LADYFINGER SPONGE LAYER
Preheat the oven to 425°F (220°C/Gas mark 7). Make the batter (see technique p. 222), spoon it into the pastry bag with the larger plain tip, and pipe a 6-in. (16-cm) disk onto a baking sheet lined with parchment paper. Bake for 10–12 minutes.

MAKING THE RHUBARB SYRUP
Bring the ingredients to a boil in a pan. Cool and remove the vanilla bean.

MAKING THE SET CUSTARD
Dissolve the gelatin powder in the water. Make a custard with the ingredients listed (see technique p. 204). Stir in the dissolved gelatin and chill for 30 minutes.

MAKING THE VANILLA-FLAVORED MASCARPONE CREAM
Fit the stand mixer with the whisk and beat the mascarpone until the consistency of Chantilly cream. Using a spatula, lightly fold in the custard, which should be at 64°F (18°C).

MAKING THE CHESTNUT CREAM
Beat the chestnut paste, rum, and honey together in a mixing bowl. Beat in the chestnut spread and softened butter, whisking until light and airy.

MAKING THE FRENCH MERINGUE
Preheat the oven to 175°F (80°C/Gas mark ¼). Make a French meringue with the ingredients listed (see technique p. 234). Line a baking sheet with parchment paper. Spoon the meringue into the pastry bag with the smaller plain tip and pipe small shells on the sheet. Bake for about 3 hours.

ASSEMBLING THE CAKE
Place the sponge layer on the baked crust and moisten it with rhubarb syrup. Lift the jelly on top and spread with the mascarpone cream. Using the pastry bag with the Mont-Blanc tip, pipe fine lines of chestnut cream close together over the cake and dot with small meringues.

LEVEL

3

MONT-BLANC

Mont-Blanc

by Yann Menguy

FORMER FERRANDI PARIS STUDENT

Makes 10

Active time
2 hours

Cooking time
5 ¼ hours

Storage
Up to 24 hours
in the refrigerator

Equipment
Stand mixer fitted
with the paddle beater
3-in. (8-cm) round
pastry cutter
Baking sheet lined
with a silicone baking mat
Pastry bag fitted
with a plain ¾-in. (18-mm) tip
Cake turntable
Flat decorating tip

Ingredients

MERINGUE
1.75 oz. (50 g) egg white
1.75 oz. (50 g) superfine
sugar
1.75 oz (50 g)
confectioners' sugar

SWEET PASTRY CRUST
9 oz. (250 g) flour
2.75 oz. (80 g)
confectioners' sugar
1 oz. (30 g) ground toasted
almonds
⅛ tsp (1 g) fine-grain salt
5.25 oz. (150 g) butter,
diced and well chilled
2.25 oz. (65 g) egg

CHESTNUT CREAM
10.5 oz. (300 g) chestnut
spread (*crème de marrons*)
1 lb. (450 g) chestnut paste
(*pâte de marrons*)
3.5 oz. (100 g) chestnut
purée
¼ tsp (2 g) fleur de sel
⅓ cup (90 ml) water
2 ¼ tbsp (35 ml)
Clément XO aged rum

VANILLA CHANTILLY CREAM
1 ¼ cups (300 ml) whipping
cream, 35% butterfat,
chilled overnight
0.5 oz. (15 g)
confectioners' sugar
1 ¼ tbsp (10 g)
chestnut honey
Seeds from ½ Bourbon
vanilla bean
Finely chopped
chestnut pieces

─────── MAKING THE MERINGUE
Preheat the oven to 150°F (65°C/Gas mark ¼). Whisk the egg whites, adding the superfine sugar in three equal amounts. When the whites form stiff peaks, whisk in all the confectioners' sugar. Spoon into the pastry bag fitted with the plain tip and pipe 10 × 2-in. (5-cm) balls of meringue onto a baking sheet lined with parchment paper. Bake for 5 hours.

─────── MAKING THE SWEET PASTRY CRUST
Preheat the oven to 325°F (160°C/Gas mark 3). Beat the dry ingredients with the butter in the stand mixer until the mixture resembles fine bread crumbs. Beat in the egg to make a smooth dough. Roll out to a thickness of ¹⁄₁₆ in. (2 mm) and cut out 10 × 3-in. (8-cm) disks. Bake on the silicone mat for 12 minutes.

─────── MAKING THE CHESTNUT CREAM
Beat all the ingredients on medium speed in the stand mixer. Push through a fine-mesh sieve to remove any small lumps. Chill until needed.

─────── MAKING THE VANILLA CHANTILLY CREAM
Pour the well-chilled cream into a well-chilled bowl and add the sugar, honey, vanilla seeds, and chestnut pieces. Lightly whip the cream until it forms soft peaks but avoid over-whipping or it will become grainy and lose its smooth texture, as the fat forms into globules.

─────── ASSEMBLING THE MONTS-BLANCS
Stick a ball of meringue onto each pastry crust with a dot of vanilla cream. Using a spatula, spread the vanilla cream over the meringues in a dome shape to cover them completely. Coat the monts-blancs with the chestnut cream, place on the cake turntable, and smooth the cream coating in a spiral using the flat decorating tip. Decorate as you wish.

LEVEL

1

CHOCOLATE GANACHE LAYER CAKE

Entremets Ganache

Serves 6–8

Active time
1 hour

Cooking time
25 minutes

Chilling time
1 hour

Storage
Up to 2 days in the refrigerator

Equipment
Silicone baking mat
Electric hand beater
Instant-read thermometer
Long, thin, serrated knife

Ingredients

CHOCOLATE GENOISE
½ cup (3.5 oz./100 g) sugar
⅔ cup (5.25 oz./150 g) lightly beaten egg (about 3 eggs)
½ cup minus 1 tbsp (1.75 oz./50 g) flour
3 tbsp (1 oz./30 g) cornstarch
Scant ½ tsp (1.5 g) baking powder
3 tbsp (0.75 oz./20 g) unsweetened cocoa powder

CHOCOLATE SYRUP
Scant ½ cup (110 ml) water
½ cup (3.5 oz./100 g) sugar
3 tbsp (0.75 oz./20 g) unsweetened cocoa powder

GANACHE
Scant 1 cup (220 ml) whipping cream, 35% butterfat
3 tbsp (2 oz./60 g) glucose syrup
10.5 oz. (300 g) bittersweet chocolate, 50% cacao, chopped
4 tbsp (2 oz./60 g) butter, diced

GLAZE
7 oz. (200 g) ganache
(see ingredients above)
3 ½ tbsp (2.75 oz./80 g) glucose syrup

Tempered chocolate for decoration

MAKING THE CHOCOLATE GENOISE
Lay the silicone mat on a baking sheet. Whisk the sugar and egg in a bowl over a pan of hot water using the electric beater until the mixture reaches 113°F (45°C). Remove from the heat and whisk until cold. Preheat the oven to 400°F (200°C/Gas mark 6). Sift the dry ingredients together and fold in, taking care not to deflate the mixture. Spread over the mat and bake for about 25 minutes.

MAKING THE CHOCOLATE SYRUP
Heat the water, sugar, and cocoa powder in a pan until the sugar and cocoa dissolve. Cool and chill for 30 minutes.

MAKING THE GANACHE
In a saucepan, bring the cream and glucose to a boil. Pour over the chocolate, stirring until melted. Mix in the butter to make a ganache. Allow to cool: it needs to be 59°F–64°F (15°C–18°C) when spread over the cake. Reserve 7 oz. (200 g) for the glaze.

MAKING THE GLAZE
In a saucepan, heat the remaining ganache and glucose syrup to 95°F (35°C).

ASSEMBLING THE CAKE
Using the serrated knife, cut the sponge horizontally into 3 equal layers. Spread 5 oz. (150 g) of ganache over the first layer and place the second on top. Moisten with the syrup and spread another 5 oz. (150 g) of ganache over it. Top with the third layer, moisten with syrup and, using a spatula, spread the cake with a smooth coating of ganache. Chill for 30 minutes. Place the cake on a rack over a baking sheet and pour the glaze over it. Make a paper cone (see technique p. 598), fill with tempered chocolate (see techniques pp. 570 and 572) and pipe the word "Ganache" on top of the cake with a decorative flourish.

LEVEL

2

RASPBERRY GANACHE LAYER CAKE

Entremets Ganache

Serves 10

Active time
3 hours

Cooking time
20 minutes

Storage
Up to 2 days in the refrigerator

Equipment
Electric hand beater
16 × 24-in. (40 × 60-cm) baking sheet lined with parchment paper
Instant-read thermometer
Stick blender
Sheet of food-safe acetate
8 × 12-in. (20 × 30-cm) cake frame on a baking sheet

Ingredients
CHOCOLATE SPONGE
⅓ cup (3.5 oz./100 g) egg yolk (about 5 ½ yolks)
Generous ⅓ cup (2.75 oz./75 g) sugar
2 ½ tbsp (0.75 oz./20 g) flour
2 ½ tbsp (0.5 oz./15 g) potato starch
3 tbsp (0.75 oz./20 g) unsweetened cocoa powder
3 tbsp (1.5 oz./45 g) butter, melted and cooled
Scant ½ cup (3.75 oz./105 g) egg white (about 3 ½ whites)
2 ½ tbsp (1 oz./30 g) sugar
0.15 oz. (4 g) invert sugar

RASPBERRY COMPOTE
½ sheet (1 g) gelatin
5.5 oz. (160 g) whole frozen raspberries
1 tsp (6 ml) lemon juice
Generous ⅓ cup (2.75 oz./75 g) sugar
0.1 oz. (3 g) pectin NH

RASPBERRY GANACHE
½ cup plus 1 tbsp (140 ml) whipping cream, 35% butterfat
5 oz. (140 g) seedless raspberry purée
3.5 oz. (100 g) bittersweet couverture chocolate, 64% cacao (preferably Valrhona Manjari), chopped
3.5 oz. (100 g) bittersweet couverture chocolate, 70% cacao (preferably Valrhona Guanaja), chopped

BITTERSWEET CHOCOLATE GLAZE
Heaping ½ tsp (0.1 oz./3 g) gelatin powder
1 tbsp plus ½ tsp (18 ml) water for the gelatin
1 tbsp plus 2 tsp (20 ml) water for the syrup
Scant ¼ cup (1.5 oz./45 g) sugar
2 tbsp (1.5 oz./45 g) glucose syrup
2 tbsp (30 g) sweetened condensed milk
1.5 oz. (45 g) bittersweet chocolate, 60% cacao

DECORATION
1.75 oz. (50 g) bittersweet couverture chocolate, 64% cacao

MAKING THE CHOCOLATE SPONGE
Preheat the oven to 325°F (170°C/Gas mark 3). Whisk together the egg yolks and sugar. Sift the flour with the potato starch and cocoa and lightly fold in, along with the melted butter. Whisk the egg whites and sugar with the electric beater and fold into the yolk mixture with the invert sugar. Spread over the baking sheet, ⅛ in. (3 mm) thick, and bake for about 12 minutes.

MAKING THE RASPBERRY COMPOTE
Soften the gelatin in the cold water. Put the still-frozen raspberries and lemon juice in a pan. Combine the sugar and pectin and stir in before the raspberries have reached 122°F (50°C). Boil for 2 minutes, squeeze excess water from the gelatin, and stir in until melted. Remove from the heat.

MAKING THE RASPBERRY GANACHE
Bring the cream to a boil, add the raspberry purée, and bring to a boil again. Pour over the chopped chocolates and blend with the stick blender to make a ganache.

MAKING THE BITTERSWEET CHOCOLATE GLAZE
Dissolve the gelatin powder in the water. Heat the water for the syrup with the sugar and glucose syrup to 221°F (105°C). Pour it over the condensed milk, add the gelatin and stir. Pour it over the chopped chocolate and blend while hot. Set aside to cool: the glaze must be at 95°F (35°C) when it is poured over the cake.

MAKING THE CHOCOLATE DECORATIONS
Melt the couverture chocolate in a bowl over a pan of hot water. When it reaches 95°F (35°C), spread it over the acetate sheet and leave it to begin to set. Cut into ¾ × 2 ½-in. (2 × 6-cm) rectangles and allow to set for a few minutes.

ASSEMBLING THE CAKE
Place the sponge in the cake frame. Spread a thin layer of raspberry compote over it with a spatula. When it has set, spread a layer of raspberry ganache on top and repeat these layers twice more. Coat with the chocolate glaze at 95°F (35°C) and decorate with the chocolate rectangles.

ENTREMETS GANACHE "MY WAY"

Réinterprétation Entremets "Ganache"

by Ophélie Barès

FORMER FERRANDI PARIS STUDENT

Makes 4 individual cakes

Active time
1 hour

Cooking time
15 minutes

Chilling time
24 hours

Storage
Up to 48 hours
in the refrigerator

Equipment
Stick blender
Stand mixer fitted
with the whisk attachment
Baking sheet lined
with a silicone baking mat
Acetate sheet
Pastry bag fitted
with a plain ½-in. (10-mm) tip

Ingredients

MILK CHOCOLATE GANACHE
2 ¼ cups (535 ml) whipping cream, 35% butterfat, chilled, divided
1.5 oz. (45 g) glucose syrup
10 oz. (285 g) Valrhona Jivara milk chocolate, chopped

CHOCOLATE SPONGE
4.25 oz. (120 g) egg
6 oz. (170 g) superfine sugar, divided
2 oz. (60 g) almond flour
1.5 oz. (40 g) flour
1.5 oz. (45 g) unsweetened cocoa powder
½ cup (130 ml) sunflower oil
6.25 oz. (180 g) egg white

CHOCOLATE YUZU SYRUP
Scant ¼ cup (50 ml) water
2.75 oz. (75 g) sugar
Scant ¼ cup (50 ml) yuzu juice
1 ½ tbsp (10 g) unsweetened cocoa powder

CHOCOLATE DECORATIONS
7 oz. (200 g) bittersweet couverture chocolate, 64% cacao, chopped

Unsweetened cocoa powder for dusting

——— MAKING THE MILK CHOCOLATE GANACHE
In a saucepan, bring a scant 1 cup (195 ml) of the cream and the glucose syrup to a boil. Pour over the chopped chocolate a third at a time, stirring until smooth. Stir in the rest of the cold cream, mixing well, and process with the stick blender. Cover with plastic wrap and chill for 24 hours.

——— MAKING THE CHOCOLATE SPONGE
Preheat the oven to 350°F (175°C/Gas mark 4). Whisk the eggs with 4 oz. (110 g) of the sugar to the ribbon stage. Meanwhile, sift together the almond flour, flour, and cocoa powder. Mix a small amount of the egg mixture with the oil and pour it back into the rest of the mixture. Whisk the egg whites to soft peak stage and whisk in the remaining sugar until stiff. Carefully fold half the whisked whites into the egg mixture with a spatula, followed by the sifted dry ingredients. Fold in the remaining whites and spread over the silicone mat. Bake for 12 minutes.

——— MAKING THE CHOCOLATE YUZU SYRUP
In a saucepan, heat the water and sugar until the sugar has dissolved, then bring to a boil. Remove from the heat, whisk in the yuzu juice and cocoa powder, and set aside.

——— MAKING THE CHOCOLATE DECORATIONS
Melt the chocolate over a bain-marie and then temper it (see techniques pp. 570 and 572). Spread the chocolate over the acetate sheet using a spatula and, as it starts to set, mark into 16 × 4 ½ × 1 ½-in. (11 × 3.5-cm) rectangles. Allow to set completely.

——— ASSEMBLING THE ENTREMETS
Moisten the sponge with the syrup. Whisk the ganache to aerate it and spread three-quarters over the sponge. Cut the sponge widthwise into 6 strips, 3 ½ in. (9 cm) wide. Stack 3 strips on top of one another and repeat with the remaining 3 strips. Chill for a few minutes in the refrigerator and then cut each stack into 3 ½-in. (9-cm) squares to make 4 cakes. Place the chocolate rectangles around the sides of each cake. Spoon the remaining ganache into the pastry bag and pipe pointed mounds on top of each cake. Dust generously with cocoa powder and, using a baking sheet, lightly press down on the points to flatten them.

LEVEL

1

MOCHA CAKE

Moka Café

Serves 8

Active time
2 hours

Cooking time
25 minutes

Chilling time
15 minutes

Storage
Up to 3 days in the refrigerator (best eaten the day after it was made, to give the sponge time to absorb the coffee flavor)

Equipment
Stand mixer
Instant-read thermometer
8-in. (20-cm) round cake pan
Long, thin, serrated knife
Small and large angled spatulas
Pastry bag fitted with a fluted ½-in. (10-mm) tip

Ingredients

GENOISE
⅔ cup (5.25 oz./150 g) lightly beaten egg (about 3 eggs)
Scant ½ cup (3 oz./90 g) sugar
⅔ cup plus 1 tbsp (3 oz./90 g) flour, sifted, plus extra for dusting
Butter for greasing

COFFEE-FLAVORED BUTTERCREAM
1 cup minus 1 tbsp (6.25 oz./180 g) sugar
¼ cup (60 ml) water
½ cup (4.25 oz./120 g) lightly beaten egg (about 2 ½ eggs)
2 sticks plus 6 tbsp (11.25 oz./320 g) butter, diced, at room temperature
Coffee flavoring or dissolved instant coffee to taste

COFFEE-FLAVORED SYRUP
¾ cup (5.25 oz./150 g) sugar
Scant ⅔ cup (150 ml) water
Coffee flavoring to taste

DECORATION
Roasted sliced almonds
Chocolate-coated coffee beans

MAKING THE GENOISE
Butter and flour the cake pan. Preheat the oven to 350°F (180°C/Gas mark 4). Fit the stand mixer with the whisk and beat the eggs and sugar together to the ribbon stage—the temperature should be 95°F–104°F (35°C–40°C). Using a spatula, lightly fold in the flour. Pour the batter into the prepared pan and bake for 20–25 minutes

MAKING THE COFFEE-FLAVORED BUTTERCREAM
In a saucepan, dissolve the sugar in the water and heat to 243°F (117°C). Meanwhile, whisk the eggs in the stand mixer until frothy. When the syrup reaches the correct temperature, whisk it into the eggs in a thin stream at medium speed. Continue whisking until the mixture cools to 68°F–77°F (20°C–25°C). Whisk in the butter until the mixture is creamy and then add the coffee flavoring.

MAKING THE COFFEE-FLAVORED SYRUP
Dissolve the sugar in the water and bring to a boil. Stir in the coffee flavoring and allow it to cool completely.

ASSEMBLING THE CAKE
Cut the genoise horizontally into 3 equal layers, ensuring they are sliced completely flat so they can be coated evenly with the buttercream. Brush 1 layer with syrup and spread about 5 oz. (150 g) buttercream over it. The buttercream needs to be soft or it could tear the sponge when you spread it; if it seems too firm, whisk it until sufficiently softened. Brush the second sponge layer with syrup on one side and place it, syrup side down, over the buttercream. Brush the top with syrup and spread with another 5 oz. (150 g) buttercream. Brush the third layer with syrup and place it, syrup side down, on top. Cover the entire cake with a thin layer of buttercream. To do this, hold the cake on the palm of one hand and, using the small angled spatula, spread the buttercream smoothly around the sides. Place the cake back on a work surface and, using the large spatula, coat the top of the cake with a smooth layer of buttercream. Neaten the top edge and chill for about 15 minutes to firm up the buttercream slightly. Coat the chilled cake with a second layer of buttercream in the same way. Draw the blade of the serrated knife backward and forward over the top of the cake (the buttercream must still be soft when marking the pattern), smoothing any excess buttercream down the sides and neatening the top edge. Press the roasted sliced almonds around the cake two-thirds of the way up the sides. Using the pastry bag fitted with the fluted tip, pipe the remaining buttercream on top of the cake. Decorate with chocolate-coated coffee beans and chill. The cake should be served at room temperature, so remove it from the refrigerator 30 minutes ahead.

LEVEL

2

IRISH CREAM–MOCHA CAKE

Moka

Serves 6–8

Active time
3 hours

Infusing time
Overnight

Cooking time
30 minutes

Chilling time
3 hours

Storage
Up to 3 days in the refrigerator

Equipment
7-in. (18-cm) cake ring,
1 ½ in. (3.5 cm) high, buttered,
on a baking sheet
Stand mixer
Instant-read thermometer
Stick blender
6-in. (16-cm) silicone cake mold
Kitchen torch
Angled spatula
Pastry bag fitted
with a Saint-Honoré tip

Ingredients

INFUSED COFFEE CREAM
1.45 oz. (40 g) coffee beans
2 cups (500 ml) whipping cream,
35% butterfat

COFFEE SPONGE
9.5 oz. (280 g) almond paste,
50% almonds
3 ½ tbsp (1.45 oz./40 g) light
brown sugar
1 ½ tbsp (0.2 oz./5 g) instant coffee
granules
Scant cup (7 oz./200 g) egg
(about 4 eggs)
5 tbsp (2.75 oz./75 g) melted,
browned butter, cooled
½ cup (2.25 oz./65 g) flour

COFFEE-FLAVORED BUTTERCREAM
1 ¼ cups (8.5 oz./240 g) sugar
¼ cup (60 ml) water
½ cup (4.25 oz./120 g) lightly
beaten egg (about 2 ½ eggs), or

½ cup plus 2 tsp (4.25 oz./120 g)
egg white (about 4 whites)
2 sticks plus 6 tbsp
(11.25 oz./320 g) butter, diced,
at room temperature
Coffee flavoring or dissolved
instant coffee to taste

IRISH CREAM LAYER
1 ½ sheets (0.1 oz./3 g) gelatin
¼ cup (1.75 oz./50 g) sugar
1 vanilla bean, split lengthwise
and seeds scraped out
¾ cup (200 ml) infused coffee
cream (see ingredients above)
⅓ cup (3.5 oz./100 g) egg yolk
(about 5 ½ yolks)
3 tbsp (50 ml) Baileys' Irish Cream
Light brown sugar for sprinkling

COFFEE-FLAVORED SYRUP
½ cup plus 1 ½ tbsp (150 ml)
espresso coffee
¼ cup (1.75 oz./50 g) sugar
1 tsp (5 ml) rum

GLAZE
2 ½ sheets (0.14 oz./4.5 g) gelatin
½ cup (125 ml) whole milk
1 scant tsp (1 g) instant coffee
granules
2 tbsp (1.5 oz./45 g) glucose syrup
5.75 oz. (165 g) white chocolate,
chopped
5.7 oz. (160 g) *pâte à glacer ivoire*
(white glazing paste)

DECORATION
Chocolate strip and small
chocolate disks
Chocolate-coated coffee bean
Edible gold leaf

INFUSING THE CREAM (1 DAY AHEAD)
Place the coffee beans in the cream and infuse in the refrigerator overnight.

MAKING THE COFFEE SPONGE
Preheat the oven to 350°F (180°C/Gas mark 4). Fit the stand mixer with the paddle beater and beat together the almond paste, sugar, and instant coffee. Add the eggs, one at a time. Continue beating until the mixture reaches the ribbon stage. Add a little of the batter to the browned butter, return it to the bowl and mix thoroughly. Lightly fold in the flour, pour into the ring, and bake for 20–30 minutes. Remove the ring and allow to cool.

MAKING THE COFFEE-FLAVORED BUTTERCREAM
Dissolve the sugar in the water and cook to 243°F (117°C). Whisk the eggs or egg whites in the stand mixer until soft peaks form. Pour in the hot syrup in a thin stream, whisking continuously at medium speed until the temperature cools to 86°F (30°C). Whisk in the butter until creamy and then stir in the coffee flavoring.

MAKING THE IRISH CREAM LAYER
Soak the gelatin in a bowl of cold water. Using the ingredients listed, including the infused coffee cream, make a custard (see technique p. 204). Squeeze out the gelatin sheets, stir them into the custard with the Baileys' Irish Cream and process until smooth with the stick blender. Pour into the silicone mold and freeze until solid. Sprinkle with light brown sugar and, using the kitchen torch, caramelize the sugar. Return to the freezer.

MAKING THE COFFEE-FLAVORED SYRUP
Heat the coffee and sugar to 104°F (40°C) to dissolve the sugar. Allow to cool. Stir in the rum and chill in the refrigerator until needed.

MAKING THE GLAZE
Soak the gelatin in a bowl of cold water. Heat the milk, instant coffee, and glucose syrup to 221°F (105°C). Squeeze the water from the gelatin and stir in until dissolved. Pour the hot mixture over the white chocolate and glazing paste, stirring until melted. Blend with the stick blender to obtain a smooth mixture and strain through a fine-mesh sieve.

ASSEMBLING THE CAKE
Slice the coffee sponge into 2 layers, each just under ½ in. (1 cm) thick. Brush 1 layer with syrup, place in the cake ring and, using the angled spatula, spread a thin layer of buttercream around the insides of the ring and over the sponge. Place the Irish Cream layer on top and spread with another thin layer of buttercream. Brush the second layer of sponge with syrup and place on the buttercream. Smooth more buttercream over the top. Chill for about 2 hours. Lift the cake onto a rack set over a rimmed baking sheet and lift off the ring. (You can use a sheet of food-safe acetate when assembling the cake so it is easier to remove the ring.) Coat the top and sides of the cake by pouring over the glaze at 77°F (25°C)—any hotter and you risk melting the buttercream and the glaze will not stick—and allow to set. Surround with a strip of chocolate and top with small chocolate decorations (see techniques pp. 592–98), the remaining buttercream piped using the Saint-Honoré tip, a chocolate-coated coffee bean, and edible gold leaf. To marble the glaze, add ⅛ tsp (1 g) white titanium dioxide and coffee essence to a neutral mirror glaze. Run a spatula over it to obtain the marbled effect.

LEVEL

3

MOCHA

Moka

by Julien Alvarez

WORLD PASTRY CUP CHAMPION, 2011

Serves 6

Active time
2 ½ hours

Cooking time
15 minutes

Storage
Up to 24 hours
in the refrigerator

Equipment
Instant-read thermometer
3 × 6-in. (16-cm) cake rings
Food processor
Electric hand beater
Stick blender
Spray gun
7-in. (18-cm) cake ring
Pastry bag without a tip

Ingredients
ÉCLAT D'OR/AZÉLIA CRISP
1 oz. (29.8 g) Valrhona
Azélia hazelnut milk
chocolate, 35% cacao
1 oz. (29.8 g) hazelnut
praline paste
1 oz. (29.8 g) hazelnut paste
1 oz. (29.8 g) Valrhona
Éclat d'Or (*feuilletine*
flakes)
1 pinch (0.8 g) fleur de sel

COFFEE GENOA BREAD
3 oz. (89.9 g) almond paste,
66% almonds
1 pinch (0.5 g) salt
2.75 oz. (73.8 g) egg
½ oz. (16.2 g) egg yolk
7 tsp (18 g) flour
⅓ tsp (1.8 g) potato starch
0.5 oz. (14.4 g) butter, melted
1 tsp (5.4 g) coffee paste

BITTER CITRUS MARMALADE
¾ tsp (3.3 ml) cold water
¹⁄₁₀ tsp (0.5 g) gelatin powder
2.75 oz. (76.6 g) oranges
4 tsp (19.2 ml) yuzu juice
2 ½ tbsp (38.3 ml) fresh
mandarin juice
⅛ (0.8 g) vanilla bean
2 oz. (57.7 g) sugar, divided
⅓ tsp (1.9 g) pectin
⅓ tsp (1.9 ml) Grand Marnier
Cordon Rouge liqueur

MILK CHOCOLATE AND COFFEE
CREAM MOUSSE
1 tbsp (14.4 ml) cold water
½ tsp (2.4 g) gelatin powder
2 ½ tbsp (37.9 ml) whole milk
2 ½ tbsp (37.9 ml) whipping
cream, 35% butterfat
0.25 oz. (7.4 g) Maragogype
"elephant" coffee beans
1.25 oz. (37.9 g) egg yolk,
beaten
2.75 oz. (82.1 g) Valrhona
Jivara milk couverture
chocolate, 40% cacao
1 tsp (1.1 g) instant coffee
⅓ cup (78.9 ml) whipping
cream, 35% butterfat

ABSOLU COFFEE GLAZE
1 lb. 2 oz. (500 g) Valrhona
Absolu glaze
2 ¾ tbsp (40 ml) espresso
coffee
2 tsp (10 ml) Trablit coffee
extract

──────── MAKING THE ÉCLAT D'OR/AZÉLIA CRISP
Melt the Azelia chocolate to 113°F (45°C) and mix with the hazelnut praline and paste. Add the *feuilletine* flakes and salt and fold in carefully. Roll out to a thickness of ⅛ in. (4 mm) and chill in the refrigerator to harden. Cut a 6-in. (16-cm) disk and reserve until ready to use.

──────── MAKING THE COFFEE GENOA BREAD
Preheat the oven on the convection setting to 325°F (160°C/Gas mark 3). Blend the almond paste and salt in the food processor. Gradually mix in the eggs and yolks and whisk until light and airy. Carefully fold in the sifted flour and potato starch. Blend the hot melted butter with the coffee paste and add to the batter. Pour into a 6-in. (16-cm) ring and bake for 15 minutes.

──────── MAKING THE BITTER CITRUS MARMALADE
Pour the water over the gelatin, whisking until smooth and leave in the refrigerator to soak for at least 20 minutes. Coarsely chop the oranges, removing the white pith in the center. In a saucepan, make a syrup with the yuzu juice, mandarin juice, vanilla bean, and 1.5 oz (38.3 g) of the sugar, and poach the chopped oranges in this. Blend briefly, mix the remaining sugar with the pectin, add it gradually to the pan, and bring back to a boil. Add the bloomed gelatin and Grand Marnier and blend again until smooth. Set aside in the refrigerator.

──────── MAKING THE MILK CHOCOLATE AND COFFEE CREAM MOUSSE
Pour the water over the gelatin, whisking until combined and leave in the refrigerator to soak for at least 20 minutes. Bring the milk and cream to a boil in a saucepan. Coarsely chop the coffee beans and infuse in the hot cream for at least 10 minutes. Strain through a fine-mesh sieve and adjust the flavor by adding more milk. Pour over the beaten egg yolks and cook to 185°F (85°C), whisking constantly. Pour over the lightly melted chocolate, instant coffee, and bloomed gelatin. Blend until smooth and then fold in the whipped cream at 86°F–95°F (30°C–35C).

──────── MAKING THE ABSOLU COFFEE GLAZE
In a saucepan, bring all the ingredients to a boil and transfer to the spray gun.

──────── ASSEMBLING THE MOCHA
Place the praline crisp in a 6-in. (16-cm) ring. Cut the disk of Genoa bread in half horizontally to make 2 equal layers. Place the first on top of the praline crisp, spoon 5.5 oz. (160 g) of the citrus marmalade into the pastry bag and pipe over. Cover with the second layer of Genoa bread and freeze until firm. Pour the cream mousse into the 7-in. (18-cm) ring and place the layered Genoa bread and praline crisp inside. Chill in the refrigerator until set. Unmold, turn the dessert the right way up, and spray with the glaze. Add decorations of your choice.

PINEAPPLE AND THAI BASIL CAKE

Ananas-Basilic Thaï

Serves 6–8

Active time
3 hours

Cooking time
30 minutes

Freezing time
2 ½ hours

Storage
Up to 2 days in the refrigerator

Equipment
2 × 7-in. (18-cm) cake rings
on baking sheets lined with
parchment paper

6-in. (16-cm) cake ring
on a baking sheet lined
with parchment paper

Instant-read thermometer
Stick blender

Ingredients

PINEAPPLE SPONGE LAYER
4 tbsp (1.75 oz./55 g) butter,
plus extra for greasing
¼ cup (1.75 oz./50 g) sugar
Generous ¼ cup (2.25 oz./65 g)
lightly beaten egg
(about 1 ½ eggs)
½ cup (2.25 oz./65 g) flour
¼ tsp (1 g) baking powder
1 tbsp (15 ml) whipping cream,
35% butterfat, at room
temperature
1 oz. (25 g) pineapple purée,
at room temperature
5.25 oz. (150 g) pan-fried
pineapple

LIGHT SHORT PASTRY
1.5 oz. (45 g) white chocolate
5 tbsp (2.75 oz./75 g) butter,
softened
Heaping 1 tbsp (0.5 oz./15 g)
light brown sugar
Scant ⅓ cup (1 oz./30 g)
almond flour
2 ¾ tsp (0.5 oz./15 g) egg yolk
(about 1 yolk)
⅛ teaspoon (1 g) fleur de sel
⅓ cup (1.5 oz./40 g) flour

FROZEN PINEAPPLE AND BASIL LAYER
1 ½ sheets (0.1 oz./3 g) gelatin
1.5 oz. (40 g) pineapple,
in small dice
1 tbsp (1 oz./25 g) agave syrup
4.5 oz. (125 g) pineapple purée
2 tbsp (5 g) Thai basil, chopped
1 ½ tbsp (25 ml) vodka

PINEAPPLE MOUSSE
7 oz. (200 g) pineapple purée,
plus extra if needed
1 oz. (25 g) lemon purée
2 tbsp (5 g) chopped Thai basil
2 ½ tbsp (1 oz./30 g) sugar
3 sheets (0.2 oz./6 g) gelatin
3 tbsp (1.75 oz /50 g) egg yolk
(about 3 yolks)
Scant 1 cup (200 ml) whipping
cream, 35% butterfat, whipped

WHITE GLAZE
2 sheets (0.12 oz./4 g) gelatin
2 tbsp (35 ml) water
5 tbsp (2 oz./60 g) sugar
2 tbsp plus 2 tsp (2 oz./60 g)
glucose syrup
3 tbsp (1.5 oz./40 g)
sweetened condensed milk
2 oz. (60 g) white chocolate,
chopped

DECORATION
10.5 oz. (300 g) white chocolate

MAKING THE PINEAPPLE SPONGE
Preheat the oven to 300°F (150°C/Gas mark 2). Butter a 7-in. (18-cm) cake ring. Cream the butter and sugar and beat in the eggs. Sift the flour and baking powder together and fold in. Stir in the cream and pineapple purée. Pour into the ring, top with the pan-fried pineapple and bake for 20 minutes. Remove the ring and cool on a rack. Keep the oven at the same temperature.

MAKING THE LIGHT SHORT PASTRY
Butter the second 7-in. (18-cm) ring. Melt the chocolate in a bowl over a pan of hot water. Whisk the butter and brown sugar until pale, stir in the almond flour, egg yolk, and fleur de sel and fold in the flour. Stir in the melted chocolate, pour into the ring and bake until lightly browned. Cool in the ring (it is very fragile when hot) before carefully removing the ring.

MAKING THE FROZEN PINEAPPLE AND BASIL LAYER
Soak the gelatin in cold water. Pan-fry the diced pineapple with the agave syrup without caramelizing. Stir in the pineapple purée and basil and heat to 140°F (60°C). Strain through a fine-mesh sieve, pressing down to extract all the juice. Stir in the vodka. Squeeze excess water from the gelatin and stir in until dissolved. Pour into the 6-in. (16-cm) ring and freeze for 1 ½ hours.

MAKING THE PINEAPPLE MOUSSE
Heat the pineapple and lemon purées, Thai basil, and sugar in a saucepan. Strain through a fine-mesh sieve. Add enough pineapple purée to the liquid so it weighs 8 oz. (225 g). Soak the gelatin in a bowl of cold water. Return the pineapple mixture to the saucepan and bring to a boil. Stir in the egg yolks and continue as for making a custard (see technique p. 204) without boiling the mixture again. Squeeze excess water from the gelatin and stir in. Cool to 64°F (18°C) and then fold in the whipped cream with a spatula.

MAKING THE WHITE GLAZE
Soak the gelatin in cold water. In a saucepan, heat the water, sugar, and glucose syrup to 215° F (102°C). Stir in the condensed milk. Squeeze excess water from the gelatin and stir in. Pour over the chocolate and process with the stick blender. When used, the glaze must be about 95°F (35°C).

ASSEMBLING THE CAKE
Lay the sponge in one of the larger rings and spread some of the pineapple mousse over it in a smooth layer. Carefully put the frozen layer in the center and cover with another layer of mousse. Top with the pastry and spread with more mousse. Freeze for 1 hour. Carefully remove the ring and place the assembled cake on a rack over a baking sheet. Smooth the mousse with a spatula before pouring over the white glaze. Melt the white chocolate and spread it over a strip of acetate long enough to wrap around the cake and about two-thirds of its depth. When the chocolate is starting to set but is not hard, wrap the strip around the cake and leave until firmly set before carefully pulling away the acetate strip. Add decorations of your choice.

SOUR CHERRY AND MASCARPONE CAKE

Entremets Griotte-Mascarpone

Serves 6–8

Active time
2 hours

Cooking time
40 minutes

Chilling time
1 hour 20 minutes

Freezing time
3 hours

Storage
Up to 2 days in the refrigerator

Equipment
6-in. (16-cm) cake ring
on a baking sheet lined
with parchment paper

Instant-read thermometer
Electric hand beater
6-in. (16-cm) silicone cake pan
Silicone baking mat
Pastry bag fitted
with a plain ½-in. (10-mm) tip
Stick blender
Angled spatula
Food-safe acetate strip
and sheet

Ingredients

HAZELNUT STREUSEL
3 ½ tbsp (1.75 oz./50 g)
butter, diced
¼ cup (1.75 oz./50 g)
light brown sugar
½ cup minus 1 tbsp
(1.75 oz./50 g) flour
Heaping ¼ cup (1 oz./25 g)
ground hazelnuts
Heaping ¼ cup (1 oz./25 g)
ground almonds
Scant ¼ cup (0.75 oz./20 g)
slivered almonds
1 tonka bean
1 pinch of fleur de sel

MASCARPONE MOUSSE
4 sheets (0.25 oz./8 g) gelatin
1 cup (240 ml) whole milk
1 tbsp plus 2 tsp (0.75 oz./20 g)
sugar
Scant ¼ cup (50 ml) whipping
cream, 35% butterfat
Seeds from ½ vanilla bean
1 tonka bean (see method)
¼ cup (2 oz./60 g) egg yolk
(about 3 ½ yolks)
¼ cup (3 oz./85 g) glucose syrup
1 cup (9 oz./250 g) mascarpone

SOUR CHERRY CRÉMEUX
1 ¼ sheets (2.5 g) gelatin
5 oz. (150 g) sour cherry purée
3 tbsp (45 ml) whipping cream,
35% butterfat
Scant ¼ cup (1.5 oz./45 g) sugar
1 tbsp plus 1 scant tsp (0.5 oz./12 g)
cornstarch

ALMOND AND LEMON SPONGE
¾ tsp (5 g) invert sugar
Scant ¼ cup (1 oz./30 g)
confectioners' sugar
1 tbsp (0.3 oz./8 g) flour
⅔ cup (2.25 oz./65 g) almond flour
Scant 2 tbsp (1 oz./30 g) egg yolk
(about 1 ½ yolks)
1 tbsp plus 1 tsp (0.75 oz./20 g)
lightly beaten egg (about ½ egg)
Finely grated zest of ½ lemon
1 tbsp plus 1 tsp (0.75 oz./20 g)
butter, melted
3 ½ tbsp (1.75 oz./50 g) egg white
(about 1 ½ whites)
1 ½ tbsp (0.7 oz./18 g) sugar

CHOCOLATE GLAZE
Scant ½ cup (111 ml) water
½ cup (3.5 oz./100 g) sugar
Generous ¼ cup (3.5 oz./100 g)
glucose syrup
Heaping ½ tsp (3 g) gelatin
powder
Scant ⅓ cup (2.5 oz./70 g)
sweetened condensed milk
3.5 oz. (100 g) white chocolate,
chopped
Red food coloring as needed

MAKING THE HAZELNUT STREUSEL
Work the butter, light brown sugar, flour, ground hazelnuts and almonds, and salt together to make a fairly smooth dough. Chill for 20 minutes. Preheat the oven to 350°F (180°C/Gas mark 4). Break up the dough into small chunks, spread them out in the cake ring, and grate over about a tenth of the tonka bean. Bake for about 20 minutes.

MAKING THE MASCARPONE MOUSSE
Soak the gelatin in a bowl of cold water. Heat the milk, sugar, cream, and vanilla seeds in a saucepan and grate in another tenth of the tonka bean. Whisk the egg yolks with the glucose syrup, drizzle over a little of the hot milk, whisking constantly. Return the mixture to the pan and continue as for making a custard (see technique p. 204). Remove from the heat, squeeze excess water from the gelatin and stir in until dissolved. Strain the custard through a fine-mesh sieve into a bowl set over a larger bowl containing ice cubes. When the custard has cooled to 68°F (20°C), gradually stir it into the mascarpone. Chill for 1 hour and then, using the electric beater, whisk to the ribbon stage.

MAKING THE SOUR CHERRY CRÉMEUX
Soak the gelatin in cold water. Heat the sour cherry purée and cream in a saucepan to 104°F (40°C). Stir in the sugar and cornstarch and bring to a boil, stirring constantly. Remove from the heat, squeeze excess water from the gelatin and stir in. Pour into the silicone baking pan and freeze for 1 hour.

MAKING THE ALMOND AND LEMON SPONGE
Preheat the oven to 400°F (200°C/Gas mark 6). Place the silicone mat on a baking sheet. In a mixing bowl, combine the invert sugar, confectioners' sugar, flour, and almond flour. Whisk together the egg yolk and egg and gradually add to the sugar and almond mixture, whisking constantly. Mix the lemon zest with the melted butter and stir in. Whisk the egg whites with the sugar to soft peak stage and fold in carefully until combined. Spoon into the pastry bag and pipe a 6-in. (16-cm) disk onto the baking sheet. Bake for 15–20 minutes.

MAKING THE CHOCOLATE GLAZE
Bring ⅓ cup (75 ml) of the water, the sugar and glucose to a boil in a pan. Soak the gelatin in the rest of the water. Stir the condensed milk into the pan, remove from the heat, and stir in the dissolved gelatin. Pour over the chocolate, add the food coloring and process with the stick blender until smooth. When used, the glaze should be at 86°F (30°C).

ASSEMBLING THE CAKE
Line the cake ring with a strip of acetate. Place it on a sheet of acetate and pour half the mascarpone mousse into the center, spreading it to the sides of the ring with the spatula. Spoon a layer of sour cherry crémeux on top and spread more mousse over it. Top with the sponge, spread with more mousse and then scatter over the streusel crumbs. Put in the freezer until frozen (about 2 hours) and then immediately remove the acetate base and strip and pour over the glaze. Add decorations as you wish, surrounding the cake with a chocolate strip tinted red.

A FEAST OF SUMMER BERRIES

Régal du Chef aux Fruits Rouges

Serves 6–8

Active time
3 hours

Cooking time
30 minutes

Storage
Up to 2 days in the refrigerator

Equipment
6-in. (16-cm) and 7-in. (18-cm) cake rings on baking sheets lined with parchment paper

Stand mixer fitted with the paddle beater

Instant-read thermometer
Silicone baking mat
5-in. (13-cm) and 6 ½-in. (17-cm) round silicone molds

Ingredients

ROSE AND RASPBERRY GENOISE
2 oz. (60 g) almond paste
⅓ cup (2.5 oz./70 g) sugar
¾ cup (6.25 oz./180 g) lightly beaten egg (about 4 eggs)
¾ cup plus 2 tbsp (3.5 oz./100 g) flour
3 tbsp (1.5 oz./40 g) butter, melted, plus extra for greasing
1 tsp (6 g) natural raspberry flavoring (or to taste)

WHITE JOCONDE SPONGE
1 ½ cups (4.75 oz./135 g) almond flour
1 cup (4.75 oz./135 g) confectioners' sugar
¾ cup (6.25 oz./180 g) lightly beaten egg (about 4 eggs)
Generous ¼ cup (1.25 oz./35 g) flour
½ cup plus 2 tsp (4.25 oz./120 g) egg white (about 4 whites)
1 ½ tbsp (0.7 oz./18 g) sugar
1 tbsp plus 2 tsp (25 g) butter, melted
Pink and white food coloring, as needed

RASPBERRY AND STRAWBERRY SYRUP
1.75 oz. (50 g) raspberry purée
2.75 oz. (75 g) strawberry purée
2 tbsp (30 ml) water
Scant ¼ cup (55 ml) simple syrup (made of equal parts water and sugar)

SET RASPBERRY COMPOTE
1 tsp (5 g) gelatin powder
1 ½ tbsp (25 ml) water
7 oz. (200 g) raspberry purée, divided
Heaping 1 tbsp (0.5 oz./15 g) sugar
Scant 1 tsp (4 ml) lemon juice

VANILLA CREAM
1 tsp plus heaping ¼ tsp (6 g) gelatin powder
2 tbsp (30 ml) water
Scant ½ cup (100 ml) whole milk
1 vanilla bean, split lengthwise and seeds scraped out
2 ½ tbsp (1.5 oz./45 g) egg yolk (about 2 ½ yolks)
3 tbsp (1.25 oz./35 g) sugar
1 cup plus scant ½ cup (350 ml) whipping cream, 35% butterfat, divided

RASPBERRY JELLY
Scant 1 tsp (4 g) gelatin powder
1 tbsp plus 1 tsp (20 ml) mineral water
7 oz. (200 g) raspberry purée
Heaping 1 tbsp (0.5 oz./15 g) sugar
½ tsp (3 ml) lemon juice

FRUIT DECORATION
Raspberries to fill the center
Confectioners' sugar for dusting
A few cress leaves

MAKING THE ROSE AND RASPBERRY GENOISE
Preheat the oven to 350°F (180°C/Gas mark 4). Butter the 6-in. (16-cm) cake ring. Crumble the almond paste with the sugar and a little of the egg. Gradually beat in the remaining egg to the ribbon stage. Stir the flour into the melted butter and fold in with the flavoring. Pour into the ring and bake for 18 minutes.

MAKING THE WHITE JOCONDE SPONGE
Grind the almond flour until very fine. In the stand mixer, beat the almond flour, confectioners' sugar, whole eggs, and flour. Whisk the egg whites with the sugar to soft peaks. Fold the two mixtures together and then add the butter. Spoon a tenth of the batter into another bowl and tint it pink with the coloring. Spread it randomly over the baking mat in thin swirls to create a marbled effect and freeze until frozen. Heat the oven to 425°F (210°C/Gas mark 7). Color the remaining batter white and spread over the top of the frozen pink batter in a thick layer. Bake for 11 minutes, then cool on a rack.

MAKING THE RASPBERRY AND STRAWBERRY SYRUP
In a saucepan, heat the raspberry and strawberry purées to 104°F (40°C). Stir in the water and syrup.

MAKING THE SET RASPBERRY COMPOTE
Dissolve the gelatin in the water. In a saucepan, bring half the raspberry purée to a boil with the sugar and lemon juice. Pour over the dissolved gelatin and stir to combine. Pour into the 6 ½-in. (17-cm) silicone mold and chill in the refrigerator.

MAKING THE VANILLA CREAM
Dissolve the gelatin in the water. Heat the milk and infuse with the vanilla bean and seeds. Whisk the egg yolks and sugar until pale. Whisk in a little of the milk, return the mixture to the saucepan, add 2 tbsp (30 ml) of the cream and heat to 185°F (85°C). Stir in the dissolved gelatin, strain through a fine-mesh sieve and allow to cool. Whisk the remaining cream to soft peaks and fold into the custard, which should be smooth and quite firm.

MAKING THE RASPBERRY JELLY
Dissolve the gelatin in the water. In a saucepan, bring the raspberry purée, sugar, and lemon juice to a boil. Stir in the dissolved gelatin. Pour into the 5-in. (13-cm) silicone mold and chill in the refrigerator.

ASSEMBLING THE CAKE
Line the sides of the larger ring with a strip of marbled Joconde sponge. Brush the genoise with the syrup and place it in the ring. Place the disk of set raspberry compote on top and spread with a layer of vanilla cream to come halfway up the ring. Place the disk of raspberry jelly over the vanilla cream and spread more vanilla cream over it, stopping just under ½ in. (1 cm) from the top of the Joconde sponge lining the sides. Fill with raspberries, dust with confectioners' sugar, and sprinkle over a few leaves of cress.

SUMMER

QUILTED STRAWBERRY MOUSSE CAKE

Le Coussin de la Reine

Serves 6–8

Active time
1 ½ hours

Infusing time
24 hours

Cooking time
20 minutes

Freezing time
1 ½ hours

Storage
Up to 2 days in the refrigerator

Equipment
Pastry bag fitted
with a plain ½-in. (12-mm) tip
Instant-read thermometer
7-in. (18-cm) silicone cake pan
Velvet spray gun
8-in. (20-cm) cake ring
Sheet of food-safe acetate

Ingredients

VANILLA-FLAVORED CREAM
¼ cup (60 ml) whipping cream,
35% butterfat
¼ vanilla bean, split lengthwise
and seeds scraped out

ALMOND DACQUOISE
Heaping 1 cup (4 oz./115 g)
almond flour
⅓ cup (1.5 oz./40 g) flour
Scant ½ cup (2.25 oz./65 g)
confectioners' sugar
½ tsp (1 g) finely grated lime zest
Scant ¾ cup (6.5 oz./185 g)
egg white (about 6 whites)
¾ cup (4.75 oz./135 g) sugar

LIGHTLY-CANDIED WILD STRAWBERRIES
5 oz. (140 g) wild strawberry
purée
0.75 oz. (20 g) invert sugar
1 tbsp plus 2 tsp
(0.75 oz./20 g) sugar
½ tsp (2 g) pectin NH
0.75 oz. (20 g) wild strawberries
1 tsp (5 ml) lime juice

PÂTE À BOMBE
2 tbsp (30 ml) water
Scant ¼ cup (1.5 oz./45 g) sugar
¼ cup (2 oz./60 g) egg yolk
(about 3 ½ yolks)
1 tbsp plus 2 tsp (1 oz./25 g)
lightly beaten egg (about ½ egg)

VANILLA-FLAVORED MOUSSE
3 ½ sheets (0.25 oz./7 g) gelatin
¼ cup (60 ml) vanilla-flavored
cream (see ingredients above)
1 cup (250 ml) *fromage blanc*
(or substitute strained Greek
yogurt, quark, or ricotta)
1 tbsp (0.75 oz./20 g) honey
2.25 oz. (65 g) *pâte à bombe*
(see ingredients above)
Scant ½ cup (100 ml) whipping
cream, 35% butterfat

RED VELVET SPRAY
12.5 oz. (350 g) white chocolate
5.25 oz. (150 g) cocoa butter
1 knife tip bright red food coloring

DECORATION
Edible silver pearls
A few wild strawberries

INFUSING THE CREAM (24 HOURS AHEAD)
Bring the whipping cream to a boil in a saucepan. Remove from the heat, add the vanilla bean and seeds, and infuse in the refrigerator for 24 hours.

MAKING THE ALMOND DACQUOISE
Preheat the oven to 350°F (180°C/Gas mark 4). Line a baking sheet with parchment paper. Sift the almond flour, flour, and sugar and add the lime zest. Whisk the egg whites and sugar to soft peaks and fold in the dry ingredients. Spoon into the pastry bag and pipe 2 × 7-in. (18-cm) disks on the baking sheet. Bake for 18 minutes with the oven door slightly ajar.

MAKING THE LIGHTLY-CANDIED WILD STRAWBERRIES
Heat the strawberry purée and invert sugar in a saucepan to 104°F (40°C). Mix the sugar with the pectin, stir in, and bring to a boil. Remove from the heat and add the whole strawberries and lime juice. Pour into the silicone cake pan and freeze for about 30 minutes.

MAKING THE PÂTE À BOMBE
Bring the water and sugar to a boil, remove from the heat and cool to 176°F (80°C). While the syrup is cooling, beat the egg yolk and egg. Add the syrup in a thin stream, whisking constantly. Whisk until cold.

MAKING THE VANILLA-FLAVORED MOUSSE
Soak the gelatin in a bowl of cold water. Scald the vanilla-flavored cream and stir it into the *fromage blanc*. Squeeze excess water from the gelatin, stir it in with the honey, and then stir in the *pâte à bombe*. Whisk the cream and carefully fold it in.

MAKING THE RED VELVET SPRAY
Melt the chocolate and cocoa butter in a bowl over a pan of hot water. Stir in the food coloring and spoon into the spray gun.

ASSEMBLING THE CAKE
Lay the acetate sheet on a baking sheet and place the ring on it. Pour a layer of vanilla-flavored mousse into the ring and spread to the sides. Sit a disk of dacquoise on the mousse and the still-frozen strawberry layer on top. Spread with a thin layer of mousse, top with the second dacquoise and cover with more mousse. Place the cake in the freezer until frozen. Carefully remove the ring. Turn the cake upside down and place on a rack. Cover the surrounding work surfaces and spray the cake with the red velvet spray to completely cover it. Mark lines as shown with the side of a ruler and decorate with edible silver pearls and quartered strawberries.

AUTUMN

PEAR, CREAM BRÛLÉE, AND COFFEE CAKE

Entremets Automne

Serves 6

Active time
2 hours

Cooking time
1 hour

Freezing time
1 hour

Storage
Up to 2 days in the refrigerator

Equipment
5 ½-in. (14-cm) round silicone mold
5 ½-in. (14-cm) round cake pan
Kitchen torch
Instant-read thermometer
Spray gun
6-in. (16-cm) cake ring

Ingredients

PEAR CLAFOUTIS
3 tbsp (1.5 oz./40 g) butter, softened
⅓ cup (1.5 oz./40 g) confectioners' sugar
⅔ cup (2 oz./60 g) almond flour
2 ½ tsp (0.3 oz./8 g) custard powder or cornstarch
1 tbsp (0.75 oz./20 g) egg yolk (about 1 yolk), at room temperature
1 tbsp (0.5 oz./16 g) lightly beaten egg (about ½ egg), at room temperature
1 tbsp plus 1 tsp (20 ml) whipping cream, 35% butterfat
2.5 oz. (70 g) pears, in large dice

BUTTERNUT CREAM BRÛLÉE
1 tbsp (0.5 oz./15 g) gelatin powder
⅓ cup plus 2 tsp (90 ml) water
¾ cup (215 ml) whipping cream, 35% butterfat
⅓ cup (2.25 oz./65 g) sugar
¼ cup (2.5 oz./70 g) egg yolk (about 4 yolks)
½ tsp (2 g) *quatre-épices* spice mix (or allspice, ground mixed spice, or pumpkin pie spice)
9.25 oz. (260 g) butternut purée
Granulated sugar for sprinkling

COFFEE MOUSSE
Scant 1 tsp (4 g) gelatin powder
1 tbsp plus 1 tsp (20 ml) water
⅓ cup (75 ml) whole milk
Scant 2 tbsp (1 oz./30 g) egg yolk (about 1 ½ yolks)
1 tsp (5 g) coffee paste
1.75 oz. (50 g) Italian meringue (see technique p. 232)
Scant 1 cup (200 ml) whipping cream, whipped

FLOCKED FROSTING
3.5 oz. (100 g) bittersweet chocolate, 64% cacao
3.5 oz. (100 g) cocoa butter

MAKING THE PEAR CLAFOUTIS
Preheat the oven to 325°F (160°C/Gas mark 3). Beat the butter with the confectioners' sugar. Mix in the almond flour and custard powder or cornstarch. Whisk in the egg yolk and egg and then whisk in the cream. Pour into the silicone mold, arrange the diced pears on top, and bake for 20–25 minutes. Reduce the oven temperature to 195°F (90°C/Gas mark ¼).

MAKING THE BUTTERNUT CREAM BRÛLÉE
Dissolve the gelatin in the water. Make a custard (see technique p. 204) with the next 3 ingredients, using the cream instead of milk. Stir in the spice mix and butternut purée, followed by the dissolved gelatin. Pour into the cake pan and bake for about 20 minutes until set. Cool and then freeze for about 1 hour. When frozen, sprinkle with sugar and caramelize the top with the kitchen torch.

MAKING THE COFFEE MOUSSE
Dissolve the gelatin in the water. Make a custard (see technique p. 204) using the next 2 ingredients and flavor it with the coffee paste. Stir in the dissolved gelatin and allow to cool to 64°F (18°C). Carefully fold in the Italian meringue and whipped cream, using a spatula.

MAKING THE FLOCKED FROSTING
Melt the chocolate and cocoa butter in a bowl over a pan of hot water. Transfer the mixture to the spray gun.

ASSEMBLING THE CAKE
Spread a layer of coffee mousse around the sides of the cake ring. Carefully place the pear clafoutis in the ring, followed by the butternut cream brûlée, caramelized side down. Spread another layer of coffee mousse on top and smooth with a spatula. Place in the freezer until frozen and spray with the chocolate flocked frosting. Add decorations of your choice.

AUTUMN

QUINCE, GINGER, AND CHOCOLATE CAKE

Entremets Coing-Gingembre

Serves 6–8

Active time
4 hours

Cooking time
2 hours 40 minutes

Freezing time
1 hour

Storage
Up to 3 days in the refrigerator

Equipment
6-in. (16-cm) silicone mold, ¾ in. (2 cm) deep
Electric hand beater
6-in. (16-cm) silicone mold, 1 in. (2.5 cm) deep
Instant-read thermometer
Stick blender
6-in. (16-cm) silicone mold, ⅔ in. (1.5 cm) deep
7-in. (18-cm) cake ring, 1 ¾ in. (4.5 cm) deep
Silicone baking mat
Strip of food-safe acetate
Angled spatula

Ingredients

PECAN MADELEINE SPONGE BASE
5 tbsp (2.5 oz./70 g) butter
2 tbsp plus 1 tsp (1.2 oz./35 g) clarified butter
2 tbsp (30 ml) whole milk
0.5 oz. (15 g) invert sugar
⅓ cup (2.75 oz./75 g) lightly beaten egg (about 1 ½ eggs)
Scant ⅓ cup (2 oz./60 g) sugar
Seeds from 1 vanilla bean
¾ cup plus 2 tbsp (3.5 oz./100 g) flour
1 ¼ tsp (5 g) baking powder
Heaping ¼ cup (1 oz./30 g) pecans, chopped

FROZEN ROASTED QUINCE LAYER
2 quinces
1 tbsp (20 g) butter, melted
½ cup (3.5 oz./100 g) sugar

GINGER CRÉMEUX
1 sheet (2 g) gelatin
⅓ cup (80 g) whipping cream, 35% butterfat
1.5 oz. (40 g) ginger purée or juice
Scant 2 tbsp (1 oz./30 g) egg yolk (about 1 ½ yolks)
3 ½ tbsp (1.75 oz./50 g) lightly beaten egg (about 1 egg)
2 ½ tbsp (1 oz./30 g) sugar
3 tbsp (1.5 oz./45 g) butter, preferably 84% butterfat, diced
20 cubes of candied ginger

CHOCOLATE MOUSSE
Heaping ½ tsp (3 g) gelatin powder
1 tbsp plus ½ tsp (18 ml) water
Scant ¼ cup (50 ml) whole milk
¼ cup (60 ml) whipping cream, 35% butterfat
2 ½ tbsp (2 oz./60 g) glucose syrup
4 oz. (120 g) bittersweet chocolate, 66% cacao, chopped
⅔ cup (150 ml) whipping cream, 35% butterfat

MILK CHOCOLATE GLAZE
2 tsp (0.35 oz./10 g) gelatin powder
½ cup (135 ml) water, divided
¾ cup (5 oz./150 g) sugar
½ cup minus 1 tbsp (5.25 oz./150 g) glucose syrup
Scant ½ cup (3.5 oz./100 g) evaporated milk
5 oz. (150 g) milk chocolate

MAKING THE PECAN MADELEINE SPONGE BASE
Preheat the oven to 325°F (170°C/Gas mark 3). Line the 6-in. (16-cm) silicone mold, ¾ in. (2 cm) deep, with parchment paper. In a saucepan, melt the butter, stir in the clarified butter, bring to a boil, and remove from the heat. Scald the milk with the invert sugar. With the electric beater, whisk the egg, sugar, and vanilla seeds. Whisk in the hot milk, sift the flour and baking powder together and fold in. Stir in the hot butter, pour into the mold and sprinkle with the chopped pecans. Bake for 10 minutes.

MAKING THE FROZEN ROASTED QUINCE LAYER
Preheat the oven to 425°F (220°C/Gas mark 7). Peel, core and finely slice the quinces. Grease the 6-in. (16-cm) silicone mold, 1 in. (2.5 cm) deep, with the melted butter and sprinkle with the sugar. Arrange the quince slices in lines in the mold, alternating the direction. Cover with foil and bake for 2 hours. Reduce the temperature to 320°F (160°C/Gas mark 3), remove the foil, and bake for 30 minutes so all the moisture evaporates. Cool and then freeze.

MAKING THE GINGER CRÉMEUX
Soak the gelatin in cold water. Bring the cream and ginger purée or juice to a boil in a saucepan. Whisk the egg yolks, whole egg, and sugar until pale and thick. Whisk a little hot cream into the yolk mixture, return it to the saucepan and cook, stirring constantly, to 180°F (82°C). Remove from the heat, squeeze excess water from the gelatin, and stir in. Transfer to a mixing bowl and allow to cool. When the temperature is just below 104°F (40°C), add the butter and process with the stick blender until smooth. Pour into the 6-in. (16-cm) silicone mold, ⅔ in. (1.5 cm) deep, and scatter the ginger cubes over the top. Freeze for 30 minutes, until frozen.

MAKING THE CHOCOLATE MOUSSE
Dissolve the gelatin in the water. Bring the milk, cream, and glucose syrup to a boil. Pour over the chocolate, stir until melted and then stir in the dissolved gelatin. Process with the stick blender until smooth and let cool to 77°F (25°C). Whip the cream until it holds soft peaks and fold in.

MAKING THE MILK CHOCOLATE GLAZE
Dissolve the gelatin in ¼ cup (60 ml) of the water. Bring the rest of the water to a boil with the sugar and glucose syrup. Stir in the dissolved gelatin and evaporated milk. Pour over the milk chocolate and process with the stick blender until smooth.

ASSEMBLING THE CAKE
Place the 7-in. (18-cm) cake ring on the silicone baking mat and line the sides with the acetate strip. Place the sponge disk in the ring and spread a layer of chocolate mousse over it, just under ½ in. (1 cm) deep, right to the sides of the ring. Place the ginger crémeux on top, followed by the frozen quince layer. Cover the cake with the remaining chocolate mousse, smooth it with the angled spatula and place in the freezer until frozen. Put the cake on a rack and cover with the milk chocolate glaze. Add decorations of your choice and chill in the refrigerator until ready to serve.

COFFEE, HAZELNUT, AND CHOCOLATE CAKE

LE 55 FBG, W.H.

Serves 6

Active time
2 ½ hours

Chilling time
24 hours

Cooking time
40 minutes

Storage
Up to 2 days in the refrigerator

Equipment
Stand mixer
2 × 4 ½ × 7-in. (11 × 18-cm) oval cake frames
6 × 3 ½-in. (16 × 9-cm) oval cake frame
Silicone baking mat
Electric hand beater
Instant-read thermometer

Ingredients

CHOCOLATE SHORT PASTRY CRUST (MAKE 24 HOURS AHEAD)
1 stick plus 2 tbsp (5.25 oz./150 g) butter
½ cup (3.5 oz./100 g) light brown sugar
Scant ⅔ cup (1.75 oz./50 g) ground hazelnuts, roasted
3 ½ tbsp (1 oz./25 g) unsweetened cocoa powder
0.5 oz. (15 g) *feuilletine* flakes (or use crushed wafers)
0.25 oz. (10 g) cocoa nibs
½ tsp (2 g) fleur de sel
1 tbsp plus 1 tsp (0.75 oz./20 g) lightly beaten egg (about ½ egg)
1 ⅔ cups (7 oz./200 g) flour
¼ tsp (1 g) baking soda

COFFEE CRÉMEUX
¼ cup (55 ml) whipping cream, 35% butterfat
¼ cup (55 ml) whole milk
Heaping ¼ cup (0.5 oz./15 g) instant coffee granules
¾ tbsp (0.5 oz./15 g) egg yolk (about 1 yolk)
1 ¾ tbsp (0.75 oz./20 g) sugar
0.75 oz. (25 g) coffee-flavored bittersweet couverture chocolate
1 oz. (30 g) milk couverture chocolate

SHORTBREAD
1 stick plus 2 tsp (4.5 oz./125 g) butter
Scant ⅓ cup (2 oz./60 g) sugar
1 cup (4.5 oz./130 g) flour
¼ tsp (1 g) salt

CRISP HAZELNUT LAYER
3 oz. (80 g) dark gianduja (bittersweet chocolate with about 30% hazelnuts)
1.5 oz. (45 g) *feuilletine* flakes (or use crushed wafers)
3.5 oz. (100 g) shortbread (see ingredients above), crumbled

CHOCOLATE SPONGE
2.75 oz. (75 g) bittersweet couverture chocolate
1.25 oz. (35 g) almond paste, 66% almonds
1 tbsp (0.75 oz./20 g) egg yolk (about 1 yolk)
1 tbsp plus 1 tsp (0.75 oz./20 g) butter, softened
⅓ cup (3 oz./85 g) egg white (about 3 whites)
2 ½ tbsp (1 oz./30 g) sugar

CHOCOLATE BAVARIAN CREAM
2 sheets (0.2 oz./4 g) gelatin
⅓ cup (85 ml) whole milk
⅓ cup (85 ml) whipping cream, 35% butterfat
Heaping 1 tbsp (0.5 oz./15 g) sugar
Scant 2 tbsp (1 oz./30 g) egg yolk (about 1 ½ yolks)
3.25 oz. (90 g) milk couverture chocolate
1.25 oz. (35 g) bittersweet couverture chocolate
1 ¼ cups (300 ml) whipping cream, 35% butterfat
¼ tsp (1 g) finely grated lemon zest
¼ tsp (1 g) finely grated orange zest

CARAMEL GLAZE
1 tsp plus heaping ¼ tsp (6 g) gelatin powder
2 tbsp plus 2 tsp (40 ml) water
Scant ½ cup (100 ml) milk
1 ¼ cups (9 oz./250 g) sugar, divided
Scant 1 cup (200 ml) whipping cream, 35% butterfat
4 tbsp (2.5 oz./70 g) glucose syrup
2 ½ tbsp (0.5 oz./15 g) potato starch

MAKING THE CHOCOLATE SHORT PASTRY CRUST
Fit the stand mixer with the paddle beater and beat the butter with the brown sugar. Beat in the ground hazelnuts, cocoa powder, *feuilletine*, cocoa nibs, and fleur de sel. Add the egg, combine well, and then fold in the flour and baking soda. Roll out the dough ⅛ in. (3 mm) thick and line one of the larger oval cake frames. Chill for 24 hours. Preheat the oven to 325°F (165°C/Gas mark 3) and bake for 10–12 minutes.

MAKING THE COFFEE CRÉMEUX
Bring the cream and milk to a boil. Stir in the coffee, steep for 15 minutes and then strain through a fine-mesh sieve. Beat the egg yolk with the sugar, whisk in a little of the warm milk, and make a custard (see technique p. 204). Melt both chocolates in a bowl set over a pan of boiling water. Pour over the custard and process with the stick blender until smooth. Pour into the other 4 ½ × 7-in. (11 × 18-cm) frame and freeze.

MAKING THE SHORTBREAD
Preheat the oven to 325°F (160°C/Gas mark 3). Fit the stand mixer with the paddle beater and mix all the ingredients together to make a dough. Roll the dough between two sheets of parchment paper and slide onto a baking sheet. Bake for 11 minutes and allow to cool.

MAKING THE CRISP HAZELNUT LAYER
Melt the gianduja in a saucepan and then stir in the *feuilletine* and chopped shortbread. Spread into the smaller frame and chill until set.

MAKING THE CHOCOLATE SPONGE
Preheat the oven to 350°F (180°C/Gas mark 4). Lay the silicone mat on a baking sheet. Melt the chocolate in a bowl over a pan of hot water. Beat the almond paste with the electric beater, gradually adding the egg yolk. Beat in the butter and the melted chocolate. In another bowl, whisk the egg whites with the sugar to fairly firm peaks. Combine the two mixtures using a spatula, spread over the baking sheet and bake for about 8 minutes.

MAKING THE CHOCOLATE BAVARIAN CREAM
Soak the gelatin in cold water. Using the ingredients listed, make a custard (see technique p. 204). Melt the chocolates in a bowl over a pan of hot water. Squeeze excess water from the gelatin, stir it into the custard, and strain. Pour it over the melted chocolate and process until smooth. Cool to 77°F–86°F (25°C–30°C). Lightly whip the cream with the zests and fold in.

MAKING THE CARAMEL GLAZE
Dissolve the gelatin powder in the water. Bring the milk to a boil with half the sugar, the cream, and glucose syrup. Cool to 113°F (45°C), then stir in the remaining sugar and potato starch. Bring to a boil again, remove from the heat, and stir in the dissolved gelatin. Use the glaze at 77°F (25°C).

ASSEMBLING THE DESSERT
Take the pastry crust in its frame and spread a ½-in. (1-cm) layer of the Bavarian cream over it, spreading it around the sides of the frame. Place the hazelnut layer on the cream, then a layer of chocolate sponge cut to size, cover with more cream and top with the coffee crémeux. Smooth more Bavarian cream over the entire dessert and freeze. Glaze when frozen.

NUTCRACKER SWEET

Casse-Noisette Gianduja-Caramel

WINTER

Serves 8

Active time
3 hours

Cooking time
30 minutes

Freezing time
2 hours

Storage
Up to 3 days in the refrigerator

Equipment
Silicone baking mat
Pastry bag fitted
with a plain ½-in. (15-mm) tip
Instant-read and candy
thermometers
2 × 2 ¼ × 12-in. (6 × 30-cm) molds
Electric hand beater
Stick blender

Ingredients

ALMOND DACQUOISE
Scant ¼ cup (1.75 oz./50 g)
egg white (about 1 ½ whites)
1 tbsp (0.5 oz./13 g) sugar
1 tbsp (0.3 oz./9 g) flour
3 tbsp (0.75 oz./22 g)
confectioners' sugar
¼ cup (1 oz./25 g) almond flour
Heaping ¼ cup (1 oz./25 g)
ground hazelnuts

FROZEN CARAMEL CRÉMEUX
⅓ cup (2.25 oz./65 g) sugar
1 ½ tbsp (0.5 oz./12 g) glucose
syrup
2 tbsp (30 ml) whipping cream,
35% butterfat
3 tbsp (1.75 oz./50 g) butter, diced

FROZEN CHOCOLATE CRÉMEUX
Scant ¼ cup (50 ml) milk
Scant ¼ cup (50 ml) whipping
cream, 35% butterfat
2 ½ tbsp (1.5 oz./40 g) egg yolk
(about 2 yolks)

Heaping 1 tbsp (0.5 oz./15 g)
sugar
1 oz. (25 g) bittersweet
chocolate, preferably Valrhona
Caraïbe 66%
1 oz. (30 g) milk chocolate,
preferably Valrhona Jivara 35%

CRISP BASE
2 oz. (50 g) hazelnut praline paste
0.3 oz. (8 g) milk chocolate,
35% cacao
0.3 oz. (8 g) bittersweet chocolate,
66% chocolate
1 oz. (25 g) *feuilletine* flakes
(or use crushed wafers)
1 oz. (25 g) chopped caramelized
roasted hazelnuts

GIANDUJA MOUSSE
1 tsp (5 g) gelatin powder
2 tbsp (30 ml) water
3 tbsp (1.75 oz./50 g) egg yolk
(about 3 yolks)
1 tbsp plus 1 tsp (1 oz./30 g)
glucose syrup
1 tbsp (0.5 oz./13 g) sugar
3 tbsp (45 ml) whole milk
4.75 oz. (135 g) dark gianduja
(bittersweet chocolate
with about 30% hazelnuts)
1 cup (250 ml) whipping cream,
35% butterfat

GLAZE
1 tsp (5 g) gelatin powder
2 tbsp (30 ml) water
½ cup (125 ml) whole milk
2 tbsp (1.5 oz./40 g) glucose syrup
0.25 oz. (7 g) hazelnut paste
3.5 oz. (100 g) milk chocolate,
35% cacao
2.75 oz. (75 g) gianduja
6 oz. (175 g) *pâte à glacer lactée
blonde* (light glazing paste)

MAKING THE ALMOND DACQUOISE
Preheat the oven to 350°F (180°C/Gas mark 4). Lay the silicone mat on a baking sheet. Make a dacquoise with the ingredients listed (see technique p. 224). Pipe a 1 ½ × 10-in. (4 × 25-cm) oval on the mat and bake for 20 minutes.

MAKING THE FROZEN CARAMEL CRÉMEUX LAYER
In a saucepan, cook the sugar and glucose syrup to 347°F (175°C): a light caramel. Meanwhile, heat the cream. When the caramel reaches the required temperature, carefully deglaze with the cream and then stir in the butter. Pour the caramel into one of the molds and freeze until frozen.

MAKING THE FROZEN CHOCOLATE CRÉMEUX
Using the ingredients listed, make a custard (see technique p. 204). Heat to 181°F (83°C) and then cool to 104°F (40°C). Melt the chocolates to 95°F (35°C). Pour the warm custard over the melted chocolate to make a ganache. Pour it over the caramel crémeux and freeze until both layers are frozen.

MAKING THE CRISP BASE
Melt the praline paste and chocolate together and stir in the remaining ingredients. Mix well.

MAKING THE GIANDUJA MOUSSE
Dissolve the gelatin in the water. Make a *pâte à bombe*, using the electric beater to whisk the yolks, syrup, sugar, and milk in a bowl over hot water, to 160°F (70°C). Stir in the gelatin. Melt the gianduja to 113°F (45°C). Whisk the cream to soft peaks and then whisk the gianduja, cream, and *pâte à bombe* together. Finish by folding them together with a spatula.

MAKING THE GLAZE
Dissolve the gelatin in the water. Bring the milk, glucose syrup, and hazelnut paste to a boil. Stir in the chocolate, gianduja, and glazing paste until melted. Remove from the heat, stir in the gelatin, and process with the stick blender. Keep at room temperature. The glaze needs to be used at 77°F–86°F (25°C–30°C).

ASSEMBLING THE CAKE
Spread a little gianduja mousse over the second mold. Place the two frozen layers in the mold and spread more mousse over them. Cut the dacquoise to size and place it over the mousse. Freeze until frozen. Spread the crisp base over the frozen cake, filling the mold to the top and smoothing the surface level. Return to the freezer until frozen. Carefully turn out the cake onto a serving dish and pour over the glaze while still frozen. Add decorations of your choice.

FESTIVE OCCASIONS

FESTIVE OCCASIONS

Birthdays can be celebrated with all types of desserts, but certain occasions in France traditionally call for a specific cake. For example, for many French people it would not be Epiphany without a *galette des rois* (kings' cake) or Christmas without a *bûche de Noël* (Yule log). To anyone who has grown up eating such cakes, the flavors are deeply familiar and steeped in memories of special times spent with family and friends. Tradition can be delicious!

A BRIEF HISTORY OF FESTIVE FRENCH CAKES
Galette des rois *(kings' cake)*
The French tradition of eating this cake to celebrate Epiphany is centuries old. Until the 1950s, Parisians celebrated with a simple puff pastry cake without any filling, but in the 1960s bakeries began adding a layer of almond cream or frangipane and this has now become a popular modern classic. Hidden inside is a charm, usually a tiny ceramic figure, and the lucky person who finds it in their slice becomes king or queen for the day.

Bûche de Noël *(Yule log)*
This Christmas cake celebrates the tradition of burning a large log in the hearth on Christmas Eve, but as fireplaces disappeared this custom evolved into eating a log-shaped cake instead. Traditionally a rolled sponge, today it comes in many different shapes and colors, with pastry chefs reinventing it each Christmas.

Croquembouche
This spectacular pyramid of choux puffs held together with caramel is the traditional cake served in France at weddings, baptisms, and communions. It is also known as a pièce montée, literally an "assembled piece," and has been served at celebrations in France since the 19th century.

TRADITIONAL OR MODERN?

The traditional filling for a *galette des rois* is almond cream—either plain or mixed with pastry cream to make frangipane—but today bakers and pastry chefs use many unconventional fillings, such as the sour cherry and grapefruit filling in this chapter. When making your own kings' cake, the choice of a traditional or modern filling is completely up to you but it's important that you incorporate as little air as possible when folding the ingredients together. The filling should not be whisked, as any air beaten in will expand during baking, causing it to puff up and alter the shape of the cake.

MIGNARDISES: SMALL BITES *À LA FRANÇAISE*

Sometimes called petits fours, these small pastries are often served in France at soirées and cocktail parties. Their name comes from the French word *mignard*, meaning "dainty" or "pretty," and in many cases *mignardises* are miniature versions of larger pastries, both traditional and modern. The only rule for *mignardises* is that they can be eaten in one bite but, beyond this constraint, the options are infinite. They can be tartlets, religieuses, éclairs, financiers, lollipops, and much more. When making *mignardises* using your favorite pastry recipes, it is important to keep ingredients in the same proportions, adjusting them as necessary. And, given their size, decorations and finishing touches for these miniature masterpieces require precision and meticulous attention to detail.

WORKING WITH POURING FONDANT

Made of water, sugar, and glucose, pouring fondant is used to ice éclairs, religieuses, and napoleons, whatever their size. To use pouring fondant, it is important to first bring it to the ideal working temperature, which is 95°F–99°F (35°C–37°C). This can be done in a bowl over a pan of hot water (hot-water bath) or in a microwave (see technique p. 169) but if your fondant is too hot, it will become dull and brittle. To thin the fondant and give it a more fluid consistency, you can add a little water, or, better still, simple syrup. To color fondant, you can use cocoa powder, coffee extract, pistachio paste, or powdered food colorings. When covering a cake with two layers of icing, be sure to stir the fondant while the first layer is drying to prevent crystals from forming in the remaining fondant.

LEVEL

1

COFFEE YULE LOG

Bûche de Noël Café

Serves 6–8

Active time
2 hours

Cooking time
5 minutes

Storage
Up to 1 week in the refrigerator

Equipment
Silicone baking mat
Electric hand beater
Instant-read thermometer
Stand mixer
Pastry bag fitted with a large, serrated, basketweave tip
Paper piping cone

Ingredients

GENOISE
½ cup (3.5 oz./100 g) sugar
⅔ cup (5.25 oz./150 g) lightly beaten egg (about 3 eggs)
½ cup plus 1 tbsp (2.75 oz./70 g) flour
3 tbsp (1 oz./30 g) cornstarch

SOAKING SYRUP
½ cup minus 1 tbsp (110 ml) water
½ cup (3.5 oz./100 g) sugar

COFFEE BUTTERCREAM
Scant ½ cup (100 ml) water
1 ⅓ cups (9 oz./250 g) sugar
Scant ½ cup (3.5 oz./100 g) lightly beaten egg (about 2 eggs)
2 sticks plus 7 tbsp (11.5 oz./325 g) butter, diced, at room temperature
2 tbsp (30 ml) coffee extract

DECORATION
Green food coloring

MAKING THE GENOISE

Preheat the oven to 450°F (230°C/Gas mark 8). Lay the silicone mat on a baking sheet. Using the electric beater, whisk the sugar and eggs together in a bowl over a pan of hot water until the temperature reaches 113°F (45°C). Remove the bowl to a work surface and whisk until cold. The mixture should be pale and thick and when you lift the beaters the batter should fall off in a thick ribbon that stays on the surface for several seconds. Sift the flour and cornstarch together and, using a spatula, lightly fold in until just combined, taking care not to deflate the mixture. Pour onto the silicone mat, spread lightly in an even layer and bake for about 5 minutes until just springy to the touch.

MAKING THE SOAKING SYRUP

Heat the water and sugar in a saucepan until the sugar dissolves and then bring to a boil. Remove from the heat and allow to cool before using.

MAKING THE COFFEE BUTTERCREAM

Put the water and sugar in a saucepan over medium heat and, when the sugar has dissolved, heat to 243°F (117°C). Meanwhile, whisk the eggs in a bowl until pale and frothy. When the syrup is ready, pour it onto the eggs in a thin, steady stream, whisking constantly. Strain the mixture through a fine-mesh strainer into the bowl of the stand mixer fitted with the whisk attachment. Beat until the mixture cools to 68°F–77°F (20°C–25°C) and then beat in the butter until smooth. Spoon about ½ cup (3.5 oz./100 g) of the buttercream into a separate bowl. Stir the coffee extract into the rest and spoon this into the pastry bag with the basketweave tip.

ASSEMBLING THE LOG

Brush the syrup over the sponge to moisten it thoroughly. Using a spatula, spread it with a very thin layer of coffee buttercream, about 1/16 in. (2 mm) thick, and roll up from one short side like a jelly roll. Cut a diagonal slice at 45 degrees off each end and lay the slices, cut side down, on top for knots. Spread plain buttercream over the ends and knots, with a dab of coffee buttercream in the center. Pipe the rest of the coffee buttercream in lines down the length of the log to cover it in a thick layer. Roughen the surface with the tines of a fork dipped in ice-cold water to resemble bark. Warm the blade of a knife and smooth the ends and knots neatly. Color the remaining plain buttercream green, spoon it into the paper cone (see technique p. 598), and pipe a winding green stem with ivy leaves down the log. Add decorations of your choice such as fir trees, holly leaves, and snowflakes.

2

CHOCOLATE AND BANANA YULE LOG

Bûche Banane-Chocolat

Serves 8

Active time
2 hours

Chilling time
2 hours 50 minutes

Cooking time
40 minutes

Freezing time
3 hours

Storage
Up to 2 days in the refrigerator

Equipment
Electric hand beater
Stick blender
Silicone baking mat
11 × 2-in. (28 × 5-cm) baking frame
12 × 1-in. (30 × 3-cm) insert
for the Yule log (*bûche*) mold
Stand mixer
Instant-read thermometer
12 × 2 ½-in. (30 × 6-cm) Yule log
(*bûche*) mold

Ingredients

CHOCOLATE CRÉMEUX
Scant ½ cup (100 ml) milk
Scant ½ cup (100 ml) whipping
cream, 35% butterfat
1 ½ tbsp (1 oz./25 g) egg yolk
(about 1 ½ yolks)
2 ½ tsp (0.35 oz./10 g) sugar
2.25 oz. (65 g) bittersweet
couverture chocolate,
70% cacao, finely chopped
0.2 oz. (5 g) cacao paste

HAZELNUT CRUMBLE
5 tbsp (2.75 oz./75 g) butter
Heaping ½ cup
(2.75 oz./75 g) sugar
⅔ cup (2.75 oz./75 g) flour
Heaping ¾ cup
(2.75 oz./75 g) hazelnut flour

CRUNCHY HAZELNUT CHOCOLATE
2.75 oz. (75 g) white couverture
chocolate, finely chopped
10.5 oz. (300 g) baked hazelnut
crumble (see ingredients above)

1.5 oz. (45 g) hazelnuts, roasted
and finely chopped
1 tbsp (0.5 oz./15 g) butter, diced,
at room temperature
1.25 oz. (35 g) hazelnut praline
paste

FLAMBÉED BANANA LAYER
7 oz. (200 g) bananas
½ tsp (2 ml) lemon juice
Packed 2 tbsp (1 oz./30 g)
light brown sugar
1 ½ tbsp (25 ml) dark rum
5 tsp (0.75 oz./20 g) sugar
1 ¼ tsp (0.2 oz./5 g) pectin NH

DACQUOISE
Scant ½ cup (3 oz./90 g) egg
white (about 3 whites),
at room temperature
Scant ¼ cup (1.5 oz./40 g) sugar
Scant ½ cup (1.5 oz./40 g) hazelnut
flour
Scant ½ cup (1.5 oz./40 g)
almond flour
1 ½ tbsp (0.5 oz./15 g) flour
Scant ½ cup (2 oz./60 g)
confectioners' sugar

LIGHT VANILLA CREAM
1 ½ sheets (0.1 oz./3 g) gelatin
1 vanilla bean
¾ cup plus 1 tbsp (200 ml) milk
½ cup minus 1 ½ tbsp
(2.75 oz./80 g) sugar, divided
Heaping 1 tbsp (0.75 oz./20 g)
egg yolk (about 1 yolk)
1 tbsp (0.35 oz./10 g) custard
powder or cornstarch
1 tbsp (0.35 oz./10 g) flour
1 cup (250 ml) whipping cream,
35% butterfat

BITTERSWEET CHOCOLATE GLAZE
½ cup plus 2 tsp (135 ml) water
¾ cup (5.25 oz./150 g) sugar
Scant ½ cup (5.25 oz./150 g)
glucose syrup
2 tsp (0.35 oz./10 g) 180 Bloom
powdered gelatin
Scant ½ cup (3.5 oz./100 g)
sweetened condensed milk
5.25 oz. (150 g) bittersweet
chocolate, 60% cacao,
finely chopped

MAKING THE CHOCOLATE CRÉMEUX
Bring the milk and cream to a boil in a pan. Whisk the yolk and sugar until thickened. Make a custard with the yolks, sugar, milk, and cream (see technique p. 204). Mix the chocolate and cacao paste together, pour the custard over, and blend until smooth. Cover the surface with plastic wrap and chill for 2 hours.

MAKING THE HAZELNUT CRUMBLE
Using your fingertips, mix all the ingredients together on a work surface or in a bowl, without making a dough. Chill for about 20 minutes. Preheat the oven to 325°F (160°C/Gas mark 3). Lay the silicone mat on a baking sheet, spread the crumble over it, and bake for about 20 minutes until golden. Allow to cool.

MAKING THE CRUNCHY HAZELNUT CHOCOLATE
Crush the cooled crumble into crumbs. Melt the white chocolate in a bowl over a pan of hot water, remove from the heat, and stir in the remaining ingredients using a spatula. Sit the frame on a baking sheet lined with parchment paper, pour in the crumble mixture, and freeze for 30 minutes.

MAKING THE FLAMBÉED BANANA LAYER
Peel and slice the bananas, coat with the lemon juice, and cook them in a skillet with the brown sugar over medium heat until caramelized. Add the rum and flambé carefully with a long-reach lighter. When the flames die down, mix the sugar and pectin together and add. Cook for 5 minutes over high heat, pack into the insert mold, and freeze until needed.

MAKING THE DACQUOISE
Preheat the oven to 350°F (180°C/Gas mark 4). Lay the silicone mat on a baking sheet. Whisk the egg whites and sugar in the stand mixer to firm peaks, sieve together the flours and confectioners' sugar and fold in. Spread evenly over the silicone sheet, bake for 20 minutes, and allow to cool.

MAKING THE LIGHT VANILLA CREAM
Soak the gelatin in cold water. Split the vanilla bean lengthwise and scrape out the seeds. Using this and the next 5 ingredients, prepare a pastry cream (see technique p. 196). Squeeze excess water from the gelatin and stir it into the cream until dissolved. Press a piece of plastic wrap over the surface of the cream, allow to cool, and then chill for 30 minutes. Whip the whipping cream until it holds soft peaks and carefully fold it into the pastry cream.

MAKING THE BITTERSWEET CHOCOLATE GLAZE (TO BE PREPARED AFTER LOG IS ASSEMBLED)
Heat 5 tbsp (75 ml) of the water with the sugar and glucose to 221°F (105°C). Dissolve the gelatin in the remaining water. Pour the hot syrup over the condensed milk and stir in the gelatin. Pour over the chopped chocolate and blend until smooth. Cool to 95°F (35°C) before using.

ASSEMBLING THE LOG
Spread vanilla cream into the mold. Add the chocolate crémeux and unmold the banana layer into the center. Cut the dacquoise to fit and place on top. Cover with vanilla cream and finish by adding the crunchy hazelnut chocolate. Freeze for 2 hours. Unmold the log and pour over the chocolate glaze at 95°F (35°C). Add decorations of your choice.

GIRLY YULE LOG

Bûche Fondante Girly

by Christophe Felder

MASTER PÂTISSIER

Serves 8–10

Active time
5 hours

Cooking time
30 minutes

Chilling time
30 minutes

Freezing time
1 hour

Storage
Up to 24 hours
in the refrigerator

Equipment
Electric hand beater
Yule log molds
Instant-read thermometer
2 pastry bags fitted
with a plain ¼-in. (6-mm) tip
and a fluted ¼-in. (6-mm) tip
Ribbed or basketweave
embossed rolling pin
Gold cake board

Ingredients
GENOA BREAD GENOISE
3.5 oz. (100 g) egg
2.75 oz. (80 g) egg yolk
6 oz. (170 g) superfine sugar
1 ⅓ tsp (10 g) invert sugar
½ tsp (3 g) HF emulsifier
(optional)
1 oz. (30 g) almond paste
4.25 oz. (120 g) egg white
1 pinch of salt
4.5 oz. (130 g) cake flour
1.75 oz. (50 g) potato starch

KIRSCH SYRUP
2 tbsp (30 ml) kirsch (eau
de vie from Alsace, 40%)
⅓ cup (80 ml) hot water
2.5 oz. (70 g)
superfine sugar

PASTRY CREAM
1 ⅓ cups (320 ml) whole milk
½ vanilla bean,
split lengthwise and
seeds scraped out
1 oz. (30 g) egg yolk
1.75 oz. (55 g)
superfine sugar
1 oz. (30 g) cornstarch
1 ¼ tsp (3 g) fat-free
powdered milk

LOW-SUGAR ITALIAN MERINGUE
¼ cup (60 ml) water
3.75 oz. (110 g) sugar
2.5 oz. (70 g) egg white

LIGHT BUTTERCREAM
7.5 oz. (210 g) pastry cream
(see ingredients above)
6.25 oz. (180 g) best-quality
butter, at room temperature
2.5 oz. (70 g) low-sugar
Italian meringue
(see ingredients above)

MOUSSELINE PASTRY CREAM
2 tbsp (30 ml) kirsch
10.5 oz. (300 g) pastry cream
(see ingredients above)
12.5 oz. (350 g)
light buttercream
(see ingredients above)
1 drop of red food coloring

DECORATION
Confectioners' sugar
12.5 oz. (350 g)
pink almond paste
A few drops of red food
coloring
2 small pink meringues
(see technique p. 234, adding food
coloring with vinegar in step 1)
Pink and white
chocolate disks

_____ MAKING THE GENOA BREAD GENOISE
Preheat the oven to 350°F (180°C/Gas mark 4). Beat the eggs and egg yolks with 4.25 oz. (120 g) of the sugar until light. Add the invert sugar, emulsifier, and softened almond paste, mixing well. Whisk the egg whites with the remaining sugar and salt until stiff. Sift together the flour and starch. Fold the whites into the egg mixture and then carefully fold in the sifted flour and starch. Pour into 1 or 2 yule log molds (depending on their size) and bake for about 30 minutes. Slice horizontally into 3 layers.

_____ MAKING THE KIRSCH SYRUP
Whisk the kirsch, hot water, and sugar together. Let the sugar dissolve fully, stirring from time to time. Set aside at room temperature.

_____ MAKING THE PASTRY CREAM
Bring the milk to a boil in a saucepan with the vanilla bean and seeds. Whisk the egg yolks with the sugar until thick and light. Sift together the starch and milk powder and then carefully fold in. Whisk some of the hot milk into the egg mixture, add the rest of the milk, and return to the heat. Stir until it just comes to a boil, remove from the heat, and set aside.

_____ MAKING THE LOW-SUGAR ITALIAN MERINGUE
Heat the water with 3.5 oz. (100 g) of the sugar until the sugar dissolves and then cook to 243°F (117°C). Beat the egg whites to soft peaks and add the remaining sugar, continuing to whisk until stiff. Using the electric beater, whisk the hot sugar syrup into the egg whites until they are completely cold. Set aside 2.5 oz. (70 g) for this recipe, covering the remaining meringue with plastic wrap and freezing for future use.

_____ MAKING THE LIGHT BUTTERCREAM
Loosen the pastry cream. Warm the butter slightly and whisk until creamy. Carefully add it to the pastry cream until evenly combined. Fold in the Italian meringue and set aside at room temperature.

_____ MAKING THE MOUSSELINE PASTRY CREAM
Heat the kirsch over a bain-marie to 86°F (30°C). Loosen the cold pastry cream with a spatula and then warm it over a bain-marie to 86°F (30°C). Pour in the kirsch and fold in the buttercream. Stir in a little red food coloring. Set aside at room temperature.

_____ ASSEMBLING THE YULE LOG
Place the first layer of genoise on the cake board, moisten it with kirsch syrup and, using the pastry bag with the plain tip, pipe a layer of mousseline cream over it. Carefully place a second genoise layer on top and moisten it with syrup. Pipe over another thin layer of mousseline cream, place the last layer of moistened genoise on top, and cover the entire cake with mousseline cream, smoothing the surface with a spatula. Freeze the cake for 1 hour and then chill in the refrigerator for 30 minutes (to avoid condensation). Dust a work surface with confectioners' sugar and roll out the almond paste about 1/16–1/8 in. (2–3 mm) thick. Roll the embossed rolling pin over it. Remove the cake from the refrigerator and cover it smoothly with the textured almond paste. Whip the remaining mousseline cream, spoon it into the pastry bag with a fluted tip, and pipe rosettes on top of the log. Finish with pink meringues and pink and white chocolate disks.

LEVEL

1

KINGS' CAKE

Galette à la Frangipane

Serves 8

Active time
3 hours

Chilling time
24 hours

Freezing time
Overnight

Cooking time
40 minutes

Storage
Up to 2 days

Equipment
Pastry bag fitted
with a plain ½-in. (10-mm) tip
Ceramic charm or dried bean
Pastry pincher

Ingredients

PUFF PASTRY
¾ tsp (4 g) salt
Scant ½ cup (100 ml) cold water
Heaping 1 tbsp (0.35 oz./10 g)
confectioners' sugar, sifted
1 ⅔ cups (7 oz./200 g) flour, sifted
Scant 3 tbsp (1.5 oz./40 g) butter,
melted and cooled
1 stick plus 2 tbsp (5 oz./140 g)
butter, preferably 84% butterfat

FRANGIPANE CREAM
3 ½ tbsp (1.75 oz./50 g) butter,
at room temperature
¼ cup (1.75 oz./50 g) sugar
Scant 3 tbsp (1.5 oz./40 g) lightly
beaten egg (about 1 egg),
at room temperature
2 tsp (10 ml) whipping cream,
35% butterfat
½ cup (1.75 oz./50 g) almond flour
1 tsp (5 ml) rum
Few drops of vanilla extract
1 oz. (25 g) pastry cream
(see technique p. 196)

EGG WASH
Scant ¼ cup (1.75 oz./50 g) lightly
beaten egg (about 1 egg)

SIMPLE SYRUP
3 tbsp plus 1 tsp (50 ml) water
¼ cup (1.75 oz./50 g) sugar
2 tsp (10 ml) rum

MAKING THE PUFF PASTRY
Use the ingredients to make a 5-turn puff pastry (see technique p. 66), adding the sugar with the flour. Divide the dough into 2 × 9-oz. (250-g) squares. Fold the corners of the squares to the center, turn over and shape each into a ball. Flatten, cover in plastic wrap, and chill for 24 hours.

MAKING THE FRANGIPANE CREAM
Cream the butter and sugar together in a large mixing bowl until light. Mix in the egg and whipping cream and then stir in the almond flour, rum, and vanilla. Add the pastry cream and mix until well blended. Line a baking sheet with parchment paper and spoon the frangipane cream into the pastry bag. Pipe the cream in a tight spiral, 8 in. (20 cm) in diameter, on the baking sheet, starting at the center and working outwards. Tuck the charm or bean into the cream, cover with plastic wrap, and freeze overnight.

ASSEMBLING THE CAKE
The next day, roll out each disk of pastry, with the folds underneath, into 9-in. (23-cm) rounds. Turn one over so the folds are facing up (the cream will cover the folds) and brush the edges with water. Place the disk of frangipane cream in the center. Cover with the second puff pastry round, with the folds facing down and in contact with the cream. Press the pastry edges together using the pastry pincher (see technique p. 28) to seal them and prevent the filling leaking out during baking. Dampen a baking sheet by brushing with water. Turn the cake over and lift it onto the sheet. Brush the pastry with egg wash and chill for 30 minutes. Preheat the oven to 375°F (190°C/Gas mark 5). Brush with egg wash again and, using the paring knife, mark curved lines in the pastry, ¼ in. (6 mm) apart, starting at the center and working to the outside. Place in the oven, lower the temperature to 340°F (170°C/Gas mark 3), and bake for 40 minutes. While the cake is baking, prepare the syrup. Heat the water and sugar in a saucepan over medium heat and, when the sugar has dissolved, bring to a boil. Remove from the heat and stir in the rum. As soon as the cake is taken out of the oven, brush it with a little syrup to give the pastry a nice sheen without making it soggy. Serve warm or at room temperature.

LEVEL

2

PISTACHIO AND SOUR CHERRY KINGS' CAKE

Galette Pistache-Griotte

Serves 8

Active time
3 hours

Chilling time
2 ½ hours

Freezing time
30 minutes

Cooking time
40 minutes

Storage
Up to 2 days

Equipment
Food-grade acetate sheet, measuring 4 × 8 in. (10 × 20 cm)
7-in. (18-cm) cake ring or silicone tart mold
9-in. (22-cm) cake ring
Ceramic charm or dried bean
Pastry pincher

Ingredients
INVERSE PUFF PASTRY
Beurre manié
½ cup (1.75 oz./55 g) flour
1 stick plus 3 tbsp (5.5 oz./160 g) butter, preferably 84% butterfat, well chilled

Water dough
1 ¼ cups (5.5 oz./160 g) flour
6 tbsp (90 ml) water
1 tsp (0.2 oz./5 g) salt

Colored water dough
1.75 oz. (50 g) plain water dough (see ingredients above)
2 tsp (0.2 oz./6 g) cornstarch
Heaping ½ tsp (3 g) butter
Scant 2 tsp (0.2 oz./6 g) water-soluble powdered red food coloring

ALMOND CREAM WITH SOUR CHERRIES
3 ½ tbsp (1.75 oz./50 g) butter, at room temperature
¼ cup (1.75 oz./50 g) sugar
3 ½ tbsp (1.75 oz./50 g) lightly beaten egg (about 1 egg)
Heaping 1 tbsp (0.75 oz./20 g) pistachio paste
½ cup (1.75 oz./50 g) almond flour
1 tsp (5 ml) kirsch
2 oz. (60 g) pitted sour cherries, quartered

EGG WASH
Scant ¼ cup (1.75 oz./50 g) lightly beaten egg (about 1 egg)
1 tbsp (0.75 oz./20 g) egg yolk (about 1 yolk)
2 tsp (10 ml) whipping cream, 35% butterfat
Powdered red food coloring

SIMPLE SYRUP
Scant ¼ cup (50 ml) water
¼ cup (1.75 oz./50 g) sugar

DECORATION
Scant ⅓ cup (1.75 oz./50 g) pistachios, finely chopped
3 tbsp (1 oz./25 g) confectioners' sugar
A few whole cherries
Edible gold leaf

MAKING THE INVERSE PUFF PASTRY
Prepare the pastry (see technique p. 72) in the following way. Make the beurre manié and flatten it with a rolling pin into an 8-in. (20-cm) square. Cover in plastic wrap and chill for about 20 minutes. Make the water dough and flatten 7 oz. (200 g) of it into a 4 × 8-in. (10 × 20-cm) rectangle. Cover with plastic wrap and chill for about 20 minutes. Using your hands, work the cornstarch, butter, and red coloring into the remaining 1.75 oz. (50 g) of water dough. Flatten into a 4 × 8-in. (10 × 20-cm) rectangle on the acetate sheet and chill. Incorporate the beurre manié into the plain water dough, make 2 double turns and 2 single turns, chilling between each turn. Roll the dough into a 4 × 8-in. (10 × 20-cm) rectangle, the same size as the colored water dough, brush the surface with water, and lift the colored dough on top. Cut into 2 squares, each weighing about 8.5 oz. (240 g), and roll each into a 9-in. (23-cm) square. Cover in plastic wrap and chill.

MAKING THE ALMOND CREAM WITH SOUR CHERRIES
Prepare the almond cream (see technique p. 208), adding the pistachio paste, almond flour, kirsch, and cherries. Spoon into the 7-in. (18-cm) cake ring, on a baking sheet lined with parchment paper, or the silicone mold, push in the charm or bean, and freeze for 30 minutes.

ASSEMBLING THE CAKE
Remove the almond cream from the freezer, turn it out, and place it in the center of one of the rolled-out squares of dough (red size down). Brush the edges of the square with water and lift the second square of dough, red side up, over the almond cream. Press the dough edges together to seal them. Position the 9-in. (22-cm) ring in the center of the square and press down firmly to cut out a circle, removing the excess dough. Seal the pastry edges again with a pastry pincher, marking at ½-in. (12-mm) intervals all the way around, to prevent the filling leaking out during baking (see technique p. 28). Dampen a baking sheet by brushing with water, turn the cake over and lift onto the sheet. Chill for 15 minutes. Prepare the red egg wash. Preheat the oven to 375°F (190°C/Gas mark 5) and then brush the pastry with the egg wash. Mark curved lines in the pastry using the paring knife, either evenly spaced or in a decorative pattern as in the photo, leaving a narrow border around the edge for the pistachios.
Place in the oven, lower the temperature to 340°F (170°C/Gas mark 3), and bake for 40 minutes, until golden but ensuring the red color is preserved. While the cake is baking, prepare the simple syrup. Heat the water and sugar in a saucepan over medium heat until the sugar has dissolved, then bring to a boil. As soon as the cake is taken out of the oven, brush the syrup over the pastry and stick the chopped pistachios around the edge. Add additional decorations, if wished, such as a dusting of confectioners' sugar over the pistachios and a few whole cherries and small pieces of edible gold leaf arranged on top, just before serving.

PINK GRAPEFRUIT KINGS' CAKE

Galette Pamplemousse Rose

by Gontran Cherrier

FORMER FERRANDI PARIS STUDENT

Serves 6

Active time
2 hours

Macerating time
Overnight

Chilling time
4 hours plus 2 nights

Cooking time
1 hour

Storage
Up to 2 days

Equipment
9-in. (24-cm) tart ring

Ingredients

SEGMENTS
1 pink grapefruit
¼ cup (60 ml) Campari
(red aperitif liqueur flavored
with orange peel)
Scant ⅓ cup (90 ml) water
5.5 oz. (160 g) sugar

RYE PUFF PASTRY
2.75 oz. (80 g) butter, melted
½ cup (130 ml) water
1 ½ tsp (7 g) salt
9.5 oz. (275 g) strong
white bread flour
2.5 oz. (70 g) rye flour
9 oz. (250 g) butter, preferably
84% butterfat

ALMOND CREAM
2.5 oz. (70 g) butter
2.5 oz. (70 g) sugar
2.5 oz. (70 g) ground almonds
2.5 oz. (70 g) egg,
at room temperature
1 tbsp (10 g) custard powder

Confectioners' sugar for dusting

——— PREPARING THE SEGMENTS

A day ahead, remove the segments from the grapefruit (about 5.25 oz./150 g). In a saucepan, make a simple syrup with the Campari, water, and sugar. Pour over the segments and set aside in the refrigerator overnight.

——— MAKING THE RYE PUFF PASTRY

A day ahead, combine the melted butter, cold water, and salt. Knead in the sifted flours to make a water dough (*détrempe*). Cover with plastic wrap and chill for 2 hours to relax the gluten. Give the dough a double turn, incorporating the 84%-fat butter, let rest in the refrigerator for at least 2 hours, give it a single turn, and then chill overnight. The next day, give the dough a double and a single turn and then roll it out to a thickness of 1/16 in. (2 mm). Use the tart ring to cut out 2 × 9-in. (24-cm) disks and chill until needed.

——— MAKING THE ALMOND CREAM

Cream the butter and sugar, mix in the ground almonds, and gradually beat in the eggs. Lastly stir in the custard powder. Drain and coarsely chop the grapefruit segments and add them to the almond cream.

——— ASSEMBLING THE KINGS' CAKE

Spread the almond cream with the grapefruit pieces over the center of one of the pastry disks. Dampen the pastry edges by brushing with water and place the second pastry disk on top. Seal the edges well and, using a paring knife, mark with a decorative pattern. Chill in the refrigerator overnight.

Preheat the oven to 400°F (200°C/Gas mark 6) and bake for 25 minutes. Cover the top with a sheet of parchment paper and a rack or light baking sheet to ensure the top remains flat and bake for an additional 20 minutes. Remove from the oven, turn over onto the baking sheet or an oven grid. Increase the temperature to 450°F–475°F (230°C–240°C/Gas mark 8–9). Dust the surface with confectioners' sugar and return to the hot oven until caramelized.

LEVEL

1

CROQUEMBOUCHE

Serves 12–15

Active time
2 ½ hours

Cooking time
40 minutes

Chilling time
30 minutes

Storage
Up to 12 hours

Equipment
Instant-read thermometer
Silicone baking mat
Food-grade acetate sheet
7-in. (18-cm) cake ring
3-in. (6-cm) dessert ring
9-in. (24-cm) dessert ring
Pastry bag fitted with
a plain ½-in. (10-mm) tip

Ingredients

NOUGATINE
1 ¼ cups (7 oz./ 200 g)
chopped almonds
½ cup (125 ml) water
1 ⅓ cups (9 oz./250 g) sugar
⅓ cup (4.5 oz./125 g)
glucose syrup

POURED SUGAR DISKS
½ cup plus 1 tsp (130 ml) water
1 ¾ cups (11.5 oz./330 g) sugar
½ cup plus 2 tsp (3.5 oz./100 g)
glucose syrup
Powdered brown food coloring

CHOUX PASTRY
Scant ½ cup (100 ml) water
Scant ½ cup (100 ml) whole milk
¾ tsp (4 g) salt
1 tsp (4 g) sugar
6 tbsp (3.25 oz./90 g) butter,
diced
½ cup plus 1 tbsp (2.5 oz./70 g)
flour, sifted
¾ cup plus 2 tbsp (7 oz./200 g)
lightly beaten egg (about 4 eggs),
at room temperature

PASTRY CREAM
Generous 1 ½ cups (400 ml) whole
milk
Scant ⅔ cup (4.25 oz./120 g) sugar
1 vanilla bean, split lengthwise
and seeds scraped out
⅓ cup (2.75 oz./80 g) lightly
beaten egg (about 1 ½ eggs)
4 tsp (1 oz./25 g) egg yolk
(about 1 ½ yolks)
3 tbsp (1 oz./30 g) custard
powder or cornstarch
3 tbsp (1 oz./30 g) flour
Scant 3 tbsp (1.5 oz./40 g) butter,
diced, at room temperature

CARAMEL
⅓ cup (75 ml) water
1 ⅓ cups (9 oz./250 g) sugar
1 tbsp (1 oz./25 g) glucose syrup

DECORATION
Pearl sugar

MAKING THE NOUGATINE
Preheat the oven to 325°F (160°C/Gas mark 3). Spread the almonds over a lined baking sheet and dry them out in the oven for 15 minutes. Reduce the temperature to 300°F (150°C/Gas mark 2). Heat the water and sugar in a saucepan and when the sugar dissolves, bring to a boil. Stir in the glucose syrup, skim off any foam, and cook, without stirring, until golden. When the temperature reaches 330°F (165°C), remove from the heat and stir in the almonds. Pour the nougatine onto the silicone mat, cover with the acetate sheet to prevent sticking, and roll over with a rolling pin until just over ⅓ in. (1 cm) thick. Place the 7-in. (18-cm) ring on top and tap it around the edge with the pin to cut through the nougatine. Allow the disk to cool. Return the remaining nougatine to the oven to soften, roll it out very thinly and, using a knife or cookie cutters, cut out shapes for decoration and set aside.

MAKING THE POURED SUGAR DISKS
Line a baking sheet with parchment paper and place the 3-in. (6-cm) ring and 9-in. (24-cm) ring on top. Heat the water and sugar in a pan over medium heat, brushing the sides with a damp brush to remove any crystals. When the sugar has dissolved, bring to a boil and stir in the glucose syrup. Cook to about 320°F (160°C), remove from the heat, and stir in enough food coloring to tint the caramel mahogany. Pour the syrup into the rings. Once the disks have set, remove the rings.

MAKING THE CHOUX PASTRY
Preheat the oven to 400°F (200°C/Gas mark 6). Butter 2 baking sheets or use nonstick. Make the choux pastry (see technique p. 162), spoon into the pastry bag, and pipe 60 × 1-in. (3-cm) puffs onto the sheets. Bake for about 20–25 minutes, until golden. Cool the puffs before filling.

MAKING THE PASTRY CREAM
Prepare the pastry cream (see technique p. 196). Press a piece of plastic wrap over the surface, cool, and then chill in the refrigerator. Fill the choux puffs with the cream (see technique p. 168) just before making the caramel and assembling the croquembouche.

MAKING THE CARAMEL
Fill a large bowl with cold water and ice. Proceed as for the poured sugar disks. At 320°F (160°C), plunge the base of the pan in the ice water to prevent further cooking.

ASSEMBLING THE CROQUEMBOUCHE
Line a baking sheet with parchment paper and put the pearl sugar in a bowl. Dip the tops of the filled puffs in the hot caramel and place, caramel uppermost, on the sheet. Before the caramel sets, dip half the puffs in the pearl sugar. Place the 9-in. (24-cm) sugar disk on a flat serving plate or cake board. Center the 7-in. (18-cm) ring on top and place the nougatine disk inside. Make the first choux layer by dipping one side of each puff into the hot caramel and sticking it to the nougatine base with the glazed top facing out, to make a tight circle around the inside of the ring. Continue in the same way, making a second, smaller circle just inside the first with puffs dipped in pearl sugar. Carefully remove the ring by lifting it up and over the puffs. Continue building smaller concentric circles and alternating the plain and sugar-coated layers until you have a cone. Top the cone with the 3-in. (6-cm) caramel disk, using a little hot caramel for glue. Decorate with the nougatine shapes.

CHEFS' NOTES

• If the caramel thickens during glazing and assembly, gently reheat it to make it liquid again.

• Keep a bowl of ice water nearby when working with the hot caramel. If you burn your fingertips, quickly dip them in the water.

CROQUEMBOUCHE WITH SESAME NOUGATINE

Croquembouche à la Nougatine de Sésame aux Eclats de Grué de Cacao

LEVEL 2

Serves 12–15

Active time
3 ½ hours

Cooking time
1 hour

Storage
Up to 12 hours

Equipment
2 pastry bags fitted with plain ½-in. (10-mm) tips
Silicone baking mat
Food-safe acetate sheet
7-in. (18-cm) cake ring
3-in. (6-cm) dessert ring
9-in. (22-cm) cake ring
Instant-read thermometer
Isosceles triangle template with 8-in. (20-cm) base and 16-in. (40-cm) sides
1-in. (3-cm) and 2-in. (5-cm) round cookie cutters

Ingredients

CHOUX PASTRY
Scant ½ cup (100 ml) water
Scant ½ cup (100 ml) whole milk
¾ tsp (4 g) salt
1 tsp (4 g) sugar
6 tbsp (3 oz./90 g) butter, diced
½ cup plus 1 tbsp (2.5 oz./70 g) flour, sifted
¾ cup plus 2 tbsp (7 oz./200 g) lightly beaten egg (about 4 eggs), at room temperature

LIGHT CHOCOLATE PASTRY CREAM
2 cups (500 ml) whole milk
¾ cup (5.25 oz./150 g) sugar
½ cup (3.5 oz./100 g) lightly beaten egg (about 2 eggs)
Scant 2 tbsp (1 oz./30 g) egg yolk (about 1 ½ yolks)
½ cup (2.75 oz./80 g) cornstarch
3 ½ tbsp (1.75 oz./50 g) butter, diced, at room temperature
2 oz. (60 g) pure cacao paste
Generous ¾ cup (200 ml) whipping cream, 35% butterfat

SESAME NOUGATINE WITH ROASTED CACAO NIBS
5 cups (1 ¾ lb./800 g) sesame seeds
2 cups (500 ml) water
5 ¼ cups (2 lb. 3 oz./1 kg) sugar
1 ½ cups (1 lb. 2 oz./500 g) glucose syrup
7 oz. (200 g) roasted cacao nibs

CARAMEL
2 ½ cups (1 lb. 2 oz./500 g) sugar
⅔ cup (150 ml) water
2 tbsp plus 1 tsp (1.75 oz./50 g) glucose syrup
Generous ¼ tsp (1 g) water-soluble powdered brown food coloring

DECORATION
Pearl sugar

MAKING THE CHOUX PASTRY
Preheat the oven to 400°F (200°C/Gas mark 6). Make the choux pastry (see technique p. 162), spoon into one pastry bag, and pipe 60 × 1-in. (3-cm) puffs onto 2 baking sheets. Bake for about 20–25 minutes, until golden. Cool.

MAKING THE LIGHT CHOCOLATE PASTRY CREAM
Make the pastry cream (see technique p. 196) and stir in the cacao paste while the cream is still warm. Cover the surface with plastic wrap, cool, and chill until cold. Whip the cream until it holds soft peaks. Whisk the pastry cream to make it smooth and fold in the whipped cream. Chill until needed.

MAKING THE SESAME NOUGATINE WITH ROASTED CACAO NIBS
Preheat the oven to 325°F (160°C/Gas mark 3) and dry out the sesame seeds on a lined baking sheet for 5 minutes. Reduce the temperature to 300°F (150°C/Gas mark 2). Heat the water and sugar in a saucepan. When the sugar has dissolved, bring to a boil, then stir in the syrup, skim, and cook until golden. Remove from the heat and stir in the sesame seeds and cacao nibs. Spread out on the silicone mat, cover with the acetate sheet, and roll to just over ⅓ in. (1 cm) thick. Lay the 7-in. (18-cm) ring on top and tap with the pin to cut through the nougatine. Let the disk cool and put the remaining nougatine back in the oven to keep it soft.

MAKING THE CARAMEL
Place the 3-in. (6-cm) and 9-in. (22-cm) rings on a lined baking sheet. Fill a bowl with cold water and ice. Dissolve the sugar in the water, brushing the sides of the pan to clean them. Bring to a boil, stir in the glucose syrup, and cook to 320°F (160°C). Stir in the food coloring and plunge the base of the pan in the cold water to prevent further cooking. Pour into the rings to make a 9-in. (22-cm) disk for the base and a 3-in. (6-cm) disk for the top, as well as a triangle with a 2 ½-in. (6-cm) base and 5-in. (12-cm) sides. Keep the rest of the caramel at 320°F (160°C) by returning it to the heat occasionally, so it remains fluid.

ASSEMBLING THE CROQUEMBOUCHE
Pipe the chocolate cream into the cooled choux puffs (see technique p. 168). Dip the tops in the hot caramel and dip half the puffs in the pearl sugar. Place, caramel uppermost, on a lined baking sheet. Place the 9-in. (22-cm) caramel disk on a flat serving plate or cake board. Center the 7-in. (18-cm) ring on top and place the nougatine disk inside. Make the first choux layer by dipping each puff into the hot caramel and sticking it to the nougatine base with the glazed top facing out, making a tight circle around the inside of the ring. Make a second, smaller circle just inside the first with puffs dipped in pearl sugar. Carefully remove the ring by lifting it up and over the puffs. Continue building smaller concentric circles and alternating the plain and sugar-coated layers of puffs to make a cone. Roll out the remaining nougatine about ⅛ in. (3–4 mm) thick. Cut out a triangle using the template. Cut out holes using the cookie cutters and curve into a semi-circle. Cool and then stick it around the base with caramel. Cut a 2 ½ × 7-in. (6 × 18-cm) rectangle into 9 alternate triangles, with 1-in. (2-cm) bases, from the remaining nougatine. Cool in a rounded shape, stick around the base and top, and stick the 2 ½-in. (6-cm) caramel disk and triangle on top.

LEVEL

3

CROQUEMBOUCHE

by Frédéric Cassel

BEST PASTRY CHEF OF THE YEAR, 1999 AND 2007

Serves 15

Active time
3 hours

Cooking time
40 minutes

Storage
Up to 24 hours
in the refrigerator

Equipment
Stand mixer fitted
with the paddle
beater attachment

2 pastry bags fitted
with plain ½-in.
(10-mm) and ⅓-in.
(8-mm) tips

Deck oven (optional)
Copper sugar
saucepan
Silicone baking mat
7-in. (18-cm) tart ring

Ingredients

CHOUX PASTRY
1 cup (250 ml) whole milk
9 cups (2.15 liters) water
2 ½ tsp (10 g) superfine sugar
2 tsp (10 g) fleur de sel
8 oz. (225 g) butter
9.5 oz. (275 g) strong white
bread flour, sifted
14 oz. (400 g) egg

ALMOND NOUGATINE
12.5 oz. (360 g) chopped almonds
⅓ cup (80 ml) water
1 lb. 1 oz. (480 g) superfine sugar
12.5 oz. (360 g) glucose syrup

VANILLA PASTRY CREAM
2 cups (500 ml) whole milk
4.5 oz. (125 g) brown sugar
1 vanilla bean, split lengthwise
and seeds scraped out
2.75 oz. (80 g) egg yolk
1.5 oz. (45 g) custard powder
0.75 oz. (20 g) unsalted butter

CARAMEL
¾ cup (400 ml) water
2 ¼ lb. (1 kg) superfine sugar
7 oz. (200 g) glucose syrup

——————— MAKING THE CHOUX PASTRY
Preheat the oven to 400°F (210°C/Gas mark 6). Bring the milk, water, sugar, fleur de sel, and butter to a boil in a saucepan. Remove from the heat and beat in the flour with a spatula. Return to a low heat, stir vigorously until the mixture pulls away from the sides of the pan, and then cook for an additional 2–3 minutes to dry out the dough. Transfer to the stand mixer and gradually beat in the eggs. Beat until the dough is of dropping consistency but still firm enough to hold its shape. Spoon into the pastry bag fitted with the ½-in. (10-mm) tip and pipe small choux puffs about 1 ¼ in. (3 cm) in diameter. Bake, ideally in a deck oven, for about 20–25 minutes.

——————— MAKING THE ALMOND NOUGATINE
Reduce the oven temperature to 325°F (160°C/Gas mark 3) and toast the chopped almonds on a baking sheet for 15 minutes, until golden. In the copper saucepan, cook the water and sugar over low heat until the sugar dissolves, then bring to a boil, keeping the sides of the pan clean with a damp brush. Add the glucose syrup and cook rapidly over high heat to a blond caramel. Stop the cooking process and add the toasted almonds all at once, mixing in with a spatula. Gently reheat the saucepan so the nougatine is not sticking to it and then pour onto the silicone mat. Let cool slightly, then roll out the nougatine and cut into the desired shape (see assembling step below).

——————— MAKING THE VANILLA PASTRY CREAM
In a saucepan, bring the milk to a boil with half the sugar and the vanilla bean and seeds. Whisk the remaining sugar with the egg yolks in a mixing bowl, add the custard powder, and mix well. Pour one-third of the boiling milk into the egg mixture, whisking continuously, then pour the mixture back into the saucepan and bring to a boil. Add the butter and chill as rapidly as possible in the refrigerator.

——————— MAKING THE CARAMEL
In the copper saucepan, cook the water and sugar over low heat until the sugar dissolves, then bring to a boil, keeping the sides of the pan clean with a damp brush. Add the glucose syrup and cook rapidly over high heat to a blond caramel.

——————— ASSEMBLING THE CROQUEMBOUCHE
Using the 7-in. (18-cm) ring as a guide, cut a round of nougatine the same size for the base. Using a template, cut 2 half-moon shapes to make the sides. Spoon the pastry cream into the bag with the ⅓-in. (8-mm) tip, fill the choux puffs (see technique p. 168) and glaze the tops with the caramel. Lay 1 nougatine half-moon flat on a work surface, stick 2 rows of choux puffs (caramelized side outwards) on it and another 2 rows on those. Stick the other half-moon of nougatine on top. Stick the croquembouche upright on the nougatine base with caramel. Add decorations of your choice.

CITRUS TARTLETS

Tartelettes aux Agrumes

Makes 50

Active time
1 hour

Chilling time
About 2 hours

Cooking time
15 minutes

Storage
Up to 24 hours in the refrigerator

Equipment
Electric hand beater
1 ¼-in. (3-cm) round cookie cutter
Pastry bag fitted with a sultan tip

Ingredients

BRETON SHORTBREAD
⅔ cup (5.25 oz./150 g) butter, diced and softened
¾ cup (5 oz./140 g) sugar
¼ tsp (2 g) salt
¼ cup (2 oz./60 g) egg yolk (about 3 ½ yolks)
1 ½ cups (7 oz./ 200 g) flour
½ tsp (2 g) baking powder

CITRUS MOUSSELINE
3 sheets (0.2 oz./6 g) gelatin
2 tbsp plus 1 tsp (35 ml) water
Generous 1 cup (265 ml) orange juice
½ tsp (1.5 g) finely grated orange zest
⅓ cup (3.25 oz./90 g) egg yolk (about 5 yolks)
⅔ cup (4.5 oz./130 g) sugar
¼ cup (1.5 oz./40 g) potato starch
¾ cup (6.5 oz./190 g) butter, diced
1 cup (9 oz./265 g) pomelo purée
Scant ½ cup (100 ml) whipping cream, 35% butterfat, whipped

DECORATION
2 grapefruit
2 oranges
2 lemons
Tiny sprigs of lemon cress

MAKING THE BRETON SHORTBREAD
In a mixing bowl, whisk the butter, sugar, and salt together using the electric beater, until light and creamy. Whisk in the egg yolks, sift in the flour with the baking powder and mix together with a spatula, without overworking the mixture, to make a soft dough. Cover in plastic wrap and chill for 1 hour. Preheat the oven to 325°F (170°C/Gas mark 3). Roll out the dough, ¼ in. (5 mm) thick, and cut out 50 disks using the cookie cutter. Lift the disks onto a baking sheet lined with parchment paper and bake for 12–15 minutes until golden and crisp.

MAKING THE CITRUS MOUSSELINE
Soak the gelatin in the water. Proceed as for a pastry cream using the next 5 ingredients (see technique p. 196), replacing the milk with the orange juice and whisking the potato starch with the egg yolks. While the cream is still warm, add the butter and stir in until melted. Squeeze excess water from the gelatin and stir in until dissolved. Finally stir in the pomelo purée. Press a piece of plastic wrap over the surface of the custard, cool, and then chill in the refrigerator for 1 hour or until needed. Just before assembling the tartlets, whisk the cream to soften it and gently fold in the whipped cream.

ASSEMBLING THE TARTLETS
Spoon the mousseline into the pastry bag and pipe a swirl on the top of each shortbread base. Peel and segment the citrus fruits, cutting each segment into small slices. Decorate the tartlets with the citrus fruit slices and tiny sprigs of lemon cress.

LEMON, LIME, AND JASMINE TARTLETS

Tartelettes Citron-Jasmin

Makes 50

Active time
1 ½ hours

Cooking time
1 hour 10 minutes

Chilling time
3 hours

Storage
Up to 2 days in the refrigerator

Equipment
Electric hand whisk
Instant-read thermometer
Stick blender
6-in. (15-cm) square baking frame
Silicone baking mat
2 pastry bags fitted with plain
¼-in. (6-mm) tips
Pastry bag fitted with a fluted
¼-in. (6-mm) tip

Ingredients

LEMON AND LIME CRUST
1 ½ cups (6.5 oz./190 g) butter, softened
2 ¼ cups (7.5 oz./210 g) sugar
Generous ½ tsp (3.5 g) salt
⅓ cup (2.75 oz./75 g) lightly beaten egg (about 1 ½ eggs)
3 tbsp (1.75 oz./50 g) egg yolk (about 3 yolks)
2 tbsp plus 2 tsp (40 ml) lemon juice
¼ tsp (1 g) lime zest
5 cups (1 lb. 2 oz./500 g) flour

JASMINE CRÉMEUX
1 cup (250 ml) whole milk
1 cup (250 ml) whipping cream, 35% butterfat
2 tbsp (1 oz./30 g) loose leaf jasmine tea
7 tbsp (3 oz./85 g) sugar
½ tsp (2 g) pectin NH
¼ cup (2.5 oz./70 g) lightly beaten egg yolk (about 4 yolks)

LIME CREAM
3 sheets (0.2 oz./6 g) gelatin
Generous 1 cup (8 oz./225 g) sugar
2 ½ tbsp (1 oz./25 g) lime zest
¾ cup (175 ml) lime juice
Generous ¾ cup (7 oz./200 g) lightly beaten egg (about 4 eggs)
1 ¼ cups (10.25 oz./290 g) butter, diced
Scant ½ cup (100 ml) whipping cream, 35% butterfat, whipped

JELLED LEMON CUBES
3 sheets (0.2 oz./6 g) gelatin
1 ¼ cups (300 ml) lemon juice
¼ cup (1.5 oz./45 g) sugar

SWISS MERINGUE
½ cup (3.5 oz./100 g) sugar
3 tbsp (1.75 oz./50 g) egg white (about 1 ½ whites)

DECORATION
Lemon cress leaves
Edible gold leaf

MAKING THE LEMON AND LIME CRUST
In a mixing bowl, whisk together the butter, sugar, salt, eggs, egg yolks, lemon juice, and zest until creamy. Sift in the flour and mix in well. Work the dough with your hands on a work surface until smooth. Cover in plastic wrap and chill for about 30 minutes. Preheat the oven to 325°F (170°C/Gas mark 3.) Roll out using a textured rolling pin and cut into ⅓ × 1 ¼-in. (1 × 3-cm) rectangles. Line a baking sheet with parchment paper and lift the rectangles onto it. Bake for about 8 minutes until golden.

MAKING THE JASMINE CRÉMEUX
In a saucepan, heat the milk and cream. Add the tea, cover the pan with plastic wrap and infuse for 15 minutes off the heat. Strain, stir in the sugar and pectin, and bring to a boil. Whisk one-third into the egg yolks, pour back into the saucepan and cook, stirring constantly, to 175°F (85°C). Cool and then chill for at least 1 hour.

MAKING THE LIME CREAM
Soak the gelatin in cold water. Mix the sugar and zest together. Pour the lime juice into a saucepan, add the sugar and zest, heat until the sugar dissolves, and bring to a boil. Add the eggs and, stirring continuously, bring back to a boil. Strain, squeeze excess water from the gelatin and stir until dissolved. Cool to 100°F (40°C), add the butter and, when melted, blend with the stick blender until smooth. Cool, gently fold in the whipped cream, and chill for 1 hour.

MAKING THE JELLED LEMON CUBES
Soak the gelatin in cold water. Heat one-quarter of the lemon juice in a saucepan with the sugar and, when the sugar has dissolved, squeeze excess water from the gelatin and stir in until dissolved. Stir in the rest of the lemon juice. Place the frame on the silicone mat and carefully pour in the mixture. Cool and then chill until set. Remove the frame and cut into ¼-in. (5-mm) cubes.

MAKING THE SWISS MERINGUE
Preheat the oven to 175°F (80°C/Gas mark ¼). Make a Swiss meringue (see technique p. 236). Line a baking sheet with parchment paper, spoon the meringue into a pastry bag with a plain tip, and pipe small pointed shells on the sheet. Bake for about 1 hour until crisp and dry.

ASSEMBLING THE TARTLETS
Spoon the jasmine crémeux into the second pastry bag with the plain tip and the lime cream into the pastry bag with the fluted tip. Pipe small balls of jasmine crémeux and small rosettes of lime cream neatly on the shortbreads and tuck the meringues and lemon cubes between them. Decorate with cress leaves and edible gold leaf.

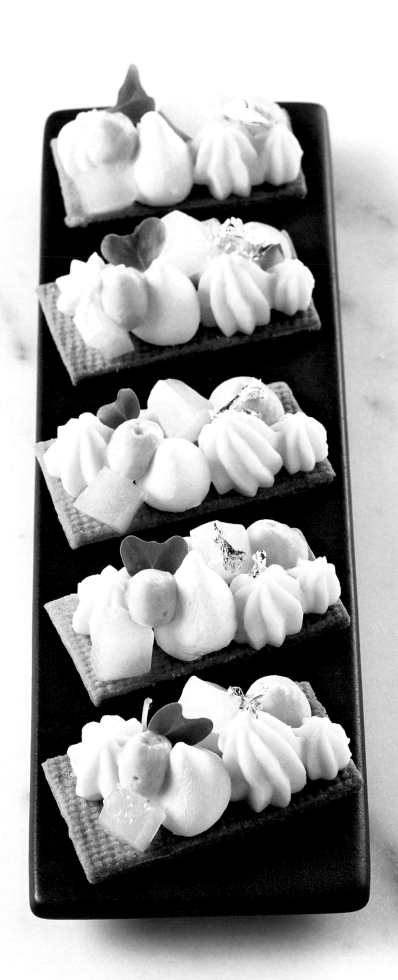

CHOCOLATE BARK ÉCLAIRS

Caroline Chocolat Mendiant

Makes 50

Active time
1 hour

Cooking time
30–40 minutes

Chilling time
40 minutes

Storage
Up to 2 days in the refrigerator

Equipment
2 pastry bags fitted with plain ⅓-in. (10-mm) and ¼-in. (6-mm) tips

Instant-read thermometer
Stick blender

Ingredients

CHOUX PASTRY
½ cup (125 ml) water
½ cup (125 ml) whole milk
1 tsp (5 g) salt
1 tsp (5 g) sugar
7 tbsp (3.5 oz./100 g) butter, diced
1 ¼ cups (5.25 oz./150 g) flour, sifted
1 cup (9 oz./250 g) egg (about 5 eggs)

CHOCOLATE CRÉMEUX
Scant 1 cup (200 ml) whole milk
Scant 1 cup (200 ml) whipping cream, 35% butterfat
Scant ⅓ cup (2.75 oz./80 g) egg yolk (about 4 ½ yolks)
Scant ¼ cup (1.5 oz./40 g) sugar
5.5 oz. (160 g) bittersweet chocolate, 70% cacao, chopped

DECORATION
Bittersweet chocolate pouring fondant icing
Halved pistachios
Diced dried apricots
Chopped roasted hazelnuts

MAKING THE CHOUX PASTRY
Heat the water, milk, salt, sugar, and butter in a saucepan and, when the butter melts, bring to a fast boil. Remove from the heat and tip in all the flour, beating vigorously until smooth. Return the pan to a high heat and stir constantly to dry out the mixture. Remove from the heat and beat in the eggs, one at a time, with a spatula. Preheat the oven to 350°F (180°C/Gas mark 4). Spoon the pastry into the pastry bag with the ⅓-in. (10-mm) tip and pipe mini éclairs, 2 in. (5 cm) long and ⅝ in. (1.5 cm) wide, onto a nonstick baking sheet (see technique p. 166). Bake for 30–40 minutes.

MAKING THE CHOCOLATE CRÉMEUX
Bring the milk and cream to a boil in a saucepan. Meanwhile, whisk the egg yolks and sugar together until pale and thickened. Whisk in a little of the hot milk and cream, pour back into the saucepan and cook, stirring constantly, to 180°F–184°F (82°C–84°C) until the mixture coats the back of a spoon. Strain the crémeux through a fine-mesh sieve onto the chopped chocolate and blend, keeping the arm of the stick blender immersed in the crémeux so as not to incorporate any air. Chill for 30–40 minutes.

ASSEMBLING THE ECLAIRS
Melt the chocolate fondant icing (see technique p. 169). Spoon the chocolate crémeux into the pastry bag with the ¼-in. (6-mm) tip and fill the éclairs with it (see technique p. 168). Dip the tops of the éclairs in the chocolate fondant icing and decorate with the pistachios, apricots, and hazelnuts before it sets.

VANILLA AND RASPBERRY RELIGIEUSES

Religieuses Vanille-Framboise

Makes 50

Active time
1 ½ hours

Cooking time
30 minutes

Chilling time
2 hours

Freezing time
1 hour

Storage
Up to 2 days in the refrigerator

Equipment
⅓-in. (1-cm) and ¾-in. (2-cm) round cookie cutters

3 pastry bags, 2 fitted with plain ⅓-in. (10-mm) tips and 1 fitted with a plain ¼-in. (4-mm) tip

Instant-read thermometer
Stick blender
Silicone tray with tiny round ball molds

Ingredients

VANILLA CRISP COATING (CRAQUELIN)
¼ cup (1.75 oz./50 g) butter
¼ cup (1.75 oz./50 g) sugar
2 tbsp (0.35 oz./10 g) ground hazelnuts
2 tbsp (0.35 oz./10 g) ground almonds
Scant ¼ cup (0.75 oz./20 g) flour
Seeds from 1 vanilla bean

CHOUX PASTRY
½ cup (125 ml) water
½ cup (125 ml) whole milk
1 tsp (5 g) salt
1 tsp (5 g) sugar
7 tbsp (3.5 oz./100 g) butter
1 ¼ cups (5.25 oz./150 g) flour
1 cup (9 oz./250 g) egg
(about 5 eggs)

VANILLA CRÉMEUX
2 sheets (0.2 oz./4 g) gelatin
⅓ cup (3 oz./80 g) egg yolk
(about 4 ½ yolks)
⅓ cup (2.5 oz./70 g) sugar
1 ½ cups (340 ml) whipping cream, 35% butterfat
1 vanilla bean, split and seeds scraped out

RASPBERRY CRÉMEUX
1 sheet (2 g) gelatin
¾ cup (7 oz./200 g) raspberry purée
¼ cup (2 oz./60 g) egg yolk
(about 3 ½ yolks)
⅓ cup (2.75 oz./75 g) lightly beaten egg (about 1 ½ eggs)
¼ cup (1.75 oz./50 g) sugar
⅓ cup (2.75 oz./ 75 g) butter, diced

RED ICING
2 sheets (0.2 oz./4 g) gelatin
Scant ½ cup (115 ml) whipping cream, 35% butterfat
6.75 oz. (190 g) white chocolate, chopped
¼ cup (2.75 oz./75 g) clear neutral glaze
Fat-soluble powdered red food coloring

VANILLA "CAVIAR"
¾ sheet (1.5 g) gelatin
Scant ½ cup (100 ml) milk
1 vanilla bean, split and seeds scraped out

DECORATION
25 raspberries
Edible silver leaf

MAKING THE VANILLA CRISP COATING (CRAQUELIN)
Mix all the ingredients together with your hands to make a sweet dough. Roll out between 2 sheets of parchment paper to a thickness of 1/16 in. (2 mm), and cut out 50 small and 50 larger disks using the cookie cutters. Set aside.

MAKING THE CHOUX PASTRY
Preheat the oven to 350°F (180°C/Gas mark 4). Heat the water, milk, salt, sugar, and butter in a pan and, when the butter melts, bring to a fast boil. Remove from the heat and tip in all the flour, beating vigorously until smooth. Return the pan to a high heat and stir constantly to dry out the mixture. Remove from the heat and beat in the eggs, one at a time, with a spatula. Spoon the pastry into a pastry bag fitted with a ⅓-in. (10-mm) tip and pipe 50 × ⅓-in. (1-cm) puffs and 50 × 1 ¼-in. (3-cm) puffs onto nonstick baking sheets. Top the small puffs with the smaller disks of vanilla *craquelin* and the large puffs with the larger disks and bake for 20–30 minutes.

MAKING THE VANILLA CRÉMEUX
Soak the gelatin in a bowl of cold water. Whisk the egg yolks and sugar together until pale and thickened. Pour into a saucepan, add the cream and vanilla bean and seeds, and cook, stirring constantly, until the temperature reaches 180°F–184°F (82°C–84°C) and the mixture coats the back of a spoon. Squeeze excess water from the gelatin and stir in until dissolved. Remove from the heat, strain into a mixing bowl, and process briefly with the stick blender until smooth. Allow to cool. Spoon into the second pastry bag with a ⅓-in. (10-mm) tip and fill the large choux puffs (see technique p. 168).

MAKING THE RASPBERRY CRÉMEUX
Soak the gelatin in a bowl of cold water. Heat all the ingredients, except the butter, in a saucepan and bring just to a boil. Squeeze excess water from the gelatin and stir in until dissolved. When the mixture has cooled to about 95°F (35°C–40°C), mix in the butter and process using the stick blender. Pour into a bowl and chill in the refrigerator. Spoon into the pastry bag fitted with a ¼-in. (4-mm) tip and fill the small choux puffs.

MAKING THE RED ICING
Soak the gelatin in a bowl of cold water. Bring the cream to a boil in a saucepan. Squeeze excess water from the gelatin and stir into the cream until dissolved. Pour over the chopped chocolate and neutral glaze, and mix to make a ganache. Stir in the food coloring and allow to cool to about 85°F (30°C–35°C), before icing the tops of the small puffs (see technique p. 169). Leave to set.

MAKING THE VANILLA "CAVIAR"
Soak the gelatin in cold water. Bring the milk and vanilla bean and seeds to a boil. Squeeze excess water from the gelatin and stir in until dissolved. Pour into the silicone mold, cool, and freeze.

ASSEMBLING THE RÉLIGIEUSES
Cut the raspberries in half horizontally, to make raspberry "rings." Place a raspberry ring on each large puff and top with a small puff, iced side uppermost. Arrange one or more vanilla "caviar" balls on top and decorate with a little edible silver leaf.

PISTACHIO AND SOUR CHERRY BITES

Mignardises Pistache-Griotte

Makes 50

Active time
1 ½ hours

Chilling time
2 ½ hours

Cooking time
30 minutes

Storage
Up to 2 days in the refrigerator

Equipment
Stand mixer
1-in. (2.5-cm) round cookie cutter
Instant-read thermometer
Silicone tray with half-sphere molds, about 1 in. (2.5 cm) in diameter
Pastry bag fitted with a basketweave tip

Ingredients
CHOCOLATE SHORTBREAD
3 tbsp (1.75 oz./50 g) egg yolk (about 3 yolks)
½ cup (3.5 oz./100 g) sugar
Scant ½ cup (3.5 oz./100 g) butter, diced and softened
1 cup (4.5 oz./125 g) flour
¼ tsp (1 g) salt
⅓ cup (1.25 oz./35 g) unsweetened cocoa powder
1 ½ tsp (6 g) baking powder

LIGHT PISTACHIO CREAM
Scant ½ cup (100 ml) whipping cream, 35% butterfat
⅓ cup (85 ml) whole milk
Seeds from ½ vanilla bean
1 tbsp (0.75 oz./18 g) egg yolk (about 1 yolk)
5 tsp (0.75 oz./20 g) superfine sugar
2 tsp (4 g) flour
1 ¼ tsp (4 g) custard powder
1.25 oz. (35 g) pistachio paste
2.5 oz. (70 g) white chocolate, chopped
Scant 1 cup (8 oz./225 g) whipped cream

PISTACHIO AND SOUR CHERRY BALLS
12.5 oz. (360 g) almond paste, 50% almonds, chopped
¾ cup (6.25 oz./180 g) lightly beaten egg (about 4 eggs)
1 ½ tsp (0.35 oz./10 g) honey
2.5 oz. (70 g) pistachio paste
½ cup (3.75 oz./110 g) butter, diced and softened
50 pitted sour cherries

BITTERSWEET CHOCOLATE DECORATIONS
7 oz. (200 g) bittersweet couverture chocolate, 66% cacao

DECORATION
Apricot glaze
Pistachio powder

MAKING THE CHOCOLATE SHORTBREAD
Fit the stand mixer with the paddle beater and beat the egg yolks and sugar until pale and thickened. Beat in the butter and then the flour, salt, cocoa powder, and baking powder. Transfer to a work surface and finish kneading the dough by hand until smooth. Cover in plastic wrap and chill for 40 minutes. Preheat the oven to 325°F (165°C/Gas mark 3). Roll out the dough ⅛ in. (3 mm) thick and cut out disks with the cookie cutter. Lift onto baking sheets lined with parchment paper and bake for 12 minutes.

MAKING THE LIGHT PISTACHIO CREAM
Bring the cream, milk, and vanilla seeds to a boil in a saucepan. Beat the egg yolk and sugar in a mixing bowl until pale and thickened, sift in the flour and custard powder, and stir in. Stir in one-third of the hot cream, pour back into the saucepan, and cook, stirring constantly, until the temperature reaches 175°F (83°C) and the mixture coats the back of a spoon. Stir in the pistachio paste and white chocolate until melted. Cover a baking sheet with plastic wrap, spread the cream over it, and press another piece of plastic wrap over the surface. Cool and then fold in the whipped cream. Chill until needed.

MAKING THE PISTACHIO AND SOUR CHERRY BALLS
Preheat the oven to 350°F (180°C/Gas mark 4). Fit the stand mixer with the paddle beater and beat together the almond paste, eggs, honey, and pistachio paste. Beat in the butter until smooth. Pour the mixture into the silicone molds and place a sour cherry in each. Bake for 15 minutes.

MAKING THE CHOCOLATE DECORATIONS
Temper the chocolate (see techniques pp. 570 and 572). Cut parchment paper into 4 × 2-in. (10 × 5-cm) strips. Make a paper piping cone (see technique p. 598) and spoon the tempered chocolate into it. Snip off the tip and pipe lines across the parchment strips. Leave until the chocolate is starting to set and then lay the strips over a rolling pin so the chocolate lines set in curved shapes. Allow to set in the refrigerator.

ASSEMBLING THE BITES
Dip the balls in warm apricot glaze and coat in pistachio powder. Place, flat side down, on the shortbread disks and top with the chocolate decorations, curves upright. Spoon the pistachio cream into the pastry bag and pipe a little cream on top of each one.

PARIS-BREST ALMOND FINANCIERS

Moelleux Financiers Paris-Brest

Makes 50

Active time
1 hour

Cooking time
20 minutes

Chilling time
1 ½ hours

Storage
Up to 2 days in the refrigerator

Equipment
12 × 16-in. (30 × 40-cm) rectangular frame, ½ in. (1.3 cm) high
Electric hand beater
Instant-read thermometer
Pastry bag fitted with
a Saint-Honoré tip

Ingredients

FINANCIER BASE
1 ¼ cups (5.5 oz./150 g) flour
1 ½ cups (5.5 oz./150 g) almond flour
¾ cup (5.5 oz./150 g) sugar
1 ¼ cups (5 oz./150 g) confectioners' sugar
1 ½ tsp (0.35 oz./10 g) invert sugar
1 ½ cups (10.5 oz./300 g) butter, diced
1 ¼ cups (9 oz./250 g) egg white (about 8 whites)

PRALINE CREAM
Scant 1 cup (200 ml) whole milk
2 oz. (50 g) praline paste
1 ½ tbsp (1 oz./25 g) egg yolk (about 1 ½ yolks)
¼ cup (1.5 oz./40 g) sugar
2 tbsp (0.75 oz./20 g) custard powder
7 tbsp (3.5 oz./100 g) butter, diced and softened

COATING
3.5 oz. (100 g) bittersweet couverture chocolate, 58% cacao, chopped
2 tsp (10 ml) grape seed oil
1 ½ tsp (0.35 oz./10 g) brown glazing paste
4 tbsp (0.75 oz./20 g) chopped almonds

DECORATION
Chopped toasted hazelnuts

MAKING THE FINANCIER BASE
Preheat the oven to 325°F (160°C/Gas mark 3). Put the frame on a baking sheet lined with parchment paper. Using the electric beater, mix the flours, sugars, and invert sugar together. Melt the butter in a saucepan and continue to cook until it browns. Whisk the egg whites into the dry ingredients and then the warm, browned butter. Spoon the mixture into the frame and bake for 20 minutes. Allow to cool and cut into ¾ × 2 ¼-in. (2 × 6-cm) rectangles.

MAKING THE PRALINE CREAM
Bring the milk to a boil in a saucepan with the praline paste. Whisk the egg yolks with the sugar and custard powder until pale and thickened, and then cook as for a pastry cream (see technique p. 196). Remove from the heat, stir in half the butter while the mixture is still warm and allow to cool. Whisk in the rest of the butter, continuing to whisk until smooth. Chill in the refrigerator until needed.

MAKING THE COATING
Melt all the ingredients together in a saucepan. Use at 85°F (30°C).

ASSEMBLING THE FINANCIERS
Dip the tops and sides of the rectangles of cake in the coating, leaving the bottoms uncoated, and place on a sheet of parchment paper to set. Spoon the praline cream into the pastry bag and pipe waves on top of each rectangle. Decorate with chopped hazelnuts.

BANANA AND CHOCOLATE TARTLETS

Tartelettes Banane-Chocolat

Makes 25

Active time
1 ½ hours

Cooking time
15 minutes

Freezing time
2 ¼ hours

Storage
Up to 2 days in the refrigerator

Equipment
Tartlet molds
6-in. (20-cm) square baking frame
Silicone baking mat
Instant-read thermometer
Stick blender
⅓-in. (1-cm) round cookie cutter
2 pastry bags fitted with plain
¼-in. (5-mm) tips

Ingredients

CHOCOLATE SHORT PASTRY CRUST
⅓ cup plus 1 tbsp (1.5 oz./45 g) unsweetened cocoa powder
⅔ cup (2.75 oz./80 g) flour
½ cup (2.75 oz./75 g) confectioners' sugar
¼ cup (1.75 oz./50 g) butter, diced
2 ½ tbsp (1.25 oz./35 g) lightly beaten egg (about 1 egg)

BANANA FLAMBÉ LAYER
7 oz. (200 g) bananas
2 tbsp (1 oz./30 g) brown sugar
¼ cup (50 ml) dark rum
1 ¼ tsp (5 g) pectin NH
5 tsp (0.75 oz./20 g) sugar

CHOCOLATE CRÉMEUX
Scant ½ cup (100 ml) whole milk
Scant ½ cup (100 ml) whipping cream, 35% butterfat
2 ½ tsp (0.35 oz./10 g) sugar
1 ½ tbsp (1 oz./25 g) egg yolk (about 1 ½ yolks)
2.75 oz. (75 g) bittersweet couverture chocolate, 70% cacao, chopped

BITTERSWEET CHOCOLATE GLAZE
3 sheets (0.2 oz./6 g) gelatin
2 tbsp (30 ml) water
⅓ cup (2.75 oz./75 g) sugar
3 ½ tbsp (2.75 oz./75 g) glucose syrup
3 ½ tbsp (50 ml) sweetened condensed milk
2.75 oz. (75 g) bittersweet couverture chocolate, 60% cacao, chopped

DECORATION
Lightly caramelized banana slices
1 sheet edible gold leaf

MAKING THE CHOCOLATE SHORT PASTRY CRUST
Preheat the oven to 325°F (170°C/Gas mark 3). Make a sweet short pastry, adding the cocoa powder and flour to the sugar, butter, and eggs (see technique p. 60). Line the tartlet molds with the pastry and blind bake for 10 minutes.

BANANA FLAMBÉ LAYER
Put the frame on the silicone mat on a baking sheet. Peel and dice the bananas and cook them in a skillet with the brown sugar. Once they are a rich caramel color, flambé them with the rum. Mix the pectin with the sugar and add. Cook for another 2 minutes and then transfer to the frame. Cool and freeze.

CHOCOLATE CRÉMEUX
Make a custard with the first 4 ingredients (see technique p. 204). Pour over the chocolate and blend until smooth. Cool and then chill.

MAKING THE BITTERSWEET CHOCOLATE GLAZE
Soak the gelatin in a bowl of cold water. Heat the water, sugar, and glucose syrup in a saucepan to 225°F (105°C). Pour onto the condensed milk, stirring continuously. Squeeze excess water from the gelatin and stir in until dissolved. Pour over the chocolate and blend until smooth while still warm. Cool to 95°F (35°C) before using.

ASSEMBLING THE TARTLETS
Carefully remove the tartlet crusts from the molds. Cut out 25 disks from the banana flambé layer using the cookie cutter and place one in each tartlet crust. Spoon the chocolate crémeux into a pastry bag and pipe into the tartlets, filling the crusts by three-quarters. Freeze for about 15 minutes. Spoon the chocolate glaze (which should be at 95°F/35°C) into the second pastry bag and pipe the glaze over the chocolate crémeux. Decorate with caramelized banana slices and tiny pieces of gold leaf.

MOJITO CREAMS

Mojito

Makes 25

Active time
1 ½ hours

Cooking time
25 minutes

Chilling time
2 hours

Freezing time
About 1 hour

Storage
Up to 2 days in the refrigerator

Equipment
8-in. (20-cm) square baking frame
Embossed silicone baking mat
2 pastry bags fitted with plain
¼-in. (5-mm) tips
Instant-read thermometer
Electric hand beater
Stick blender
Silicone tray with at least 25 × 1-in.
(2-cm) square molds
Pastry bag fitted with a fluted
1⁄16-in. (2-mm) tip

Ingredients
MELT-IN-THE-MOUTH SHORTBREAD
1.75 oz. (50 g) white chocolate,
chopped
⅓ cup (2.75 oz./80 g) butter, diced
and softened
3 tbsp (1.25 oz./35 g) sugar
½ cup (1.25 oz./35 g) almond flour
1 tbsp (0.5 oz./15 g) egg yolk
(about 1 yolk)
⅔ cup (2.75 oz./80 g) flour
⅛ tsp (1 g) fleur de sel

ALMOND AND LIME SPONGE
1.25 oz. (35 g) almond paste,
50% almonds, softened
3 tbsp (1.25 oz./35 g) sugar
¼ tsp (1 g) lime zest
⅓ cup (2.5 oz./70 g) lightly
beaten egg (about 1 ½ eggs)
⅓ cup (1.5 oz./40 g) flour
3 tbsp (1.5 oz./40 g) butter, melted
and cooled

LIME, MINT, AND RUM LAYER
¼ cup (60 ml) white rum
¼ cup (60 ml) lime juice
1 ½ tsp (8 g) chopped fresh mint
¼ cup (2.75 oz./75 g) cane syrup
2 tbsp (1 oz./30 g) brown sugar
3 tsp (0.5 oz./12 g) pectin
Powdered mint green food
coloring

MINT AND LIME MOUSSE
0.35 oz. (10 g) fresh mint
2 tbsp (30 ml) lime juice
3 tbsp (1.75 oz./50 g) egg yolk
(about 3 yolks)
3 tbsp (1.25 oz./35 g) sugar
2 tbsp (1.5 oz./45 g) honey
Finely grated zest of ½ lime
5 tsp (25 ml) white rum
1 cup (9 oz./250 g) *fromage blanc*
(or Greek-style yogurt), 40% fat
4 sheets (2.5 oz./8 g) gelatin
⅔ cup (140 ml) whipping cream,
35% butterfat, whipped

WHITE GLAZE
3 ½ sheets (0.2 oz./7 g) gelatin
¼ cup (50 ml) water
½ cup (3.5 oz./100 g) sugar
¼ cup (3.5 oz./100 g) glucose
syrup
¼ cup (70 ml) sweetened
condensed milk
3.5 oz. (100 g) white chocolate,
chopped

DECORATION
Small segments of lime
Sprigs of lemon cress

MAKING THE MELT-IN-THE-MOUTH SHORTBREAD
Put the baking frame on a nonstick baking sheet. Preheat the oven to 300°F (150°C/Gas mark 2). Melt the chocolate in a bowl over a pan of hot water. In a mixing bowl, cream the butter, sugar, and almond flour together. Beat in the egg yolk and then stir in the flour. Pour in the melted chocolate and add the fleur de sel. Stir until well blended and smooth. Transfer to the frame and bake for about 15 minutes. Remove from the oven and immediately cut into small 1 ⅓-in. (3.5-cm) squares.

MAKING THE ALMOND AND LIME SPONGE
Place the silicone mat on a baking sheet. Preheat the oven to 325°F (170°C/Gas mark 3). Combine the almond paste, sugar, and lime zest in a mixing bowl using a spatula. Gradually mix in the eggs, gently fold in the flour, and then the melted butter. Spread the mixture over the silicone mat, about ¼ in. (5 mm) thick, and bake for about 10 minutes. Cool and then cut into ¾-in. (2-cm) squares.

LIME, MINT, AND RUM LAYER
Heat the rum, lime juice, mint, and cane syrup in a saucepan. Strain by pressing through a fine-mesh sieve and cool a little. Mix the sugar with the pectin and food coloring, stir in, return to the pan, and bring to a boil. Cool, transfer to a pastry bag with a plain tip, and chill until needed.

MAKING THE MINT AND LIME MOUSSE
Heat the mint in the lime juice, let infuse for about 10 minutes, and then strain. Whisk in the egg yolks and sugar and, when the sugar has dissolved, heat to 175°F (85°C). Whisk with the electric beater until cool. Stir the honey, lime zest, rum, and *fromage blanc* or yogurt together in a mixing bowl. Soften the gelatin in a bowl of cold water. Squeeze excess water from the gelatin, melt it over low heat, and stir into the *fromage blanc* mixture gradually until combined. Lightly fold one-third of the whipped cream into the egg yolk mixture (*pâte à bombe*), fold in the *fromage blanc* mixture, and then carefully fold in the rest of the whipped cream. Spoon most of the mousse into the second pastry bag with the plain tip (reserving the rest for decoration) and chill until needed.

MAKING THE WHITE GLAZE
Soak the gelatin in a bowl of cold water. Heat the water, sugar, and glucose in a saucepan to 225°F (102°C) and then stir in the condensed milk. Squeeze excess water from the gelatin and stir in until the gelatin has dissolved. Pour over the white chocolate and blend until smooth. Cool to approximately 95°F (35°C) before using.

ASSEMBLING THE MOJITO CREAMS
Pipe mousse into the silicone molds until they are about three-quarters full. Pipe the lime layer into the center of the squares and top each with a square of almond sponge. Freeze until firm. Carefully unmold before covering with the white glaze (which should be at approximately 95°F/35°C). Place the mousse squares on top of the shortbreads. Spoon the reserved mousse into the pastry bag with the 1⁄16-in. (2-mm) fluted tip, pipe small rosettes of mousse on each shortbread, and decorate with tiny segments of lime and sprigs of lemon cress.

PASSION FRUIT LOLLIPOPS

Sucettes Passion

Makes 15

Active time
45 minutes

Chilling time
2 hours

Cooking time
10 minutes

Storage
Up to 2 days in the refrigerator

Equipment
Instant-read thermometer
Stick blender
Pastry bag fitted
with a plain ¼-in. (5-mm) tip
15 lollipop sticks

Ingredients

PASSION FRUIT LOLLIPOPS
½ sheet (1 g) gelatin
Scant ½ cup (3.5 oz./100 g)
passion fruit pulp
2 tbsp (1 oz./30 g) egg yolk
(about 1 ½ yolks)
3 tbsp (1.5 oz./40 g) lightly beaten
egg (about 1 egg)
2 tbsp (1 oz./25 g) sugar
3 tbsp (1.5 oz./40 g) butter, diced
15 × 1-in. (2.5-cm) hollow white
chocolate balls (available from
Valrhona)

GLAZE
1 ½ sheets (0.1 oz./3 g) gelatin
⅓ cup (75 ml) whipping cream,
35% butterfat
4.5 oz. (125 g) white chocolate,
chopped
2 tbsp (1.75 oz./50 g) mirror glaze
Fat-soluble powdered food
coloring of your choice

MAKING THE PASSION FRUIT LOLLIPOPS
Soak the gelatin in a bowl of cold water to soften it. Put all the other ingredients, except the butter and chocolate balls, in a saucepan. Squeeze excess water from the gelatin, add to the pan, and bring to a gentle boil, stirring until the mixture gels. Cool to approximately 95°F–105°F (35°C–40°C), add the butter, and process until smooth using the stick blender. Spoon into the pastry bag and pipe the mixture into the hollow white chocolate balls. Cool, inserting the sticks into the holes where you added the filling as they cool, and then chill for at least 2 hours.

MAKING THE GLAZE
Soak the gelatin in a bowl of cold water to soften it. Bring the cream to a boil in a saucepan, squeeze excess water from the gelatin, and stir in until dissolved. Pour over the chocolate and mirror glaze, and blend to make a smooth ganache. Stir in the food coloring and cool to 95°F (35°C) before using.

ASSEMBLING THE LOLLIPOPS
Once the lollipops are well chilled, coat them with the glaze.

RASPBERRY LOLLIPOPS

Sucettes Framboise

Makes 15

Active time
45 minutes

Cooking time
10 minutes

Chilling time
2 hours

Storage
Up to 2 days in the refrigerator

Equipment
Stick blender
Pastry bag fitted
with a plain ¼-in. (5-mm) tip
Instant-read thermometer
15 lollipop sticks

Ingredients

RASPBERRY LOLLIPOPS
½ sheet (1 g) gelatin
Scant ½ cup (3.5 oz./100 g)
raspberry purée
2 tbsp (1 oz./30 g) lightly beaten
egg (about 1 egg)
2 ½ tbsp (1.5 oz./40 g) egg yolk
(about 2 yolks)
2 tbsp (1 oz./25 g) sugar
3 tbsp (1.5 oz./40 g) butter, diced
15 × 1-in. (2.5-cm) hollow
bittersweet chocolate balls
(available from Valrhona)

GLAZE
1 ½ sheets (0.1 oz./3 g) gelatin
⅓ cup (75 ml) whipping cream,
35% butterfat
4.5 oz. (125 g) white chocolate,
chopped
2 tbsp (1.75 oz./50 g) mirror glaze
Fat-soluble powdered food
coloring of your choice

DECORATION
A few fresh raspberries
Edible silver leaf

MAKING THE RASPBERRY LOLLIPOPS
Soak the gelatin in a bowl of cold water to soften it. Put all the other ingredients, except the butter and chocolate balls, in a saucepan. Squeeze excess water from the gelatin, add to the pan, and bring to a gentle boil, stirring until the mixture gels. Cool to approximately 95°F–105°F (35°C–40°C), add the butter, and process until smooth using the stick blender. Spoon into the pastry bag and pipe the mixture into the hollow chocolate balls. Cool, inserting the sticks into the holes where you added the filling as they cool, and then chill for at least 2 hours.

MAKING THE GLAZE
Soak the gelatin in a bowl of cold water to soften it. Bring the cream to a boil in a saucepan, squeeze excess water from the gelatin, and stir in until dissolved. Pour over the chopped chocolate and mirror glaze and blend to make a smooth ganache. Stir in the food coloring and cool to 95°F (35°C) before using.

ASSEMBLING THE LOLLIPOPS
Once the lollipops are well chilled, coat them with the glaze and decorate with small pieces of raspberry and silver leaf.

CANDIES, CONFECTIONS & JAMS

CANDIES, CONFECTIONS, AND JAMS (COOKED SUGAR)

What do candies, confections, and jams have in common? All of them are made from cooked sugar, a technique in its own right. To master the subtleties you need a watchful eye—and to invest in an accurate candy thermometer. With both, you'll have no trouble getting it right!

CHOOSING THE RIGHT SUGAR

A BRIEF HISTORY OF FRENCH CONFECTIONERY

Nougat is one of the oldest known confections, its name deriving from the Latin nux gatum (walnut cake). There are references to nougat dating back to 1701, when the dukes of Berry and Bordeaux traveled to Montélimar. Today the town is the major center of nougat production in France.

Pralines were named after Marshal du Plessis Praslin, Duke of Choiseul, whose cook, Clément Juluzot, created them in the 17th century. They are regarded as the very first candies ever made.

Marshmallows were originally made from the root of the marshmallow plant and honey, but the root has not been used for a long time and now only the name remains.

Salted butter caramel is a recent French specialty, being created in 1977 by Henri Le Roux at Quiberon in Brittany.

All the candies, confections, and jams in this chapter are made using white sugar. If you want to replace this with any of the brown sugars, you need to bear in mind that they all contain impurities, which are likely to burn. This could have a major impact not just on the success of the recipe but also on the consistency of the finished candy.

DEGREES BRIX

Degrees Brix measure the percentage of dry matter present in a liquid using an instrument called a refractometer. Professionals use this, as it is a very reliable way of calculating the percentage of sucrose in a solution. A similar system, called degrees Baumé, which is mentioned in some books, has not been in use in France since the 1960s so is not used here. One degree Brix is equal to 1 g sucrose in 100 g of solution.

FINGERS OR A CANDY THERMOMETER?

Before accurate thermometers were widely available, the stages of sugar cooking had to be measured using a bowl of ice water—and the cook's fingers! It involved plunging one's hand in the cold water before scooping up a little boiling syrup and dropping it in the water to determine what stage it had reached: thread, soft-ball, etc. We still use the same names for these stages but today, in your own kitchen, nothing beats a good candy thermometer for checking when your syrup is nearly there!

CALIBRATE YOUR THERMOMETER

To be sure your thermometer is giving accurate readings, bring a pan of water to a boil and check the temperature. If the reading on the thermometer is 212°F (100°C), it's working perfectly.

AVOID GETTING BURNT!

Cooking sugar at high temperatures requires concentration and organization. To prevent accidents, first clear your work surface and have a bowl of cold water close by. However, if you do burn yourself, immediately put your hand under cold running water and leave it there for 10 minutes or longer. If necessary, seek emergency medical care. Stay safe!

SUGAR COOKING STAGES

SMALL THREAD		
Temperature	**Finger test**	Fairly fluid syrup. When pulled between the thumb and index finger, the thread breaks
219°F–221°F (104°C–105°C)	**Uses**	Jams, jellies, and fruit jellies

PEARL		
Temperature	**Finger test**	Thick syrup. When pulled between the thumb and index finger, it stretches into a fine thread
225°F (107°C)	**Uses**	Glazing chestnuts, jelly candies

SOFT-BALL		
Temperature	**Finger test**	When dropped into cold water, forms a ball that can be flattened between the fingers
239°F (115°C)	**Uses**	Soft fondant icing

FIRM-BALL		
Temperature	**Finger test**	When dropped into cold water, forms a malleable ball
243°F (117°C)	**Uses**	Soft caramel candies, praline pastes

HARD-BALL		
Temperature	**Finger test**	When dropped into cold water, forms a firm ball that holds its shape
248°F–250°F (120°C–121°C)	**Uses**	Italian meringue, buttercreams, firm fondant icing

SOFT-CRACK		
Temperature	**Finger test**	Hardens in cold water and forms a malleable thread
266°F–275°F (130F–135°C)	**Uses**	Marshmallow, hard candies, almond paste

HARD-CRACK		
Temperature	**Finger test**	Hardens in cold water, forming a firm but very brittle thread
284°F–293°F (140°C–145°C)	**Uses**	Spun, poured, pulled, and blown sugar. Barley sugar candies and lollipops

LIGHT CARAMEL		
Temperature	**Finger test**	Sugar turns golden or light amber
320°F (160°C)	**Uses**	Poured, pulled, blown, and bubble sugar. Croquembouches, glazing choux puffs, etc.

CARAMEL		
Temperature	**Finger test**	Sugar turns medium brown
356°F (180°C)	**Uses**	Cream caramel, praline pastes, caramel cages, spun sugar (angel's hair), salted butter caramel sauce

JAMS

THE BASICS

Jam is made with fruit and sugar, which are cooked together until sufficient liquid has evaporated to preserve the jam. When making jam, it is important to keep the following in mind: the amount of pectin the fruit contains; the amount of acidity in the fruit; and how much water the fruit naturally contains. Depending on the acidity and sugar levels, you will need 1 lb. 10 oz.–2 ¼ lb. (750 g–1 kg) sugar for every 2 ¼ lb. (1 kg) fruit.

WHAT IS PECTIN?

Pectin occurs naturally in fruit and is one of the factors in making jams set. It is concentrated in the skin, core, and seeds, but pectin levels vary widely from one type of fruit to another, and according to how ripe the fruit is. Fruit that is over-ripe does not contain sufficient pectin, so it is important to select fruit with the right degree of ripeness to ensure jellies and jams set well. Fruit that is slightly under-ripe contains less pectin but more acid, which helps a jam set, but the acidity level must not be more than ⅙ of the weight of the fruit. To compensate for the lack of natural pectin in some fruits, it is sufficient to add just one fruit that is rich in pectin—such as an apple or pear—to a recipe. Or, you can add commercially-made pectin in powdered form.

ADDING PECTIN

The following recipes use commercial pectin NH, which is available online or from specialist food stores. It ensures a firmer set than ordinary powdered pectin, which is more readily available. Before adding pectin, it should be mixed with some of the sugar in the recipe to ensure it disperses evenly. Sugar to which pectin has already been added (known as jam sugar) can also be used with low pectin fruit but not with fruits that have a naturally high pectin content already, as the finished jam would be too firmly set and have an unpleasant taste. Jam sugar can be bought online.

ADDING LEMON JUICE: NOT JUST FOR ITS FLAVOR

By modifying the pH of a jam mixture, lemon juice helps the pectin work. 2 tablespoons of lemon juice is sufficient for 2 ¼ lb. (1 kg) of fruit.

CAN JELLIES BE MADE FROM ALL TYPES OF FRUIT?

Jellies can only be made from fruits with a high pectin content, such as red currants, apples, black currants, blackberries, and quinces.

PREPARING THE JARS CORRECTLY

Jars need to be sterilized before they can be used. Select jars in perfect condition without any chips or cracks and wash them well. Put the jars and their lids in a pan of boiling water and keep them immersed in the hot water for 20 minutes, separating the jars with clean dishcloths so they do not knock together. Or, if you prefer, stand the jars on a baking sheet and heat in a 300°F (150°C/Gas mark 2) oven for 20 minutes.

Pour the hot jam into the jars (which should be kept warm after sterilization or they could crack). Fill the jars to within 1 in. (2 cm) of the rim. Screw the lids on tightly and turn the jars upside down so the jam is automatically pasteurized. When cold, turn the jars the right way up. Jams prepared in this way can be kept for up to 1 year.

FLAVOR PAIRINGS

There are many ways to flavor jams, such as by adding spices, dried flowers, herbs, or other aromatics according to personal taste (see flavor pairing table pp. 518–19).

FRUITS	LEVEL OF PECTIN CONTENT	FRUITS	LEVEL OF PECTIN CONTENT	FRUITS	LEVEL OF PECTIN CONTENT
Apple	High	Guava	High	Pineapple	Low
Apricot	Medium	Kiwi	Low	Plum	High
Black currant	High	Lemon	High	Quince	High
Blueberry	Medium	Nectarine	Low	Raspberry	Medium
Cherry	Low	Orange	High	Red currant	High
Grape	Low	Peach	Low	Rhubarb	Low
Grapefruit	High	Pear	Low	Strawberry	Low

FLAVOR PAIRING TABLE

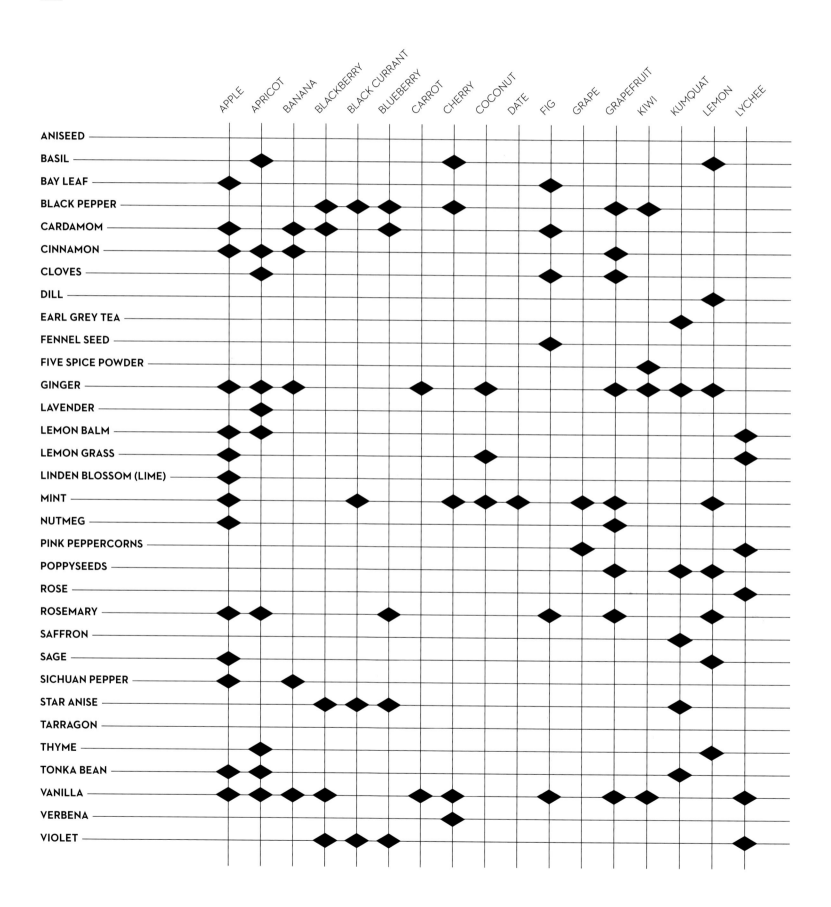

	APPLE	APRICOT	BANANA	BLACKBERRY	BLACK CURRANT	BLUEBERRY	CARROT	CHERRY	COCONUT	DATE	FIG	GRAPE	GRAPEFRUIT	KIWI	KUMQUAT	LEMON	LYCHEE
ANISEED																	
BASIL		◆						◆								◆	
BAY LEAF	◆										◆						
BLACK PEPPER				◆	◆	◆		◆					◆	◆			
CARDAMOM	◆		◆	◆		◆					◆						
CINNAMON	◆	◆	◆										◆				
CLOVES		◆									◆		◆				
DILL																◆	
EARL GREY TEA															◆		
FENNEL SEED											◆						
FIVE SPICE POWDER													◆				
GINGER	◆	◆	◆				◆		◆				◆	◆	◆	◆	
LAVENDER		◆															
LEMON BALM	◆	◆															◆
LEMON GRASS	◆								◆							◆	
LINDEN BLOSSOM (LIME)	◆																
MINT	◆			◆				◆	◆	◆		◆	◆		◆		
NUTMEG	◆												◆				
PINK PEPPERCORNS												◆					◆
POPPYSEEDS													◆		◆	◆	
ROSE																	◆
ROSEMARY	◆	◆				◆					◆		◆				
SAFFRON															◆		
SAGE	◆														◆		
SICHUAN PEPPER	◆		◆														
STAR ANISE				◆	◆	◆									◆		
TARRAGON																	
THYME		◆													◆		
TONKA BEAN	◆	◆													◆		
VANILLA	◆	◆	◆	◆			◆	◆			◆	◆	◆	◆		◆	
VERBENA								◆									
VIOLET				◆	◆	◆											◆

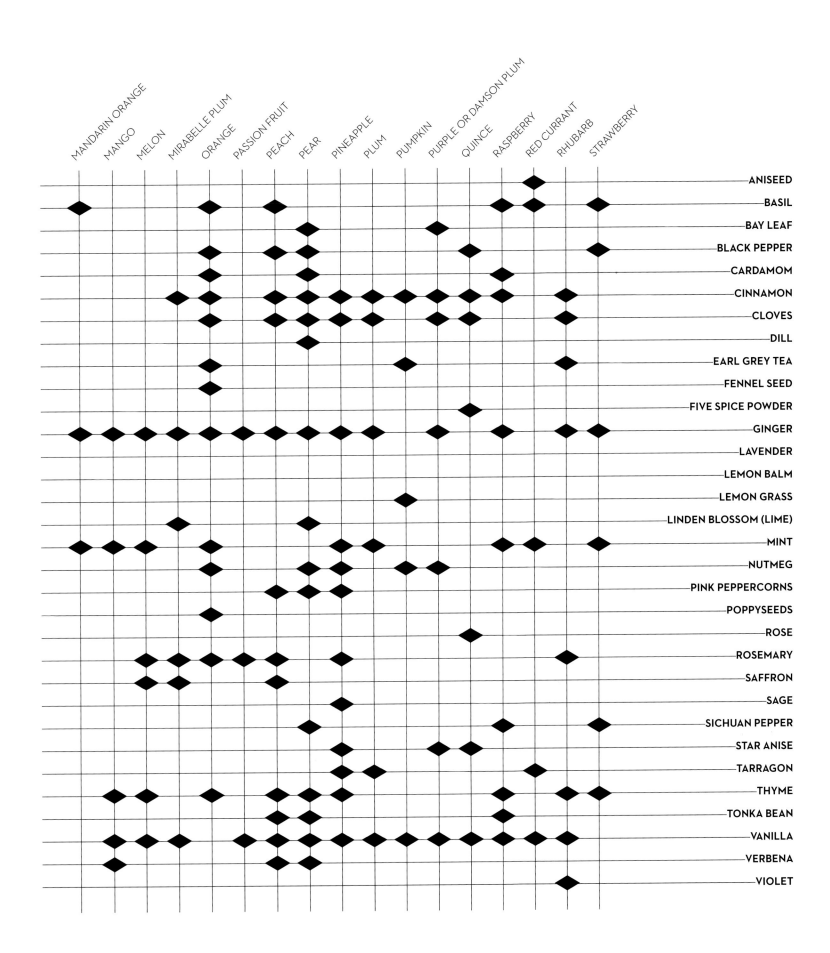

Sugar Cooking

Ingredients

5 ¼ cups (2 ¼ lb./1 kg) sugar

Scant ⅓ cup (3.5 oz./100 g) glucose syrup

1 cup plus scant ½ cup (350 ml) water

Equipment

Candy thermometer

1 • Soft-ball

Boil the syrup to 239°F (115°C). It will form a small, soft ball that can be flattened when pressed.

CHEFS' NOTES

• Before bringing the syrup to a boil, the sugar must be dissolved completely. Once it has dissolved, never stir the syrup as this could cause crystals to form.

• Have a bowl of very cold water close by. When the syrup reaches the required temperature, take the saucepan off the heat to prevent further cooking. Drop a teaspoonful of the syrup into the water where it will solidify and cool sufficiently for you to handle it.

• Always take great care when cooking sugar as boiling syrup can cause very serious burns.

2 • Hard-ball
Boil the syrup to 248°F–250°F (120°C–121°C). It will form a firm ball that remains rigid when pressed.

3 • Soft-crack
Boil the syrup to 266°F–275°F (130°C–135°C). It will be impossible to form the solidified syrup into a ball, but it will remain malleable.

4 • Hard-crack
Boil the syrup to 284°F–293°F (140°C–145°C). The solidified syrup will no longer be malleable and will crack.

5 • At temperatures above 320°F (160°C) the syrup becomes a caramel.

Chocolate Hazelnut Spread

Pâte à Tartiner

Makes 4 × 1-cup (250-ml) jars

Active time
15 minutes

Cooking time
5 minutes

Storage
Up to 2 weeks in the refrigerator

Equipment
4 × 1-cup (250-ml) jars
Stick blender

Ingredients
1 cup plus scant ½ cup (350 ml) whipping cream, 35% butterfat
2 ½ tbsp (1.75 oz./50 g) honey
5.25 oz. (150 g) bittersweet chocolate, 50% cacao
12.5 oz. (350 g) duja paste
(see technique p. 547)

1• In a saucepan, bring the cream and honey to a boil.

3• Pour the hot cream over the chocolate and duja paste.

4• Process with the stick blender until you have a smooth and glossy ganache.

2 • Chop the chocolate into small pieces and place in a mixing bowl with the duja paste.

5 • Pour the spread into the jars and allow it to cool completely before closing with tight-fitting lids.

Salted Butter Caramel Spread

Pâte à Tartiner Caramel Beurre Salé

Makes 4 × 1-cup (250-ml) jars

Active time
30 minutes

Cooking time
15 minutes

Storage
Up to 2 weeks in the refrigerator

Equipment
4 × 1-cup (250-ml) jars
Candy thermometer
Stick blender

Ingredients
Scant ⅓ cup (3.5 oz./100 g)
glucose syrup
or light corn syrup

2 ½ cups (1 lb. 2 oz./500 g)
sugar

1 cup (250 ml) whipping cream,
35 % butterfat

3 ½ sticks (14 oz./400 g) butter,
softened

¼ teaspoon (1 g) fleur de sel
(or other sea salt flakes)

1• Warm the glucose syrup, gradually adding the sugar. When the sugar has dissolved, bring to a boil and cook until you have a dark brown caramel.

3• Cool the mixture to 104°F (40°C), transfer it to a mixing bowl and stir in the butter and fleur de sel.

4• Using the stick blender, process until creamy and smooth.

2 • Bring the cream to a boil in another pan. Gradually stir it into the caramel to prevent it cooking further, taking great care as the mixture could spit or splash and burn your hand.

5 • Pour into the jars and cool completely before closing the jars and refrigerating.

Nougat

Makes 32

Active time
30 minutes

Cooking time
15 minutes

Drying time
24 hours

Storage
Up to 2 months, well covered
in plastic wrap, in an airtight
container

Equipment
Silicone baking mat
Stand mixer
Candy thermometer
2 × 5 ½-in. (16-cm) square
confectionery frames, 4 cm high
Long serrated knife

Ingredients
2 cups plus scant 1 cup
(14 oz./400 g) almonds, skins on
½ cup plus 2 tsp (135 ml) water
2 cups (14 oz./400 g) sugar
Generous ½ cup (7 oz./200 g)
glucose syrup
1 cup plus scant ½ cup
(1 lb. 2 oz./500 g) honey
⅓ cup (2.5 oz./70 g) egg white
(about 2 ½ whites)
1 cup (4.5 oz./130 g) shelled,
raw pistachios
4 sheets edible rice paper
(wafer paper), cut to the size
of the confectionery frames

1 • Line a baking sheet with the silicone mat, spread the almonds
out on it, and roast in a 300°F (150°C/Gas mark 2) oven for
15 minutes. Don't let the almonds cool completely as they need to
be warm when added to the nougat mixture.

CHEFS' NOTES

• The egg whites must not be whisked too firmly
before the syrup is added.

• The texture of the nougat can vary depending on the type
of honey used: lavender honey is best.

• Greasing the knife with a little cacao butter
makes it easier to cut the nougat.

• It is difficult to make reduced quantities of this recipe
due to the small number of egg whites used.

• If the syrup is boiled to a higher temperature,
the nougat will be harder and more brittle.

4 • Gradually whisk in the sugar and glucose syrup mixture.

2 • In a medium saucepan, heat the water with the sugar and the glucose syrup until the sugar dissolves. Boil to 293°F (145°C).

3 • As honey expands when it boils, heat it in a large pan over medium heat. Meanwhile, whisk the egg whites in the stand mixer until frothy. When the honey reaches 265°F (130°C), slowly pour it over the egg whites, whisking continuously.

5 • Continue whisking for about 5 minutes, or until the mixture has cooled to 160°F (70°C).

6 • If you can roll a small amount of the mixture into a ball between your fingers, it is the correct consistency. ➔

Nougat (continued)

7 • Replace the whisk with the paddle beater and beat the mixture until it has cooled to 140°F (60°C). Add the still-warm almonds and the pistachios but do not overmix as the nuts could crumble.

8 • Lay the frames on the silicone mat and place a sheet of rice paper in each (see Chefs' Notes). Pour in the mixture and press another sheet of rice paper on top.

10 • Neaten the edges of the rice paper by trimming away any overlap.

11 • Cool completely in a dry atmosphere. After 24 hours, unmold by sliding the blade of a knife between the nougat and the sides of the frames.

CHEFS' NOTES

To make unmolding easier, brush the inside of the confectionery frames with oil before pouring in the nougat.

9 • Place a sheet of parchment paper over the two frames and flatten the surface of the nougat with a rolling pin.

12 • Using the serrated knife, cut the nougat into ½-in. (1-cm) thick bars.

13 • Wrap the nougat in clear candy wrap and store in a cool, dry place.

Fruit Jellies

Pâtes de Fruits

Makes about 50

Preparation time
1 hour

Cooking time
30 minutes

Drying time
24 hours

Storage
Up to 2 weeks, well covered in plastic wrap or clear candy wrap

Equipment
Copper pan
6-in. (16-cm) square stainless steel confectionery frame, ¾ in. (2 cm) high, sides brushed with oil, and placed on a silicone baking mat

Candy thermometer

Ingredients
1 lb. 2 oz. (500 g) raspberry purée
½ cup (6 oz./175 g) glucose syrup
½ cup (3.5 oz./100 g) superfine sugar
0.35 oz. (10 g) yellow pectin
2 ½ cups (1 lb. 2 oz./500 g) granulated sugar, plus extra for coating the jellies
0.07 oz. (2 g) tartaric acid dissolved in ½ tsp (2 ml) hot water or ¾ tsp (4 ml) lemon juice

Uses
Individual candies, plain or coated in chocolate

1• Whisk the raspberry purée and glucose syrup together in a copper pan. Mix the superfine sugar with the pectin and whisk in. Place over medium heat until the sugar dissolves, and then cook to 104°F (40°C).

4• Immediately pour into the confectionery frame and allow to cool and set.

5• Unmold and cut into 1-in. (3-cm) squares.

CHEFS' NOTES

For firmer or softer jellies, it is necessary to experiment with the cooking temperatures.
The lower the temperature, the softer the jellies will be. At a higher temperature,
they will be firmer and can be stored for longer.

2 • Bring to a boil and cook for 2–3 minutes. Add the granulated sugar in two or three stages, keeping the mixture at a boil, and cook to 221°F–223°F (105°C–106°C), stirring constantly so it does not burn.

3 • Remove from the heat and whisk in the dissolved tartaric acid or lemon juice.

6 • Roll the jellies in sugar until coated. Before wrapping them, leave them in a cool, well-ventilated place for 24 hours so the sugar forms a crust and does not become damp.

Salted Butter Caramels

Caramels au Beurre Salé

Makes 40

Active time
30 minutes

Cooking time
10 minutes

Resting time
2 hours

Storage
Up to 2 weeks in an airtight container

Equipment
Candy thermometer
2 confectionery frames measuring 6 ¼ in. × 4 ¾ in. (16 cm × 12 cm), ¼ in. (0.5 cm) high, sides brushed with oil

Silicone baking mat

Ingredients
1 ¼ cups (9 oz./250 g) sugar
2 ½ tbsp (2 oz./50 g) glucose syrup
½ cup (125 ml) whipping cream, 35% butterfat
1 stick plus 3 tbsp (5.5 oz./160 g) butter, diced, at room temperature
Scant ½ tsp (0.1 oz./2.5 g) fleur de sel (or other sea salt flakes)

1 • Heat the sugar and glucose syrup in a saucepan without adding any water and, when the sugar has dissolved, boil until caramelized, to 347°F–356°F maximum (175°C–180°C). Meanwhile, bring the cream to a boil.

3 • Remove from the heat and gradually add the butter, stirring until smooth. Return to medium heat and continue cooking to 248°F (120°C).

4 • Stir in the salt. Place the confectionery frames on the silicone baking mat and pour in the mixture.

2 • Gradually pour the hot cream into the caramel to prevent it cooking further, taking great care to avoid spattering. Stir with a spatula to combine the mixtures.

5 • Allow to cool and rest for at least 2 hours before cutting into the shapes of your choice.

Marshmallow

Guimauve

Makes 60

Active time
45 minutes

Cooking time
15 minutes

Setting time
12–24 hours

Storage
Up to 1 week
in an airtight container

Equipment
Candy thermometer
Stand mixer
2 pastry bags fitted
with plain ⅓-in. (10-mm)
and ½-in. (15-mm) tips
2 silicone baking mats

Ingredients
7 ½ sheets (0.5 oz./15 g) gelatin
Scant ½ cup (110 ml) water
1 ¾ cups (11.5 oz./330 g) sugar
1 ½ tbsp (1.25 oz./35 g)
glucose syrup
⅓ cup (2.75 oz./80 g) egg white
(about 2 ½ whites)
1 oz. (30 g) Granny Smith
apple flavoring
(or another of your choice)
Coloring (optional)
⅔ cup (3.5 oz./100 g) cornstarch
¾ cup (3.5 oz./100 g)
confectioners' sugar

Uses
Individual marshmallows,
plain or dipped in couverture
chocolate

1• Soak the gelatin sheets in plenty of cold water for 15 minutes.

4• Continue beating until the mixture reaches the ribbon stage. Beat in the apple flavoring and add food coloring (if using), whisking until the mixture is the desired shade.

Filter the egg whites through a fine-mesh strainer before whisking.

2 • While the gelatin soaks, heat the water, sugar, and glucose syrup in a saucepan and, when the sugar dissolves, boil to 257°F (125°C).

3 • Meanwhile, whisk the egg whites in the stand mixer until frothy. Add the hot sugar syrup in a thin stream, whisking constantly. Squeeze excess water from the gelatin and put in the still-hot saucepan to melt, before whisking into the meringue mixture.

5 • Spoon the meringue into the pastry bags and pipe long ropes onto one of the baking mats, using the smaller tip, and shells onto the other mat, using the larger tip.

6 • The mixture must now be left undisturbed to jellify for 12–24 hours at room temperature (63°F/17°C), to maximize the setting properties of the gelatin. ➔

Marshmallow (continued)

7 • Very carefully peel the marshmallows off the silicone mats.
Lightly oil a knife and cut the long ropes into shorter lengths.
Shape them as you wish, for example by tying into knots.

8 • Mix the cornstarch and confectioners' sugar together and use
to coat the marshmallows, removing any excess by placing the
marshmallows, a few at a time, in a sieve and shaking it gently.

Chocolate-Coated Caramelized Almonds and Hazelnuts

Amandes et Noisettes Caramélisées au Chocolat

Makes 2 ¼ lb. (1 kg)

Active time
30 minutes

Cooking time
15 minutes

Storage
Up to 3 weeks
in an airtight container

Equipment
Copper pan
Candy thermometer
Drum sifter

Ingredients
1 heaping cup (5.25 oz./150 g) blanched almonds

1 heaping cup (5.25 oz./150 g) skinned hazelnuts

1 cup (7 oz./200 g) granulated sugar

Scant ⅓ cup (70 ml) water

2 tsp (0.35 oz./10 g) butter

3.5 oz. (100 g) milk couverture chocolate

14 oz. (400 g) bittersweet couverture chocolate, 58% cacao

7 tbsp (1.75 oz./50 g) unsweetened cocoa powder

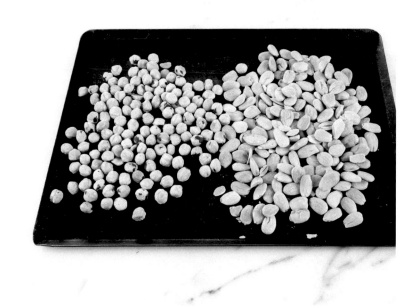

1· Spread the nuts over a baking sheet and roast them in a 300°F (150°C/Gas mark 2) oven for about 15 minutes, until lightly browned.

CHEFS' NOTES

• It is necessary to partially caramelize the nuts to prevent them absorbing moisture.

• Add the tempered chocolate gradually, a small amount at a time, so the hazelnuts and almonds keep their natural shape.

• Do not wait for the last coating of chocolate to set completely before adding the first half of the cocoa powder. However, after adding the rest of the cocoa, leave until the chocolate is firmly set.

2· Add the sugar to the water in the copper pan, heat until the sugar melts, and then boil to 243°F (117°C): the firm-ball stage. Add the nuts and stir until the sugar crystallizes. ⊕

Chocolate-Coated Caramelized Almonds and Hazelnuts (continued)

3 • Return the pan to medium heat to partially caramelize the nuts and then stir in the butter, mixing well.

4 • Tip them onto a work surface and, when cool enough to handle, separate into individual nuts. When they are cold, put the nuts in a large bowl.

6 • Temper the bittersweet chocolate (see techniques pp. 570 and 572) and coat the nuts with it twice in the same way, stirring constantly and letting the chocolate set for 2 minutes between each coating.

7 • Add half the cocoa powder and mix until the nuts are coated. Leave for 2 minutes before adding the rest.

5 • Temper the milk chocolate (see techniques pp. 570 and 572). Pour the chocolate, a little at a time, over the nuts, mixing well with a spatula so each nut is coated. Leave for about 2 minutes to set.

8 • Allow to set completely before transferring the nuts to the drum sifter and shaking gently to remove excess cocoa powder. Store in sealed confectionery bags, gift boxes, or an airtight container.

Layered Jelly and Marshmallow Candies

Bonbons Gélifiés

Makes about 80

Active time
30 minutes

Cooking time
10 minutes

Setting time
2–3 days

Storage
Up to 4 days
in an airtight container

Equipment
Candy thermometer
Stand mixer
Funnel with a piston
(or pastry bag)
Disposable pastry bag
without a tip
4 polycarbonate or
thermoformed chocolate molds

Ingredients
Candies
0.25 oz. (7 g) yellow pectin
1 ½ cups (10.5 oz./300 g)
sugar, divided
⅔ cup (150 ml) water
9 oz. (250 g) strained
passion fruit pulp
Scant ⅓ cup (3.5 oz./100 g)
glucose syrup
0.2 oz. (5 g) citric acid solution:
0.1 oz. (2.5 g) citric acid dissolved
in ½ tsp (2.5 ml) hot water

Marshmallow layer
2 tbsp plus 2 tsp (40 ml) water
⅔ cup (4.5 oz./125 g) sugar
3.5 oz. (100 g) invert sugar,
divided
5 sheets (0.35 oz./10 g) gelatin
0.05 oz. (1 g) citric acid solution:
0.05 oz. (0.5 g) citric acid
dissolved in ⅛ tsp (0.5 ml) hot
water, or ¼ tsp (1 ml) lemon juice
2 tsp (10 ml) orange flower water

Coating
⅓ cup (1.75 oz./50 g) cornstarch
⅓ cup (1.75 oz./50 g)
confectioners' sugar
½ cup (3.5 oz./100 g) granulated
(or superfine) sugar

1• **Making the candies:** Mix the pectin with ½ cup (3.5 oz./100 g) of the sugar. Heat the water, fruit pulp, and glucose syrup in a saucepan to 104°F (40°C). Whisk in the pectin and sugar and bring to a boil.

4• Making the marshmallow layer: Heat the water, sugar, and 1.5 oz. (40 g) of the invert sugar in a saucepan to 230°F (110°C). Soak the gelatin in cold water until softened, squeeze out excess water, and melt the sheets for several seconds in a microwave oven.

2 • Add the rest of the sugar in two equal quantities and, when the sugar has dissolved, heat to 225°F (107°C).

3 • Stir in the citric acid solution. If you are making a marshmallow layer, use the funnel with a piston (or a pastry bag) to fill the molds by two-thirds. Otherwise, fill the molds completely. Allow to set at room temperature for 1–2 days.

5 • Place the remaining invert sugar in the bowl of the stand mixer fitted with a whisk and pour the hot mixture over it. Add the melted gelatin, citric acid solution (or lemon juice), and orange flower water.

6 • Whisk at high speed until the mixture cools to 68°F (20°C). Spoon the mixture into the pastry bag and snip off the tip of the bag to make a small hole, 1/16–1/8 in. (2–3 mm) in diameter. ⊕

Layered Jelly and Marshmallow Candies (continued)

7 • Fill the molds to the top with the marshmallow mixture. Allow to cool and set at room temperature for 24 hours.

8 • Before unmolding, mix the cornstarch and confectioners' sugar together and sift over the top.

CHEFS' NOTES

• You can try other fruit pulps without changing the rest of the recipe.

• These jelly candies are good on their own.
Pour the mixture into a confectioners' frame, leave it to set,
and then cut into small squares or bars.

• A pinch of citric acid crystals can be mixed
with the final sugar coating if you want the candies to have a sharper flavor,
one that is similar to the store-bought candies we all know and love.

9 • Unmold carefully and finish by rolling the candies in the granulated or superfine sugar.

Pink Candy-Coated Almonds

Pralines Roses

Makes about 1 ¼ lb. (600 g) candied almonds

Active time
25 minutes

Cooking time
10–15 minutes

Storage
Up to 2 weeks
in an airtight container

Equipment
Copper pan
Candy thermometer
Drum sifter

Ingredients
1 ½ cups (7 oz./200 g) almonds, skins on
2 cups (14 oz./400 g) sugar
½ cup plus 1 tbsp (160 ml) water
½ vanilla bean, slit lengthwise and seeds scraped out
Red coloring

1• Sort through the almonds and rinse them under running water to remove any dust. Spread them out on a nonstick baking sheet and roast in a 300°F (150°C/Gas mark 2) oven for 15 minutes. Allow to cool and then tip the almonds into the copper pan.

2• Put the sugar, water, and vanilla seeds in a saucepan and, when the sugar has dissolved, bring to a boil. Boil for 1 minute, keeping the sides of the pan clean by brushing with a damp brush. Skim off any foam from the surface.

3• Set aside a scant 1 cup (200 ml) of the syrup in a mixing bowl and cook the remaining 1 cup (250 ml) of syrup in the saucepan to 240°F (115° C). ⊕

CHEFS' NOTES

• For a thinner caramel coating, use equal quantities of sugar and water. For a thicker coating, use twice the weight of sugar as water.

• For a stronger caramel taste, cook for a little longer once the nuts are coated.

• Other types of nuts can be used, or you can replace the coloring with flavorings such as orange flower water, spices, etc.

4 • Pour the syrup in the saucepan onto the almonds and, using a spatula, stir until the sugar crystallizes.

5 • Stir enough red food coloring into the syrup in the mixing bowl until tinted the desired shade.

6 • Place the pan of almonds over medium heat and stir until pale-colored. Stirring constantly, add small amounts of the red syrup, continuing until the almonds are coated to the thickness you desire.

7 • Tip the almonds onto a sheet of parchment paper and allow to cool to room temperature. Shake them gently in the drum sifter to remove the excess crystallized sugar.

Duja Paste

Makes 1 lb. 2 oz. (500 g)

Active time
15 minutes

Cooking time
15 minutes

Storage
Up to 2 days in the refrigerator, tightly covered in plastic wrap

Equipment
Food processor

Ingredients
9 oz. (250 g) skinned hazelnuts
Scant 2 cups (9 oz./250 g) cornstarch-free confectioners' sugar

CHEFS' NOTES

To make a gianduja filling for chocolates, simply stir in melted milk couverture chocolate, equal in weight to 30% of the combined weight of the nuts and sugar.

1• Spread the hazelnuts out on a nonstick baking sheet and roast them in a 300°F (150°C/Gas mark 2) oven for 15 minutes. Transfer to a mixing bowl and allow to cool.

2• Add the sugar to the nuts and mix well.

3• Process the mixture to a smooth paste in the food processor.

Praline Paste, Dry Caramel Method

Makes 1 lb. 2 oz. (500 g)

Active time
30 minutes

Cooking time
15 minutes

Storage
Up to 2 weeks,
in an airtight container

Equipment
Nonstick baking sheet
or silicone baking mat

Food processor

Ingredients
4.5 oz. (125 g) skinned hazelnuts
4.5 oz. (125 g) blanched almonds
1 ⅓ cups (9 oz./250 g) sugar

1 • Spread the nuts out on a nonstick baking sheet and roast them until well browned in a 300°F (150°C/Gas mark 2) oven for about 15 minutes. Allow to cool.

CHEFS' NOTES

Although the nuts and caramel should be cooked until brown,
take care not to let either darken too much
or the paste will have an unpleasant bitter flavor.

4 • Break the nut brittle roughly into pieces and place in a food processor.

2 • Heat the sugar in a heavy saucepan, without adding any water, until it melts and cooks to a rich brown caramel.
Add the roasted nuts, mixing well with a spatula until the nuts are completely coated.

3 • Return the caramelized nuts to the nonstick baking sheet (or a silicone baking mat) and allow to cool until the caramel becomes hard.

5 • Process to a smooth paste.

Praline Paste, Liquid Caramel Method

Makes 1 lb. 2 oz. (500 g)

Active time
40 minutes

Cooking time
15 minutes

Storage
Up to 2 weeks, well covered in plastic wrap, in an airtight container

Equipment
Copper pan
Candy thermometer
Nonstick baking sheet or silicone baking mat
Food processor

Ingredients
1 ⅓ cups (9 oz./250 g) sugar
Scant ½ cup (100 ml) water
4.5 oz. (125 g) blanched almonds, unroasted
4.5 oz. (125 g) skinned hazelnuts, unroasted

1 • Add the sugar to the water in the copper pan, heat until the sugar has dissolved, and cook to 243°F (117°C): the firm-ball stage.

CHEFS' NOTES

• Take care not to roast the nuts or cook the caramel for too long, as if they are allowed to darken too much the praline will have an unpleasant bitter flavor.

• For extra flavor, add ½ vanilla bean to the cooked sugar with the nuts and leave it in when you process the praline to a paste.

• You can also add the finely grated zest of a lemon just before processing.

4 • To check the nuts are sufficiently roasted, carefully lift one out and cut it in half. When the mixture is ready, transfer it to a nonstick baking sheet (or silicone baking mat).

2 • Add the nuts and stir well with a spatula until the sugar becomes opaque and starts to crystallize.

3 • The sugar crystals will stick to the nuts, so continue cooking and stirring until the sugar caramelizes and, at the same time, the nuts become roasted.

5 • When cool, break the caramelized nuts roughly into large chunks and place in a food processor.

6 • Process to a smooth paste.

Raspberry Jam

Confiture de Framboises

Makes 3 × 1 lb. 2-oz. (500-g) jars

Active time
45 minutes

Cooking time
Varies according to time taken to reach setting point

Storage
Up to 3 months at room temperature and up to 1 year if pasteurized (see p. 517)

Equipment
3 × 1 lb. 2-oz. (500-g) jars, sterilized and warmed

Tin-plated copper or stainless steel preserving pan

Candy thermometer

Skimmer

Ingredients
2 ¼ lb. (1 kg) fresh raspberries

3 cups (1 lb. 5 oz./600 g) granulated sugar

Generous ¼ cup (3.5 oz./100 g) honey

0.25 oz. (6 g) pectin NH (see Chefs' Notes)

½ cup (3.5 oz./100 g) superfine sugar

2 tsp (10 ml) lemon juice

1· Wash and drain the raspberries. Carefully pat them dry. Put the raspberries, granulated sugar, and honey in the preserving pan.

CHEFS' NOTES

• Pectin NH is used in commercial kitchens to ensure a perfect set. It can be bought online or from specialist food stores.

• Make the jam using no more than 2 ¼ lb. (1 kg) of fruit.

• When cooled, you can use this jam in desserts, entremets, and everyday cakes.

3· Regularly skim any foam off the surface and continue to cook until the temperature reaches 220°F (104°C). Stir in the lemon juice.

CHEFS' NOTES

For additional ideas for combinations, see the flavor pairing table p. 518.

2 • Mix well and place over medium heat.
When the temperature reaches about 176°F (80°C),
mix the pectin and superfine sugar together and stir in.

4 • Ladle the hot jam into the warm sterilized jars, close them tightly,
and turn upside down until completely cooled.

Strawberry Jam

Confiture de Fraises

Makes 3 × 1 lb. 2-oz. (500-g) jars

Active time
45 minutes

Cooking time
Varies according to time taken to reach setting point

Storage
Up to 3 months at room temperature and up to 1 year if pasteurized (see p. 517)

Equipment
3 × 1 lb. 2-oz. (500-g) jars, sterilized and warmed

Tin-plated copper or stainless steel preserving pan

Candy thermometer

Skimmer

Ingredients
2 ¼ lb. (1 kg) strawberries
3 cups (1 lb. 5 oz./600 g) granulated sugar
1 ¼ cups (300 ml) water
0.25 oz. (6 g) pectin NH
½ cup (3.5 oz./100 g) superfine sugar
2 tsp (10 ml) lemon juice

CHEFS' NOTES

• Make the jam using no more than 2 ¼ lb. (1 kg) of fruit.

• Mix the superfine sugar with the pectin and add to the other ingredients before bringing to a boil.

1 • Wash and drain the strawberries.
Carefully pat them dry and remove the hulls. Cut the larger strawberries into halves, leaving the others whole.

3 • Mix the pectin with the superfine sugar and stir into the pan. Continue cooking until the jam reaches 220°F (104°C). Stir in the lemon juice.

CHEFS' NOTES

For additional ideas for combinations, see the flavor pairing table p. 518.

2 • Heat the granulated sugar and water in the preserving pan until the sugar dissolves and then cook to 250°F (120°C). Add the strawberries and skim off any foam.

4 • Ladle the hot jam into the warmed jars, close them tightly, and turn upside down until completely cooled.

PINEAPPLE, VANILLA, AND RUM JAM

Confiture d'Ananas à la Vanille et au Rhum

by Christine Ferber

PASTRY CHEF OF THE YEAR, 1998

Makes 6–7 × 8-oz. (220-g) jars

Active time
20 minutes

Chilling time
Overnight

Cooking time
Varies according to time taken to reach setting point

Equipment
Copper or stainless steel jam pan
Jelly jars with lids, sterilized
Skimmer

Ingredients
5 ½ lb. (2.5 kg) pineapple (about 2 ¼ lb./1 kg when peeled and cored)
4 ¾ cups (2 lb./900 g) sugar
1 vanilla bean, split in half
Juice of ½ small lemon
⅔ cup (150 ml) rum

——— DAY 1
Using a sharp knife, cut away the thick skin of the pineapple. Cut lengthwise into quarters and remove the fibrous core. Cut the quarters crosswise into thin slices. Place the pineapple slices, sugar, split vanilla bean, and lemon juice in the jam pan. Bring to a simmer while gently stirring, then pour the contents of the pan into a large bowl. Cover with a sheet of parchment paper, cool, and store in the refrigerator overnight.

——— DAY 2
The next day, pour the contents of the bowl back into the jam pan. Bring to a boil while gently stirring. Continue cooking at a rolling boil over high heat for about 10 minutes, stirring constantly and carefully skimming off any foam that forms on the surface. Add the rum. Bring back to a boil and cook for another 5 minutes, stirring gently. To check if the jam has reached setting point, drizzle a few drops onto a cold saucer: it should form a soft gel. When ready, remove the vanilla bean and place it in one of the jars as decoration. Take the pan off the heat, immediately fill the jars with the hot jam, and screw the lids on tightly.

CHEFS' NOTES

For a zestier jam, add a dash of ginger, pepper, and gingerbread spices—it's great with broiled chicken. The alcohol in this recipe helps improve the keeping qualities of the jam.

Orange Marmalade

Confiture d'Oranges

Makes 3 × 14-oz. (400-g) jars

Active time
45 minutes

Cooking time
Varies according to time taken
to reach setting point

Storage
Up to 3 months at room
temperature and up to 1 year if
pasteurized (see p. 517)

Equipment
3 × 14-oz (400-g) jars,
sterilized and warmed
Tin-plated copper or stainless
steel preserving pan
Candy thermometer
Skimmer

Ingredients
1 lb. 10 oz. (750 g) juicing
oranges, such as Valencia
1 ½ cups (10.5 oz./300 g)
granulated sugar
⅓ cup (90 ml) water
0.3 oz. (8 g) pectin NH
½ cup (3.5 oz./100 g)
superfine sugar
⅓ cup (4.25 oz./120 g)
multifloral honey
2 tsp (10 ml) lemon juice

CHEFS' NOTES

• Make the marmalade using
no more than 1 lb. 10 oz. (750 g) of fruit.

• To reduce the bitterness of the oranges,
blanch them whole two or three times, cooling them each time
in a bowl of ice water.

1 • Wash and drain the oranges.
   Wipe them so they are completely dry. Cut off the tops
   and bottoms and discard. Chop the rest of the fruit,
   leaving the peel on.

4 • Finally stir in the lemon juice.

For additional ideas for combinations, see the flavor pairing table p. 518.

2 • Make a syrup in the preserving pan with the granulated sugar and water. When the temperature reaches 300°F (150°C), add the chopped oranges. Skim regularly, removing the seeds that rise to the top.

3 • Keep the pan over the heat. Combine the pectin with the superfine sugar and stir in, followed by the honey. Cook until the marmalade reaches 220°F (104°C).

5 • Ladle the hot marmalade into the warmed jars, close them tightly, and turn upside down until completely cooled.

Apricot Jam

Confiture d'Abricots

Makes 3 × 1 lb. 2-oz. (500-g) jars

Active time
45 minutes

Cooking time
Varies according to time taken to reach setting point

Storage
Up to 3 months at room temperature and up to 1 year if pasteurized (see p. 517)

Equipment
3 × 1 lb. 2-oz. (500-g) jars, sterilized and warmed

Tin-plated copper or stainless steel preserving pan

Candy thermometer

Skimmer

Ingredients
2 ¼ lb. (1 kg) fresh apricots
3 cups (1 lb. 5 oz./600 g) granulated sugar
1 ¼ cups (300 ml) water
Seeds from 1 vanilla bean
0.2 oz. (5 g) pectin NH
½ cup (3.5 oz./100 g) superfine sugar
2 tsp (10 ml) lemon juice

1 • Wash and drain the apricots.
Dry them completely, halve and remove the pits.
Cut the larger halves into quarters and leave the smaller ones as halves.

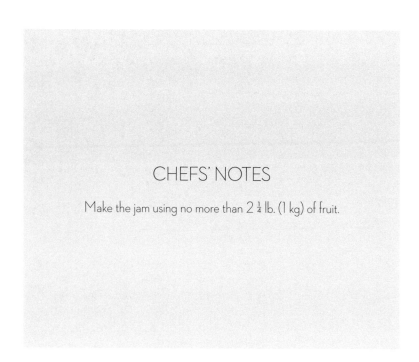

CHEFS' NOTES

Make the jam using no more than 2 ¼ lb. (1 kg) of fruit.

3 • Keeping the pan over the heat, combine the pectin with the superfine sugar and stir in. Continue cooking until the temperature reaches 221°F–223°F (105°C–106°C). Stir in the lemon juice.

For additional ideas for combinations, see the flavor pairing table p. 518.

2 • Mix the granulated sugar and water in the preserving pan, heat to 250°F (120°C) and then add the apricots and vanilla seeds. Skim regularly.

4 • Ladle the hot jam into the jars, close them tightly, and turn upside down until completely cooled.

CARAMEL APPLE JAM

Confiture de Pommes au Caramel

by Christine Ferber

PASTRY CHEF OF THE YEAR, 1998

Makes 8–9 × 8-oz. (220-g) jars

Active time
15 minutes

Macerating time
1 hour

Chilling time
Overnight

Cooking time
Varies according
to time taken
to reach
setting point

Equipment
Copper or stainless
steel jam pan
Skimmer
Jelly jars with lids,
sterilized

Ingredients
2 ¾ lb. (1.2 kg) apples
(about 2 ¼ lb./1 kg when peeled
and cored)
5 ¾ cups (2 ½ lb./1.1 kg) sugar
Juice of ½ small lemon
1 cup (250 ml) hot water

——— DAY 1

Peel the apples, cut them in half, remove the cores, and slice the apples into thin matchsticks. In a large bowl, combine the apple matchsticks, 4 ½ cups (2 lb./850 g) of the sugar, and the lemon juice. Cover with a sheet of parchment paper and set aside to macerate for 1 hour. Meanwhile, make the caramel by slowly melting the remaining sugar in the jam pan, stirring with a wooden spoon until it becomes a medium-colored caramel. As soon as it reaches this stage, pour the hot water over the caramel to slow the cooking. Bring back to a boil, add the apple mixture to the caramel in the pan, and bring to a simmer, stirring gently. Pour this mixture into a large bowl, cover with a sheet of parchment paper, cool, and store in the refrigerator overnight.

——— DAY 2

The next day, pour the contents of the bowl back into the jam pan. Bring to a boil while stirring gently. Continue cooking at a rolling boil over high heat for about 5–10 minutes, stirring constantly and carefully skimming off any foam that forms on the surface. Check if the jam is at setting point by drizzling a few drops onto a cold saucer: it should form a soft gel. When ready, remove from the heat and immediately fill the jars with the hot jam, screwing the lids on tightly.

CHEFS' NOTES

This jam is delicious with cinnamon-flavored whipped cream and walnut cookies.

CHOCOLATE

CHOCOLATE

In order to achieve perfect results, working with chocolate requires precision and a clear understanding of the crystallization process of cocoa butter.

WHAT IS COUVERTURE CHOCOLATE?
—

Couverture chocolate is very rich in cocoa butter (containing 30%–42%), which means it melts more easily and is more fluid than other chocolates. This makes pouring and molding easier and results in a superior texture when the chocolate cools. Tempered couverture chocolate is used in this book to make molded chocolates and chocolate bars, for coating bonbons, and much more.

WHAT IS TEMPERING?
—

Tempering is an important step in working with chocolate as it stabilizes the cocoa butter in the chocolate. This helps ensure the set chocolate has a glossy finish and a firm snap when broken. Untempered chocolate can look dull, or an unattractive cloudy-white; it has a dense, crumbly texture and does not keep well. For making chocolate bonbons or molded chocolates, it is essential to master the tempering technique.

THE KEY STEPS IN TEMPERING CHOCOLATE
—

There are different ways to temper chocolate but they all follow the same basic steps. First, the chocolate must be melted and then cooled to a given temperature when the cocoa butter will begin to crystallize. The chocolate must then be reheated gently until it reaches the temperature at which the cocoa butter becomes fluid again and easy to work with. As it hardens, tempered chocolate will maintain its sheen and snap but, to achieve this, it is crucial to know the correct temperatures for working with different chocolates, bearing in mind the tempering curves are different for bittersweet, milk, and white.

THE RIGHT SIZE
—

Before tempering, begin by chopping the chocolate into equal-sized pieces so it melts evenly. Break bars into small squares, or finely chop them, so they melt quickly. You can also use small, flat disks of couverture chocolate which are sold under a variety of names, including pistoles, fèves, wafers, and pastilles.

A PROPER HOT WATER BATH
—

In order for chocolate to melt correctly, it should be placed in a heatproof bowl and set over a saucepan of barely simmering water. The bottom of the bowl should not touch the water.

STIR, BUT NOT TOO MUCH
—

Although it is important to stir chocolate as it heats up to ensure it melts evenly, it is equally important not to beat in any air, so use a spatula to do this rather than a whisk.

WHAT ABOUT PROPORTIONS?
—

It is difficult to melt and temper small quantities of chocolate, as the total mass is important in regulating the temperature. For this reason, it is best not to reduce the quantities of ingredients given in the recipes in this chapter as the end results could be disappointing. If any tempered chocolate is left over, it can be cooled and kept for future use without harm to its quality or texture.

WORKING TEMPERATURES FOR DIFFERENT CHOCOLATES

TYPE OF CHOCOLATE	MELTING TEMPERATURE	PRE-CRYSTALLIZATION TEMPERATURE	WORKING TEMPERATURE
Bittersweet chocolate	122°F–131°F (50°C–55°C)	82°F–84°F (28°C–29°C)	88°F–90°F (31°C–32°C)
Milk chocolate	113°F–122°F (45°C–50°C)	81°F–82°F (27°C–28°C)	84°F–86°F (29°C–30°C)
White or colored chocolate	113°F (45°C)	79°F–81°F (26°C–27°C)	82°F–84°F (28°C–29°C)

Pay close attention to the melting temperatures, because white and milk chocolates burn easily.

To ensure your chocolate is properly tempered, test it by dipping a knife blade into the chocolate and placing it in the refrigerator for about 3 minutes to see if it sets properly.

If you are not happy with the texture, it is best to re-melt the chocolate and repeat the tempering process.

TEMPERING CURVES

BITTERSWEET CHOCOLATE

122°F–131°F (50°C–55°C) — 82°F–84°F (28°C–29°C) — 88°F–90°F (31°C–32°C)

MILK CHOCOLATE

113°F–122°F (45°C–50°C) — 81°F–82°F (27°C–28°C) — 84°F–86°F (29°C–30°C)

WHITE OR COLORED CHOCOLATE

113°F (45°C) — 79°F–81°F (26°C–27°C) — 82°F–84°F (28°C–29°C)

WHAT ARE THE MAIN TEMPERING METHODS?

In addition to the tabling method (the most widely used by professionals, see p. 572) and the water bath method (see p. 570), the following methods can also be used to temper chocolate:

– **Seeding:** Melt two-thirds of the chocolate you wish to temper to 113°F (45°C). Gradually add in the remaining third in small pieces and stir until completely melted. Once the temperature has dropped to the lower pre-crystallization temperature for the type of chocolate you are using, reheat the chocolate to 90°F (32°C).

– **Adding micronized cocoa butter (Mycryo):** Melt your chocolate until it reaches 95°F (35°C) and add a quantity of Mycryo cocoa butter equal to 1% of the total weight of the chocolate you wish to temper. The chocolate is ready to use once it cools to 90°F (32°C). This method is fast but is not suitable for large quantities of chocolate.

CORRECTLY TEMPERED CHOCOLATE	INADEQUATELY TEMPERED CHOCOLATE
Glossy	Lacks sheen
Crisp, hard texture	Quickly melts when touched
Shrinks slightly as it cools so is easier to unmold	Difficult to unmold
Well-defined flavors	Dull gray or whitish discoloration
Smooth, pleasant mouthfeel	Grainy texture
Keeps well	Does not keep well
Snaps cleanly when broken	Fat bloom occurs quickly with its characteristic white blotches

THE COUVERTURE CHOCOLATE THICKENS WHILE YOU ARE WORKING WITH IT.	
Causes	Considerable cooling (crystallization) of the chocolate.
Solutions	Add a small amount of hot, melted couverture chocolate or place under a heat source, such as a heat gun.

THE FINISHED CHOCOLATES ARE NOT GLOSSY.	
Causes	Inadequately tempered chocolate. Room and/or refrigerator temperature too cold. Molds or acetate sheets not clean.
Solutions	The room temperature should be 66°F–73°F (19°C– 23°C) and the refrigerator 46°F–54°F (8°C–12°C). Molds and acetate sheets must be perfectly clean: wipe with soft, absorbent cotton.

THE CHOCOLATES DO NOT RELEASE CONSISTENTLY FROM THE MOLDS AND BREAK EASILY.	
Causes	Cold couverture chocolate poured into warmer (room temperature) molds.
Solutions	Respect the tempering curves. The molds must be perfectly clean: wipe with cotton balls. The molds should be at room temperature, 72°F (22°C).

THE CHOCOLATES RELEASE FROM THE MOLDS BUT TURN WHITE (DULL FINISH AND POOR CONTRACTION).	
Causes	Cold couverture chocolate poured into a cold mold.
Solutions	Respect the tempering curves and monitor the temperature. The molds should be at room temperature, 72°F (22°C).

THE CHOCOLATES STICK TO THE MOLDS AND HAVE A STREAKED APPEARANCE.	
Causes	Cold couverture chocolate poured into a warm or hot mold.
Solutions	Respect the tempering curves and monitor the temperature. The molds should be at room temperature, 72°F (22°C).

THE CHOCOLATES CRACK AND SPLIT.	
Causes	Chocolate cooled too quickly after molding.
Solutions	Let the chocolate set on a worktop before placing it in the refrigerator at 46°F–54°F (8°C–12°C).

THE CHOCOLATES TURN GRAY OR WHITE (BLOOM).	
Causes	Warm chocolate placed in a refrigerator that is too cold. Too much humidity, resulting in condensation.
Solutions	Respect the tempering curves and monitor the temperature. The refrigerator should be set at 46°F–54°F (8°C–12°C).

THE CHOCOLATES HAVE MARKS ON THE SURFACE.	
Causes	Dirty, inadequately wiped molds that are dull rather than shiny.
Solutions	Remove grease from your molds with cotton balls moistened with 90° alcohol. Dry and polish your molds with fresh cotton balls.

PROPER STORAGE: KEEP YOUR CHOCOLATES FRESH
—

Chocolate should be stored in an airtight container in a cool, dry place away from sunlight. Humidity, heat, and light all adversely affect its storage time and texture. Because it contains cocoa butter, chocolate tends to absorb other strong smells, so it must be kept well wrapped.

Tempering Chocolate, Water Bath Method

Active time
25 minutes

Equipment
Instant-read thermometer

Ingredients
Bittersweet, milk, or white
couverture chocolate

CHEFS' NOTES

• Be sure no water gets into the chocolate,
as even the tiniest drop will make the chocolate seize
and become unworkable.

• When placing the bowl over the pan of hot water,
make sure the bottom of the bowl does not touch the water.

1 • Chop the chocolate and place in a bowl over a saucepan
of barely simmering water. Stir until melted, 122°F (50°C)
for bittersweet chocolate, and 113°F (45°C) for milk and white.

2 • When the chocolate has melted, stand the bowl in a larger bowl
filled with ice cubes and water. Stir to lower the temperature
of the chocolate.

3 • Cool bittersweet chocolate to 82°F–84°F (28°C–29°C), milk
to 81°F–82°F (27°C–28°C), and white to 79°F–81°F (26°C–27°C).
Put the bowl back over the pan and raise the temperature
to 88°F (31°C) for bittersweet, 84°F (29°C) for milk,
and 82°F (28°C) for white.

Tempering Chocolate, Tabling Method

Active time
25 minutes

Equipment
Instant-read thermometer
Marble slab
Angled spatula
Scraper

Ingredients
Bittersweet, milk, or white
couverture chocolate

1 • Chop the chocolate and place in a heatproof bowl over a pan of barely simmering water.
Stir until melted, 122°F (50°C) for bittersweet and 113°F (45°C) for milk and white chocolate.
Once melted, pour two-thirds onto a clean, dry marble slab to cool.

CHEFS' NOTES

• No water must get into the chocolate, as even the tiniest drop will make the chocolate seize and become unworkable.

• When placing the bowl over the pan of hot water, make sure the bottom of the bowl does not touch the water.

2 • Using the angled spatula and scraper, work the chocolate from the outside toward the center.

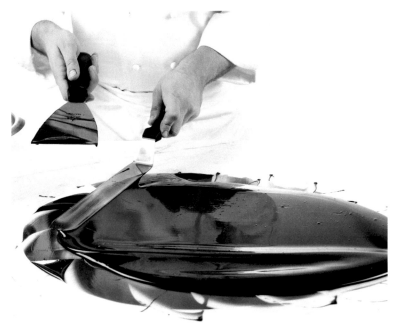

3 • Spread out the chocolate again and repeat the process to cool it down.

4 • When the temperature reaches 82°F–84°F (28°C–29°C) for bittersweet chocolate, 81°F–82°F (27°C–28°C) for milk, and 79°F–81°F (26°C–27°C) for white, it needs to be raised again.

5 • Gradually stir the melted chocolate back into the bowl containing the remaining warm chocolate until the temperature reaches 88°F–90°F (31°C–32°C) for bittersweet, 84°F–86°F (29°C–30°C) for milk, and 82°F–84°F (28°C–29°C) for white.

Chocolate Eggs

Active time
10 minutes

Setting time
20–50 minutes

Storage
Up to 2 months, well wrapped and protected from light, heat, and strong smells

Equipment
Instant-read thermometer
Chocolate half-shell egg molds
Scraper

Ingredients
Tempered bittersweet, milk, or white couverture chocolate (see techniques pp. 570 and 572)

1• Pour the tempered chocolate into the molds to fill them completely. For slightly thicker shells, brush a thin layer of chocolate over the molds first.

CHEFS' NOTES

• Ensure the molds are at room temperature before turning the chocolate shells out.

• Clear plastic molds make it easier to see when the chocolate has pulled away from the sides and is ready to be released.

• Before using the molds, it is important to check their condition, as a scratched or dirty mold will prevent the set chocolate from pulling away properly. Use soft cotton balls and a toothpick to clean them thoroughly.

4• With the molds still upside down, run the scraper over the surface to clean the edge of each half-shell.

2 • Tap the molds on a work surface to burst any air bubbles.

3 • Turn the molds upside down over a sheet of parchment paper to allow excess chocolate to drain out.
For thicker chocolate egg shells, repeat steps 1 to 3.

5 • Keeping the molds inverted, allow the chocolate to set for about 5 minutes. With a scraper or chef's knife, neaten the edges of the chocolate so it is level with the tops of the molds.

6 • Let the chocolate contract, ideally at 65°F (18°C) or on the top shelf of the refrigerator, for 20 minutes. When the chocolate shells are firmly set and have contracted slightly from the sides of the molds, they are ready to be turned out. Carefully turn the molds upside down to do this.

Chocolate Bars

Active time
15 minutes

Cooking time
15 minutes (for the nuts)

Setting time
50 minutes

Storage
Up to 2 months, well wrapped and protected from light, heat, and strong smells

Equipment
Instant-read thermometer
Disposable pastry bag
Chocolate bar mold

Ingredients
Tempered bittersweet, milk, or white couverture chocolate (see techniques pp. 570 and 572)
Nuts (hazelnuts, almonds, etc.)

1• Preheat the oven to 300°F (150°C/Gas mark 3). Spread out the nuts on a baking sheet lined with parchment paper and toast for about 15 minutes. Pour the tempered chocolate into the pastry bag, snip off the tip, and pipe into the mold, filling it to the top.

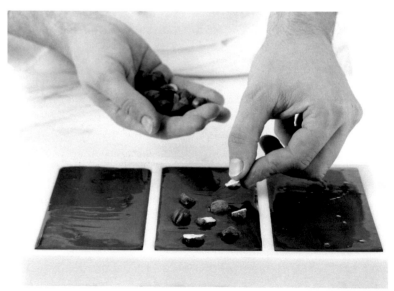

2• Tap the mold against a work surface to burst any air bubbles.

3• Arrange the cooled, toasted nuts evenly over the still liquid chocolate.

4 • Allow the chocolate to set and contract from the edges of the mold. Turn the mold over to release the chocolate bars.

Almond Praline Truffles

Rochers

Makes 40

Active time
45 minutes

Cooking time
45 minutes

Setting time
3 hours

Chilling time
20 minutes

Storage
Up to 1 month
in an airtight container

Equipment
Instant-read thermometer
Dipping fork
or spiral dipping tool

Ingredients
Generous ½ cup (2.75 oz./75 g) chopped almonds

2 ½ tsp (0.35 oz./10 g) superfine sugar

2 oz. (60 g) bittersweet couverture chocolate, 58% cacao

6.25 oz. (180 g) almond praline paste

Coating
5.25 oz. (150 g) bittersweet couverture chocolate, 58% cacao

1• Heat the almonds and sugar in a saucepan over medium heat until the sugar dissolves and caramelizes. Transfer to a sheet of parchment paper to cool.

4• Divide the mixture roughly into 3 parts, shape it into 5.25-oz. (150-g) logs, about 8 in. (20 cm) long, and cut into 0.3–0.35-oz. (8–10-g) slices, about ⅔ in. (1.5 cm) thick. Roll the slices between your hands to shape into balls. Chill for 20 minutes.

5• Temper the coating chocolate (see techniques pp. 570 and 572) and stir in the cooled caramelized almonds.

2 • Melt the chocolate in a bowl over a pan of simmering water to 86°F (30°C) and then stir in the praline paste. Transfer to a baking sheet, cover with plastic wrap, and allow to set in the refrigerator for about 1 hour.

3 • Once set, knead the chocolate mixture until it is smooth and pliable.

6 • Dip the truffles using your hands, or a dipping fork or spiral tool, until fully coated. Allow to set for about 2 hours on a sheet of parchment paper.

Palets Or

Makes about 30

Active time
About 45 minutes

Infusing time
30 minutes

Setting time
2 hours

Storage
Up to 2 weeks
in an airtight container

Equipment
Instant-read thermometer
Pastry bag fitted with
a ½-in. (12-mm) tip
Acetate sheet
Dipping fork
or spiral dipping tool

Ingredients
Ganache
½ cup minus 1 tbsp (100 ml)
whipping cream, 35% butterfat
1 vanilla bean, split lengthwise
and seeds scraped out
1 ½ tsp (0.35 oz./10 g) honey
3 oz. (90 g) bittersweet
couverture chocolate,
58 % cacao, chopped
3.5 oz. (100 g) bittersweet
chocolate, 50% cacao, chopped
Scant 3 tbsp (1.5 oz./40 g)
butter, diced, at room
temperature

Coating
10 ½ oz. (300 g) bittersweet
couverture chocolate,
58% cacao

Decoration
Sheets of edible gold leaf

1 • Heat the cream, vanilla bean and seeds, and honey in a pan over medium heat and bring to a boil. Remove from the heat and infuse for 30 minutes.

4 • Spoon the ganache into the pastry bag and pipe small mounds onto a baking sheet lined with parchment paper.

5 • Lay the acetate sheet on top and press it down lightly using a baking sheet. Allow to cool and set for about 1 hour.

CHEFS' NOTES

Take care when making the ganache as it is fragile and overmixing may cause it to separate.

2 • Melt the couverture and bittersweet chocolate in a bowl over a pan of barely simmering water until the temperature reaches 95°F (35°C). Strain the infused cream onto the melted chocolate and stir to make a smooth ganache.

3 • When the ganache cools to 86°F (30°C), add the butter and stir until smooth (see Chefs' Notes).

6 • Temper the coating chocolate (see techniques pp. 570 and 572). When the ganache has set, dip each disk into the chocolate until evenly coated.

7 • Allow to set on a baking sheet lined with parchment paper for 1 hour. Top each disk with a small piece of edible gold leaf.

Truffles

Truffes

Makes 30

Active time
45 minutes

Infusing time
30 minutes

Setting time
2 hours

Storage
Up to 2 weeks
in an airtight container

Equipment
Instant-read thermometer
Dipping fork

Ingredients
Scant ½ cup (100 ml) heavy
cream, 35% butterfat

½ vanilla bean, split lengthwise
and seeds scraped out

1 ¼ tsp (0.3 oz./8 g) honey

3.5 oz. (100 g) bittersweet
couverture chocolate,
70% cacao, chopped

2 ½ tbsp (1.25 oz./35 g) butter,
diced and softened

⅔ cup (2.75 oz./75 g)
unsweetened cocoa powder

Coating
3.5 oz. (100 g) bittersweet
couverture chocolate,
58% cacao

1 • Heat the cream, vanilla bean, and seeds in a pan over medium
heat. Bring to a boil, remove from the heat, and infuse
for 30 minutes. Add the honey and bring back to a boil.

4 • Cut the set ganache into 1 ¼-in. (3-cm) squares and roll into balls.

5 • Put the cocoa powder on a plate. Temper the couverture
chocolate (see techniques pp. 570 and 572) and, using a dipping fork
or your hands, dip the ganache balls in the chocolate
until evenly coated.

2 • Put the chopped chocolate in a bowl and strain the hot cream over it, stirring gently until you have a smooth ganache.

3 • When the ganache has cooled to 86°F (30°C), stir in the butter. Pour onto a baking sheet lined with parchment paper and allow to set for 1 hour.

6 • As soon as you have dipped them, roll the truffles in the cocoa powder with the aid of a dipping fork, until they are coated. Allow to set for 1 hour and then carefully shake the truffles in a sifter to remove excess cocoa.

Crispy Praline Chocolates

Pralinés Feuilletines

Makes about 30

Active time
1 hour

Cooking time
5–10 minutes

Setting time
1 hour

Storage
Up to 2 weeks
in an airtight container,
at 63°C (17°C) maximum

Equipment
Instant-read thermometer
10-in. (26-cm) square
confectionery frame,
½ in. (1 cm) high

Dipping fork

Ingredients
1 oz. (25 g) cocoa butter
1 oz. (25 g) milk couverture
chocolate
9 oz. (250 g) praline paste
1.75 oz. (50 g) *feuilletine* flakes
(about 2 ¼ cups)

Coating
10.5 oz. (300 g) bittersweet
couverture chocolate,
58% cacao

1• Melt the cocoa butter and milk chocolate in a saucepan
over low heat. Remove from the heat and stir in the praline paste
and *feuilletine* flakes.

4• When the praline has cooled, remove the frame
and cut into pieces the shape and size of your choice.

5• Temper the coating chocolate (see techniques pp. 570 and 572).
Using the dipping fork, dip the pralines until evenly coated,
allowing excess chocolate to drip back into the bowl.

Cut up the praline as soon as it has cooled to ensure the pieces have neat edges.

2 • Stir lightly with a spatula until the mixture cools to 70°F (20°C).

3 • Line a baking sheet with parchment paper and stand the frame on top. Pour the praline mixture into the frame, smoothing it level with a spatula.

6 • Place on a baking sheet lined with parchment paper and mark the tops with the dipping fork. Leave to set for about 1 hour.

Gianduja Rosettes

Makes 30

Active time
45 minutes

Chilling time
1 hour

Setting time
1 hour

Storage
Up to 2 weeks
in the refrigerator,
in an airtight container

Equipment
Instant-read thermometer
Pastry bag fitted with a fluted
½-in. (10-mm) tip
2 food-safe acetate sheets
Pastry bag without a tip

Ingredients
9 oz. (250 g) gianduja chocolate,
diced
30 whole roasted hazelnuts

Chocolate base
5.25 oz. (150 g) bittersweet
couverture chocolate,
58% cacao, tempered
(see techniques pp. 570 and 572)

1 • Melt the gianduja in a bowl set over a saucepan of barely
simmering water until the temperature reaches 113°F (45°C).

4 • Decorate each rosette with a whole hazelnut
and chill for about 1 hour.

5 • Spoon the tempered bittersweet chocolate into the pastry bag
without a tip and pipe out small rounds slightly smaller than
the gianduja rosettes onto the other acetate sheet.

2 • Remove from the heat and let the gianduja cool until it has the consistency of softened butter.

3 • Spoon into the pastry bag with the fluted tip and pipe rosettes about 1 in. (3 cm) in diameter onto one of the acetate sheets.

6 • Place a rosette on each chocolate round and press down gently so the chocolate spreads to the same size as the rosettes. Leave to set for about 1 hour and then peel off the acetate sheet.

DECORATIONS

DECORATIONS

Since we also eat with our eyes, presentation is an integral part of pâtisserie work and finishing touches can make cakes and pastries even more irresistible. Below is a summary of the main ingredients and techniques that are used to decorate entremets, tarts, petits fours, and homemade cakes.

A HISTORIC CONE
A pastry chef from Bordeaux by the name of Lorsa was the first to use a paper cone in 1805 to decorate his cakes.

INGREDIENT OR PREPARATION	USES
Confectioners' sugar	Dusting, icing pithiviers, soufflés
Buttercream	Piped decorations, borders, flowers, and other designs (see p. 202)
Pouring fondant	Icing, decorating using a paper cone (see p. 598)
Marzipan	Covering cakes, making ribbons, modeling flowers, fruits, animals (see p. 601)
Glazing paste (*pâte à glacer*)	Icing
Ganache	Icing, frosting, and decorating
Clear glaze (*nappage*)	Giving entremets, tarts, tartlets, babas, and savarins a glossy finish. Preserving the shine on napoleons and other cakes.
Couverture chocolate	Chocolate or praline fillings, chocolate cigarettes, cones, fans, cut-out shapes, silhouettes, vermicelli, and piped chocolate
Gianduja chocolate	Decorating using a paper cone, molded and cut-out shapes for decoration
Royal icing	Decorating using a paper cone, making flowers. Can be colored.
Candied fruits	Decorations (cherries, angelica, orange peel, pineapple, pear, and citrus fruits)
Nougatine	Molded or cut-out decorations, cones.
Italian meringue	Masking entremets, cakes, and tarts. Piped decorations toasted briefly in the oven until golden (see p. 232)
Choux pastry	Decorative buns piped from a pastry bag and baked, e.g. Gateau Saint-Honoré (see p. 162)
Almonds, hazelnuts, walnuts, and other nuts and seeds	Used whole, caramelized, flaked, slivered, crushed
Pulled sugar	Flowers, leaves, ribbons, baskets, and more
Caramel	Spun caramel, cages, sweets
Opalines	Decorations of different shapes depending on design of the stencil used (see p. 606)

Chocolate Cigarettes

Active time
10 minutes

Storage
Up to 2 weeks
in an airtight container,
at 70°F (20°C) maximum

Equipment
Angled spatula
Small and large triangular
scrapers
Marble slab

Ingredients
Tempered chocolate
(see techniques pp. 570 and 572)

CHEFS' NOTES

When lifting chocolate decorations onto cakes or pastries,
don't use your hands. Either lift and position them with a spatula
or wear thin disposable gloves. Otherwise, you'll mark the chocolate
with your fingers—or even melt the decorations if your hands are warm.

1• Pour the tempered chocolate slowly onto the marble slab
and, using the angled spatula, spread it out in an even layer,
about 1/16–1/8 in. (2-3 mm) thick. Let the chocolate set lightly,
so it is firm but not hard.

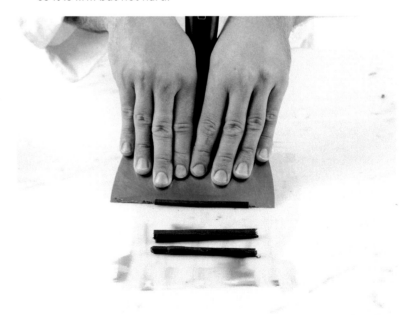

2• Push the small scraper along the edges of the chocolate
to make a neat rectangle.

3• With even pressure, push the large scraper down the length
of the chocolate to shave off long, thin rolls.

Chocolate Fans

Active time
10 minutes

Storage
Up to 2 weeks
in an airtight container,
at 70°F (20°C) maximum

Equipment
Angled spatula
Scraper
Marble slab

Ingredients
Tempered chocolate
(see techniques pp. 570 and 572)

1• Pour the tempered chocolate onto the marble slab and spread evenly using the spatula into a rectangle about 1/16–1/8 in. (2–3 mm) thick. Let the chocolate set lightly, so it is firm but not hard. Run the scraper along the edges to neaten.

2• Press down firmly with your index finger on the corner of the scraper and push it forward steadily so the chocolate is shaved off in a fan shape. Repeat to make more fans.

Chocolate Curls

Active time
15 minutes

Storage
Up to 2 weeks
in an airtight container,
at 70°F (20°C) maximum

Equipment
Angled spatula
Marble slab

Ingredients
Tempered chocolate
(see techniques pp. 570 and 572)

1• Pour the tempered chocolate slowly onto the marble slab.

2 • Spread the chocolate out in an even layer, about 1/16–1/8 in. (2–3 mm) thick, using the angled spatula and let it set lightly so it is firm but not hard.

3 • With the tip of a large, sharp knife, mark equally spaced diagonal lines across the chocolate (to ensure the curls are of roughly equal size).

4 • With the knife at a slight angle, quickly scrape the blade across the chocolate, working from the bottom upward.

5 • You can make curls of different sizes depending on the pressure you exert on the knife and the speed at which you scrape it across the chocolate.

Chocolate Transfer Sheets

Makes 1 sheet

Active time
15 minutes

Storage
Up to 2 weeks
in an airtight container,
at 70°F (20°C) maximum

Equipment
1 chocolate transfer sheet
of your choice, measuring
about 10 × 16 in. (30 × 40 cm)

Angled spatula

Ingredients
3.5 oz. (100 g) tempered
chocolate (see techniques
pp. 570 and 572)

1 · Lay the chocolate transfer sheet on the work surface,
printed side up, and slowly pour the chocolate onto it.

4 · Use a ruler and knife or a cookie cutter to mark the chocolate into
your desired shapes. Leave until the chocolate is completely set.

2 • Using the spatula, spread the chocolate over the sheet in a thin, even layer, about 1⁄16 in. (2–3 mm) thick, until the sheet is completely covered.

3 • Carefully move the chocolate-covered sheet to a clean surface and leave until the chocolate is firm but has not set hard.

5 • Very carefully turn the sheet over and peel it away from the chocolate.

6 • Separate the individual shapes.

Paper Piping Cone

Active time
5 minutes

Equipment
1 rectangular sheet
of parchment paper

Ingredients
Tempered chocolate
(see techniques pp. 570 and 572)

1• Cut the parchment paper diagonally in half to make two right-angled triangles. Set one triangle aside.

4• Fold over the protruding parchment at the top into the cone.

5• Crease the fold firmly so the cone is secure and will not unroll.

CHEFS' NOTES

You can also fill your paper cone with chocolate or caramel spread (pâte à tartiner) **(see techniques p. 522 and 524)** for decorating.

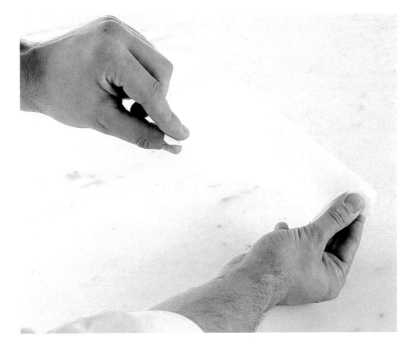

2 • Hold the center of the longest side of the triangle. With your other hand, bring one of the points over to start forming a cone, holding it in place.

3 • Bring up the other point to make a cone with a tightly closed point.

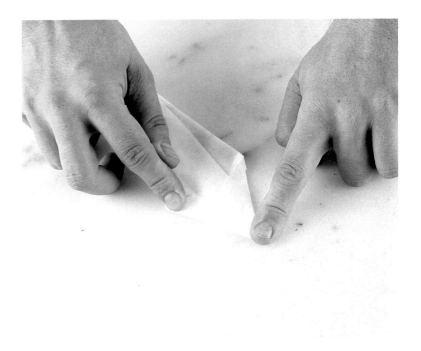

6 • Spoon tempered chocolate into the cone to fill it by about one-third.

7 • Pinch the top edges of the cone together and then fold them over diagonally. ⊙

599

Paper Piping Cone (continued)

8 • Turn the cone over and roll the top down tightly until you reach the chocolate.

9 • The cone is now almost ready to use. Snip off the tip, cutting a hole the size you require—the smaller the hole, the finer your piping will be.

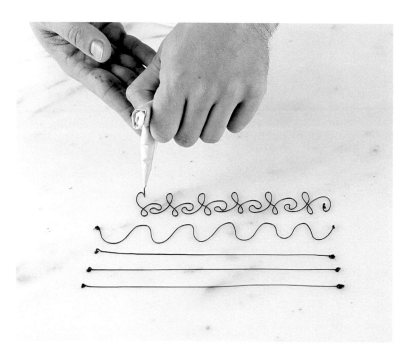

10 • You can now pipe decorations such as lines, waves, freehand patterns, lace borders, or a personal message.

Marzipan Roses

Makes 1 rose, 1 rosebud, and 5 leaves

Active time
15 minutes

Storage
Up to 1 week

Equipment
2 food-grade plastic or acetate sheets

Ingredients
2 oz. (60 g) marzipan

1 • Shape some of the marzipan into a log ¾ in. (2 cm) in diameter, and cut into ¼-in. (5-mm) rounds.

2 • Lay the rounds flat between the plastic or acetate sheets.

3 • Press down with the palm of your hand and then with a finger to flatten the rounds until they are very thin. These are to make the rose petals. ⊕

Marzipan Roses (continued)

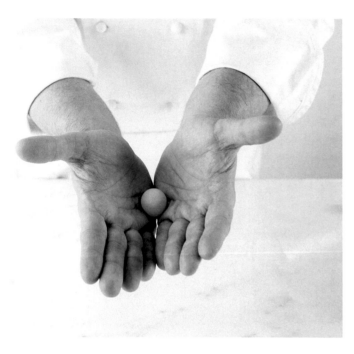

4 • Roll more marzipan into a ball, about ¾ in. (2 cm) in diameter, to make the center of the rose.

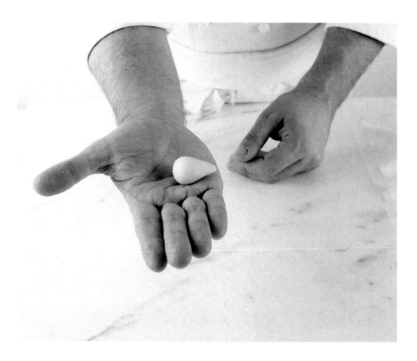

5 • Form the ball into a teardrop shape with your hands.

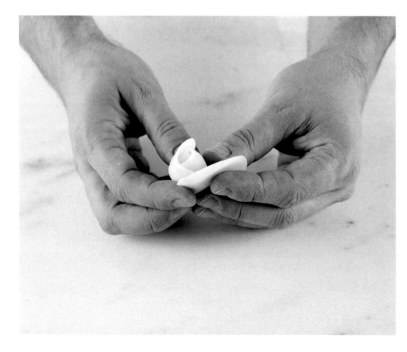

8 • Add a second petal in the same way, starting on the opposite side of the rose center. Add more petals, overlapping them slightly as you work around.

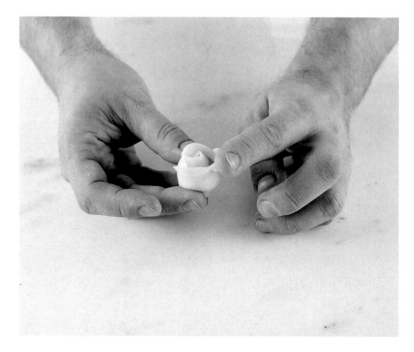

9 • If you wish, curve the tops of the outer petals back a little to make the rose look more realistic.

6 • Press one of the thin rounds of marzipan against the rose center to make the first petal.

7 • Wrap the petal around the center, pressing it gently in place, and closing the petal tightly at the top.

10 • Adjust the position of the petals, taking care not to dislodge them. Press the excess marzipan away at the base to give the rose a good shape.

11 • Stop adding petals once you have a nicely shaped rose the size you require. ⊕

Marzipan Roses (continued)

12 • Trim off the surplus marzipan with a small knife so the rose has a flat base.

13 • Roll small pieces of marzipan into balls about ½ in. (1 cm) in diameter and mold into teardrop shapes. Place between the plastic or acetate sheets.

14 • Press down with the palm of your hand and then your finger to flatten the shapes into thin leaves. Mark veins on the leaves with the tip of a knife.

15 • Carefully lift the leaves off the sheet and press them attractively around the base of the rose.

Opalines

**Makes decorations
for a cake to serve 4–6**

Active time
30 minutes

Cooking time
8–10 minutes

Storage
Up to 3 days
in an airtight container

Equipment
Candy thermometer
Baking sheet lined
with a silicone baking mat
Food processor
Fine-mesh sieve
Chablon stencil mat
of your choice
Spatula

Ingredients
4 oz. (115 g) pouring fondant
3 ½ tbsp. (2.6 oz./75 g)
glucose syrup
1 tsp (5 g) butter

1• Heat the fondant, glucose syrup, and butter in a saucepan
and bring the mixture to a boil. Continue to boil until it reaches
311°F (155°C) and turns golden.

CHEFS' NOTES

• You can color your opalines by adding food coloring
to the fondant mixture in step 1 or by using a flavored fondant,
such as chocolate.

• You can also sprinkle grated citrus zest, poppy seeds,
or sesame seeds over the ground caramel before baking.

• Any leftover ground caramel can be stored
in an airtight container for future use.

4• Lay the stencil on the silicone mat, still on the baking sheet,
and sift the ground caramel onto the mat to fill in the cut-out
design on the stencil.

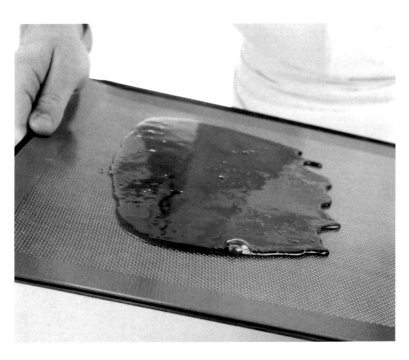

2 • Slowly pour this caramel onto the silicone mat lining the baking sheet and tilt the sheet so the caramel spreads out evenly. Let the caramel cool completely.

3 • Once the caramel has hardened, break it into small pieces and grind the pieces to a fine powder in the food processor. Preheat the oven to 300°F (150°C/Gas mark 2).

5 • Carefully lift off the stencil and place the baking sheet in the oven. Bake until the ground caramel melts (about 8–10 minutes).

6 • Let the *opalines* cool completely, then carefully release them from the mat with the spatula. Store in an airtight container in a dry place until ready to use.

FROZEN DESSERTS

FROZEN DESSERTS

Making ice cream, sorbet, and other frozen desserts at home entails a very different process from professionally made ice creams, which need to meet exacting standards and regulations. But the underlying principles remain the same.

ICE CREAM IS MUCH MORE THAN FROZEN CREAM

To understand recipes for ice creams and sorbets, you need to appreciate the concept of the ratio of dry to wet ingredients. Dry ingredients include everything that is suspended in the water in the ice cream (also called the "ice cream mix"): sugar, fruit purée, chocolate, and milk fat and proteins. Generally speaking, an ice cream mix is approximately 56–70% water (from the milk and cream and that contained in fruit) and 30–44% solids ("dry" ingredients). The ice cream's texture and structure depend on the dry ingredients' makeup.

WHY USE DIFFERENT TYPES OF SUGAR?

Different sugars have different effects on freezing temperature and final texture. Each plays a role in creating the ideal ice cream texture. In addition to regular sugar (sucrose), the most common are:
– **glucose powder:** since it inhibits sucrose crystallization, it makes for smoother ice cream. If too much is used, the ice cream becomes rubbery. It has a lower sweetness value than sucrose;
– **dextrose:** a glucose extract with a higher sweetness value than glucose powder but lower than sucrose. It makes ice cream smoother by lowering the freezing point;
– **invert sugar:** its sweetness value is notably higher than sucrose. Like the others, it makes ice cream smoother, but should be used only for ice creams that are naturally harder because of their high fat content (chocolate, praline, pistachio). It is not recommended for sorbets made with acidic fruits (red fruits, citrus) since it inhibits their preservation. It can be replaced with honey—a natural invert sugar—but this will affect the flavor.
In the home kitchen, these sugars can all be replaced by sucrose (ordinary sugar) in the same measure. The resulting ice cream will be slightly sweeter.

THE ROLE OF FAT IN ICE CREAM

Fat is added to ice cream in the form of egg yolks and milk products: butter, cream, whole milk. It is important to use whole milk and to choose good-quality products for the mix, because the structure and smoothness of the end product depend on it. Fat hardens during freezing, which contributes to the texture and mouthfeel.

WHY USE POWDERED MILK?

Powdered milk is a dried, defatted milk extract: it increases the percentage of dry ingredients in the mix, which stabilizes it by absorbing part of the water contained in the mix, in turn limiting the unpleasant gritty texture on the palate. Always be sure to use skim milk powder, which contains no fat. You can have too much of a good thing: an excess tends to make ice cream sandy. Measure carefully!

WHY COMBINE STABILIZERS AND EMULSIFIERS?

Ice cream and sorbet mixes made according to professional recipes often use additives to stabilize water and emulsify fat. They help:
– make smoother ice creams;
– improve texture by eliminating the formation of crystals;
– slow down melting when serving;
– improve storage properties.

These products can be bought in professional stores or online but are not required for ice creams prepared at home that will be eaten immediately or stored for short periods (up to 7 days). The recipes in this book may be made without using them.

WHY DOES THE ICE CREAM MIXTURE NEED TO AGE?

Aging refers to the refrigeration time before churning that is necessary for developing flavor and texture. For homemade sorbets without stabilizers, aging is not needed and they can be churned immediately. However, ice creams always need some aging time, as specified in the recipes: be sure to follow the times closely.

HOW LONG WILL HOMEMADE ICE CREAM KEEP?

Homemade ice cream without stabilizers should be consumed within a week, but it will be at its best right after being churned. Most of the ice-cream recipes here include stabilizers.

WHAT MAKES HOMEMADE ICE CREAM DIFFERENT FROM PROFESSIONAL?

The many differences between homemade and professionally made ice cream are due to:
- the sugars used;
- the percentage of fat and dry ingredients;
- the use of stabilizers;
- freezer temperature;
- the ice cream maker, which determines overrun (the amount of air incorporated into the mixture).
Commercially sold ice creams must adhere to government and trade organization standards, which regulate the ingredients and additives that are permitted. All the recipes presented here conform to French regulations for artisanal ice creams.

SERVING ICE CREAMS AND FROZEN DESSERTS

Ice creams and frozen desserts should be transferred from the freezer to the refrigerator 20–30 minutes before serving, so they soften sufficiently for scooping or portioning.

A note on measurements:
The precise amounts in these recipes make it difficult to convert into imperial or volume measures.
Weighing ingredients and switching your scale to metric will give you the best results.

A BRIEF HISTORY OF ICE CREAM AND FROZEN DESSERTS

Parfait
Developed under Napoleon III, this frozen dessert with a pâte à bombe base and whipped cream was traditionally only flavored with coffee. Nowadays, it can be made with fruits or chocolate.

Baked Alaska (omelette norvégienne)
Created in 1867 by Balzac, the chef of the Grand Hôtel in Paris, this frozen dessert is made of sponge cake and ice cream or sorbet covered in meringue and flambéed at the table. Baked Alaska is a spectacular dessert that provides a cold and hot sensation in a single bite.

Frozen Nougat
A relatively recent invention (the earliest recipes date from the 1970s), frozen nougat is a light dessert: a mixture of Italian honey meringue and whipped cream with roasted nuts and dried fruits.

Profiteroles
Originally a savory dish based on bread dough, profiteroles didn't become a dessert until they were made with choux pastry in the 19th century. It was Antonin Carême who had the idea to fill the puffs with whipped or pastry cream, but nobody knows who thought of serving them with ice cream and drizzling them with chocolate sauce.

Fresh Mint Ice Cream

Serves 6-8

Active time
40 minutes

Aging time
4-12 hours

Storage
Up to 2 weeks in the freezer

Equipment
Acetate sheets
Instant-read thermometer
Stick blender
Ice cream maker
Gelato pan

Ingredients
0.75 oz. (23 g) fresh mint
4 oz. (116 g) sucrose (sugar)
1.25 oz. (33 g) glucose powder
0.5 oz. (17 g) dextrose
0.15 oz. (4 g) stabilizer
2 cups (500 ml) whole milk, 3.6% butterfat
Scant ½ cup (120 ml) whipping cream, 35% butterfat
1.5 oz. (40 g) nonfat milk powder
¼ cup (2.5 oz./73 g) egg yolk (about 4 yolks)
1 drop of mint extract

1 • Place the mint leaves and half the sucrose between two acetate sheets. Mix the other half with the glucose powder, dextrose, and stabilizer.

CHEFS' NOTES

Crushing the leaves lets you extract the natural flavors without the bitterness from the fibrous parts.

4 • In a saucepan, heat the milk and cream. When it reaches 95°F (35°C), add the powdered milk and the mix of sucrose, glucose powder, dextrose, and stabilizer.

2 • Using a rolling pin, crush the mint and sugar.

3 • Transfer the resulting paste to a bowl. Set aside.

5 • When the mixture reaches 113°F (45°C), add the egg yolk. At 185°F (85°C), continue cooking for about 1 minute.

6 • Turn off the heat before adding the mint paste, to preserve its natural color. Mix together for 1 minute using a spatula. Add the mint extract. ⊕

Fresh Mint Ice Cream (continued)

7 • Blend the mixture using a stick blender.

8 • Strain the mixture well, without pressing on the fibers to avoid any bitterness being transferred to the mixture.

9 • Pour the mixture into a container and cool quickly in the refrigerator. Age at 39°F (4°C) for 4–12 hours.

10 • Blend once more before churning in the ice cream maker according to the manufacturer's instructions. Scoop the ice cream into a gelato pan, smooth the surface, and freeze at -31°F (-35°C) before storing it at -4°F (-20°C).

Egg-Enriched Vanilla Ice Cream

Serves 6–8

Active time
40 minutes

Aging time
4–12 hours

Storage
Up to 2 weeks in the freezer

Equipment
Instant-read thermometer
Stick blender
Ice cream maker
Gelato pan

Ingredients
2 ¼ cups (534 ml) whole milk, 3.6% butterfat
⅔ cup (150 ml) whipping cream, 35% butterfat
1 vanilla bean, split lengthwise and seeds scraped out
1.5 oz. (41 g) nonfat milk powder
4.75 oz. (134 g) sucrose (sugar)
1.25 oz. (33 g) glucose powder
0.5 oz. (17 g) dextrose
0.2 oz. (5 g) stabilizer
¼ cup (2.5 oz./73 g) egg yolk (about 4 yolks)

1 • Heat the milk, cream, and vanilla bean and seeds in a saucepan. When the mixture reaches 95°F (35°C), add the milk powder and, combining them together first, the sucrose, glucose powder, dextrose, and stabilizer.

4 • Strain the mixture well.

5 • Pour the mixture into a container and cool quickly in the refrigerator. Age at 39°F (4°C) for at least 4–12 hours.

• Coffee ice cream: Replace the vanilla
with 2 oz. (60 g) crushed coffee beans, infusing them in the milk.

• Pistachio ice cream: Substitute 2 oz. (60 g) pistachio paste for the vanilla.

• Praline ice cream: Omit the vanilla, ¼ cup (50 ml) of the cream,
and 1.75 oz. (50 g) of the sucrose and add 4.5 oz. (130 g) praline paste.

2 • When it reaches 113°F (45°C), add the egg yolk.
Continue cooking at 185°F (85°C) for about 1 minute.

3 • Blend the mixture using a stick blender.

6 • Blend once more before churning in the ice cream maker
according to the manufacturer's instructions. Scoop the ice
cream into a gelato pan, smooth the surface, and freeze
at -31°F (-35°C) before storing it at -4°F (-20°C).

SALTED CARAMEL ICE CREAM

Serves 6–8

Active time
40 minutes

Aging time
4–12 hours

Storage
Up to 2 weeks in the freezer

Equipment
Instant-read thermometer
Stick blender
Ice cream maker
Gelato pan

Ingredients
2 ¼ cups (531 ml) whole milk,
3.6% butterfat
3.25 oz. (93 g) sugar,
to make the caramel
3 oz. (87 g) atomized
glucose powder
1.75 oz. (50 g) sucrose (sugar)
0.75 oz. (21.75 g) nonfat
milk powder
0.1 oz. (3.25 g) stabilizer
4 tbsp (2 oz./60 g) lightly salted
butter, diced
1 ½ tbsp (1 oz./25 g) egg yolk
(about 1 ½ yolks)

Warm the milk in a saucepan. In another saucepan, make a dry caramel with the sugar, then remove from the heat and add the milk to stop the cooking process.

Return the pan with the caramel milk mixture to the heat. Combine the glucose powder, sucrose, powdered milk, and stabilizer in a small bowl and add to the mixture when it reaches 95°F (35°C), then add the butter. When the mixture reaches 104°F (40°C), add the egg yolk and cook at 185°F (85°C) for 2 minutes. Blend with a stick blender for 1 minute.

Pour the mixture into a container and cool quickly in the refrigerator. Age at 39°F (4°C) for at least 4–12 hours.

Blend once more before churning in the ice cream maker according to the manufacturer's instructions.

Scoop into a gelato pan, smooth the surface, and freeze at -31°F (-35°C) before storing it at -4°F (-20°C).

CHOCOLATE ICE CREAM

Serves 6–8

Active time
40 minutes

Aging time
4–12 hours

Storage
Up to 2 weeks in the freezer

Equipment
Instant-read thermometer
Stick blender
Ice cream maker
Gelato pan

Ingredients
1.25 oz. (32 g) nonfat milk powder
5.25 oz. (150 g) sucrose (sugar)
0.2 oz. (5 g) stabilizer
1.5 oz. (40 g) cacao paste
2.75 oz. (75 g) Valrhona Caraïbe couverture chocolate, 66% cocoa, chopped
2 cups plus 1 tbsp (518 ml) whole milk, 3.6% butterfat
Scant 1 cup (200 ml) whipping cream, 35% butterfat
1.5 oz. (45 g) invert sugar
2 ½ tbsp (1.5 oz./40 g) egg yolk (about 2 yolks)
Scant ¼ cup (50 ml) chocolate liqueur (optional)

Mix together the powdered milk, sucrose, and stabilizer. Melt the cacao paste and the couverture chocolate in a bowl set over a pan of hot water.

In another saucepan, heat the milk, cream, and invert sugar. When it reaches 95°F (35°C), add the powdered milk, sucrose, and stabilizer mixture. When it reaches 104°F (40°C), add the egg yolk. Continue cooking at 185°F (85°C) for about 1 minute. Add the melted chocolate mixture, blend, then strain through a fine-mesh sieve.

Pour the mixture into a container and cool quickly in the refrigerator. Age for at least 4–12 hours at 39°F (4°C).

If you wish, add the chocolate liqueur. Blend once more before churning in the ice cream maker according to the manufacturer's instructions.

Scoop into a gelato pan, smooth the surface, and freeze at -31°F (-35°C) before storing it at -4°F (-20°C).

Pear Liqueur Granita

Serves 8

Active time
10 minutes

Freezing time
2–3 hours

Storage
Up to 2 weeks in the freezer

Equipment
Gelato pan

Ingredients
4 ¼ cups (1 liter) water
9 oz. (250 g) sucrose (sugar)
Juice of ½ lemon
Scant 1 cup (200 ml)
pear liqueur

1• Put the water and sucrose in a saucepan.
Bring to a boil to make a syrup.

4• Pour the pear liqueur into the well-chilled syrup.

5• Pour into a container and place in the freezer.

2 • Pour the syrup into a bowl and cool in the refrigerator.

3 • Add the lemon juice and chill.

6 • Using a fork, scrape the ice as it forms during freezing. Place the container back in the freezer. Repeat as many times as necessary to obtain a granita texture.

7 • Place in a gelato pan and store in the freezer.

Exotic Fruit Sorbet

Serves 6–8

Active time
40 minutes

Aging time
4 hours

Storage
Up to 2 weeks in the freezer

Equipment
Instant-read thermometer
Stick blender
Ice cream maker
Gelato pan

Ingredients
12 oz. (334 g) mango
(prepared weight)
6 oz. (167 g) banana
(peeled weight)
2.75 oz. (75 g) kiwi
4.75 oz. (135 g) sucrose
(sugar)
1.75 oz. (50 g) atomized
glucose powder
0.45 oz. (14 g) dextrose
0.1 oz. (3 g) stabilizer
⅔ cup (143 ml) water
2.25 oz. (67 g) passion fruit
purée

1• Peel the mango, cut the flesh away from the pit,
and cut into pieces. Peel and slice the banana and kiwi.

4 • Add the bananas and cook for at least 1 minute to destroy
the enzyme that turns them black.

2 • In a small bowl, combine the sucrose, glucose powder, dextrose, and stabilizer.

3 • Heat the water in a saucepan. When it reaches 104°F (40°C), add the sucrose mixture and bring to a boil.

5 • Pour into a bowl and blend with a stick blender to make a purée.

6 • Add the mango pieces and the passion fruit purée. ⊕

Exotic Fruit Sorbet (continued)

7 • Blend for 2 minutes before adding the kiwi. Blend again but briefly to avoid releasing the bitterness of the kiwi seeds.

8 • Pour the mixture into a container and cool quickly in the refrigerator. Age for at least 4 hours.

9 • Blend the mixture once more before churning it in the ice cream maker according to the manufacturer's instructions. Scoop it into a gelato pan.

10 • Smooth the surface. Freeze at -31°F (-35°C) before storing the sorbet at -4°F (-20°C).

ORANGE SORBET IN A SHELL

Oranges Givrées

Serves 8

Active time
40 minutes

Freezing time
20 minutes

Aging time
4 hours

Storage
Up to 2 weeks in the freezer

Equipment
Instant-read thermometer
Stick blender
Ice cream maker
Gelato pan
Pastry bag fitted
with a fluted ½-in. (10-mm) tip

Ingredients

SHELLS
8 oranges
1 cup (250 ml) simple syrup
(equal parts sugar and water
by weight, boiled until the sugar
is completely dissolved)

ORANGE SORBET
5.5 oz. (154.5 g) sucrose (sugar)
1.35 oz. (38 g) atomized glucose
powder
0.4 oz. (13 g) dextrose
0.2 oz. (5 g) stabilizer
0.5 oz. (15 g) nonfat milk powder
(optional) (see Chefs' Notes)
2 ¾ cups (687 ml) water
Scant 3 cups (705 ml) freshly
squeezed orange juice

PREPARING THE SHELLS
Wash the oranges and then cut a small slice off the bottom (so they stand upright). Cut off the tops and set aside to use as lids. Squeeze the fruits gently to make it easier to remove the pulp. Use a spoon to scrape out the innards of the oranges, then pour the syrup inside the shells and lids to reduce the bitterness in the pith. Place them in the freezer. Squeeze and strain the removed orange pulp. Set aside for the sorbet.

MAKING THE ORANGE SORBET
Combine the powders: sugar, glucose powder, dextrose, stabilizer, and powdered milk. Heat the water in a saucepan. When it reaches 104°F (40°C), add the powders and bring to a boil. Add the orange juice. Blend with the stick blender, then cool in the refrigerator and age for at least 4 hours. Blend once more before churning it in the ice cream maker according to the manufacturer's instructions. Scoop into a gelato pan and freeze at -31°F (-35°C) before storing it at -4°F (-20°C).

ASSEMBLING THE ORANGES
Remove the frozen orange shells and lids from the freezer. Fill the pastry bag with the sorbet and pipe into the shells. Replace the lids and serve.

CHEFS' NOTES

• You can substitute lemons for oranges
and make a lemon sorbet
(see recipe p. 632).

• The powdered milk in this recipe is optional:
it helps make the sorbet opaque and stabilize the water.

LEMON SORBET

Serves 6–8

Active time
30 minutes

Aging time
4 hours

Storage
Up to 2 weeks in the freezer

Equipment
Instant-read thermometer
Stick blender
Ice cream maker
Gelato pan

Ingredients
6.5 oz. (191 g) sucrose (sugar)
1.25 oz. (35 g) atomized glucose powder
1 oz. (25.5 g) dextrose
0.5 oz. (5 g) stabilizer
0.35 oz. (9 g) nonfat milk powder
1 ⅔ cups (398 ml) water
Scant 1 ½ cups (332 ml) lemon juice

Combine the powders: sucrose, glucose powder, dextrose, stabilizer, and powdered milk.

Heat the water in a saucepan. When it reaches 104°F (40°C), add the powders and bring to a boil. Add the lemon juice. Blend with the stick blender, then cool in the refrigerator and age for at least 4 hours.

Blend once more before churning in the ice cream maker according to the manufacturer's instructions.

Scoop into a gelato pan, smooth the surface, and freeze at -31°F (-35°C) before storing it at -4°F (-20°C).

RASPBERRY SORBET
(WITHOUT STABILIZER)

Serves 6–8

Active time
30 minutes

Aging time
2 hours

Storage
Up to 1 week in the freezer

Equipment
Instant-read thermometer
Stick blender
Ice cream maker
Gelato pan

Ingredients
2.75 oz. (75 g) sucrose (sugar)
0.5 oz. (17 g) atomized glucose powder
0.3 oz. (8 g) dextrose
Scant ½ cup (100 ml) water
1 lb. 7 oz. (667 g) raspberry purée
3 tbsp plus ½ tsp (33 ml) lemon juice

Combine the sucrose, glucose, and dextrose.

Heat the water in a saucepan. When it reaches 104°F (40°C), add the powders and bring to a boil. Cool quickly in the refrigerator.

Add the raspberry purée and lemon juice and blend. Age for at least 2 hours.

Blend once more before churning in the ice cream maker according to the manufacturer's instructions.

Scoop into a gelato pan and freeze at -31°F (-35°C), before storing it at -4°F (-20°C).

FROZEN COFFEE PARFAIT

Parfait Glacé au Café

Serves 8

Active time
35 minutes

Aging time
4 hours

Freezing time
At least 4 hours

Cooking time
25 minutes

Storage
Up to 2 weeks in the freezer

Equipment
Stand mixer fitted
with the whisk attachment
Large rimmed baking sheet
Instant-read thermometer
6-in. (16-cm) square mold,
1.5 in. (4 cm) deep

Ingredients

SPONGE BASE
Scant ½ cup (3.5 oz./100 g)
lightly beaten egg (about 2 eggs)
2 ½ tbsp (1oz./30 g) sugar
1 ½ tbsp (1 oz./30 g) honey
½ cup minus 1 tbsp (1.75 oz./50 g)
flour, sifted
1 ½ tbsp (0.35 oz./10 g)
almond flour, sifted

COFFEE SYRUP
Scant ½ cup (100 ml) strong
coffee
¼ cup (1.75 oz./50 g) sugar
2 tsp (10 ml) dark rum (optional)

COFFEE PARFAIT
⅔ cup (150 ml) whole milk,
3.6% butterfat
½ vanilla bean, split lengthwise
and seeds scraped out
½ cup (1.5 oz./40 g) coffee beans,
crushed
½ cup (5.25 oz./150 g) egg yolk
(about 8 yolks)
¾ cup (5.25 oz./150 g) sugar
¾ cup plus 1 ½ tbsp (200 ml)
whipping cream, 35% butterfat,
whipped

MAKING THE SPONGE BASE
Preheat the oven to 375°F (190°C/Gas mark 5). In the bowl of the stand mixer, beat the eggs with the sugar and honey until pale and fluffy. Fold in the sifted flour and almond flour. Pour onto the baking sheet lined with parchment paper and bake in the oven for 25 minutes, until the base has risen and is springy to the touch.

MAKING THE COFFEE SYRUP
Heat the coffee and sugar in a saucepan until the sugar has dissolved. Remove from the heat and, when cooled, add the rum, if using.

MAKING THE COFFEE PARFAIT
In a saucepan, infuse the milk with the vanilla bean, seeds, and crushed coffee beans over low heat. Strain and top up with milk, if necessary, to retain ⅔ cup (150 ml). Whisk the egg yolks and sugar until pale and thick. Pour a little of the warm infused milk over the egg yolk mixture, then pour everything back into the saucepan and cook to 185°F (85°C). Pour into the bowl of the stand mixer and whisk until completely cooled. Gently fold in the whipped cream, then pour into the square mold.

ASSEMBLING THE PARFAIT
Cut a 6-in. (15-cm) square out of the sponge base. Moisten with coffee syrup and set it in the mold on top of the parfait. Freeze for at least 4 hours. Unmold the parfait and decorate as desired, for example with milk chocolate decorations (see techniques pp. 592–97), whipped cream, and chocolate-covered coffee beans.

CHEFS' NOTES

• For a fruit parfait, replace the milk with fruit purée.

• To add alcohol to the parfait, replace the milk with water to make a syrup and add 15% of the alcohol of your choice to the final mixture.

• To help the parfait hold its shape when served, add 1 ½ sheets (3 g) of gelatin just after cooking to 185°F (85°C), before whisking in the stand mixer to cool.

• For a deeper flavor, you can roast the coffee beans in the oven at 300°F (150°C/Gas mark 2) for 15 minutes before infusing.

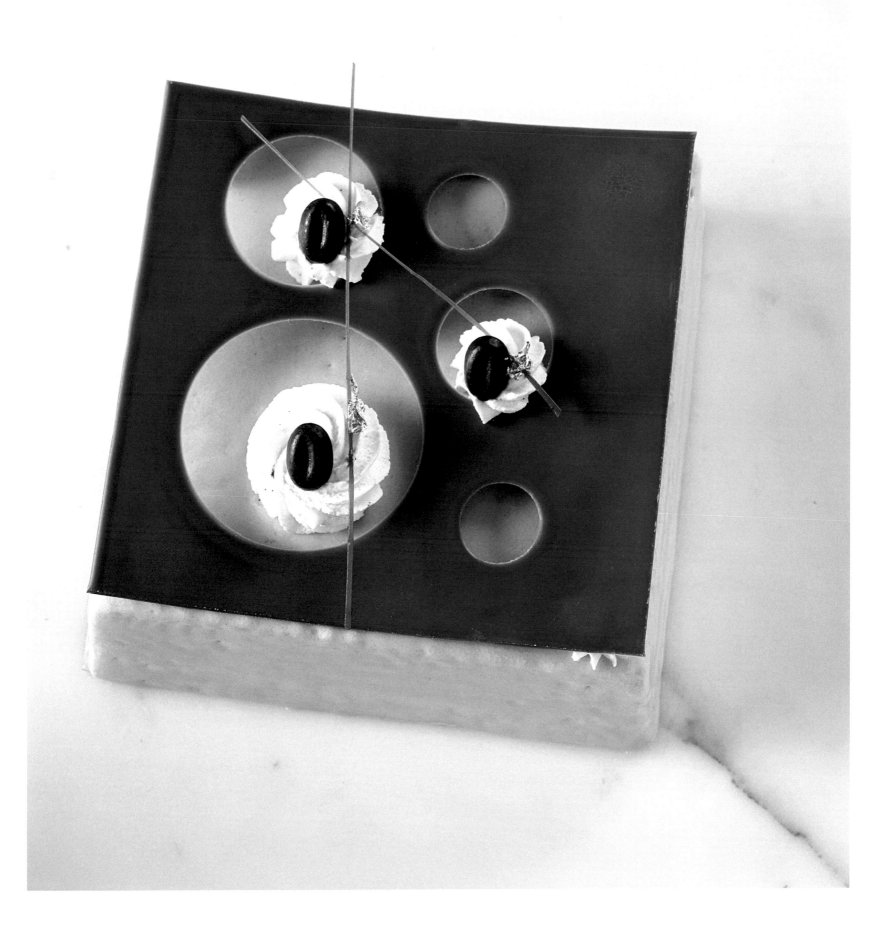

FROZEN NOUGAT

Nougat Glacé

Serves 8

Active time
40 minutes

Cooking time
25 minutes

Freezing time
4 hours

Storage
Up to 2 weeks in the freezer

Equipment
Electric hand beater
12 × 16-in. (30 × 40-cm)
baking sheet
Instant-read thermometer
10 × 6-in. (25 × 15-cm)
pastry frame, 2.5 in. (6 cm) high
Pastry bag fitted
with a fluted ½-in. (10-mm) tip
Kitchen torch

Ingredients
HONEY SPONGE
⅓ cup (2.75 oz./80 g)
egg yolk (about 4 ½ yolks)
Scant ½ cup (3 oz./85 g) sugar,
divided
4 tsp (1 oz./30 g) honey
½ cup (4.25 oz./120 g)
egg white (about 4 whites)
¾ cup plus 2 tbsp
(3.5 oz./100 g) flour
⅓ cup (1 oz./25 g) almond flour

NOUGAT
⅔ cup (3.5 oz./100 g) almonds
1 ½ sheets (0.1 oz./3.5 g) gelatin
¼ cup (1.75 oz./50 g) sugar
½ cup (5.75 oz./165 g) honey
½ cup (3.5 oz./100 g) egg white
(about 3 ½ whites)
Seeds of 1 vanilla bean
Ground anise for decoration
1 cup (230 ml) whipping cream,
35% butterfat
3 tbsp (42 ml) Grand Marnier
¼ cup (1.25 oz./35 g) whole
pistachios, shelled
¼ cup (1.25 oz./35 g) candied
orange peel, diced
½ cup (2.5 oz./70 g) candied fruit

ITALIAN MERINGUE
½ cup (3.5 oz./100 g) sugar
3 tbsp (40 ml) water
¼ cup (1.75 oz./50 g) egg white
(about 1 ½ whites)

GRAND MARNIER SYRUP
⅔ cup (150 ml) water
¼ cup (1.75 oz./50 g) sugar
1 tsp (5 ml) Grand Marnier

DECORATION
Fresh or dried fruit

MAKING THE HONEY SPONGE
Preheat the oven to 375°F (190°C/Gas Mark 5) and line the baking sheet with parchment paper. Using an electric hand beater, beat the egg yolk and ⅓ cup (2.47 oz./70 g) of the sugar until pale, then beat in the honey. In another bowl, whisk the egg whites and the remaining 4 tsp (0.5 oz./15 g) sugar until stiff peaks form. Gently fold the yolk mixture into the egg whites. Sift together the flour and almond flour and fold into the mixture. Pour onto the prepared baking sheet and bake for 10 minutes, until risen and springy to the touch. Set aside.

MAKING THE NOUGAT
Spread the almonds on a baking sheet and toast for 15 minutes at 300°F (150°C/Gas mark 2). When cool, coarsely chop them. Soak the gelatin in cold water. In a saucepan, cook the sugar to 225°F (110°C). In another saucepan, bring the honey to a boil. Beat the egg whites to stiff peaks, then pour in the honey and cooked sugar and whisk to make an Italian meringue (see technique p. 232). Add the vanilla seeds and anise to the mixture. Squeeze excess water from the gelatin, melt, and stir it in. Whip the cream until peaks form, then add the Grand Marnier. Gently fold the whipped cream into the cooled meringue. Add the whole pistachios, diced orange peel, and candied fruit.

MAKING THE ITALIAN MERINGUE
Prepare an Italian meringue (see technique p. 232).

MAKING THE GRAND MARNIER SYRUP
Heat the water and sugar in a saucepan and bring to a boil. Let cool before adding the alcohol.

ASSEMBLING THE DESSERT
Cut two rectangles from the honey sponge to fit the frame. Moisten with the Grand Marnier syrup. Place one piece of sponge cake into the pastry frame, spread the nougat into the frame, and top with the second piece of sponge cake. Freeze for 4 hours. Spoon the Italian meringue into a pastry bag fitted with a fluted tip and decorate the top of the dessert. Use the torch to lightly scorch the meringue. Garnish with a few fruits immediately before serving.

CHEFS' NOTES

Cream tends to curdle when put in contact with alcohol. Make sure that the cream is pliable enough to allow the two substances to mix perfectly.

BAKED ALASKA

Omelette Norvégienne

Serves 8

Active time
1 ½ hours

Aging time
4 hours

Cooking time
15 minutes

Freezing time
4 hours

Storage
Up to 2 weeks in the freezer

Equipment
Instant-read thermometer
Stick blender
Ice cream maker
Gelato pan
Rimmed baking sheet
Electric hand beater
6 ½-in. (16-cm) pastry ring,
1 ½ in. (4 cm) high
Pastry bag fitted with a ½-in.
(10-mm) plain tip (optional)

Ingredients

VANILLA ICE CREAM
2 ¼ cups (534 ml) whole milk,
3.6% butterfat
⅔ cup (150 ml) whipping cream,
35% butterfat
1 vanilla bean, split lengthwise
and seeds scraped out
1.5 oz. (41 g) nonfat milk powder
4.75 oz. (134 g) sucrose (sugar)

1.25 oz. (33 g) glucose powder
0.5 oz. (17 g) dextrose
0.2 oz. (5 g) stabilizer
⅓ cup (2.6 oz./73 g) egg yolk
(about 4 yolks)

LADYFINGER SPONGE
2 ½ tbsp. (1.5 oz./40 g)
egg yolk (about 2 yolks)
3 ½ tbsp (1.5 oz./43 g) sugar,
divided
2 tsp (0.5 oz./15 g) honey
¼ cup (2 oz./60 g) egg white
(about 2 whites)
½ cup minus 1 tbsp
(1.75 oz./50 g) flour
2 ¼ tbsp (0.5 oz./12 g)
almond flour

CALVADOS SYRUP
½ cup (125 ml) water
⅔ cup (4.5 oz./125 g) sugar
2 ½ tbsp (35 ml) Calvados

MERINGUE
⅔ cup (5.25 oz./150 g)
egg white (about 5 whites)
½ cup (3.5 oz./100 g)
superfine sugar
¼ cup (1.75 oz./50 g)
egg yolk (about 3 yolks)

DECORATION
½ cup (3.5 oz./100 g) toasted
slivered almonds
¾ cup (3.5 oz./100 g)
confectioners' sugar
Alcohol for flambéing
(Grand Marnier, Calvados,
or other liqueur)

MAKING THE VANILLA ICE CREAM
Make the vanilla ice cream (see technique p. 618). Age at 39°F (4°C) for at least 4 hours. Blend once more before churning it in the ice cream maker according to the manufacturer's instructions.

MAKING THE LADYFINGER SPONGE
Preheat the oven to 375°F (190°C/Gas mark 5) and line the baking sheet with parchment paper. Using an electric hand beater, beat the egg yolks with 3 tbsp (35 g) of the sugar and the honey until thick. Whisk the egg whites with the remaining ½ tbsp (8 g) of sugar until peaks form. Fold the egg yolk mixture into the meringue, then sift together the flour and almond flour and fold in. Pour onto the prepared baking sheet and bake in the oven for about 10 minutes.

MAKING THE CALVADOS SYRUP
In a saucepan, bring the water and sugar to a boil. Let cool, then add the Calvados.

MAKING THE MERINGUE
Using an electric hand beater, whisk the egg whites with the sugar until peaks form. Beat the egg yolks and gently fold into the egg whites.

ASSEMBLING THE BAKED ALASKA
When the ladyfinger sponge has cooled, cut out 2 × 6 ½-in. (16-cm) diameter circles. Place the first circle in the bottom of the pastry ring. Moisten it with the Calvados syrup using a pastry brush, then spread the vanilla ice cream on top. Moisten the second sponge circle and place it on top. Freeze for at least 4 hours.
Preheat the oven to 475°F (250°C/Gas mark 9). Using a straight spatula or pastry bag, cover the frozen dessert with the meringue. Sprinkle with the toasted slivered almonds and dust with confectioners' sugar. Place briefly in the oven until lightly browned. Keep in the freezer until ready to serve. Just before serving, place the baked Alaska on a flameproof plate. Heat the alcohol in a small saucepan and flambé the liqueur before pouring it over.

CHEFS' NOTES

• Be sure to use a flameproof deep platter
or serving plate to avoid setting your table on fire.

• You can substitute regular Italian meringue
for the meringue used here (**see technique p. 232**).

PROFITEROLES

Serves 8

Active time
2 hours

Aging time
4 hours

Freezing time
1 hour

Cooking time
25 minutes

Storage
Up to 2 weeks in the freezer

Equipment
2 pastry bags fitted
with a plain ½-in. (10-mm) tip
and a fluted ½-in. (10-mm) tip

Instant-read thermometer
Stick blender
Ice cream maker
Gelato pan

Ingredients

CHOUX PASTRY
¼ cup plus 1 tbsp (70 ml) water
¼ cup (60 ml) milk
1 ¼ tsp (5 g) sugar
⅛ tsp (1 g) salt
4 tbsp (1.75 oz./50 g) butter, diced
⅔ cup (2.75 oz./75 g) flour, sifted
½ cup (125 g) lightly beaten egg
(about 2 ½ eggs)
Pearl sugar for decoration
Chopped almonds for decoration

VANILLA ICE CREAM
2 ¼ cups (534 ml) whole milk,
3.6% butterfat
⅔ cup (150 ml) whipping cream,
35% butterfat
1 vanilla bean, split lengthwise
and seeds scraped out
1.5 oz. (41 g) nonfat milk powder
4.75 oz. (134 g) sucrose (sugar)
1.25 oz. (33 g) atomized
glucose powder
0.5 oz. (17 g) dextrose
0.2 oz. (5 g) stabilizer
⅓ cup (2.6 oz./73 g) egg yolk
(about 4 yolks)

CHOCOLATE SAUCE
½ cup (125 ml) whipping cream,
35% butterfat
⅓ cup (75 ml) water
½ cup (3.25 oz./95 g) sugar
⅓ cup (1.5 oz./40 g) unsweetened
cocoa powder
1 ½ tsp (0.5 oz./12 g) glucose syrup
3.25 oz. (95 g) bittersweet
chocolate, 70% cacao, chopped

MAKING THE CHOUX PASTRY (A DAY AHEAD)
Preheat the oven to 375°F (190°C/Gas Mark 5). In a saucepan, bring the water, milk, sugar, salt, and butter to a boil. Remove from the heat, add the sifted flour all at once, then mix using a spatula until it forms a thick paste. Dry out the paste over the heat for 10 seconds, until the dough no longer sticks to the sides of the pan. Transfer it to a metal bowl to stop the cooking process. Add the beaten egg, a little at a time. Check the batter's consistency with a spatula: when you draw a line through it, it should close up slowly. If needed, add more egg. Spoon into the pastry bag fitted with the plain ½-in. (10-mm) tip and pipe about 40 small puffs (4 or 5 puffs per person) onto a nonstick baking sheet. Sprinkle with the almonds and pearl sugar and bake for 25 minutes.

MAKING THE VANILLA ICE CREAM
Make the vanilla ice cream (see technique p. 618). Age at 39°F (4°C) for at least 4 hours. Blend once more before churning in the ice cream maker according to the manufacturer's instructions.

MAKING THE CHOCOLATE SAUCE
In a saucepan, bring the cream, water, sugar, cocoa powder, and glucose syrup to a boil. Pour over the chopped chocolate and blend well as for a ganache. Set aside.

ASSEMBLING THE PROFITEROLES
Cut the top third off each choux puff to form a lid. Fill the pastry bag fitted with the fluted ½-in. (10-mm) tip with vanilla ice cream and generously fill the puffs, forming attractive rosettes. Place the lid on top. Keep in the freezer until ready to serve. Serve with the warm chocolate sauce: allow about 3 tbsp (40 ml) of sauce per person.

CHEFS' NOTES

You can freeze the cut puffs, which prevents the ice cream
from melting as quickly when you fill them.

VANILLA AND RASPBERRY VACHERIN

Vacherin Vanille-Framboise

Serves 8

Active time
3 hours

Aging time
6 hours

Freezing time
1 hour

Cooking time
1 ½ hours

Storage
Up to 2 weeks in the freezer

Equipment
Instant-read thermometer
Stick blender
Ice cream maker
Gelato pans
6 ½-in. (16-mm) round silicone mold
4 pastry bags, 2 fitted with fluted ½-in. (10-mm) tips, 1 with a plain ½-in. (10-mm) tip, and 1 with a Saint-Honoré tip
Baking sheet lined with a silicone baking mat
Electric hand beater
7-in. (18-cm) dessert ring

Ingredients

VANILLA ICE CREAM
2 ¼ cups (534 ml) whole milk, 3.6% butterfat
⅔ cup (150 ml) whipping cream (35% butterfat)
1 vanilla bean, split lengthwise and seeds scraped out
1.5 oz. (41 g) nonfat milk powder
4.75 oz. (134 g) sucrose (sugar)
1.25 oz. (33 g) glucose powder
0.5 oz. (17 g) dextrose
0.2 oz. (5 g) stabilizer
¼ cup (2.5 oz./73 g) egg yolk (about 4 yolks)

RASPBERRY SORBET
Scant 1 cup (6 oz./170 g) sugar
1 oz. (30 g) atomized glucose powder
0.25 oz. (6 g) stabilizer
Scant 1 cup (200 ml) water
1 lb. 7 oz. (650 g) raspberry purée
4 tsp (20 ml) lemon juice

RASPBERRY COULIS
4 oz. (115 g) raspberry purée
2 tsp (0.35 oz./10 g) sugar
0.5 oz. (13 g) invert sugar
1 ½ tsp (7 ml) crème de framboise or kirsch

FRENCH MERINGUE
Scant ½ cup (3.5 oz./100 g) egg white (about 3 ½ whites)
1 cup (6 oz./175 g) superfine sugar
3 tbsp (1 oz./25 g) confectioners' sugar

RASPBERRY GLAZE
3.5 oz. (100 g) clear neutral glaze
0.35 oz. (10 g) crystal glucose
1 oz. (30 g) raspberry purée
Red powdered food coloring

MASCARPONE WHIPPED CREAM
⅔ cup (150 ml) whipping cream, 35% butterfat
⅔ cup (75 g) mascarpone
⅓ cup (45 g) confectioners' sugar
Seeds of ½ vanilla bean

Fresh raspberries for decorating

MAKING THE VANILLA ICE CREAM
Make the vanilla ice cream (see technique p. 618). Age at 39°F (4°C) for at least 4 hours. Blend once more before churning in the ice cream maker according to the manufacturer's instructions.

MAKING THE RASPBERRY SORBET
Mix together ¼ cup (1.75 oz./50 g) of the sugar, the glucose, and the stabilizer. In a saucepan, heat the water and the remaining sugar to make a syrup. When it reaches 104°F (40°C), add the powders and bring to a boil. Add the raspberry purée and lemon juice, and blend. Cool quickly in the refrigerator, then age for at least 2 hours. Blend once more before churning in the ice cream maker according to the manufacturer's instructions.

MAKING THE RASPBERRY COULIS
Mix the raspberry purée with the sugars, then stir in the crème de framboise or kirsch. Pour into the silicone mold. Store in the freezer until ready to assemble the vacherin.

MAKING THE FRENCH MERINGUE
Preheat the oven to 225°F (100°C/Gas mark ¼). Make a French meringue using the ingredients listed (see technique p. 234). Spoon into the pastry bag fitted with the plain tip and pipe a 7 ½-in. (18-cm) disk and tear-shaped shells of about 2 in. (5 cm) on a baking sheet lined with a silicone mat. Bake for 1 ½ hours.

MAKING THE RASPBERRY GLAZE
Bring all the ingredients to room temperature (70°F/20°C) and then blend well, adding the food coloring according to the manufacturer's instructions. Strain and set aside.

MAKING THE MASCARPONE WHIPPED CREAM
Whip together the cream, mascarpone, sugar, and vanilla seeds until peaks form, as for a Chantilly cream (see technique p. 201).

ASSEMBLING THE VACHERIN
Place the meringue base at the bottom of the dessert ring. Cover with vanilla ice cream to halfway up the height of the ring. Place the frozen coulis disk on it, then cover with raspberry sorbet to the top of the ring, reserving some to decorate the top. Freeze for 1 hour. Fill one pastry bag with a fluted tip with raspberry sorbet and the other with the mascarpone whipped cream. Remove the dessert ring and decorate the top, piping alternate rosettes of raspberry sorbet and mascarpone whipped cream around the edge. Stick the meringue shells around the outside leaving a small gap between each one. Pipe whipped cream between them using the Saint-Honoré tip. Carefully pour the raspberry glaze in the center, decorate with fresh raspberries, and serve.

APPENDIXES

GLOSSARY

A

ACETATE

Food-safe acetate sheets and strips are recommended for chocolate work, because they are more rigid than parchment paper and are perfectly smooth. When tempered chocolate sets on acetate, the surface in contact with the sheet develops a glossy sheen. Acetate strips—also known as cake collars—can be used to line dessert rings when assembling layered desserts for easy removal and perfect edges.

B

BAIN-MARIE (WATER BATH)

A way of keeping certain cooked foods warm and gently heating delicate mixtures, such as chocolate or egg-based creams and custards, that can separate or burn easily. A stovetop bain-marie consists of a heatproof bowl set over a saucepan of barely simmering water. A double boiler can be used instead. In the oven, using a bain-marie for flans and custards prevents the eggs from curdling and the tops from drying out.

BLANCHING

Sometimes called parboiling, this refers to the process of plunging ingredients into boiling water briefly and then draining and refreshing them in cold water to stop the cooking process and preserve the color of the ingredient. Blanching pre-cooks or softens foods and tempers strong flavors like the bitterness in citrus peels. Blanching certain fruits or nuts softens the skins so they are easier to remove.

BLIND BAKING

The process of baking a tart shell on its own, before adding a filling, sometimes referred to as pre-baking. Blind baking is typically used for tarts with very moist fillings (such as custards), that could produce soggy crusts, or for tarts with fillings that do not require baking.

BUTTERING PANS

Greasing the insides of pans, rings, or other baking dishes with a thin, even layer of butter to prevent dough and batter from sticking. There are several effective ways to butter pans, including with a little soft butter on your finger or a clean piece of paper towel, or with a pastry brush dipped in melted or clarified butter.

C

CARAMELIZING (COOKING SUGAR)

When sugar is heated above 320°F (160°C), either alone (dry method) or with water (wet method), it caramelizes. As it caramelizes, sugar liquefies, browns, and becomes more flavorful, but it eventually burns and becomes bitter. As sugar can burn quickly, it must be closely watched and removed from the heat as soon as the desired color is reached. Always use extreme caution when working with hot caramel, as it can cause very serious burns. The term caramelize also refers to the process of toasting the sugar on top of custards or cakes under the broiler or with a salamander or kitchen torch.

CLARIFIED BUTTER

Pure butterfat obtained by melting regular butter and removing the milk solids, water, and other impurities. Clarified butter keeps longer than regular butter and does not burn as easily (see p. 35).

COATING THE BACK OF A SPOON

When certain sauces or custards are sufficiently cooked, they will adhere to your spoon or spatula, coating it evenly. If you trace a line through the mixture with your finger, the line should remain unfilled for a few moments.

CREAMING BUTTER AND SUGAR

The process of beating butter and sugar together until they are light and smooth, with the sugar completely dissolved. This not only makes the butter more pliable, but also incorporates air into it and thus helps produce lighter and fluffier baked goods.

CRÉMEUX

A thick and creamy custard that is firm enough to be used as a filling for macarons or as a layer in elaborate pastries and mousse cakes. Crémeux are typically made by adding gelatin to a *crème anglaise*-style custard, and the flavoring options are numerous.

CRIMPING

Pinching the edges of unbaked tart or pie dough with your fingers or a pastry pincher, making small ridges around the rim. This border not only serves as decoration, but also plays a role in the baking process. In the oven, the crimped edge will turn golden and harden more quickly than the rest of the dough, which helps hold up the sides of the tart.

CRYSTALLIZATION

When the cocoa butter in couverture chocolate has fully crystallized (or set), it makes chocolate candies that are easy to unmold, with a glossy finish and a nice snap to the bite. For this to occur, the chocolate must first be tempered (see pp. 567–73).

CURDLING

When overbeaten egg whites turn grainy or egg custards split, they are said to curdle: the egg proteins clump together, resulting in an unpleasant texture.

D

DESSERT RINGS, *see* RINGS AND FRAMES

DICING
Cutting an ingredient into even cubes, either small or very small, depending on the recipe. Dicing butter into small ¼-inch (6-mm) cubes, for example, makes it easier to mix into doughs and batters.

E

EGG WASH
Beaten raw egg (sometimes mixed with a liquid like water, milk, or cream) that is brushed onto pastry or bread before baking to promote browning and add shine. A pastry brush with soft bristles is the best tool for applying a thin, even coat.

EMULSION
A smooth, uniform blend of two liquids that do not naturally mix, such as oil and water. Making an emulsion requires vigorous hand whisking or blending in a food processor or blender. This breaks one of the liquids down into tiny droplets and disperses it throughout the other liquid, forming a temporary suspension. Adding an emulsifier like egg yolk stabilizes the emulsion.

ÉTUVE (DRYING OR STEAMER OVEN)
Mainly found in professional kitchens, this oven can be set to a wide range of very precise temperatures, rising to a maximum of 572°F (300°C). It is used for drying or steaming delicate ingredients and also for proofing (proving) yeast doughs.

F

FEUILLETINE
Fine crispy flakes of crushed Gavottes cookies with a caramelized praline flavor, known as *pailleté feuilletine* in French. They are often used in layered cakes to add a crunchy texture. If these are unavailable, crushed wafers can be substituted.

FLAMBÉING
Pouring an alcoholic beverage (often rum, cognac, or liqueur) over a warm dish, igniting it, and allowing the flame to burn out. This process eliminates most of the alcohol and intensifies the flavors of the dish. For safety reasons, it is best to use a long match or long-reach lighter.

FOLDING
A gentle technique for blending a light and airy mixture into a heavier one, or vice versa, without stirring or beating. This prevents the lighter mixture (such as whisked egg whites) from deflating excessively and making the baked goods dense or chewy.

G

GLAZING
Covering a pastry or cake with a smooth, shiny layer. Glazes can either be transparent—such as apricot jam and *nappage* (clear neutral glaze)—or opaque—like chocolate glaze or the fondant icing typically used on eclairs. Pastry chefs also sprinkle their pastries with confectioners' sugar before baking, or brush them with simple syrup when fresh out of the oven to create a glossy finish.

I

INFUSING
Steeping an aromatic ingredient such as vanilla, citrus zest, or coffee beans in a hot or cold liquid like milk or cream to extract the flavor and aroma. The resulting infusion can be used to flavor preparations like buttercream, pastry cream, and ganache. In most cases, the liquid must be strained before use.

K

KNEADING
The action of blending, massaging, and working a mixture containing flour with your hands to obtain a smooth, elastic dough. Kneading develops the gluten in the dough, resulting in lighter and airier baked goods.

L

LAMINATING
The process of incorporating butter into dough by folding, turning, and rolling out multiple times to produce thin alternating layers of fat and dough, resulting in light and flaky pastries. Both puff pastries and croissants are made with laminated dough.

M

MACERATING
Soaking foods like fresh and dried fruits in liquids such as water, juice, or liquor to soften them and boost their flavor.

MASKING
Covering a cake with a thin, smooth layer of buttercream, marzipan, ganache, etc. The purpose of masking is to conceal the cake underneath, but it also secures any loose crumbs and hides imperfections, making the surface of the cake perfectly smooth before a final layer of icing or rolled fondant is applied.

MOISTENING
A technique for adding moisture and flavor to baked goods with simple syrup, alcohol, liqueur, or milk. The liquid should be

gently dabbed onto the surface of the cake with a pastry brush until the cake is thoroughly moistened, but not soggy.

P

PASTEURIZATION

The process of heating foods to an appropriate temperature, depending on their nature, to kill harmful bacteria and make the foods safe to eat. The temperatures below are particularly important to keep in mind with egg-based preparations like custards. To prevent recontamination, pasteurized foods must be cooled as quickly as possible to 39°F–43°F (4°C–6°C) and then kept refrigerated, avoiding the in-between temperatures at which bacteria can proliferate.
Low temperature pasteurization:
140°F–150°F (60°C–65°C) for 30 minutes
High temperature pasteurization:
175°F–185°F (80°C–85°C) for 3 minutes
Higher heat shorter time pasteurization:
198°F–200°F (92°C–95°C) for 1 second

PASTRY FRAMES, *see* RINGS AND FRAMES

PÂTE À BOMBE

The French term for an egg foam used to lighten and enrich mousses, parfaits, and buttercreams, made with egg yolks (and sometimes whole eggs), sugar, and water. Two methods can be used. The first is to heat a sugar syrup to around 240°F (116°C), unless otherwise indicated. The hot syrup is then whisked gradually into the eggs (previously beaten until thick and foamy) and the mixture whisked constantly to the ribbon stage.
For the second method, the eggs are whisked with sugar and water in a bowl over a pan of simmering water until their temperature reaches around 158°F (70°C). The bowl is removed from the heat and the mixture whisked to the ribbon stage. Whichever method is used, *pâte à bombe* must be cooled before being added to other ingredients.

PÂTE À GLACER (GLAZING PASTE)

A compound chocolate used for coating, glazing, and dipping. *Pâte à glacer* does not contain cocoa butter and therefore does not need to be tempered. It is semi-firm and glossy when it sets.

PEAKS

Recipes that involve whipping cream or whisking egg whites often instruct you to beat to a certain peak stage, usually soft, medium, or firm. This refers to the stiffness of the peak that forms when you lift the whisk or beaters. Soft peaks have begun to take shape, but they do not hold up for long and quickly collapse. Medium peaks are more stable than soft peaks, although the tip

of the peak curls over. Firm or stiff peaks, on the other hand, stand up straight without collapsing.

PIPING

Using a pastry bag that can be fitted with different tips to push (or pipe) out frostings, meringues, and certain batters (such as those for choux and macarons).
For instructions on piping, see technique p. 30.

PROOFING (OR PROVING)

Letting yeasted dough rise prior to baking. The proofing period gives the yeast time to react, forming air bubbles in the dough that are essential to leavening, resulting in light and airy baked goods and loaves.

PURÉEING

Grinding, pressing, or straining ingredients to make a smooth paste or thick liquid, usually in a blender or food processor, but a food mill or sieve will work, too.

R

REDUCING

Cooking a liquid at a boil or simmer to reduce the volume, thickening the liquid and concentrating the flavor.

RIBBON

The term used to describe the texture of sugar and eggs that have been beaten sufficiently for certain cakes like genoise, which rely on eggs for leavening. When it reaches the ribbon stage, the egg and sugar mixture should be airy and pale, and when you lift the whisk or beaters, the batter should form a ribbon that falls back into the bowl and lingers on the surface for several seconds before sinking back in.

RINGS AND FRAMES

Pastry chefs frequently use dessert rings (also called cake rings and ring molds), pastry (or cake or baking) frames, and tart (or flan) rings for baking cakes and tarts and layering entremets. Stood on a baking sheet or silicone mat, the rings and frames ensure tarts have a crisp bottom crust and straight sides when baked and it is easier to stack layered cakes and desserts in them. Once baking and/or assembling are complete, the ring or frame is easily lifted off. For instructions on lining tart rings, see pp. 26–29.

RUBBING IN

The process of combining flour with fat (usually chilled and diced butter) using one's fingertips until the mixture resembles coarse bread crumbs. This technique gives cookies like shortbread and certain tart crusts a deliciously crumbly texture.

S

SIMPLE SYRUP
A syrup made with equal parts sugar and water and sometimes alcohol or liqueur. To make a simple syrup, heat the water and sugar in a saucepan over medium heat until the sugar dissolves, then bring to a boil. Remove from the heat and add a splash of alcohol or liqueur if using. Once cool, simple syrup can be stored in a sealed container in the refrigerator indefinitely. Pastry chefs often use simple syrup as a glaze.

SKIMMING
Removing the foam that forms on the surface when cooking syrups, jams, jellies, and clarified butter. The foam contains impurities that can spoil the appearance of a mixture and adversely affect its storage time. Skimming is best done with a skimmer—a slotted tool made for this purpose—but other utensils such as spoons or ladles can be used.

SOFTENING BUTTER
Working room-temperature butter with a flexible spatula until smooth and easy to work with.

SOURDOUGH STARTER
The traditional way of activating the wild yeasts contained in flour and used to leaven bread doughs. Equal quantities of flour and water are combined and left to ferment for several days in a warm place as the yeasts multiply. It adds flavor to breads and improves their keeping quality.

SUPREMING (OR SECTIONING) CITRUS FRUITS
The process of cutting out the segments of citrus fruits from between the fine membranes, with no pith or membrane attached. They are called *sûpremes* in French and are often used for delicate pastries as they are decorative and easy to eat.

T

TART (OR FLAN) RINGS, *see* RINGS AND FRAMES

TEMPERING CHOCOLATE
The process of melting chocolate, cooling it to a given temperature, and reheating it slightly to stabilize the cocoa butter (see pp. 567–73).

W

WATER DOUGH (*DÉTREMPE*)
In puff pastry and croissant recipes, making the water dough with flour, water, and salt is the first step before incorporating the butter.

WELL (MAKING A WELL)
A technique for gradually mixing flour with wet ingredients, by creating a hole in the center of the flour, like the crater of a volcano. The wet ingredients are added to the well and the flour added a little at a time from the sides, being mixed in with a fork, wooden spoon, or your fingers, until completely incorporated.

INDEX

Acknowledgments

The photographer, Rina Nurra, wishes to thank:
Stévy, Carlos, and Edouard for their keen involvement, their talent, their ideas, and their good humor—and for giving this "mammoth" project a human dimension. Régis, Claude, Alain, Bruno, and the rest of the wonderful team of pastry chefs at the École Ferrandi. Allyriane, a young high-flying pastry chef who already has a keen and judicious eye, for helping out our dream team. Audrey for her valuable assistance, her cheerfulness, and for coordinating the photo shoots masterfully. The students at the school who participated directly or indirectly in the project: Lisandra, Lisa, Margot, Aurélien, Sandrine, Alba, and Florent—and apologies to anyone I may have forgotten. Clélia and Florence for their trust and their patience. Multiblitz and MMF Pro for their assistance and for providing me with equipment.

The Publisher extends thanks to:
All the teams that have worked on this book over the past year and with whom we have shared the same commitment to excellence. All the teachers and students at the École Ferrandi Paris who contributed to the recipes and the photographs. Audrey Janet, for her unwavering support and her rigor. The numerous associate chefs who have shared their knowledge and skills. The whole editorial team: Rina Nurra, a talented photographer; Alice Leroy, a graphic design whiz; Estelle Payany, an outstanding writer; Julie Haubourdin for her advice; Déborah Schwarz for her valuable assistance; Clélia Ozier-Lafontaine, for her endurance, perseverance, and kindness, which have enabled this book to be published and on time; Helen Adedotun, her British alter ego; and the freelance team who worked on the English edition, for their dedication, conscientiousness, and patience—in particular Carmella, Ansley, Alice, Wendy, and Nicole, for going the extra mile.

We would also like to thank
Marine Mora and Matfer Bourgeat
for the utensils and equipment.

9, Rue du Tapis Vert
93260 Les Lilas
France
+33 (0)1 43 62 60 40
www.matferbourgeat.com